# NEWCOMER'S
# HANDBOOK ®

## FOR MOVING TO AND LIVING IN

# ATLANTA

Including Fulton, DeKalb, Cobb, Gwinnett,
and Cherokee Counties

5th Edition

**FIRST BOOKS**

503-968-6777
www.firstbooks.com

*Scan this QR Code
to learn more about
this title*

Author/Photographer: Eileen Meslar
Editors: Linda Franklin
Series Editor: Linda Franklin
Cover design: Masha Shubin, Raspayle Wamanrao Suresh (front cover: lake, trees, grass), Yuri Konovalov (Chicago cityscape)
Interior design: Erin Johnson Design
Interior layout and composition: Masha Shubin
Maps provided by Jim Miller/fennana design

Paperback: 1-937090-50-7 | 978-1-937090-50-0
Kindle : 1-937090-51-5 | 978-1-937090-51-7
ePub: 1-937090-52-3 | 978-1-937090-52-4

Published by First Books®, 6750 SW Franklin Street, Portland, OR 97223-2542, 503-968-6777, www.firstbooks.com.

Printed in the USA

1 3 5 7 9 10 8 6 4 2

**What readers are saying about Newcomer's Handbooks:**

I recently moved to Atlanta from San Francisco, and LOVE the *Newcomer's Handbook for Atlanta*. It has been an invaluable resource—it's helped me find everything from a neighborhood in which to live to the local hardware store. I look something up in it everyday, and know I will continue to use it to find things long after I'm no longer a newcomer. And if I ever decide to move again, your book will be the first thing I buy for my next destination.

– Courtney R.
Atlanta, Georgia

I recently got a copy of your *Newcomer's Handbook for Chicago,* and wanted to let you know how invaluable it was for my move. I must have consulted it a dozen times a day preparing for my move. It helped me find my way around town, find a place to live, and so many other things. Thanks.

– Mike L.
Chicago, Illinois

Excellent reading (*Newcomer's Handbook for San Francisco and the Bay Area*) ... balanced and trustworthy. One of the very best guides if you are considering moving/relocation. Way above the usual tourist crap.

– Gunnar E.
Stockholm, Sweden

I was very impressed with the latest edition of the *Newcomer's Handbook for Los Angeles*. It is well organized, concise and up-to-date. I would recommend this book to anyone considering a move to Los Angeles.

– Jannette L.
Attorney Recruiting Administrator for a large Los Angeles law firm

In looking to move to the Boston area, a potential employer in that area gave me a copy of the *Newcomer's Handbook for Boston*. It's a great book that's very comprehensive, outlining good and bad points about each neighborhood in the Boston area. Very helpful in helping me decide where to move.

– no name given (online submit form)

# TABLE OF CONTENTS

**93** **Finding A Place To Live**
*House and apartment hunting in metro Atlanta, rental agents and online rental services, tips on what to look for in an apartment, details about leases and security deposits, insurance, tenant resources; buying a home, real estate agencies, financing, inspections, closing; online resources*

**111** **Moving and Storage**
*Truck rentals; interstate and intrastate movers; consumer complaints; storage; moving with children; moving-related tax deductions*

**123** **Money Matters**
*Banking: financial institutions, credit unions, savings and checking accounts, consumer complaints; credit cards; credit reports; taxes; starting or moving a business*

**131** **Getting Settled**
*Utilities; internet service providers; garbage and recycling; automobile registration, safety, insurance, purchasing, and parking; print and broadcast media; voter registration; driver's licenses and state IDs; passports; library cards; finding a health care provider; pet laws and services; safety and crime*

**161** **Helpful Services**
*Domestic services, pest control, mail and shipping services, consumer protection; services for people with disabilities, immigrant newcomers; gay and lesbian life*

**173** **Childcare and Education**
*Referral services for childcare, daycare, babysitting, nannies; child safety; public and private schools, homeschooling; higher education*

# NEWCOMERS' HANDBOOK
# FOR MOVING TO AND LIVING IN ATLANTA

Welcome to Atlanta, a city that combines downhome southern charm with cosmopolitan ambiance. The birthplace of the Reverend Martin Luther King, Jr., Turner Broadcasting, Coca-Cola, and CNN, Atlanta features championship sports teams, five-star restaurants, and the country's busiest international airport.

The city of Atlanta, population about 420,000, is the capital of and the largest city in Georgia, as well as the cultural and economic center of the Atlanta metropolitan area. Home to 5,268,860 people, the Atlanta metro is ninth largest in the country.

With a gross domestic product of around $304 billion, metro Atlanta is the eighth largest economy in the country, and the 17th largest in the world. The area has the third largest concentration of Fortune 500 companies, including Home Depot, Delta Airlines, Beazer Homes, and United Parcel Service. In business circles, it has long been recognized as the commercial capital of the South and continues to draw top talent and praise due to its large and diverse labor pool, numerous colleges and universities, and business-friendly local and state governments.

Atlanta is also an international city. Mainly because of busy Hartsfield-Jackson Airport, the city is home to 25 general consulates (as of 2012)—the seventh largest concentration in the country.

In the last decade, metro Atlanta has developed a profitable entertainment industry. The growth is largely owing to a state-wide tax incentive put into place in 2005 to draw film and TV producers. If you enjoy zombie movies, Atlanta gained the title "Zombie Capital of the World" following the success of AMC's TV series *The Walking Dead*. In all, film and television production pumped $1 billion into Georgia's economy in 2010, and those numbers continue to grow. Recently Atlanta hosted production of the second Hunger Games movie, *Catching Fire*.

On a more somber note, Atlanta was hard hit by the 2008 financial crisis and subsequent housing bust. Many homeowners found themselves either upside down or with large losses on their mortgages. On average home values dropped in price to levels not seen since 1996—the worst drop nationwide. The upside? It's never been a better time to buy, and deals abound. Some real estate experts say Atlanta's market is coming back—others say it continues to stall and could see a further plummet in 2013. Only time will tell.

Culturally, Atlanta boasts a flourishing arts scene, with a world-renowned symphony orchestra, a diverse and ever-growing local music industry, scores of museums and art galleries, and a wide array of theatrical productions. Other notable attributes include its climate—temperate winters and sultry summers that allow residents to play outside year-round—and its beauty. Both intown and suburban neighborhoods throughout the metro area are covered in rolling hills and so many trees that Atlanta bears the nickname "The City in a Forest." In the fall residents enjoy tree colors that rival the Appalachians, and in the spring and summer, azaleas, dogwoods, magnolias, and hydrangeas bloom all over the city. At times it's easy to forget you're in the middle of a bustling metropolis.

For all these reasons and more, Atlanta is a great place to live and work, which is why the population continues to grow. And, if you're like most newcomers, you will soon find yourself charmed by the city's potluck mix of southern amiabilities, big-city conveniences, and international clout. Make no mistake, Atlanta is a regional and international hub, a city proud of its past and poised for its future.

This book is designed to guide you through your first exciting and perhaps disquieting weeks as a newcomer to Atlanta. It offers you a survey of neighborhoods, tips on how to settle in, suggestions for rest and relaxation, as well as cultural outings, and other hints to help you acclimate to your new surroundings. The book covers not only Atlanta proper, but also nearby communities frequently populated by newcomers. Recent growth has centered primarily in the area's northern counties, but some families and singles continue to choose intown neighborhoods for their urban feel and access to work and entertainment.

# HISTORY

The land that is now Atlanta originally was the site of a Creek Indian settlement named "Standing Peachtree." The first white settlement in the area was established in 1813, when Lt. George Gilmer erected a fort here, on the banks of the Chattahoochee River, to control growing disagreements between the Creek and their Cherokee neighbors. At the time the fort was built, the area was nothing more than a small outpost on the western edge of America's frontier. It didn't actually become part of Georgia until the Creek ceded their land to the state in 1821, to avoid going to war with the white settlers. But even after the Creek nation left to resettle on lands west of the Mississippi, the Cherokees continued to live in the area alongside white settlers well into the 1830s. The relationship was tenuous, though, and in 1832, the State of Georgia began to take away Cherokee farms and distribute them to white settlers in a land lottery. Many of the settlers took control of the land at gunpoint, resulting in much bloodshed and death. The issue culminated in 1835, when a handful of Cherokee leaders, realizing the futility of further resistance, signed over the rest of their land under the Treaty of New Echota, an act that led to the infamous Trail of Tears. With treaty in hand, and President Andrew Jackson's Indian Removal Act signed into law, over 17,000 Cherokee were rounded up by federal soldiers, herded into camps, and then forced to march westward, 800 miles to Oklahoma, where they were resettled. At least 4,000 died on the journey, and those that survived suffered terribly from hunger, cold, and disease.

Throughout the 1830s, Fort Peachtree, as it had come to be called, became a thriving trading post. In fact, when the Georgia Legislature voted to establish a state-sponsored railroad system linking Georgia to the North and Midwest, this locale was considered as a possible location where the railroads could come together, though the numerous creeks and unsuitable gradients proved to be insurmountable obstacles. In 1837, after surveying half-a-dozen possible routes, railroad engineer Stephen Long chose the perfect location for the southern end of the new rail line. He staked out a point approximately eight miles south of the river and marked it with a "zero-mile" marker on land that is now Five Points in downtown Atlanta. A plaque in Underground Atlanta commemorates the location today, not far from the actual spot that Long chose.

Soon after the location was approved, railroad workers began settling into the area, and a new town, Terminus, was established, which grew quickly to include banks, warehouses, sawmills, and more. The settlement attracted merchants, farmers, and craftsmen from as far away as Virginia and the Carolinas. Textile and ironworks industries soon followed.

In 1843 the name of the town was changed to Marthasville, in honor of Martha Lumpkin, daughter of former governor Wilson Lumpkin, a man who was instrumental in bringing the railroad to the area. Two years later, the town's name changed once more, this time to Atlanta. There are several theories of how this name came to be. One claims that Atlanta was chosen because it is the feminine version of the word Atlantic; a second is that it's a shortened version of the name Atlantica-Pacifica Railroad. Governor Lumpkin, however, maintained that it was yet another tribute to his daughter Martha, whose middle name happened to be Atalanta. Whatever the case, the town continued to grow and prosper, becoming incorporated as a city in 1847.

By 1860 Atlanta was the fourth largest city in the state and was home to nearly 10,000 people—a mix of white settlers and landowners, African-American slaves, and freed slaves. Additionally, the city boasted four rail lines, close to 3,000 homes, and numerous manufacturing and retail shops. At this time, the city was led primarily by merchants and railroad men who, for economic reasons, tended to oppose the idea of secession from the Union. In fact, in the election of 1860, most of Atlanta's voters cast their ballots for Union candidates. However, when Georgia finally seceded from the United States in January 1861, Atlanta joined with the Confederacy and quickly became a major manufacturing and transportation center for Confederate forces during the Civil War. Many industries in the city were converted to wartime production, and new industries were established to produce much-needed munitions and supplies for Confederate soldiers. The two largest were the Quartermasters Depot and the Confederate Government Arsenal, which employed nearly 8,000 men and women. Because of these wartime industries and the employment opportunities associated with them, Atlanta's population swelled to 22,000 in just three short years. Unfortunately, the same productivity and rail lines that made Atlanta a crucial part of the Confederacy also made the city the prime target of Union General William T. Sherman.

In the summer of 1864, Sherman and his troops began their drive to Atlanta. A series of bloody battles ensued, and the city faced nearly daily bombardment from Union cannons. Many civilians were killed, and many homes and businesses were destroyed. On September 1, 1864, after a 117-day siege, General Hood ordered the evacuation of Atlanta, and the mayor surrendered the city to Sherman the next day.

While the terms of the surrender promised the protection of Atlanta, Sherman had a change of heart, ordering all Confederate-related buildings destroyed. And though his instructions called for the buildings to first be leveled and then torched, eager Union soldiers failed to wait for the structures to come down before setting them ablaze. Subsequently, many Atlanta homes and businesses not marked for destruction were also consumed in the fire that swept through the city. As Sherman and his troops continued their march to the sea, Atlanta was left engulfed in flames. Of the 3,600 homes and commercial buildings in Atlanta, all but 400 were destroyed in the burning. The city was left broken and bankrupt.

By 1865, despite the widespread destruction and lack of funds in the city treasury, many of the citizens who had fled the city began to return and rebuild. A plan was developed to repair damaged railroad facilities, and by the fall of that year, all five of the city's rail lines were again operational. In 1866 Atlanta was made the headquarters for area reconstruction. But it was during the Reconstruction Convention of 1867–1868 that Atlanta truly began its climb to become the city it is today. During the convention, city officials offered to provide facilities for the state government if Atlanta should be chosen as state capital. The convention accepted the proposal and Atlanta became the capital of Georgia on April 20, 1868.

At the turn of the 20th century, Georgia's new capital was the largest city in the state and the third largest in the Southeast. It was also a clear leader of commercial development in the region. Both wholesale and retail trade were prospering, the city limits were expanded, and the skyline was altered by the addition of Atlanta's earliest skyscrapers—the Equitable, Flatiron, Empire, and Candler buildings. Additionally, the city's population had tripled in just three decades to 90,000, a number that included 35,000 African Americans who were drawn to the city for its numerous educational and employment opportunities.

Though many of Atlanta's new African-American residents were shuffled into undesirable, even flood-prone sections of the city, it was these segregated neighborhoods that became home to renowned African-American colleges and universities, including the old Fourth Ward (where Morris Brown College was originally located), the south side of town (where Clark University was established), and the west side (where Atlanta University and, later, Morehouse and Spelman colleges were located). In spite of the city's racial barriers, the presence of these strong African-American colleges and accompanying communities, along with increasing economic opportunity, laid the groundwork for Atlanta's prosperous and influential African-American middle class.

Atlanta's early 20th century growth and expansion marked a turning point in how the city was viewed, both from within and without. Local leaders began to encourage not only commercial growth but cultural growth as well, in a bid to transform Atlanta into a city of national prominence. As a result, the High Museum of Art and the Atlanta Historical Society were founded. The Chamber of Commerce also launched a national ad campaign titled "Forward Atlanta," designed to lure new businesses to the city. By all accounts, the campaign was a huge success, bringing companies such as Sears-Roebuck and General Motors to the area, and creating thousands of new jobs.

At the same time, Atlanta's African-American–owned businesses, operating along Auburn Avenue, were prospering as well. Banks, hotels, restaurants, beauty schools, retail shops, and more were thriving along the thoroughfare that had been dubbed "Sweet Auburn." And the success of these local businesses had far-reaching repercussions. As the African-American–owned and –operated newspaper *Atlanta Independent* observed, "Auburn Avenue is an institution with influence and power not only among Georgians, but American Negroes everywhere. It is the heart of Negro big business, a result of Negro cooperation and evidence of Negro possibility." While Auburn Avenue was a point of pride for Atlanta's growing African-American community, it was also still a symbol of segregation, an issue that would plague and even define the city for many years to come.

In the early 1920s, downtown Atlanta, as well as the city's pattern of residential development, was affected by a new mode of transportation—the automobile. Viaducts were built to raise the city's streets above the railroad lines located in the heart of downtown. These viaducts moved the business district up, literally, creating the area now known as Underground Atlanta. The growing use of the automobile also led to the creation of new suburbs outside the city limits and a ring of middle-class communities located just two to five miles from downtown. These communities included Virginia Highland to the north, Candler Park to the east, West End to the south, and Washington Park—a African-American suburban development—to the west.

Another major development in transportation, the airplane, helped shape Atlanta at that time as well. The airplane first made its appearance here in the early part of the decade, but by 1930, thanks in large part to William B. Hartsfield, a man who would later become mayor of the city, Atlanta had established its own airfield and passenger terminal, as well as its own mail and passenger routes. This early connection to the growing airline industry is a key component in Atlanta's rise to the international city it is today.

The growth and prosperity that defined the city for decades came to a halt in the 1930s, during the Great Depression. Unlike other cities its size, though, Atlanta was poorly prepared to meet this financial emergency, and there were few agencies or programs in place to assist the rising number of unemployed. Relief for the city's poor and newly unemployed residents didn't come until after the inauguration of President Franklin D. Roosevelt, whose "New Deal" legislation provided much needed funds and resources to hard-hit areas throughout the country. Atlanta took full advantage of the opportunities offered through the "New Deal," and was, in fact, one of the first cities in the nation to have a federally operated relief program. Millions of dollars were pumped into the local economy through agencies such as the Civil Works Administration, the Public Works Administration, and the Works Progress Administration, money that went toward building and repairing local schools and hospitals, the grading of runways at the city's airport, the organization of a 45-member symphony orchestra, and the construction of a new city-wide sewer system. It was also "New Deal" funds that paid for the development and construction of the nation's first public housing projects, Techwood Homes, then a community for low-income white residents, which opened in 1936. University Homes, for African-American residents, opened in 1938. Both projects were the idea of Atlanta real estate developer Charles F. Palmer, who wanted to rid the city of its slums and replace them with federally funded public housing.

As the 1930s came to a close, Atlanta's economy picked up. Banks were back in operation, the local aviation industry continued to grow, and there was an increase in private business. The beginning of World War II helped Atlanta's economic recovery. Between 1941 and 1945 over $10 million of federal funds was invested in war industries and military bases located in the South. Atlanta, in particular, benefited from the investment, as new federal installations were established throughout the metro area and war-related industries provided thousands of new jobs. Many local men and women enlisted in the armed forces or signed on to help with the war effort. Thousands more soldiers and military support personnel either passed through the city or were stationed nearby during that time. Local businesses did their part as well. Bell Bomber (later, Bell Aircraft, and then Lockheed-Georgia) in Marietta devoted its entire production output to the war effort. And Coca-Cola, which was created here in 1886, began distributing bottles of Coke to servicemen around the world, establishing itself as a truly international company.

The growth and progress that occurred during the war years continued well into the 1950s; by 1954, there were over 800 industries in the city and almost 1,200 national corporations with offices in the metro area. Atlanta city limits were expanded to include an additional 82 square miles and 100,000 new residents. And highway construction was already well under way. Unfortunately, even as the new highway system improved Atlanta's connection to the rest of the country and fed the city's suburban growth, it did little to improve the lives of its local

African-American population. Atlanta's highway construction displaced almost 67,000 African-American residents between 1956 and 1966, creating a severe housing shortage within the community. This racial disparity, combined with years of segregation, finally came to a head in the 1960s. The local civil rights movement, led by the young Atlanta minister Martin Luther King, Jr., turned its attention to overthrowing the Jim Crow law. Local African-American college students staged sit-ins around the city in the hopes of desegregating downtown restaurants and other public facilities. In the fall of 1961, the city itself began the court-ordered desegregation of its public school system, as nine African-American students peacefully enrolled and began classes at four Atlanta area high schools: Brown, Henry Grady, Murphy, and Northside. These important events led to even more dramatic changes for the city, as the courts ordered the removal of city barricades in southwest Atlanta (originally erected to separate African-American and white neighborhoods), allowing for African-American residential expansion into what had formerly been all-white communities. This, in turn, led to the quick exodus of white residents to the suburbs. In the late 1960s, Atlanta's African-American population increased by 68,587, while the white population declined by 60,132. And by 1970, Atlanta had a majority African-American population, which still holds today.

Interestingly, as African-American Atlantans worked for civil rights, they met little resistance from the city's white business leaders. In fact, most influential businessmen in Atlanta, including Coca-Cola CEO Robert Woodruff, were concerned about the city's image in national business circles, and wanted to spare residents the acts of racial violence that had occurred in other southern cities, such as Little Rock and Birmingham. Rather than wage an ugly battle against the civil rights movement, white leaders instead nicknamed Atlanta "The City Too Busy to Hate," to differentiate it from its southern neighbors, and focused on urban renewal projects, construction of a new sports stadium, and the creation of a mass transit system that would benefit all residents, African-American and white.

Atlanta's mayor during this time was Ivan Allen, Jr., son of a prominent businessman and former president of the Atlanta Chamber of Commerce. Though Allen had originally been against African-American residential expansion, he soon became an advocate of the civil rights movement and a strong supporter of Martin Luther King, Jr. Mayor Allen even testified before the US Senate Commerce Committee in 1963 in favor of a national civil rights bill. He was the only southern elected official to do so.

By the early 1970s, Atlanta was settling into its role as a progressive and influential city. Three new sports teams—the Atlanta Braves, the Atlanta Falcons, and the Atlanta Hawks—called the city home; business continued to boom in the metro area; and the local political landscape was growing to reflect the diversity in Atlanta's population.

In 1972 Andrew Young, a colleague and former aide of Martin Luther King, Jr., became Georgia's first African-American congressman. African-American representation on the city council and in the state legislature had increased significantly.

And, perhaps most significantly, in 1973 Maynard Jackson was elected Atlanta's first African-American mayor. He would go on to serve three terms—two consecutive, with a third in 1990.

Throughout the next two decades, transportation continued to be a crucial factor in Atlanta's growth and development. City voters approved the creation and funding of the Metropolitan Atlanta Rapid Transit Authority (MARTA), a citywide public transportation system combining bus routes and rapid rail service. Hartsfield International Airport (later renamed Hartsfield-Jackson International Airport) opened a new $450 million air terminal, and is now one of the busiest hubs in the world. And Atlanta's connection to interstate highways I-85, I-75, and I-20 continued to bring new residents into the area and facilitate suburban growth. By 1980, the population of metro Atlanta had reached two million.

The advances in Atlanta's transportation industries, particularly at Hartsfield, helped the city increase its convention and tourism business in the 1990s. The renovation and expansion of the World Congress Center, the revitalization of Underground Atlanta, and the construction of new sports facilities—Turner Field for the Braves, the Georgia Dome for the Falcons, and Philips Arena for the Hawks and the Thrashers—didn't hurt either. These new facilities not only provided increased entertainment options for residents and visitors, they also helped combat the movement of retail businesses and developments to the outlying suburbs. This intown revitalization movement reached its peak in the mid-1990s as the city proudly prepared to host the 1996 Summer Olympic Games. New facilities were built, including the 21-acre Centennial Olympic Park and the Olympic Village (which was converted to student housing for Georgia Tech and Georgia State University). And older, existing buildings were given much needed and long overdue facelifts.

Since the start of the 21st century, metro Atlanta expanded to include 28 counties, and continues to become more urban and diverse over time. According to the US Census 2010, Atlanta is the country's fourth-largest black-majority city. Due to its history, Atlanta has long been seen as a center of African American political power, education, and arts. Also between 2000 and 2010, blacks moved increasingly to the suburbs, with the city's population decreasing by around 31,000 people, while whites moved into the city—growing 31% or by 22,000 new residents.

Like other sprawling metropolitan areas, Atlanta can be a transportation nightmare. You almost have to have a car or vehicle to live and work in the city, as its public transit can be spotty and include long detours. For decades Atlantans eschewed carpool programs and would rally to prevent transit coming into their community for fear of crime. However, with the current gridlock and younger generation—that mentality is changing.

In the late 1990s, the Georgia Department of Transportation tried to ease the city's traffic problems by increasing the number of passenger lanes on Atlanta's interstates and highways, and constructing a new toll road, an extension of Georgia 400, to directly connect Atlanta to the north suburbs. Significant headway was made in November 2008 when the US Department of Transportation Congestion Reduction Demonstration (CRD) Program awarded the Atlanta region a $110 million grant to support a $182 million transportation improvement project. This initiative was led by the Georgia Department of Transportation (GDOT), the State Road & Tollway Authority (SRTA), the Georgia Regional Transportation Authority (GRTA), and a number of federal, regional and local transportation partners.

The project was designed to provide more reliable travel times, commuter choices, and regional transit enhancements to residents. Actions included doubling the Xpress service in the I-85 corridor, supporting Xpress facilities throughout the region, and adding more Xpress buses. Furthermore, the program added the city's first high occupancy toll or Express Lane, where drivers can pay for a faster commute. According to SRTA, usage of the I-85 Express Lanes has more than tripled since their opening in October 2011.

Despite the efforts, Atlanta still ranks as one of the worst in the country for its traffic. According to a 2010 report from the Atlanta Regional Commission (ARC), there are around 6.8 million vehicles registered in the Atlanta region, with an average of two per household. Eighty-two percent of commuters drive to and from work alone every day, and the average commute time is 30 minutes one way. However, if you are stuck in one of Atlanta five busiest rush hours, expect that time to double.

Other noteworthy facts: you can research the busiest roads on the ARC's website, atlantaregional.com, and perhaps plan alternative routes or choose a different neighborhood if you want to avoid spending so much time in your car. The busiest interstates continue to be the Downtown Connector, I-85 and I-75 North, and Georgia 400.

## HOW TO GET AROUND

So, obviously, one of the first things you'll need to know about Atlanta is how to get around—and this is no easy concept, so feel free to buckle up. Much of metro Atlanta was planned as suburbs, with mass transportation only running within the city and just outside its boundaries. Of the nine other counties in the metro area, only a handful have access to MARTA, the city's mass transit system. As the city's population boomed and demand mounted in the late 1990s, local and state governments began to add and plan greater mass transportation and pedestrian projects. Cobb County has offered a bus system since the mid-'90s, while Gwinnett and the community of Buckhead added their own systems around 2000. Also in 2000, the state created Xpress, metro Atlanta's first commuter bus program. Overseen by the Greater Regional Transportation Authority, the system boasts some 20 routes that ferry commuters from as far south as Newnan and as far north as Cumming into the city of Atlanta.

Still, unless you work during off hours, don't expect to avoid Atlanta's gridlock traffic. Plan to make the most of on-demand traffic reports, Google Maps, or other

GPS devices to avoid snares, and, if possible, steer clear of the most congested areas altogether.

Also, newcomers will soon experience Atlanta's mishmash of roads, a good portion of which contain the word "Peachtree." Due to the way the city grew, roads were not planned on grids, and many do not faithfully go north to south or east to west, making it difficult to find your way around. Expect instead to rely on the interstates first, followed by a set of regulars—like Peachtree Road and Piedmont Road—and then Atlanta's numerous side streets to get you where you need to go. Downtown Atlanta is also one of the most difficult areas of the city to navigate, even for natives. Piedmont Park blocks out a large portion of the Midtown area; therefore, few roads go east-west straight through the city. In short, you are sure to get lost at least a few times, but don't despair. If you have a smart phone you can rely somewhat on its mapping system and GPS, and many vehicles come with GPS. And if technology fails, you can always stop and ask for directions. Most importantly, ask friends familiar to the area to share their secret shortcuts; they can save you time and traffic headaches.

Here are a few additional **tips for finding your way around**:

- I-285 makes a loop around the perimeter of the city. If someone says that a place is located "outside the perimeter," what they mean is that you must travel beyond I-285 to find it.
- Although over fifty streets contain the word "Peachtree," only one of them is the main thoroughfare. It begins downtown as Peachtree Street and changes to Peachtree Road in the Midtown area. In the heart of Buckhead, Peachtree Road forks: The east side of the fork is Peachtree Road, which travels northeast towards Gwinnett County and eventually becomes Peachtree Industrial Boulevard north of the perimeter. The west side of the fork is Roswell Road, which goes mostly north toward Sandy Springs and Roswell.
- Atlanta is divided roughly into four quadrants. Peachtree Street is the east-west dividing line and Martin Luther King Jr. Drive is the north-south dividing line on the southern edge of downtown. Therefore, if NW follows an address, this means that your destination is somewhere downtown or north of the downtown area and west of Peachtree.
- Get to know the highways. These are the only major roads that connect county to county. Often, a merchant will name a highway exit number when giving you directions. For details about Atlanta area highways, see the **Transportation** chapter of this book.
- Remember the locations of malls. These are major landmarks in the city, and often people give directions based on a locale's proximity to the nearest mall.
- Don't assume that just because two streets run parallel to each other, they will stay that way. For example, Peachtree Street and Piedmont Road, the two major north-south routes, intersect in north Buckhead. Oxford Road crosses Briarcliff twice, effectively paralleling itself.

- Remember that Atlanta streets wind unpredictably. Even if you are convinced that the route you are taking leads you in a straight line, you may not end up where you think you should. Keep your sense of humor. Atlanta is a lovely city to get lost in.
- For those who would like a hard map of Atlanta, there are a number of places to order one online. Visit **A Maps & Graphics Company** at www.amaps.com, or call 404-550-0465. Another good source is **GISential Maps** at www.mapsuper-store.com or 404-550-0465. You can also pick up Atlanta maps at local stores such as Barnes & Noble, OfficeMax, Staples, or Office Depot locations, though they may not offer as wide a selection as the specialty map stores. If all else fails, log onto the web and order an Atlanta street map from **First Books**, www.firstbooks.com.

## LOCAL LINGO

In addition to traffic tips, you may also want to investigate, and perhaps memorize, some of the local slang to help you make your way around the city. While Atlanta's local lingo isn't terribly colorful, it is laced with highway and traffic nicknames, area landmarks, and, yes, the occasional slow southern drawl. Though deep southern accents are less common, and often less noticeable, inside the perimeter, it's certain that you will run into them from time to time. You may find this drawl quaint, amusing, or just plain difficult to understand at times. Whatever the case, Atlanta's local lingo can definitely sound like a language of its own.

A complete listing is near impossible, but here are a few landmarks, roadways, and pronunciations to get you started:

**Agnes Scott:** a liberal arts college for women, located in Decatur

**The AJC:** *Atlanta Journal-Constitution*, Atlanta's daily newspaper

**Atlanta:** usually pronounced "at-LAN-ah," dropping the last "t"

**The Big Chicken:** 50-foot-tall steel chicken sign advertising a local KFC; the most recognizable landmark in Cobb County

**The Bravos:** nickname of the Atlanta Braves

**Brookwood Interchange:** where I-75 and I-85 southbound join and, when going northbound on the Downtown Connector (see below), where the two highways split

**Buckhead Loop:** the road that arcs from Piedmont Road across GA 400 to Peachtree Road

**CDC:** Centers for Disease Control and Prevention, located near Emory

**Chamblee:** pronounced "SHAM-blee"

**Cobb Cloverleaf:** I-75 and I-285 on the northwest side of the perimeter, in Cobb County

**The Concrete Campus:** Georgia State University

**The Connector:** same as the Downtown Connector

**DeKalb:** usually pronounced "Dee-CAB" or "Duh-CAB"

**Downtown Connector:** the stretch of highway at which I-75 and I-85 are combined, located between 10th Street/14th Street to the north and Langford Parkway to the south

**The Dunwoody Family:** Chamblee-Dunwoody, Peachtree-Dunwoody, and Ashford-Dunwoody roads, collectively

**East Expressway:** I-20 from downtown through the east side of metro Atlanta

**East-West Connector:** connects Town Center Mall near Kennesaw to the Cumberland Mall area in southeast Cobb (not to be confused with The Connector or the East and West expressways)

**Emory:** usually pronounced "EM-ree," can refer to the university or the hospital

**Fayetteville:** often pronounced "FATE-vul"

**Forsyth:** pronounced "Fer-SYTH," though you may also hear it pronounced "FER-syth"

**Freedom Parkway:** parkway running from the Downtown Connector to Ponce de Leon Avenue

**Glenridge Connector:** a short, highly traveled road that runs from Peachtree-Dunwoody to I-285 and then becomes Glenridge Drive

**Grady Curve:** the curve of the Downtown Connector as it circumvents downtown's central business district near Grady Hospital

**GSU:** Georgia State University

**The Highlands:** nickname for the Virginia Highland neighborhood

**The Hooch:** nickname of the Chattahoochee River, most often used in the phrase, "shooting the Hooch," which means spending the day rafting down the Chattahoochee

**Inner Loop:** the inside lanes of I-285

**The ITC:** the International Theological Center

**Jesus Junction:** the intersection of Peachtree, East Wesley, and West Wesley roads in Buckhead, so named because of the four large churches located there

**L5P:** Little Five Points (see **Neighborhoods** chapter)

**Lawrenceville:** often pronounced "LORNTZ-vul"

**The Loaf:** *Creative Loafing*, Atlanta's weekly alternative newspaper

**Marietta:** though usually pronounced "Mary-ETTA," you may occasionally run into someone who likes to call it "MAY-retta"; home of the Big Chicken

**Marietta Loop:** unofficial name of the 120 Loop, the North Marietta and South Marietta Parkways that encircle the center of Marietta

**McMansions:** the oversized homes that seem to pop up overnight in some of the more affluent neighborhoods in metro Atlanta

**Morehouse:** refers to both Morehouse College and Morehouse School of Medicine

**Northeast Expressway:** I-85 from downtown through the northeast side of metro Atlanta

**Outer Loop:** the outside lanes of I-285

**The Perimeter:** the more commonly used name for I-285, the interstate that circles Atlanta

**Pill Hill:** the intersection of Johnson Ferry Road and the Glenridge Connector in Sandy Springs, which is home to numerous major Atlanta hospitals, as well as hundreds of private doctor's offices

**Roswell:** often pronounced "RAHZ-wul"

**SoBu:** South Buckhead, an area of trendy clubs and restaurants (see **Neighborhoods** chapter)

**Southern Crescent:** the southern region of metro Atlanta, including Butts, Clayton, Coweta, Fayette, and Henry Counties

**SoVo:** *Southern Voice*, Atlanta's gay/lesbian newspaper

**Spaghetti Junction:** the soaring tangle of over- and underpasses, on-ramps and exits of I-85 at I-285; one of Atlanta's best known and appropriately nicknamed landmarks

**Spelman:** liberal arts college for women, located in Atlanta

**Stone Mountain Freeway:** unofficial term for US 78 due to its proximity to Stone Mountain

**Sunshine Slowdown:** the effect of sunlight in motorists' eyes as they travel east on I-20 in the morning and west on I-20 in the evening

**Tech:** more common nickname of the Georgia Institute of Technology

**Top End:** the northern segment of I-285 from I-75 to I-85, generally the most congested part of the Perimeter

**UGA:** University of Georgia at Athens

**Uga:** pronounced "UGH-ah"; the bulldog mascot of the University of Georgia

**West Expressway:** I-20 from downtown through the west side of metro Atlanta

**Y'all:** not limited to Atlanta, but used frequently here nonetheless; a more easygoing and southern way of saying "you" or "you all"

TODAY'S GREATER ATLANTA AREA IS COMPRISED OF 28 COUNTIES, SPAN-ning over 6,000 square miles. The epicenter, of course, is Atlanta itself, which includes parts of Fulton and DeKalb counties—both are high-lighted here, as are Atlanta's other two "inner-ring" counties, Cobb and Gwinnett. Additionally, we will cover Cherokee County, one of the state's fastest growing, which lies northwest of Atlanta. All of these counties, along with community pro-files, contact information, and county resource listings, can be found below. The remaining metro Atlanta counties each possess a number of municipalities that might be appealing to newcomers, as long as the commute to the city, which can be over an hour, is not an issue. A listing of each outer-ring county, including contact information, has been provided in the **Additional Counties** section at the end of this chapter.

## CITY OF ATLANTA—FULTON COUNTY

The City of Atlanta covers 132 square miles and is now home to about 420,000 residents. It's also host to a thriving arts scene and a wide variety of sports, enter-tainment, and dining options. The area's largest greenspace, Piedmont Park, is in the city as well.

In the not so distant past, Atlanta was shifting toward being a depressed city center with residents moving away from its intown core out to the suburbs to set up house. But the last 20 years have brought a dramatic turnaround to the city. Spurred by the Atlanta's bid to host the 1996 Summer Olympics, the 1990s ush-ered in a new wave of intown revitalization. City officials and local business leaders worked to rebuild Atlanta's historic communities and industrial areas, and that work paid off. Today the city boasts a diverse mix of residential and commercial

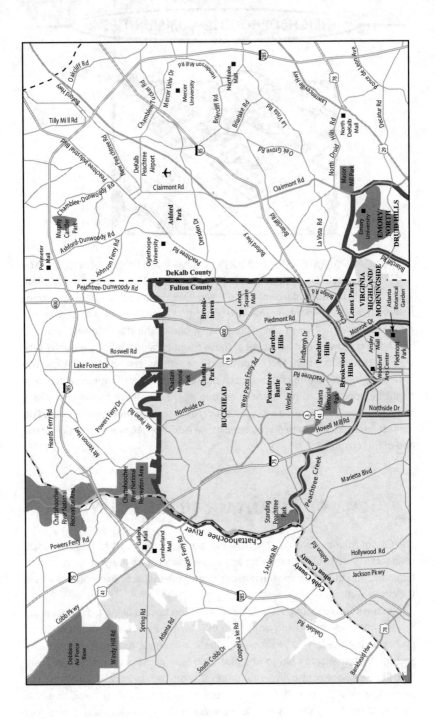

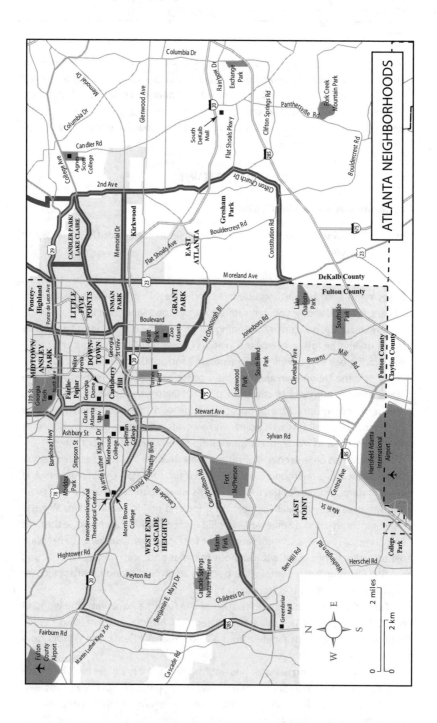

ATLANTA NEIGHBORHOODS

developments—high rises, lofts, mansions, historic homes, and townhomes, as well as malls, stadiums, museums, galleries, restaurants, night life, hotels, and more.

Most of Atlanta proper is located in Fulton County. And, in fact, that's where Downtown, with its many local and state government offices, is located. Along the east side of town, however, a few Atlanta neighborhoods overlap into DeKalb County.

## DOWNTOWN

### Castleberry Hill • Fairlie-Poplar

**Boundaries: North**: North Avenue; **East**: Boulevard; **South**: I-20; **West**: Northside Drive

The Atlanta skyline is a beautiful sight, with buildings rising up to meet the sky and towering over the bustling sidewalks and streets that teem with pedestrians and cars. On a clear day, you can catch sight of Stone Mountain in the distance, looming above the horizon as if standing watch over the city. And in all directions there is green, the lush green of the inviting Centennial Olympic Park and of the hefty shade trees that crowd over Downtown's surrounding neighborhoods.

By day, the Downtown area is a busy commercial district, home to city and state government, financial institutions, the CNN Center, the Georgia Dome, Philips Arena, and Underground Atlanta. But at night, the workaday population is replaced by residents who call this area home, and by visitors heading into Downtown to take advantage of its many sports, dining, and entertainment opportunities.

Thanks to an organized revitalization effort over the last two decades, Downtown Atlanta has undergone a massive facelift. New retail establishments and entertainment and residential developments have been constructed, and more are on the way. Centennial Olympic Park, located at Techwood Drive, Marietta Street, and International Boulevard, now fills a once-blighted area next to the CNN Center, and serves as a favorite lunch spot for Downtown workers. It also plays host to a variety of concerts throughout the year and, with its grassy areas and beautiful Olympic Ring Fountain, has become an attractive and popular place for Downtown residents and visitors to hang out.

Other Downtown destinations, such as the Georgia Aquarium, The World of Coca-Cola, Imagine It! The Children's Museum of Atlanta, and The King Center, continue to attract both families from all over metro Atlanta and visitors from around the world.

With the continuing need for housing, many of the city's older buildings have been transformed into lofts and condos. And the population has become increasingly young and well-educated—a high note for nearby retailers. According to non-profit group Central Atlanta Progress, the area saw a 61% increase in college-educated residents between the ages of 25 and 35 between 2000 and 2010.

Probably the most popular Downtown community is **Fairlie-Poplar**. Coined for the cross streets, this National Historic District in the heart of the city has long been revered for its detailed architecture and charming narrow streets. But today it's also known for its interesting mix of retail, entertainment, and loft spaces as well. It was back in the late 1990s when Georgia State University led the way for the redevelopment of Fairlie-Poplar by renovating an old movie theater into the Rialto Center for the Performing Arts. The school also moved its College of Business and its schools of Music and Public Policy into the district, and eventually constructed a student dormitory on Techwood Drive. The goal of attracting merchants to the area by providing a

*Fairlie-Poplar*

steady flux of students worked. Area businesses include the Trinity Gallery, Starbucks, Gateway News, and the Tabernacle, a hip nightclub. The Fairlie-Poplar Café and Grill, located at 85 Poplar Street, is *the* place for lunch.

Another bright spot among Downtown neighborhoods is **Castleberry Hill**. This historic warehouse district, located in southwest Atlanta, has undergone an amazing renaissance in recent years, thanks in part to a dedicated neighborhood association. What once was an overlooked, rundown industrial district is now a comfortable, cosmopolitan community, filled with artists, restaurants, and dramatic loft apartments. Residents here tend to be young, hip, and artsy. Today you'll find at least five art galleries in the neighborhood, including the renowned Marcia Wood Gallery on Walker Street, all within walking distance of the dozen or so warehouse-turned-loft buildings. For drinks, the Elliott Street Pub and Bottle Rocket are the pubs of choice. Patrons include a mix of college and graduate students, residents, Downtown workers, and tourists.

StudioPlex, a mixed-use development in the Auburn Avenue Warehouse district, is a great fit for urban dwellers. This all-in-one site offers residential loft space as well as commercial, gallery, and live-work spaces for artists.

**Website**: www.atlantaga.gov
**Area Code**: 404
**ZIP Codes**: 30303, 30308, 30312, 30313, 30314, 30301, 30370, 30379, 30371, 30365

**Post Offices**: Central City Carrier (where Downtown residents go to pick up packages), 400 Pryor St, 404-222-0765; Phoenix Station, 41 Marietta St, 404-534-2963; Civic Center, 570 Piedmont Ave NE; Gate City Station, 486 Decatur St; Morris Brown, 50 Sunset Ave NW; CNN Center, One CNN Center; 800-275-8777, www.usps.com

**Police Precincts**: 398 Centennial Olympic Park Dr NW, 404-658-7054; 247 Auburn Ave, 404-658-6452; 94 Pryor St, 404-658-6364; www.atlantapd.org

**Emergency Hospital**: Grady Memorial Hospital, 80 Jesse Hill Jr Dr, 404-616-4307; www.gradyhealthsystem.org

**Libraries**: Central Library, One Margaret Mitchell Square NW, 404-730-1700; Auburn Ave, Research Library of African American Culture and History, 101 Auburn Ave NE, 404-730-4001; Martin Luther King, Jr., 409 John Wesley Dobbs Ave, 404-730-1185; www.afplweb.com

**Public School Education**: Atlanta Public Schools, 404-802-3500; Homework Hotline, 404-827-8620; www.atlanta.k12.ga.us

**Community Publications**: *Atlanta Intown*, 404-586-0002, www.atlantaintownpaper.com/

**Community Resources**: Atlanta Downtown Neighborhood Association, www.atlantadna.org; Central Atlanta Progress, Atlanta Downtown Improvement District, 404-658-1877, www.centralatlantaprogress.org; Downtown Atlanta Ambassador Force, 404-215-9600, www.centralatlantaprogress.org; Metro Atlanta Chamber of Commerce, 404-880-9000, www.metroatlantachamber.com; Castleberry Hill Neighborhood Association, 404-228-2078, www.castleberryhill.org; StudioPlex, 404-523-4467, www.studioplexlofts.com/; Centennial Olympic Park, 404-223-4412, www.centennialpark.com; Rialto Center for the Performing Arts, 404-651-4727, www.rialtocenter.org; CNN Center, 404-827-4000, www.cnn.com; Underground Atlanta, 404-523-2311, www.underground-atlanta.com; World of Coca-Cola, 404-676-5151, www.worldofcoca-cola.com/; Imagine It! The Children's Museum of Atlanta, 404-659-5437, www.imagineit-cma.org; The Marcia Wood Gallery, 404-827-0030, www.marciawoodgallery.com; Slice, 404-588-1820, www.sliceatlanta.com

**Public Transportation**: **MARTA**, 404-848-4711, www.itsmarta.com; **East-West Line stations**: Dome/GA World Congress Center/Philips Arena, Five Points, Georgia State, and King Memorial; **North-South Line stations**: North Ave, Civic Center, Peachtree Center, Five Points, and Garnett; for detailed bus routes visit www.itsmarta.com/bus-routes-by-route

## WEST END/CASCADE HEIGHTS

**Boundaries: North**: I-20; **East**: I-29; **South**: Campbellton Road; **West**: I-285

The southwestern edge of downtown Atlanta boasts one of the largest and most prominent bastions of historically African-American education, the Atlanta University Center. This renowned educational complex consists of four separate institutions: Clark Atlanta University, Morehouse College, Morehouse School of Medicine, and Spelman College. There aren't many new retail establishments in the heart of one of Atlanta's oldest neighborhoods—most businesses have been around for years—but don't let the lack of new development fool you; local residents and business owners are proud of their community and do what they can to make their neighborhood inviting. Many area homes, apartments, and commercial buildings have been freshly painted, refurbished, or remodeled in recent years, and the once-blighted downtown neighborhood surrounding the Atlanta University Center has gone through a significant transformation, with local restaurants and boutiques displaying a much-needed facelift.

Minutes away from the commercial district, heading southwest on Ralph D. Abernathy Boulevard, is the small-town community atmosphere of the historic **West End**. Once the center of Atlanta, this neighborhood of classic Victorians and charming bungalows dates back to 1835. Journalist Joel Chandler Harris, author of the beloved Uncle Remus stories, made his home here. His house, the Wren's Nest, is one of the area's prime tourist attractions. Its restoration is just part of a widespread effort by local residents and businesses to rejuvenate the neighborhood. Although the expansion of I-20 in the mid-sixties drove some residents away, the West End was able to maintain much of its original charm. Today some new retail areas nicely coexist with old Victorian houses, offering residents middle-class comfort and suburban shopping convenience.

However, it is important to mention that despite its progress, the West End was hit very badly by the 2008 economic collapse. Around 48% of the community was affected by home foreclosures, placing the neighborhood on a number of top ten lists for communities most impacted by mortgage fraud. As a result many house hunters have been turned off by the large number of boarded-up homes in West End. But remember, markets always turn around, and buying now could save you a lot of money once the area rebounds. You just need to consider whether you are willing to live in a slightly blighted community until that rebound happens.

On a better note, the West End features a thriving exchange of African-American history and culture. The Hammonds House Galleries and Resource Center of African-American Art contains an outstanding permanent collection of African-American and Haitian art. This antebellum home also hosts various educational programs and cultural events. The Shrine of the Black Madonna Bookstore and Cultural Arts Center is the South's largest African-American bookstore and is another vibrant center of community life.

If you continue west on Cascade Road, the terrain becomes more wooded and rolling, and the pace of retail and housing developments much more hurried than in the West End. **Cascade Heights**, a small community bordered by Venetian Drive to the south and Centra Villa Drive to the east, begins as a series of

*Cascade Heights*

quiet, tree-lined streets and comfortable houses set on nice, mid-sized lots. Most of the homes here represent the bungalow and brick ranch styles similar to the ones found in other older, middle-class Atlanta neighborhoods. In recent years, though, the area has seen a massive wave of development, resulting in the construction of numerous impressive single-family homes built around culs-de-sac and small man-made lakes. Newly developed subdivisions in the Cascade Heights area, such as Cascade Manor, Cascade Glen, and Cascade Knolls, provide middle- and upper-income residents with a peaceful suburban retreat within a short drive of Downtown. The area's influx of new residents has encouraged the growth of sprawling new retail outlets that cater to expanding consumer needs. The development spreads beyond I-285, where exclusive communities are springing up alongside office parks.

Just west of Cascade Heights you'll find a pocket of land called the Cascade Springs Nature Preserve, which provides a peaceful recreation area, perfect for quiet walks. The preserve includes a quarry, nursery, hiking trails that lead past a creek, and a handicapped accessible trail.

**Website**: www.atlantaga.gov
**Area Code**: 404
**ZIP Codes**: 30310, 30311
**Post Offices**: Cascade Heights, 2414 Herring Rd SW; West End, 848 Oglethorpe Ave SW; 800-275-8777, www.usps.com
**Police Precincts**: 676 Fair St, 404-658-6274; 1125 Cascade Cir SW, 404-756-1903; 2000 Campbellton Rd, 404-755-1499; 3565 Martin Luther King Jr Dr, 404-505-3131; www.atlantapd.org
**Emergency Hospitals**: Grady Memorial Hospital, 80 Jesse Hill Jr Dr, 404-616-4307, www.gradyhealthsystem.org; Atlanta Medical Center, 303 Parkway Drive NE, Atlanta, 404-265-4000, www.atlantamedicalcenter.com

**Libraries**: Southwest Regional, 3665 Cascade Rd SW, 404-699-6363; West End, 525 Peeples St SW, 404-752-8740; www.afplweb.com

**Public School Education**: Atlanta Public Schools, 404-802-3500; Homework Hotline, 404-827-8620; www.atlanta.k12.ga.us

**Community Publications**: *Atlanta Intown*, 404-586-0002, www.atlantaintownpaper.com

**Community Resources**: Atlanta University Center, 404-523-5148, www.aucenter.edu; West End Kiwanis Club, 2343 Campbellton Rd SW, 404-344-3022; The Wren's Nest House Museum, 1050 Ralph David Abernathy Blvd SW, 404-753-7735; Hammonds House Galleries, 503 Peeples St SW, 404-752-8730, www.hammondshouse.org; The Shrine of the Black Madonna Bookstore and Cultural Arts Center, 404-752-6125, www.shrinebookstore.com; Cascade Youth Organization, 1620 Delowe St SW, 404-753-8804; Cascade Springs Nature Preserve, 404-752-5385; Metro Atlanta Chamber of Commerce, 404-880-9000, www.metroatlantachamber.com

**Public Transportation**: **MARTA**, 404-848-4711, www.itsmarta.com; **North-South Line station**: West End Station; for detailed bus routes, for detailed bus routes visit www.itsmarta.com/bus-routes-by-route

## BUCKHEAD

**Brookwood Hills • Peachtree Hills • Peachtree Battle • Garden Hills • Brookhaven**

**Boundaries: North**: Atlanta city limits; **East**: Atlanta city limits; **South**: Downtown connector; **West**: Cobb County line

Originally the home of Cherokee and Creek Indian tribes, Buckhead's beginnings can be traced to South Carolina native Henry Irby. In 1838, at a time when much of the Atlanta area was being auctioned off in lotteries to European settlers, Irby purchased 203 acres of land now known as Buckhead. He named the land "Irbyville" and at its heart built a tavern and general store. Outside the tavern he posted the now famous head of a buck, a landmark that later inspired the area's name, "Buckhead."

Over time, Buckhead evolved from a sparsely populated outpost to the neighborhood of choice for wealthy Atlantans. In 1952, the city of Atlanta annexed Buckhead, and in 1959, the neighborhood became home to the city's first shopping mall, Lenox Mall.

Today Buckhead is home to an exclusive mix of shopping, dining, and entertainment venues, as well as hundreds of old and new mansions, including the state's Governor's Mansion. The heavily wooded, rolling terrain is broken into a number of neighborhoods perfect for well-to-do professionals and their families. Homes range from renovated cottages and historic properties to new mansions and full-fledged estates. A number of historic country clubs and private schools also define the area, and the public schools are some of the best in the state.

Five miles north of Downtown in Buckhead is the **Brookwood Hills** district, recognized by the National Register of Historic Places. This neighborhood stands on the site of important Civil War clashes between Union and Confederate troops. In the late 1880s, the area drew prominent Atlanta hotel owner Joseph Thompson, who, with his wife, built a country estate near what is now the Peachtree Road–I-85 interchange. They called the estate "Brookwood." In 1912 developer B. F. Burnette began the subdivision today known as Brookwood Hills. The development boomed after World War I and is today characterized by its oak-lined streets and numerous finely crafted neo-Victorian style homes. Area amenities include the Brookwood Hills Community Club and a small commercial district located from Brighton to Collier Road. Here you'll find popular eateries and a number of art galleries. In addition, one of Atlanta's best emergency hospitals, Piedmont Hospital, is located nearby.

Just north of Brookwood Hills is the **Peachtree Hills/Peachtree Battle** neighborhood. Akin to its neighbor, this area was the site of fierce Civil War fighting during the Atlanta campaign known as "The Battle of Peachtree Creek." Those interested in the Civil War can learn about the battle by reading historical markers located throughout the neighborhood. The houses and estates along lovely Peachtree Battle Avenue and the surrounding streets are part of a planned community originally called Peachtree Heights, designed at the turn of the 20th century by architect and future Georgia governor Eurith D. Rivers. Unlike much of Atlanta, this neighborhood features wide boulevards, conceived for upper-class residents who owned automobiles. A tour of neighborhood homes reveals a variety of architectural styles, including art deco, Romanesque Revival, and the international style.

At the intersection of Peachtree Battle and Peachtree Road stands the Peachtree Battle shopping center, the commercial hub of the area. The strip is anchored by a Publix Super Market and contains various restaurants and specialty stores. Behind the shopping center, the Peachtree Hills community stretches east toward Piedmont Road. This section of the neighborhood is home to young affluent professionals and families. Increasingly, the smaller homes have been replaced or renovated. The neighborhood is also a dream come true for sports enthusiasts. Atlanta's largest tennis facility, the Bitsy Grant Tennis Center, is located here, as is the Bobby Jones Golf Course. Both facilities are open to the public.

Further north along Peachtree is **Garden Hills**, which sits like an oasis in the middle of Buckhead's busy commercial district. The area was developed by Phillips Campbell McDuffie, a prominent Atlanta lawyer and businessman active in both social and civic circles. In 1925, McDuffie formed Garden Hills Corp. and marketed the subdivision and its amenities—a stately pool and club house—as "Beautiful Garden Hills." Today the neighborhood is a favorite for active wealthy families who prefer intown living with a historic flair. A variety of early 20th century homes

*Garden Hills*

edge Garden Hills' winding tree-lined streets, not to mention its abundant parks and recreational areas. The neighborhood contains its own public swimming pool, park, and community clubhouse at the intersection of East Wesley and Rumson roads. Plus any number of shops, restaurants, or nightclubs are just a few blocks away along Peachtree Street in either Buckhead or Midtown.

North of Garden Hills, at the intersection of Peachtree and West Paces Ferry Road, is the section of Buckhead formerly known as the "Village," but now under extensive renovation. In 2007, developers planned to create 8 acres, or six city blocks, of new mixed-use development that would cater to the area's upscale tastes. However, the plan stalled with the 2008 real estate bust and sat idle until early 2012, when another developer, Oliver McMillan, took over. Now under way, the project will add 300,000 square feet of new retail space, 100,000 square feet of new office space, and 370 luxury high-rise residences. Previously called The Streets of Buckhead Project, the name was changed to Buckhead Atlanta. For more information, visit www.olivermcmillan.com/buckhead-atlanta.

Buckhead's commercial district extends on Peachtree Road past Piedmont Road to what locals call "shoppers' paradise." Lenox Square and Phipps Plaza, two of Atlanta's largest and most luxurious malls, are located here at the inter-section of Peachtree Street and Lenox Road. Shoppers come in droves to shop at large department stores, such as Neiman Marcus, Bloomingdale's, and Saks Fifth Avenue, as well as smaller boutiques such as BCBG, Max Azria, Burberry, and Brooks Brothers. While both malls are upscale and provide valet parking, Lenox Square is more trendy with the requisite mid-priced stores like Gap, The Limited, and Macy's. Phipps Plaza, on the other hand, boasts crystal chandeliers, dark wood molding, magnificent staircases, elegant white columns, and a domed skylight. The mall provides concierge, babysitting, and personal shopping services. Stores include names like Saks Fifth Avenue, Juicy Couture, Gucci, Cole Haan, and Tiffany & Co. The mall also is home to a 14-screen movie theater and popular restaurants/night spots The Tavern at Phipps and Twist. And its newest addition, The LEGOLAND Discovery

Center, is a mecca for children who love LEGO toys. Children can play with bricks, follow demonstrations, watch a 4-D movie, or ride a LEGO ride.

North of the mall area, and spilling over into DeKalb County, is the **Brookhaven** district, Atlanta's first country club community. Here you'll find a mix of old-Atlanta residences that wind around one of the city's oldest country clubs, The Capital City Club, which has operated since the end of the 19th century. Meanwhile, just blocks from these multimillion-dollar homes are a number of redeveloping areas where people are cashing in on the prime location and either tearing down inexpensive homes to build mansions or renovating attractive Craftsman-style bungalows. In addition, Oglethorpe University, a liberal arts college dating back to 1835, is also on Peachtree in Brookhaven. The small college enrolls roughly 1,100 students.

**Website**: www.atlantaga.gov

**Area Code**: 404

**ZIP Codes**: 30305, 30309, 30324, 30326, 30327, 30342, 30355, 31126

**Post Offices**: North Atlanta Carrier, 1920 Dresden Dr NE; Brookhaven, 3851 Peachtree Rd NE; Buckhead Station, One Buckhead Loop Rd NE STE 115; Glenridge, 5400 Glenridge Dr NE; Northside Carrier Facility, 3840 Roswell Rd NE; Pharr Rd, 575 Pharr Rd NE; 800-275-8777, www.usps.com

**Police Precincts**: 3120 Maple Drive NE, 404-848-7231; 3393 Peachtree Rd, 404-467-8061; www.atlantapd.org

**Emergency Hospital**: Piedmont Hospital, 1968 Peachtree Rd NE, 404-605-5000; www.piedmonthospital.org

**Libraries**: Buckhead/Ida Williams Branch, 269 Buckhead Ave NE, 404-814-3500; Northside Branch, 3295 Northside Pkwy NW, 404-814-3508; www.afplweb.com

**Public School Education**: Atlanta Public Schools, 404-802-3500; Homework Hotline, 678-553-3029; www.atlanta.k12.ga.us

**Community Publications**: *Atlanta Business Chronicle*, 404-249-1000, www.bizjournals.com/atlanta; *Northside Neighbor*, 404-256-3100, www.neighbornewspapers.com/; *The Atlanta Journal-Constitution*, (404) 332-3489, www.ajc.com; *Atlanta Magazine*, 404-527-5500, www.atlantamagazine.com

**Community Resources**: Buckhead Business Association, 404-467-7607, www.buckheadbusiness.org; Buckhead Chamber of Commerce, (770) 216-1662, www.buckhead.net; North Buckhead Civic Association, www.nbca.org/index.html; Brookwood Hills Community Club, 404-351-0327, www.brookwoodhills.com; Bitsy Grant Tennis Center, 2125 Northside Drive, www.bitsytennis.com; 404-609-7193; Bobby Jones Golf Course, 384 Woodward Way NW, 404-355-1009, www.americangolf.com/bobby-jones-golf-course; Garden Hills Pool and Clubhouse, 404-848-7220, http://gardenhillspool.com; Oglethorpe University, 404-261-1441, www.oglethorpe.edu

*Chastain Park*

**Public Transportation: The Buc** is Buckhead's free shuttle, which connects MARTA's Lenox and Buckhead stations to the many hotels, office buildings, shops, restaurants, and malls in the area. The name is an acronym for Buckhead's Uptown Connection. The shuttle runs every ten minutes between 6:30 and 9:30 a.m. for the morning commute, and between 3:30 and 7 p.m. for the evening commute, Monday through Friday, on a five-mile loop. For more information, go to www.bucride.com. **MARTA** is Atlanta's largest public transportation service and serves most of the city's metro counties and all of Fulton County. Its **North-South Line train stations** are Lindbergh, Lenox, Brookhaven, and Buckhead. For detailed bus routes, visit www.itsmarta.com/bus-routes-by-route

## CHASTAIN PARK

At the north end of Buckhead's busy Piedmont Road, behind a bank of lush trees and hidden from the stress of city life, is charming Chastain Park. Here residents enjoy a privileged and active lifestyle, with loads of activities and amenities available via the area's core, the 280-acre Chastain Memorial Park, as well as direct proximity to Buckhead and Atlanta to the south, and Sandy Springs and Roswell to the north. Homes here range from just under a million to the multi-million, with a mix of older but updated bungalows, stately mansions, and a wash of new mansions that fit with Buckhead's opulence. Most of the homes are on spacious lots, with rich and varied landscaping.

Throughout the day walkers and bikers circle Chastain Park's three-mile trail, while golfers enjoy its 18-hole course, and families spend time at the numerous sports fields and playgrounds at the park's north end. Also, for those with an equestrian bent, the park is home to Chastain Horse Park, a charming facility that houses four barns, four arenas, and a large clubhouse that includes offices, banquet facilities, a tack shop, and a photography studio. And just behind the horse park is Chastain's concert arena—the Delta Classic Chastain Amphitheater.

In addition to the extracurricular activities, Chastain Park is located in one of Atlanta's best school districts, with all of its elementary, middle and high schools consistently meeting and exceeding national standards of excellence.

**Website**: www.chastainpark.org

**Area Codes**: 404

**ZIP Code**: 30342, 30327, 30305

**Post Offices**: Glenridge Branch, 5400 Glenridge Dr; Sandy Springs Branch, 6094 Boylston Dr NE; Sandy Springs Postal Store, 227 Sandy Springs Pl; North Springs, 7527 Roswell Rd; Buckhead Station, 3495 Buckhead Loop NE STE 115, Atlanta; 800-275-8777, www.usps.com

**Police Precinct**: Atlanta Police Department, 3120 Maple Dr NE, 404-848-7231; 3393 Lenox Rd, 404-467-8061; www.atlantapd.org

**Emergency Hospitals**: Northside Hospital, 1000 Johnson Ferry Rd NE, 404-851-8000, www.northside.com; St. Joseph's Hospital, 5665 Peachtree Dunwoody Rd, 404-851-7001, www.stjosephsatlanta.org; Children's Healthcare of Atlanta at Egleston, 1001 Johnson's Ferry Rd, Atlanta, 404-205-5437, www.choa.org

**Libraries**: Buckhead Branch, 269 Buckhead Ave, 404-814-3500; Sandy Springs Branch, 395 Mount Vernon Hwy, Atlanta, 404-303-6130; www.afplweb.com

**Public School Education**: Fulton County School System, 404-763-6830, www.fulton.k12.ga.us

**Community Publications**: *Northside Neighbor*, 404-256-3100, http://neighbornewspapers.com; *Sandy Springs Reporter*, 404-917-2200, www.reporternewspapers.net

**Community Resources**: Chastain Civic Association, www.chastainpark.org; Chastain Horse Park, 404-252-4244, www.chastainhorsepark.org; Chastain Park Athletic Club, 404-841-9196, www.ussn.org; Northside Youth Association, 404-252-1483, www.nyosports.com; Tophat Soccer Club, 404-351-4466, www.tophatsoccer.com; Delta Classic Chastain Amphitheater, 404-733-4800, www.classicchastain.com; Dorothy C Benson Senior Multipurpose Complex, 6500 Vernon Woods Dr, Sandy Springs, 404-705-4900, http://bensoncenter.org

**Public Transportation**: MARTA, 404-848-4711, www.itsmarta.com; **North Line stations**: Buckhead, Sandy Springs, and North Springs; for detailed bus routes visit www.itsmarta.com/bus-routes-by-route

## MIDTOWN/ANSLEY PARK

**Boundaries: North**: Ansley Mall; **East**: Monroe Drive; **South**: Ponce De Leon Avenue; **West**: Downtown Connector

South of Buckhead, the **Ansley Park** district was originally conceived as a residential community suitable for automobile travel, with broad, rolling streets curving around wooded parcels of land. The developer, Edwin Ansley, patterned the neighborhood after the nearby Druid Hills area, which was designed by Frederick Law Olmsted. Plans provided for ample greenspace and hundreds of lots for a mixture of housing, from smaller homes to mansions. This neighborhood survived the post–World War II flight to the suburbs with little deterioration, and it has since earned a place on the National Register of Historic Places.

Ansley Park streets, which wind a hopeless tangle around the area between Peachtree Street and Piedmont Road, are some of the most confusing in the city, and only the brave or the initiated should enter without a map. This area is one of Atlanta's oldest and most comfortable neighborhoods, offering gorgeous homes to those who want to live close to the Downtown business district or the now numerous Midtown office towers. Ansley Park architecture ranges from elaborate Victorian to American Georgian to one residence that resembles a medieval fortress.

The Ansley Park/Midtown section of Atlanta is home to Piedmont Park, the city's largest park. At 180 acres, many find it the best place in the city for rollerblading, running, or walking their dogs. It's also a great place to meet people. On any given day you're likely to find families setting up for an afternoon picnic, friends playing a rousing game of touch football, or young couples out for an afternoon stroll. There is a playground, a pond, and tennis courts. Piedmont Park also plays host to many Atlanta festivals throughout the year, including the Atlanta Dogwood Festival in April and the Atlanta Lesbian and Gay Pride Festival in October.

The neighborhood that sits south of Piedmont Park, officially known as **Midtown**, was home to the counter-culture of the late 1960s. Considered to be the largest "hippie district" in the southeast, Midtown offered inexpensive dwellings to the free-love generation. However, as area residents matured and became more fiscal-minded, they began buying and renovating the neighborhood's rundown houses, and over the last few decades, this area has been completely transformed with a proliferation of office buildings and pricey high-rise apartments and condominiums. While property values have risen steadily, the persistent buyer can still find a good value. Houses range from modest 1930s bungalows to impressive turn-of-the-20th-century mansions, quite a few of which have been broken up into apartments.

The Midtown neighborhood is home to much of Atlanta's gay and lesbian community, as evidenced by the number of rainbow flags fluttering from houses and retail establishments. The gay and lesbian population here is out, loud, and very proud—numerous nightclubs, shops, and organizations in the area are gay-owned or gay-friendly, making this area an interesting and lively place to live.

Both Midtown and Ansley Park are conveniently located near several shopping areas, including Ansley Park Mall, the Midtown Promenade, and Colony Square. Residents of this area have a variety of recreational and cultural offerings

*Ansley Park*

right at their doorstep, including Piedmont Park and the Atlanta Botanical Gardens. In addition, the Woodruff Arts Center, housing the High Museum of Art; Symphony Hall; Savannah College of Art and Design; and the Alliance Theatre are located nearby. Also, Atlanta's historic movie palace, the Fox Theatre (dubbed the "Fabulous Fox" by residents) presents film series and hosts a variety of presentations, including the Atlanta Ballet's Christmas-time performance of the Nutcracker.

**Website**: www.atlantaga.gov
**Area Code**: 404
**ZIP Codes**: 30309, 30357, 30361, 30367
**Post Office**: Midtown Station, 1072 West Peachtree St, 800-275-8777, www.usps.com.
**Police Precinct**: 1320 Monroe Dr NE, 404-853-3300, www.atlantapd.org
**Emergency Hospital**: Piedmont Hospital, 1968 Peachtree Rd NE, 404-605-5000; www.piedmonthospital.org
**Library**: Peachtree, 1315 Peachtree St NE, 404-885-7830, www.afplweb.com
**Public School Education**: Atlanta Public Schools, 404-802-3500; Homework Hotline, 404-827-8620; www.atlanta.k12.ga.us
**Community Publications**: *Atlanta Intown*, 404-586-0002, www.atlantaintownpaper.com
**Community Resources**: Midtown Alliance, 404-892-4782, www.midtownalliance. org; Midtown Atlanta Neighborhood Association, www.midtownatlanta.org; Piedmont Park Conservancy, 404-875-7275, www.piedmontpark.org; the Atlanta Botanical Garden, 404-876-5859, www.atlantabotanicalgarden.org; Woodruff Arts Center, www.woodruffcenter.org; the High Museum, 404-733-HIGH, www.high.org; Atlanta Symphony Orchestra, 404-733-4900, www. atlantasymphony.org; the Alliance Theatre, 404-733-4650, http://alliancetheatre.org; the Fox Theatre, 404-881-2100, www.foxtheatre.org

**Public Transportation: MARTA**, 404-848-4711, www.itsmarta.com; **North-South Line stations**: Midtown and Arts Center; for detailed bus routes visit www. itsmarta.com/bus-routes-by-route

## VIRGINIA HIGHLAND/MORNINGSIDE

**Lenox Park • Poncey-Highland**

**Boundaries: North**: Clifton Road; **East**: Briarcliff Road; **South**: Ponce De Leon Avenue; **West**: Monroe Drive

Home to a dazzling variety of retail and residential districts, the **Virginia Highland/Morningside** neighborhood is rightfully known as one of Atlanta's most desirable places to live, and it is certainly one of the city's most artsy environs. This part of town, however, was at one time in danger of sliding into urban decay. Middle-class flight to the suburbs and a planned highway that was to bisect the neighborhood caused real estate values to plummet in the late 1950s.

Thankfully, community activists successfully prevented the highway from becoming a reality (although not before a number of houses were razed) and the neighborhood experienced a renaissance in the 1960s. Many of the homes in this neighborhood have been rescued from slow but perceptible decline by an infusion of young, urban professionals whose remodeled kitchens and carefully decorated bedrooms often appear in the pages of *Atlanta Magazine*.

This influx of well-heeled new families coincided with the emergence of restaurants, bars, antique shops, art galleries, and clothing boutiques on Highland Avenue. This retail strip stretches from University Avenue to Ponce de Leon Avenue and is frequently interrupted by lush, green blocks that have remained residential. People from all over the metro Atlanta area gravitate to area bars, blues clubs, restaurants, and art galleries. Parking becomes scarce (by Atlanta standards) near Highland on weekends, requiring would-be shoppers to walk a couple of blocks from their cars to their destinations. On the other hand, those lucky enough to live within walking distance of these businesses enjoy some of the finest dining and shopping in Atlanta just outside their doors.

On the northern edge of Morningside, around Lenox Road, is the **Lenox Park** community. Made up of grand old houses, newly developed condos, townhouses, and mid-rise luxury apartment homes, this community is one of the toniest in Atlanta. This is where you'll find many of the city's old-moneyed families living alongside the just-moved-in, two-income, upwardly mobiles. Houses in Lenox Park start at around $350,000 and range upward to well over $1 million, a worthwhile investment for those who can afford it. Not only are Lenox Park residents close to the Virginia Highland retail district, they're also right down the street from Lenox Mall and Phipps Plaza.

Notwithstanding the area's reputation as a well-to-do community, there are a fair number of apartment complexes that provide living space for those who lack the gold bullion required to purchase a Morningside or Highland house. If this is your lot and this is your spot, your best bet is simply to drive through this area searching for vacancy notices, since the better buildings seldom bother to place ads posting open apartments. Pay particular attention to the three-story buildings along St. Charles and Virginia Avenue, as these house attractive apartments with considerable character.

The northern and southern edges of Virginia Highland contain a number of less aesthetically pleasing (read 1960s architectural style) apartment complexes. But don't let the exteriors scare you off. Reasonably priced, some of these small brick complexes actually have well-maintained interiors with large rooms and beautiful hardwood floors.

The area of Virginia Highland that runs along Ponce de Leon Avenue (or "Ponce" as locals call it) was once a seedy and neglected part of town. But thanks to the 1996 Olympics, much of this **Poncey-Highland** area is now rebuilt and revitalized. Mid-rise condos and new retail establishments have replaced many of the hotels along this thoroughfare that once housed transients, prostitutes, and drug dealers. Bike paths running from Freedom Park to Stone Mountain and Downtown are in place. A Whole Foods Market offers organic groceries and take-out and the Majestic, Ponce's famous 24-hour diner, is always a good place to hang out or catch something to eat on this side of town. All of this development has paid off for Virginia Highland residents. As the Poncey-Highland community has become a safer place to live and work, more families and young professionals have moved into the area, fitting in easily with the artists, poets, and musicians who congregate here.

The western edge of the community is characterized by its easy access to Piedmont Park, Atlanta's largest greenspace. Here, too, parking can become a problem on weekends. Another local attraction, the Midtown Promenade, located on Monroe and Virginia, offers a multiplex cinema as well as restaurants and stores.

In general, the Highland/Morningside community is an attractive and convenient, but increasingly expensive, place to live. Those newcomers who are committed to making their home in this area should prepare for a lengthy apartment hunt or else resign themselves to paying a premium for the neighborhood's many fine attributes.

**Website**: www.atlantaga.gov
**Area Code**: 404
**ZIP Codes**: 30306, 31106, 30309
**Post Office**: 1190 North Highland Ave NE, 800-275-8777, www.usps.com
**Police Precinct**: Police Headquarters, 675 Ponce de Leon Ave NE, 404-817-6900, www.atlantapd.org

*Virgina Highland*

**Emergency Hospitals**: Emory University Hospital, 1440 Clifton Rd NE, 404-778-7777, www.emoryhealthcare.org; Piedmont Hospital, 1968 Peachtree Rd NE, 404-605-5000; www.piedmonthospital.org

**Library**: Ponce de Leon, 980 Ponce de Leon Ave NE, 404-885-7820, www.afplweb.com

**Public School Education**: Atlanta Public Schools, 404-802-3500; Homework Hotline, 404-827-8620; www.atlanta.k12.ga.us

**Community Publications**: *Atlanta Intown*, 404-586-0002, www.atlantaintownpaper.com

**Community Resources**: Morningside Lenox Park Association, 404-872-7714, http://mlpa.org; Virginia Highland Business Association, www.virginiahighland.com; Virginia Highland Civic Association, 404-222-8244, www.vahi.org; Whole Foods Market, 650 Ponce de Leon Ave NE, 404-853-1681; The Majestic, 1031 Ponce de Leon Ave NE, 404-875-0276; Piedmont Park Conservancy, 404-875-7275, www.piedmontpark.org; YWCA of Greater Atlanta, 957 North Highland Ave, 404-892-3476, www.ywcaatlanta.org

**Public Transportation**: **MARTA**, 404-848-4711, www.itsmarta.com; for detailed bus routes visit www.itsmarta.com/bus-routes-by-route

## LITTLE FIVE POINTS

**Boundaries: North**: Ponce de Leon Avenue; **East**: Oakdale; **South**: DeKalb Avenue; **West**: North Highland Avenue

If Buckhead is the "Beverly Hills of the East," then **Little Five Points** (or **L5P** for short) would have to be the "Haight-Ashbury" of the South. Populated by sidewalk wordsmiths hawking their poetry to pedestrians, artists selling jewelry on the street, and teenagers piercing any and all body parts, this hip little enclave is where all the cool kids come to hang out. In fact, Little Five Points has become so trendy that in recent years, residents are often in the minority, with most of the hipsters who come here to shop, drink, or listen to music trekking in from the suburbs.

The heart of this community is the retail district located at the intersection of Euclid Avenue and Moreland Avenue (which is what Briarcliff is called once it crosses Ponce to the south)—a district increasingly populated by savvy stores marketing stylized wares. Shopping here is more "alternative" than in Virginia Highland, offering the best in vintage clothes, new age paraphernalia, feminist books, and retro home furnishings. Popular stores here include The Junkman's Daughter, which has evolved from a cramped secondhand store into a sizable retail operation, anchoring a thriving strip mall on Moreland; Sevananda is the neighborhood natural foods co-op; and The Vortex, with its giant screaming-skull-head entrance, is one of the area's most recognizable and popular bars. Also check out Front Page News, a popular and reasonably priced restaurant with great outdoor seating.

Part of L5P's charm stems from its intimate size. Unlike stores on Highland, which stretch for block after block, the Little Five Points retail strip is actually very small: a few blocks on Euclid and a few blocks more on Moreland. But those few blocks pack a huge punch, offering a wide variety of ethnic restaurants, funky boutiques, and some of the best live music venues in the city.

The neighborhood has traditionally provided students and the irregularly employed with affordable (if occasionally seedy) housing. Gentrification of the retail district over the last decade, however, has noticeably escalated area rents. Still, with perseverance, the determined apartment- or house-hunter can find lodging at more favorable rates than in Morningside/Highland or Druid Hills. And the neighborhood's many restaurants and stores allow for close-to-home entertainment.

Apartment buildings can be found along Moreland, as well as on Highland, and many of the quieter back streets offer attractive housing options. Architectural styles here range from the ubiquitous ranch to the quirky Victorian. If this is where you want to live, your best bet is to drive through the area looking for "for sale" signs. And be sure to check out *Creative Loafing*, the free, weekly newspaper, as they run numerous ads for rentals in L5P.

**Website**: www.atlantaga.gov
**Area Code**: 404
**ZIP Codes**: 30307, 31107
**Post Office**: Little Five Points, 1987 Euclid Ave NE, 800-275-8777, www.usps.com
**Police Precincts**: Police Headquarters, 675 Ponce de Leon Ave NE, 404-817-6900; Little Five Points Mini Precinct, 428 Seminole Ave NE, 404-658-6782; www.atlantapd.org

*Little Five Points*

**Emergency Hospital**: Grady Memorial Hospital, 80 Jesse Hill Jr Dr, 404-616-4307, www.gradyhealthsystem.org

**Library**: Ponce de Leon, 980 Ponce de Leon Ave NE, 404-885-7820; www.afplweb.com

**Public School Education**: Atlanta Public Schools, 404-802-3500; Homework Hotline, 404-827-8620; www.atlanta.k12.ga.us

**Community Publications**: *Atlanta Intown*, 404-586-0002, www.atlantaintownpaper.com/

**Community Resources**: Little Five Points Community Center, 1083 Austin Ave NE, 404-522-2926, www.l5p.com; Little Five Points Business Association, www.little5points.com; Sevenanda Food Co-op, 467 Moreland Ave NE, 404-681-2831, www.sevananda.coop; Junkman's Daughter, 404-577-3188, www.thejunkmansdaughter.com; The Vortex, 404-688-1828, www.thevortexbarandgrill.com; Front Page News, www.fpnnews.com, 404-475-7777, Variety Playhouse, 1099 Euclid Ave, 404-524-7354, www.variety-playhouse.com

**Public Transportation**: **MARTA**, 404-848-4711, www.itsmarta.com; for detailed bus routes visit www.itsmarta.com/bus-routes-by-route

## INMAN PARK

**Boundaries: North**: DeKalb Avenue; **East**: Boulevard; **South**: Memorial Drive; **West**: Moreland Avenue

Located just south of Little Five Points, **Inman Park**, Atlanta's first planned suburb, was developed in the 1880s as a home for the city's elite. Named after civic leader Samuel M. Inman, the neighborhood was connected to nearby Downtown by Atlanta's first electric trolley car. Many of the city's most prominent business leaders resided in this illustrious enclave, including Asa Griggs Candler, the founder of the Coca-Cola Company. His celebrated estate, "Callan Castle," still remains on the corner of Euclid Avenue and Elizabeth Street.

At the turn of the 20th century, wealthy residents, drawn to other prosperous neighborhoods, such as Ansley Park, diminished Inman Park's elitism, and eventually middle-income families settled here, building more modest houses and dividing lots. Subsequently, during the mid-century flight to the new suburbs, the area fell on hard times. Numerous houses fell into disrepair, and many were condemned or destroyed. By the early 1960s, the neighborhood was considered little better than a slum until young professionals began to notice the potential of many of the older houses and the convenience of its location. Coveted renovation projects were homes from the late 19th and early 20th centuries in Queen Anne, high-style Italianate and Romanesque mansion styles.

Today Inman Park reaps the rewards of its revitalization as a popular neighborhood with numerous million-dollar properties, two historic districts, useful greenspace, and a host of retail establishments. Former industrial developments have been transformed into mixed-use complexes for businesses and residents, such as Inman Park Village and the Krog Street Market. .

Inman Park residents celebrate their history and present at the annual Inman Park Festival in late April. The festival includes a tour of the neighborhood's historic homes, as well as displays from local businesses and civic groups. In addition, be sure to check out the many historical markers in Inman Park, which chronicle a number of Civil War battles that occurred in the area and are memorialized in Grant Park's Cyclorama.

**Website**: www.atlantaga.gov

**Area Code**: 404

**ZIP Code**: 30307

**Post Office**: Ralph McGill, 822 Ralph McGill Blvd NE, 800-275-8777, www.usps.com

**Police Precincts**: Police Headquarters, 675 Ponce de Leon Ave NE, 404-817-6900; Little Five Points Mini Precinct, 428 Seminole Ave NE, 404-658-6782; www.atlantapd.org

**Emergency Hospital**: Grady Memorial Hospital, 80 Jesse Hill Jr Dr, 404-616-4307; www.gradyhealthsystem.org

**Library**: Ponce de Leon, 980 Ponce de Leon Ave NE, 404-885-7820, www.afplweb.com

**Public School Education**: Atlanta Public Schools, 404-802-3500; Homework Hotline, 404-827-8620; www.atlanta.k12.ga.us

**Community Publications**: *Atlanta Intown*, 404-586-0002, www.atlantaintownpaper.com

**Community Resources**: Inman Park Neighborhood Association, www.inmanpark.org; Inman Park Restoration, www.inmanpark.org; Inman Park Festival, www.inmanparkfestival.org; Inman Park Cooperative Preschool, 760 Edgewood Ave NE, 404-827-9796, http://ipcp.org

*Inman Park*

**Public Transportation**: **MARTA**, 404-848-4711, www.itsmarta.com; **East-West Line station**: Inman Park/Reynoldstown; for detailed bus routes visit www.itsmarta.com/bus-routes-by-route

## GRANT PARK

**Boundaries: North**: Memorial Drive; **East**: Moreland Avenue; **South**: Atlanta Avenue; **West**: Hill Street

As the gleaming emblem of the New South, Atlanta surrenders relatively few glimpses into its antebellum past. Of course, Union General William T. Sherman's decision to burn the city to the ground played a major role in obscuring Atlanta's early history. But **Grant Park** is one of the city's few neighborhoods in which the past remains clearly visible.

History buffs celebrate the neighborhood as the site of the Battle of Atlanta during the Civil War. This military action was captured in an amazingly detailed diorama known as the Cyclorama. Standing some fifty-feet high and hundreds of feet long, the cylindrical Cyclorama was painted by eleven German and Polish artists in the late 19th century and has been on display in its current site (next to Zoo Atlanta) since 1921. Today visitors from around the world come to this unique theater in the round to hear the story of the Battle of Atlanta, as the central seating rotates to facilitate viewing of the painting.

Grant Park, stretching from Cherokee to Boulevard, is the core of this district. Once home to Cherokee Indians (who were forcibly removed from the state in the 1830s), this lush, green park now provides city dwellers with open space and numerous athletic facilities.

Adjacent to the park is Zoo Atlanta, which offers visitors the chance to view a wide variety of animals in natural environments. Don't expect to see animals

*Grant Park*

behind bars here. The habitats consist of 40 acres of large, open spaces designed for the individual species. Also, the zoo is one of only a handful in the country to house pandas, and was successful in breeding its male and female in 2006, 2008, and 2010, producing three panda cubs.

In addition to its impressive assortment of animals, Zoo Atlanta entertains the public with a rainforest exhibit, storytelling, puppet shows, a miniature train, and a petting zoo for children. They've also partnered with Egleston Children's Hospital to create a wonderful playground and an "endangered species" carousel.

Many of the homes in this neighborhood were constructed in the late 19th and early 20th century, when city officials actively encouraged residential development in the region. Unfortunately, the urban flight following World War II exacted a heavy toll on Grant Park and many houses fell into a state of disrepair. Since the 1970s, however, the area has been on the upswing as families took advantage of the then soft real estate market to purchase homes that were subsequently renovated. Urban trailblazers once had to dodge bullets in this former haven for drug dealers, but today the neighborhood has settled into a gentrified revivification. In recent years, the value of homes and apartments here has begun to reflect this happy trend, making it more and more difficult to find rock-bottom rents. Still, Grant Park's many Victorian homes make this a neighborhood worth exploring.

Homebuyers and apartment hunters should take note of a dwelling's location in relation to the park. A federal prison and neighborhoods with lower-income housing to the south make southern sections of Grant Park less enticing. However, streets off Memorial Boulevard possess charming refurbished Victorian houses and a handful of cool neighborhood eateries, such Stone Soup Kitchen, a great breakfast and lunch spot that prides itself on using all local and organic ingredients.

**Website**: www.atlantaga.gov
**Area Code**: 404

**ZIP Code**: 30312

**Post Office**: Central City, 400 Pryor St SW, 800-275-8777, www.usps.com

**Police Precinct**: 880 Cherokee Ave, 404-624-0674, www.atlantapd.org

**Emergency Hospital**: Grady Memorial Hospital, 80 Jesse Hill Jr Dr, 404-616-4307, www.gradyhealthsystem.org

**Library**: Georgia-Hill Neighborhood Center, 250 Georgia Ave, 404-730-5427, www.afplweb.com

**Public School Education**: Atlanta Public Schools, 404-802-3500; Homework Hotline, 404-827-8620; www.atlanta.k12.ga.us

**Community Publications**: *The Porch Press*, 1340 Metropolitan Ave, 404-373-3130; *Atlanta Intown*, 404-586-0002, www.atlantaintownpaper.com

**Community Resources**: Grant Park Online, http://grantpark.org; Grant Park Neighborhood Association, http://grantpark.org; Grant Park Conservancy, 404-521-0938, www.gpconservancy.org; Grant Park Security Patrol, 404-577-3722, http://gpna.org/gpna/security.htm; Zoo Atlanta, 800 Cherokee Ave SE, 404-624-5600, www.zooatlanta.org; the Atlanta Cyclorama, 404-658-7625, www.bcaatlanta.com; Stone Soup Kitchen, 404-524-1222, www.stonesoupkitchen.net

**Public Transportation**: **MARTA**, 404-848-4711, www.itsmarta.com; for detailed bus routes visit www.itsmarta.com/bus-routes-by-route

**You might also want to consider:**

- Although technically not part of the city of Atlanta, another community in the area worth mentioning is the City of East Point, www.eastpointcity.org. Located just south of West End and Cascade Heights and a mere seven miles from downtown Atlanta, **East Point, www.eastpointcity.org,** is poised to become one of the next hot communities in metro Atlanta. Houses here are affordable and range from 1920s bungalows and 1950s ranch homes to recently built subdivisions. Young urbanites, drawn by East Point's lower home prices and friendly neighbors, as well as its proximity to Atlanta, have been coming in droves, breathing new life into the community. East Point's historic downtown, which boasts a handful of restaurants and blues bars, art galleries, and antique shops, is in the process of being revitalized. Growth in the city's commercial district is expected to continue as businesses and retail establishments position themselves accordingly to take advantage of the incoming young, hip, and culturally diverse population.

- **College Park, www.collegeparkga.com,** lies south of the city of Atlanta, next to Hartsfield-Jackson International Airport. The city contains some beautiful historic areas with Victorian-style homes, and a charming downtown. It is also home to Woodward Academy, one of Atlanta's top private schools, the headquarters for prosperous company John Wieland Homes, and the megachurch World Changers Ministries.

## CITY OF ATLANTA—DEKALB COUNTY

As mentioned above, most of the City of Atlanta is located within Fulton County. A handful of Atlanta communities, however, either spill over into or are completely located in neighboring DeKalb County. Because of their geographic location, residents in many of the following neighborhoods have access to both City of Atlanta and DeKalb County libraries, schools, and other public services. This overlap is sometimes confusing for new residents, particularly those who are unsure as to whether they'll be paying City of Atlanta or DeKalb County property taxes, or which school system they belong to. So, if you're considering a move to any of the following communities, be sure to find out as much as you can up front. The contact listings and community resources listed below each profile may help.

### EAST ATLANTA

#### Kirkwood • Gresham Park

**Boundaries: North**: College Avenue West; **East**: Second Avenue; **South**: Constitution Road; **West**: Moreland Avenue

Located primarily in DeKalb County (with a few streets crossing over into Fulton), **East Atlanta** is the latest intown neighborhood to experience rebirth. Like many other intown communities, this area was all but forgotten a decade ago. But thanks in part to the growing popularity of urban living and the reasonable home prices here, East Atlanta is finally experiencing a renaissance. The drug dealers are gone, and boutiques and restaurants have replaced the crack houses that once did a brisk business here. In fact, in 2007, East Atlanta was voted "Best Neighborhood" in the city by the readers of weekly newspaper *Creative Loafing*.

Less trendy and more family-friendly than nearby Little Five Points, East Atlanta Village (as the retail district is called) gives the impression of a toddler taking its first steps. It's what Virginia Highland might have been twenty years ago. Anchoring the East Atlanta retail movement are the shops along Flat Shoals and Glenwood avenues, which include a Joe's Coffee, a cozy little café that serves delicious coffee while showcasing local artists and poets, and Flatiron Bar & Grill, a great place to catch lunch or drinks while taking in the local scenery. Other popular East Atlanta attractions include various clothing boutiques, record stores, gift shops, and restaurants.

On the northern edge of East Atlanta lies the revitalized neighborhood of **Kirkwood**. Amazingly, this area has become one of the hottest home sales markets in metro Atlanta. Attracted by low prices for starter homes, a refreshing mix of residents, new families, young professionals, and artists has begun pouring in. Houses range from 1930s Craftsman-style homes desperately in need of repair

*Kirkwood*

to the rare, fully renovated Victorian. The majority of the lots are large enough to accommodate children at play, and the lawns, while not as lush as those found in more upscale communities, are at least well maintained. Kirkwood is also home to Bessie Branham Park, a neighborhood greenspace that features a baseball/softball field, basketball court, playground, picnic tables, and a newly renovated recreation center.

Two miles away, on the south side of East Atlanta, is **Gresham Park**, another neighborhood profiting from Atlanta's urban renewal movement. Like Kirkwood, there is a strong sense of community here. Neighbors know each other's names, people wave hello as you drive past, and children run and play along the quiet streets. Homes range from 1950s-style brick ranches, to older Victorians, to semi-mansions on several acres of land; such architectural diversity reflects the fact that Gresham Park was not a planned community. For the moment, home prices here are significantly lower than in other intown communities. But don't expect that to last. Like Kirkwood, Gresham Park is poised to become the next "hot" real estate market.

As more and more people seek out the urban experience, neighborhoods like Kirkwood and Gresham Park will continue to grow. For those looking to make their home in quaint, quiet communities close to Downtown, without breaking the bank, now may be the time to buy, and East Atlanta may be just the place.

**Website**: www.atlantaga.gov
**Area Code**: 404
**ZIP Codes**: 30317, 30316
**Post Offices**: East Atlanta, 1273 Metropolitan Ave SE; Eastwood, 1926 Hosea L. Williams Dr NE; 800-275-8777, www.usps.com.
**Police Precinct**: East Atlanta, 2025 Hosea L. Williams Dr SE, 404-371-5002, www. atlantapd.org

*Gresham Park*

**Emergency Hospital**: Grady Memorial Hospital, 80 Jesse Hill Jr Dr, 404-616-4307, www.gradyhealthsystem.org

**Libraries**: East Atlanta, 457 Flat Shoals Ave, 404-730-5438; Kirkwood, 11 Kirkwood Rd, 404-377-6471; www.afplweb.com; Gresham, 2418 Gresham Rd, 404-244-4374; Scott Candler, 2644 McAfee Road, 404-286-6986; Flat Shoals, 4022 Flat Shoals Pkwy, 404-244-4370; www.dekalb.public.lib.ga.us

**Public School Education**: Atlanta Public Schools, 404-802-3500; Homework Hotline, 404-827-8620; www.atlanta.k12.ga.us; DeKalb County School System, 678-676-1200, www.dekalb.k12.ga.us

**Community Publications**: *The Porch Press*, 1340 Metropolitan Ave, 404-373-3130; *Atlanta Intown*, 404-586-0002, www.atlantaintownnews.com;

**Community Resources**: East Atlanta Community Association, http://eaca.net; East Atlanta Security Patrol, http://eaca.net; Joe's Coffee, 510 Flat Shoals Ave, 404-521-1122; Flatiron Bar & Grill, 520 Flat Shoals Ave, 404-688-8864; Kirkwood Neighbors Association, www.historic-kirkwood.com; Bessie Branham Park, 2051 Delano Ave, 404-371-5010

**Public Transportation**: MARTA, 404-848-4711, www.itsmarta.com; **East-West Line station**: Eastlake Station; for detailed bus routes visit www.itsmarta.com/bus-routes-by-route

## CANDLER PARK/LAKE CLAIRE

**Boundaries: North**: Ponce de Leon Avenue; **East**: East Lake Drive; **South**: DeKalb Avenue; **West**: Oakdale

**Candler Park**, one of Atlanta's oldest suburbs, was originally founded as the City of Edgewood in 1890. As Edgewood, this community had its own government, school system, and electric company until 1908 when residents petitioned to become part of Atlanta. The neighborhood was annexed the following year.

The Candler Park community developed rapidly in the early 1900s as a mostly white, middle-class suburb. However, in the 1920s, realty companies and large property owners began to subdivide the area and sell off a large number of the smaller lots, while many of the homes here were subdivided and then rented by the week. This decline continued through the 1950s as more residents moved away from the intown community into newly developed suburbs around the perimeter. Fortunately, this trend began to change in the late 1960s, as people rediscovered Candler Park's charm and homebuyers took advantage of the housing bargains in the area, and the community found itself on an upswing that has yet to subside. Today the going rate for a house in Candler Park rivals any Virginia Highland property.

Situated around the public Candler Park Golf Course, this neighborhood is a down-to-earth, family-friendly enclave that has attracted many people looking for a conventional lifestyle. Far less commercial than nearby Little Five Points, this district is filled with a wide variety of two-story, Craftsman-style frame houses and late-period Victorians that draw a more ethnically and economically diverse population than some neighboring suburbs. Residents pride themselves on their sense of community and their rejection of the extensive commercial development of communities such as Buckhead and Virginia Highland.

Nevertheless, because of the recent flood of higher-income homebuyers and the renovation of many older houses in the area, merchants are chomping at the bit to set up shop in Candler Park. The tiny strip of stores at the corner of McLendon and Clifton has taken on a new life as a Fellini's Pizza and La Fonda restaurant have settled in, despite initial protest from locals fearing increased traffic. Other popular additions to this commercial zone include a piercing parlor, ice cream shop, the Donna Van Gogh Gallery, and Kashi Atlanta Center for Yoga, Service and Community. Regardless of the infusion of capital, this small area still retains much of its earnest charm. The Flying Biscuit Café, with its down-home southern vibe and adjoining bakery, is a wonderful eatery renowned for its sublime biscuits and friendly wait staff.

Continuing east on McLendon, one reaches the **Lake Claire** district, which, despite its name, does not possess a lake. Nor does it have a commercial district of its own. It does, however, contain a wide variety of large and small homes from 1950s bungalows to post-Victorian revivals, inhabited increasingly by members of Atlanta's artistic community. Like neighboring Candler Park, Lake Claire has recently undergone a process of revitalization that has increased property values as well as the area's popularity.

You won't find any apartment complexes in Lake Claire. Most of the properties are either single-family homes or renovated duplexes. There is, however, an occasional basement apartment for rent, but they go quickly. Be sure to check the

*Candler Park*

real estate listings in *Creative Loafing* and the *Atlanta Journal-Constitution* regularly if you want to make your home here.

A tour of the neighborhood reveals its diversity and the creativity of its inhabitants. Expect to find brightly painted houses in unusual colors that are matched only by the brilliance of the district's famous flowers.

**Website**: www.atlantaga.gov
**Area Code**: 404
**ZIP Code**: 30033
**Post Office**: Main Office, 520 West Ponce de Leon Ave, 800-275-8777, www.usps.com
**Police Precinct**: Police Headquarters, 675 Ponce de Leon Ave NE, 404-817-6900, www.atlantapd.org
**Emergency Hospitals**: DeKalb Medical Center, 2701 N Decatur Rd, 404-501-1000; www.dekalbmedicalcenter.org; Emory University Hospital, 1440 Clifton Rd NE, 404-778-7777, www.emoryhealthcare.org
**Libraries**: Kirkwood, 11 Kirkwood Rd, 404-377-6471, www.afplweb.com; Decatur, 215 Sycamore St, 404-370-3070; www.dekalb.public.lib.ga.us
**Public School Education**: Atlanta Public Schools, 404-802-3500; Homework Hotline, 404-827-8620; www.atlanta.k12.ga.us; DeKalb County School System, 678-676-1200, www.dekalb.k12.ga.us
**Community Publications**: *Candler Park Messenger*, www.candlerpark.org; *Lake Claire Newsletter*, www.lakeclaire.org/news/letter.htm; *Atlanta Intown*, 404-586-0002, www.atlantaintownnews.com
**Community Resources**: Candler Park Neighborhood Organization, www.candlerpark.org; Lake Claire Neighborhood Association, www.lakeclaire.org; Candler Park Golf Course, 404-371-1260, http://candlerpark.americangolf.com; Donna Van Gogh Gallery, 1651 McLendon Ave, 404-370-1003; 404-373-2003; Kashi Atlanta, 404-687-3353, www.kashiatlanta.org

**Public Transportation**: **MARTA,** 404-848-4711, www.itsmarta.com; **East-West Line station**: Edgewood/Candler Park; for detailed bus routes visit www. itsmarta.com/bus-routes-by-route

## EMORY/NORTH DRUID HILLS

**Boundaries: North**: Mason Mill Road; **East**: City of Decatur; **South**: Ponce de Leon Avenue; **West**: Briarcliff Road

The university neighborhood of **Emory/Druid Hills** offers a combination of lovely historic family homes and no-frills student housing. The neighborhood's quiet, family-oriented ambiance is in marked contrast to the nearby commercial districts of Virginia Highland and Little Five Points, where many of the younger residents of Emory/Druid Hills commonly find their nightlife fun.

Each school year, roughly ten thousand students congregate at Emory University—one of the South's top universities. With a campus consisting of hundreds of buildings, Emory casts a long (and occasionally unwelcome) shadow across the Druid Hills area. Constantly renovating its existing spaces and building new ones, the university keeps a small army of contractors busy and, in the process, is constantly reshaping the landscape. To the dismay of neighborhood residents, greenspaces have a tendency to disappear overnight, replaced by impressive research facilities, offices, and classrooms along Clifton Road and its few side streets.

Nevertheless, nature-lovers can still delight in the university-owned Lullwater estate, a charming park stretching from Clifton Road to Clairmont Road. The nearby Fernbank Forest offers nature on an even more spectacular scale. One of the few remaining old-growth forests in an urban area, the Fernbank Forest contains a two-mile trail open to hikers from 2 p.m. to 5 p.m., Monday–Friday, and from 10 a.m. to 5 p.m. on Saturday. The access path to the forest is at the Fernbank Science Center, on Heaton Park Drive, just north of Ponce de Leon Avenue.

South and west of the University are some of the most spectacular homes in Atlanta, particularly the ones on Lullwater, Springdale, and Oakdale Roads. This area was developed in the first decades of the 20th century according to a plan designed by noted landscape architect Frederick Law Olmsted. Because so much of Olmsted's original design remains intact here, the Druid Hills area has been placed on the National Register of Historic Places. When the producers of the movie *Driving Miss Daisy* wanted to evoke images of old southern wealth, this was the neighborhood they chose.

Not surprisingly, such splendor comes at a steep price. A few lucky (or especially determined) renters occupy carriage houses that rest behind many of the stately mansions, but such living space is hard to come by. Ads for local rentals can be found on the bulletin boards in Emory's student center, as well as in *Creative Loafing* and the *Atlanta Journal-Constitution*. There are several large apartment complexes near the intersection of Clairmont Road and North Decatur that have their own leasing offices. Some of these provide excellent living accommodations for a reasonable price and, therefore, often have a waiting list for vacancies. Residents enjoy a wide variety of shopping, dining, and culture. Located on North Decatur just outside Emory's gates, the Emory Village shopping strip is home to several gourmet coffee shops, clothing stores, and pizza restaurants. To the west, on Briarcliff Road, there's a two-story Kroger supermarket right down the street from Whole Foods. And further east on Clairmont Road, shoppers can find numerous restaurants and retail stores, including Bicycle South and Athens Pizza House.

The Fernbank Museum of Natural History (located on Clifton Road just north of Ponce de Leon Avenue) is the largest such museum in the South. Among its many attractions is an IMAX movie theater with a thirty-foot screen. Just across the street from Fernbank is the private Druid Hills Country Club.

**Website**: www.atlantaga.gov

**Area Code**: 404

**ZIP Codes**: 30307, 30322, 30329

**Post Offices**: Briarcliff, 3104 Briarcliff Rd NE; Druid Hills, 1799-X Briarcliff Rd NE; 800-275-8777, www.usps.com

**Police Precincts**: Police Headquarters, 675 Ponce de Leon Ave NE, 404-817-6900; www.atlantapd.org; Emory Police Department (emergency), 404-727-6111; Emory Police Department (non-emergency), 404-727-8005

**Emergency Hospitals**: Emory University Hospital, 1440 Clifton Rd NE, 404-778-7777, www.emoryhealthcare.org; DeKalb Medical Center, 2701 N Decatur Rd, 404-501-1000, www.dekalbmedicalcenter.org

**Libraries**: Briarcliff, 2775 Briarcliff Rd NE, 404-679-4400; Toco Hills–Avis G. Williams, 1282 McConnell Dr, 404-679-4404; www.dekalb.public.lib.ga.us; Ponce de Leon, 980 Ponce de Leon Ave NE, 404-885-7820, www.afplweb.com

**Public School Education**: DeKalb County School System, 678-676-1200, www.dekalb.k12.ga.us

**Community Publications**: *Atlanta Intown*, 404-586-0002, www.atlantaintownpaper.com

**Community Resources**: Emory University, 404-727-6123, www.emory.edu; North Druid Hills Residents Association, www.ndhra.org; Druid Hills Golf Club, 404-377-1766, www.druidhillsgolfclub.com; Fernbank Museum of Natural History, 767 Clifton Rd NE, 404-929-6300, www.fernbankmuseum.org; Fernbank Science Center, 156 Heaton Park Dr NE, 678-874-7102, www.fernbank.edu; Bicycle South, 404-636-4444, www.bicyclesouth.com

**Public Transportation**: MARTA, 404-848-4711, www.itsmarta.com; **North Line station**: Lindbergh Center; for detailed bus routes visit www.itsmarta.com/bus-routes-by-route

**You might also want to consider:**

- **Ashford Park**, just outside of Atlanta city limits in DeKalb County and with easy access to Buckhead, Chamblee, I-85, and GA 400. Homes in Ashford Park range from small ranches to million-dollar mansions (check out Redding Rd). New commercial developments continue to spring up on Dresden Rd, and the Chamblee Farmers Market is just around the corner. The Brookhaven MARTA station is also within walking distance of the northern parts of Ashford Park. For more information: Ashford Park Civic Association, www.neighborhoodlink. com/dekalbco/apca.

## NEIGHBORING COMMUNITIES

### NORTH FULTON COUNTY

North of Atlanta's city limits and further away from the inner-ring suburbs is the exurbia of North Fulton. One of the fastest growing areas in the country, North Fulton County boasts award-winning public schools and a "mediplex" along Johnson Ferry Road, in the Sandy Springs/Dunwoody area, featuring top-notch medical facilities. The county's growth, however, has created a traffic nightmare for residents in many neighborhoods. And, as of yet, there are no real solutions in sight. In some communities, rush-hour traffic is as bad on side streets as it is on the interstate. The freeway opening of the GA 400 extension in the early 1990s offered North Fulton residents a direct route into Atlanta proper, creating some-what easier access to the city's many cultural and professional opportunities.

Despite the county's growth and development over the last decade, much of North Fulton still contains lush, forested, and hilly property that is the envy of many urban dwellers. For those seeking a suburban lifestyle, with good schools, and access to Buckhead, Midtown, and Downtown, North Fulton may be the perfect place.

### SANDY SPRINGS

One of the area's busiest and most impressive retail business strips is in the North Fulton city of **Sandy Springs**. Once a Creek Indian settlement, this spot became a rest area of sorts for farmers and travelers, due to the spring that was located at the intersection of two well-traveled trails. In 1842 Wilson Spruill purchased the land, and construction of a church and a few simple log cabins followed. Sandy Springs remained a quiet farm community well into the 20th century, until the City of Atlanta, its neighbor to the south, began encroaching.

The city of Atlanta tried numerous times to annex Sandy Springs, but the community continually fought the move, and was backed up by the Georgia Supreme Court. Sandy Springs residents resented Fulton County and felt their

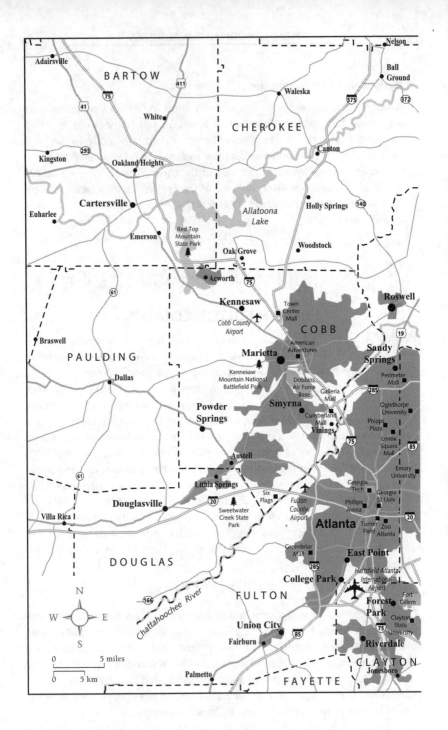

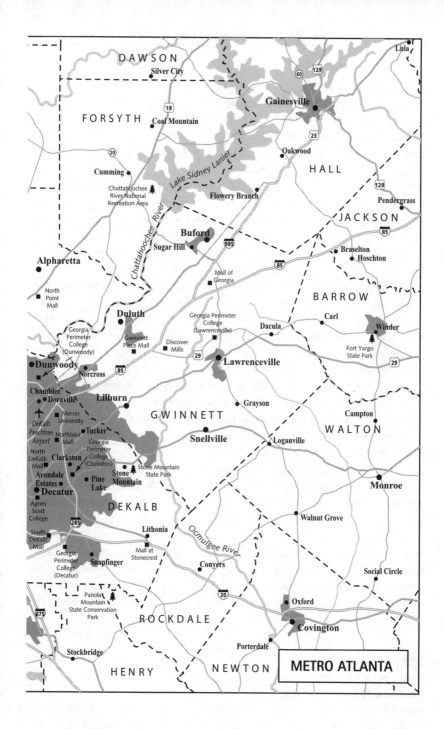

METRO ATLANTA

tax dollars were not coming back into the community. As a result, Sandy Springs brought a bill to the Georgia General Assembly each year, requesting it be made a city, but representatives from Fulton County and Atlanta continually blocked the measure for fear of losing Sandy Springs' tax dollars. It wasn't until 2005, when the Georgia Assembly was ruled by the Republican Party, that the community was successful in petitioning for cityhood. By way of referendum, 97% of residents voted for cityhood, and in December 2005, the state approved the request.

Today Sandy Springs continues to stretch its municipal wings, adding new services for residents and establishing its offices and staff. The population also continues to boom, up more than 10,000 to around 97,000 people since 2005.

It isn't hard to find the retail district in Sandy Springs. Just look for Roswell Road, and drive north or south, and you'll see any number of restaurants, shops, bars, and other establishments. However, be warned, traffic here is constant, and most locals learn to avoid the jams by sticking to side roads. But don't be fooled into thinking Sandy Springs is all like this busy strip. The neighborhoods that wind away from Roswell Road are some of the prettiest in Atlanta, with large tracts of land and an abundance of trees. House styles range from 1950s-style bungalows to 1970s brick ranches to many newly built mansions.

The neighborhoods along Mt. Vernon Highway and Hammond Drive are older, with large shady lots and houses set back away from the street, while newer homes can be found along Glenridge Road and farther south toward Buckhead in recently developed subdivisions. If you travel north along Roswell Road, away from the commercial district, there are lovely, ranch-style houses as well as larger contemporary homes lining the Chattahoochee River. These homes afford residents wonderful riverside views. This area's heavily wooded and rolling landscape attracts a large number of upwardly mobile young couples looking for the comfort of the suburbs for their growing children.

But Sandy Springs isn't just a suburb for growing families. It is also home to one of the largest populations of young singles in the metro Atlanta area and, therefore, offers a lot of newly built apartment complexes. From low-end, bare-bones studios, to trendy lofts, to lushly landscaped, upscale gated communities, those looking for a particular type of apartment can surely find it here, most likely along or very near to Roswell Road.

**Website**: www.sandyspringsga.org
**Area Codes**: 404, 770
**ZIP Code**: 30328, 30338, 30350, 30358, 31156
**Post Offices**: Glenridge Branch, 5400 Glenridge Dr; Sandy Springs Branch, 6094 Boylston Dr NE; Sandy Springs Postal Store, 227 Sandy Springs Pl; North Springs, 7527 Roswell Rd; Perimeter Station, 4707 Ashford Dunwoody Rd; 800-275-8777, www.usps.com

*Sandy Springs*

**Police Precinct**: Sandy Springs Police Department, 5995 Barfield Rd, Sandy Springs, 770-551-6911, www.sandyspringspolice.org/

**Emergency Hospitals**: Northside Hospital, 1000 Johnson Ferry Rd NE, 404-851-8000, www.northside.com; St. Joseph's Hospital, 5665 Peachtree Dunwoody Rd, 404-851-7001, www.stjosephsatlanta.org

**Library**: Sandy Springs Branch, 395 Mount Vernon Hwy, Atlanta, 404-303-6130; www.afpls.org/sandy-springs-branch6

**Public School Education**: Fulton County School System, 404-763-6830, www.fulton.k12.ga.us

**Community Publications**: *Dunwoody Crier*, 770-451-4147, www.thecrier.net; *Sandy Springs Reporter*, 404-917-2200, www.reporternewspapers.net/sandy-springs-digital-paper

**Community Resources**: City of Sandy Springs, www.sandyspringsga.org; Sandy Springs Community, www.sandysprings.org; Sandy Springs Council of Neighborhoods, P.O. Box 76154, http://sandyspringscouncil.org; Sandy Springs/Perimeter Chamber of Commerce, 404-255-5351, www.sandyspringsperimeterchamber.com; Sandy Springs Revitalization, Inc., 404-252-9352, www.sandysprings.org; Watershed Alliance of Sandy Springs, 800 Crest Valley Dr NW, 404-255-4905, http://watershedallianceofsandysprings.org; Sandy Springs/Dunwoody Community Assistance Center, 1130 Hightower Trail, 770-552-4889, www.ourcac.org; Heritage Sandy Springs, 404-851-9111, www.heritagesandysprings.org; Leadership Sandy Springs, 404-256-9091, www.leadershipsandysprings.org; Dorothy C Benson Senior Multipurpose Complex, 6500 Vernon Woods Dr, 404-705-4900, http://bensoncenter.org;

**Public Transportation**: **MARTA**, 404-848-4711, www.itsmarta.com; **North Line stations**: Dunwoody, Medical Center, Sandy Springs, and North Springs; for detailed bus routes visit www.itsmarta.com/bus-routes-by-route

## ROSWELL

North of Sandy Springs is the charming community of **Roswell**. Founded on the banks of the Chattahoochee River in 1839 by Georgia native Roswell King, this community's first claim to fame was as a small mill town. The King family's original Roswell Manufacturing Company was so successful they soon found themselves expanding by adding a second mill. King then began offering real estate and investment opportunities to his friends and associates, and soon there were homes, cottages, apartments, a general store, a church, and a school on the land surrounding the mills. The community grew and prospered until 1864 when Union troops led by General Sherman marched toward Atlanta. When Sherman discovered that clothes with the letters CSA (Confederate States of America) were being made at the mill, he ordered his troops to torch the community. Most residents were charged with treason and sent north. Amazingly, while the mill and local businesses burned, the homes and church were spared. After the war, many of the residents returned to their homes and rebuilt the mills. Textile manufacturing remained essential to Roswell's economy well into the 1970s.

Today it's obvious that Roswell is a historic town. In fact, 640 acres of the area's 33.23 square miles are now listed with the National Registry of Historic Places. Many of the area's old homes, including Barrington Hall, Mimosa Hall, and Dolvin House, still stand and are currently used as private residences. However, Bulloch Hall, the childhood home of Mittie Bulloch (President Teddy Roosevelt's mother and Eleanor Roosevelt's grandmother), is open daily to the public and is a great place to visit. Even Roswell's town square has managed to retain the feel of an old-time rural community, despite an increase in population and local traffic. The historic square is beautifully laid out in a grid pattern similar to those found in New England. Today unique stores, gift shops, and restaurants grace the square, and during the summer months it plays host to a concert series, along with numerous community-oriented festivals and events.

Around 88,000 people live in Roswell. Its main roads are Holcomb Bridge Road, running east-west, and Ga. Hwy 120/Alpharetta Highway or Crabapple Road, running north-south. Neighborhoods are a mix of historic homes, John Wielands or similar two-story four-bedroom/two-baths built in the 1980s or 1990s, and newer mansions upwards of half a million. Homes closest to the Chattahoochee Nature Center on and around Willeo Drive sit on large, tree-filled lots that offer residents a quiet, quasi-rural way of life. There are also more than enough apartment communities to please all of the young couples and suburban singles moving to the area.

**Website**: www.roswellgov.com
**Area Codes**: 770, 678
**ZIP Codes**: 30075, 30076, 30350

*Roswell*

**Post Offices**: Roswell Main Office, 8920 Eves Rd; Roswell Postal Store, 10719 Alpharetta Hwy; Crosstown Carrier Annex, 225E Crossville Rd; North Springs, 7527 Roswell Rd NE; 800-275-8777, www.usps.com

**Police Precincts**: North Fulton County Police Department, Patrol/Non-Emergency, 770-551-7600; Fulton County Police Department, Northeast Precinct, 10205 Medlock Bridge Pkwy, 770-495-8738, www.fultonpolice.org; Roswell Police Department, 39 Hill St, 770-640-4100; www.roswellgov.com/police

**Emergency Hospitals**: North Fulton Hospital, 3000 Hospital Blvd, Roswell, 770-751-2500, www.nfultonhospital.com; Northside Hospital, 1000 Johnson Ferry Rd NE, 404-851-8000, www.northside.com

**Library**: Roswell Regional, 115 Norcross St, Roswell, 770-640-3075, www.afplweb.com

**Public School Education**: Fulton County School System, 404-763-6830, www.fulton.k12.ga.us

**Community Publications**: *Alpharetta-Roswell Revue & News*, 770-442-3278, www.northfulton.com

**Community Resources**: Historic Roswell Convention and Visitors Bureau, 770-640-3253, www.visitroswellga.com; Roswell City Hall, 38 Hill St, 770-641-3727, www.roswellgov.com; Roswell Cultural Arts Center, 950 Forrest St, 770-594-6232; Chattahoochee Nature Center, 770-992-2055, www.chattnaturecenter.org; Greater North Fulton Chamber of Commerce, 11605 Haynes Bridge Rd Ste 100, Alpharetta, 770-993-8806, www.gnfcc.com; North Fulton Senior Services, 770-993-1906, www.ssnorthfulton.org

**Public Transportation**: **MARTA**, 404-848-4711, www.itsmarta.com; **North Line station**: North Springs; for detailed bus routes visit www.itsmarta.com/bus-routes-by-route

## ALPHARETTA

Further north is the community of **Alpharetta**. This North Fulton suburb was originally a successful trading post village called New Prospect Camp Ground, which was frequented by white settlers and local Indians alike. In December 1857, the village was chartered and became the county seat of Milton County, and the village was renamed Alpharetta—from the Greek word "Alpha" meaning "first" and "Retta" meaning "town." (In 1932, Milton County was absorbed into Fulton County.)

Like Roswell, this fast-growing area remained rural until the 1980s. In fact, in 1980 Alpharetta's population was still a mere 3,000. But as of 2010, thanks to the sprawling growth of the metro area and a number of Fortune 500 companies that have headquartered here, the population has swelled to almost 60,000. This growth is significant, but has not yet reached the levels of Sandy Springs and Roswell. Much of Alpharetta is still lush, green, and undeveloped, but this is quickly changing as more and more buildings replace greenspace. Driving through Alpharetta along States Bridge Road or Abbots Bridge Road, for example, you could expect to find a newly constructed apartment complex across the street from a working farm ... next door to a small subdivision ... around the corner from a strip mall. It's just this sort of ambiguity—greenspace next to homes and shopping—along with the excellent schools and access to jobs that makes Alpharetta one of the hottest markets in metro Atlanta for both residential and commercial real estate. You'll find the large colonial and ranch-style homes in this community to be a bit higher priced than comparable homes in other North Fulton suburbs. Many line the rugged bluffs overlooking the Chattahoochee River, offering lovely views. Most homes are built on nice-sized lots or in recently developed subdivisions. The newer homes coexist easily with the older homes, as the overall architectural style is fairly traditional.

Alpharetta has a strong equestrian theme, with many private horse farms stretching north into the newly incorporated city of Milton. Wills Park, with entrances on Old Milton Parkway and Wills Road, features a world-class equestrian center complete with competition course and beautiful stables. Private ranches are also plentiful.

Also, in 2008 the city opened two **Arboretums.** The attractions were funded by the city of Alpharetta's Tree Commission, the Alpharetta Convention and Visitors Bureau, and Alpharetta Arboretum, Inc. The largest arboretum is at Wills Park and features 26 types of trees. The second arboretum is at **Webb Bridge Park** and features seven types of trees, a large play area, a walking path, a playground and picnic pavilions.

**Website**: www.alpharetta.ga.us
**Area Codes**: 770, 678
**ZIP Codes**: 30004, 30005, 30022

*Alpharetta*

**Post Offices**: Alpharetta Main Office, 2400 Old Milton Pkwy; Webb Bridge Branch, 4575 Webb Bridge Rd; 800-275-8777, www.usps.com

**Police Precincts**: North Fulton County Police Department, Patrol/Non-Emergency, 770-551-7600; Fulton County Police Department, Northeast Precinct, 10205 Medlock Bridge Pkwy, 770-495-8738 www.fultonpolice.org; Alpharetta Police Department, 2565 Old Milton Pkwy, 678-297-6300; Alpharetta Community Service Division, 678-297-6309; www.alpharetta.ga.us

**Emergency Hospitals**: North Fulton Regional Hospital, 3000 Hospital Blvd, Roswell, 770-751-2500, www.northfultonregional.com

**Libraries**: Alpharetta, 238 Canton St, Alpharetta, 770-740-2425; Northeast/Spruill Oaks Regional, 9560 Spruill Rd, Alpharetta, 770-360-8820; Ocee, 5090 Abbotts Bridge Rd, Alpharetta, 770-360-8897; www.afplweb.com

**Public School Education**: Fulton County School System, 404-763-6830, www.fulton.k12.ga.us

**Community Publications**: *Alpharetta-Roswell Revue & News*, 770-442-3278, www.northfulton.com

**Community Resources**: Alpharetta City Hall, Two South Main St, 678-297-6000, www.alpharetta.ga.us; Alpharetta Environmental Education Center, 770-410-5835; Alpharetta Wills Park Equestrian Center, 678-297-6120, www.alpharetta.ga.us; Greater North Fulton Chamber of Commerce, 11695 Haynes Bridge Rd Ste 100, www.gnfcc.com; North Fulton Education Force, 770-993-8806; North Fulton Senior Services, 770-993-1906, www.ssnorthfulton.org

**Public Transportation**: **MARTA**, 404-848-4711, www.itsmarta.com; for detailed bus routes visit www.itsmarta.com/bus-routes-by-route

## DEKALB COUNTY

DeKalb (pronounced "DeeCab") County has the third largest population in metro Atlanta, and is the most ethnically diverse county in Georgia. Parts of the City of Atlanta are governed by DeKalb, and the county is the region's most urban area. The majority of DeKalb's residents are African-American, and it is the second most affluent African-American community in the country. The county also possesses a high concentration of Asians, Hispanics, and international residents. More than 16,000 refugees from over 20 countries have been resettled in DeKalb since 1980. The mix makes the county one of a kind in both flavor and commerce; it is home to more than 200 immigrant-owned businesses. The diversity is reflected in one very popular and delicious destination—the DeKalb Farmers Market—A World Market. With 140,000 square feet of goods, the market draws around 100,000 customers from all over the state every week.

DeKalb County identifies itself not only as the county with an international flavor, but also as the county with myriad biomedical facilities. The US Centers for Disease Control, the Yerkes Primate Center, Emory University's Rollins Research Center, and the American Cancer Society's national headquarters are all located here.

## DECATUR

The City of **Decatur,** the DeKalb County seat, was founded in 1823. The downtown area still conveys a small-town feeling with its Georgian-style courthouse and shops clustered around the town square. But recent development and congested one-way streets here are beginning to make downtown Decatur feel more like downtown Atlanta. On any given day, residents can expect to find streets blocked by construction equipment as new condos or office complexes are erected. Fortunately, people who work in Decatur's downtown area can take advantage of MARTA; the Decatur Station is located in the center of the community's commercial district, allowing easy access for pedestrians. Many opt to take the train in and out of downtown Decatur rather than fight traffic and scramble for parking.

Despite recent growth, Decatur's town square has preserved its small-town ambiance with wide sidewalks, wooden benches situated beneath curving light posts, and plenty of locally owned businesses. The square also plays host to a variety of events throughout the year, from family fun festivals to summertime concerts. Every July 4th, residents crowd the square to witness Decatur's famous fireworks display.

Because of its ethnic diversity, lower sales tax, and less expensive housing, Decatur attracts a mix of students, singles, young families, and retirees. West Ponce de Leon Avenue, Decatur's main street, is lined with eateries offering soul food, home cooking, Asian, Indian, or Mexican cuisines. Near the downtown area is Eddie's Attic, a long-standing and well-known folk music haven frequented by

*Decatur*

seasoned artists like the Grammy Award–winning Indigo Girls, Sugarland, Shawn Mullins, John Mayer, and even Justin Bieber.

The area also tends to attract an open-minded, easygoing crowd, including many of Atlanta's nesting gay and lesbian inhabitants who prefer the laid-back Decatur atmosphere to the busy streets of Midtown. *The Decatur Focus*, the city's official newsletter, encourages recipients to "Help Decatur be a community where neighbors help neighbors."

Just a stone's throw away from the laid-back bustle of downtown is the pastoral campus of Agnes Scott College, a women's college founded as the Decatur Female Seminary in 1888. The neighborhoods surrounding this beautiful campus are a wonderful balance to Decatur's commercial district, with shady sidewalks, quiet streets, and large Victorians and mid-sized bungalows.

South of the downtown square, families reside in smaller homes ranging from the ever-present, one-story brick ranch to old, ornate Victorians. Students of metro Atlanta's many universities find Decatur the perfect place to put down temporary roots, and they quickly fill up the smaller apartment complexes and abundant rental houses. Rents in Decatur are less expensive than intown neighborhoods such as Virginia Highland and Buckhead, though it's located only six miles from downtown Atlanta.

**Website**: www.decaturga.com

**Area Codes**: 404, 770

**ZIP Codes**: 30030, 30031, 30032, 30033, 30034, 30035

**Post Offices**: Main Office, 520 West Ponce de Leon Ave; Decatur Carrier Annex, 3651 Memorial Dr; South Decatur, 2853 Candler Rd; Scottdale, 3328 East Ponce de Leon Ave; Avondale Estates, 15 Franklin St; 800-275-8777, www.usps.com

**Police Precincts**: DeKalb County Police Department, 404-294-2519; Center Precinct, 3630 Camp Cir, 404-294-2580; South Precinct, 1816 Candler Rd, 404-

286-7911; http://web.co.dekalb.ga.us/DK_Police/index.html; DeKalb County Sheriff's Office, 404-298-8145, www.dekalbsheriff.org

**Emergency Hospital**: DeKalb Medical Center, 2701 N Decatur Rd, 404-501-1000, www.dekalbmedicalcenter.org

**Libraries**: Main Library, 215 Sycamore St, Decatur, 404-370-3070; Toco Hill-Avis G. Williams, 1282 McConnell Dr, Decatur, 404-679-4404; Brookhaven, 1242 North Druid Hills Rd, Decatur, 404-848-7140; Covington, 3500 Covington Hwy, Decatur, 404-508-7180; Flat Shoals, 4022 Flat Shoals Pkwy, Decatur, 404-244-4370; Scott Candler, 1917 Candler Rd, Decatur, 404-286-6986; William C. Brown/Wesley Chapel, 2861 Wesley Chapel Rd, Decatur, 404-286-6980; www.dekalblibrary.org

**Public School Education**: Decatur City Schools, 404-370-4400, www.csdecatur. net; Decatur City Schools Hotline, 404-419-6055; DeKalb County Board of Education, 678-676-1200, www.dekalb.k12.ga.us

**Community Publications**: *The Decatur Focus*, 404-371-8386, www.decatur-ga. com; *The Champion*, http://thechampionnewspaper.com

**Community Resources**: Decatur Business Association, 404-371-8386, http://decaturdba.com; Decatur Arts Alliance, 404-371-9583, www.decaturartsalliance. org; DeKalb History Center, 404-373-1088, www.dekalbhistory.org; Decatur Events Hotline, 404-371-8344; DeKalb County Chamber of Commerce, 404-378-8000, www.dekalbchamber.org; DeKalb County Convention & Visitors Bureau, 800-999-6055, http://visitatlantasdekalbcounty.com

**Public Transportation**: **MARTA**, 404-848-4711, www.itsmarta.com; **East/West Line station**: Decatur; for detailed bus routes visit www.itsmarta.com/bus-routes-by-route

## AVONDALE ESTATES

East of Decatur lies the city of **Avondale Estates**, a small community conceived and founded in the early 1920s by patent medicine millionaire George F. Willis. Willis envisioned a subdivision modeled after an old English village, and by 1930 he had converted 1000 acres of scenic farmland into his ideal community. Avondale Estates' public buildings and businesses were constructed in the Tudor style, gracing the commercial district with a small village ambiance that remains to this day. Homes here reflect numerous traditional styles including Tudor, English Cottage, Colonial Revival, and Craftsman.

The city, which was granted its own mayor, police department, and post office by the Georgia State government in 1926, is filled with curving, tree-lined streets. The area's small parks, its lake, pool, clubs, bird sanctuary, and tennis courts are accessible only to Avondale's residents (less than 3,000) and their guests, all of whom are identified by vehicle decals or temporary passes provided by city hall. Though this exclusivity is obviously an advantage to residents, it can be intimidating to outsiders. The community police department diligently patrols its every

*Avondale Estates*

corner, and strangers to the neighborhood won't get very far without running across a friendly but inquiring officer.

Avondale Estates was placed on the National Register of Historic Places in 1986 for being the only documented example of an early-20th-century planned town in the southeastern United States, as well as for the character of its architecture and landscape. Also noteworthy, the city housed the first Waffle House, which opened its doors Labor Day weekend of 1955. Waffle House keeps a museum at the original location at 2719 East College Avenue, Decatur.

The Avondale city government is diligent in preserving the historic value of the community, strictly limiting the type of and amount of new construction and renovation allowed within the city. Historic preservation guidelines are available for anyone considering moving into the community.

**Website**: www.avondaleestates.org

**Area Codes**: 404, 770

**ZIP Code**: 30002

**Post Offices**: Avondale Estates, 15 Franklin St; Main Office, 520 West Ponce de Leon Ave; Scottdale, 3328 East Ponce de Leon Ave; 800-275-8777, www.usps.com

**Police Precincts**: Avondale Estates Police Department, 404-294-5400; DeKalb County Police Department, 404-294-2519; Center Precinct, 3630 Camp Cir, 404-294-2580; http://web.co.dekalb.ga.us/dk_police; DeKalb County Sheriff's Office, 404-298-8145, www.dekalbsheriff.org

**Emergency Hospital**: DeKalb Medical Center, 2701 N Decatur Rd, 404-501-1000, www.dekalbmedicalcenter.org

**Libraries**: Scottdale-Tobie Grant, 644 Parkdale Dr, Scottdale, 404-508-7174; Main Library, 215 Sycamore St, Decatur, 404-370-3070; www.dekalb.public.lib.ga.us

**Public School Education**: DeKalb County Board of Education, 678-676-1200, www.dekalb.k12.ga.us

**Community Publications**: *Atlanta Intown*, 404-586-0002, www.atlantaintownpaper.com

**Community Resources**: Avondale Estates City Hall, 21 North Avondale Plaza, 404-294-5400; Avondale Community Club, 59 Lakeshore Dr, 404-284-2934, http://www.avondalecommunityclub.com; DeKalb County Chamber of Commerce, 404-378-8000, www.dekalbchamber.org; DeKalb County Convention & Visitors Bureau, 770-492-5000, http://visitatlantasdekalbcounty.com; DeKalb History Center, 404-373-8287, www.dekalbhistory.org

**Public Transportation**: **MARTA**, 404-848-4711, www.itsmarta.com; **East/West Line station**: Avondale; for detailed bus routes visit www.itsmarta.com/bus-routes-by-route

## STONE MOUNTAIN

One of DeKalb County's places of pride is the **Stone Mountain** area, which includes the 3,200-acre Stone Mountain Park, Stone Mountain Village, and neighborhoods radiating out along Memorial Drive. Of all the metro Atlanta communities, this one perhaps typifies what most Northerners might envision a small Georgia town to be like. Narrow streets and old frame houses with porches large enough for rocking chairs and swings dominate this community, giving it an old-world, rural feel not found in other Atlanta suburbs.

The community is named for the actual Stone Mountain, the world's largest monolith of exposed granite, rising over 800 feet above the ground and located in the heart of Stone Mountain Park. Local Native Americans once used the mountain for tribal rites and as a lookout point. By the time white settlers inhabited the area in the 19th century, the unusual rock formation was beginning to attract the attention of travelers and tourists. With the founding of the town of New Gibraltar (now the city of Stone Mountain), the area grew with the steady influx of tourist money.

Aside from its geological magnitude, Stone Mountain possesses an artistic magnitude of sorts, with the world's largest sculpture carved on its face. Originally conceived by noted sculptor Gutzon Borglum, who later carved the faces on Mt. Rushmore, the face of Stone Mountain depicts the three mounted figures of confederate heroes Robert E. Lee, Jefferson Davis, and Stonewall Jackson. Taking over 42 years to complete and utilizing the talents of three separate artists, the memorial was finally completed in 1972 and has been attracting onlookers ever since. Today Stone Mountain Park offers nature trails, family activities, golf courses, swimming, fishing, boating, and a skylift to the top of the mountain. There are also a petting zoo, an antique car museum, and a number of shops and restaurants.

In the shadow of the great monolith, Stone Mountain Village contains turn-of-the-century commercial buildings, which house antique stores, gift shops, restaurants, and cafés. Now home to over 7,000 residents, the village is really a place where Old South meets New South. The history here is tricky, as Stone Mountain

*Stone Mountain*

was, for many years, a predominantly white community and an annual Ku Klux Klan meeting site. But today the town is enjoying greater ethnic diversity than ever before, and residents are quick to point out that the community is concerned more with preserving its small-town character than its antiquated racist attitudes.

The homes in this area range from ornate Victorians to 1930s bungalows to newer, Craftsman-style houses. As in other suburbs, most of the older homes are on the largest lots and can be found closest to the Village, while the newer homes tend to be in planned subdivisions with smaller yards, many located on the side streets around Memorial Drive. It's important to note that one of Stone Mountain's neighborhoods, the 30083 ZIP code, was listed as one of the top 100 worst in the country when it came to foreclosures, according to a 2012 report from CNNMoney and RealtyTrac. The upside—you could find some great deals here. The downside, the neighborhoods might still be recovering from the bust.

**Website**: www.stonemountaincity.org
**Area Codes**: 404, 770
**ZIP Codes**: 30083, 30086, 30087, 30088
**Post Offices**: Stone Mountain Main Post Office, 5181 West Mountain St; Stone Mountain Memorial Branch, 5152 Memorial Dr; Mountain Park Post Office, 1785 East Park Place Blvd; 800-275-8777, www.usps.com
**Police Precincts**: City of Stone Mountain Police Department, 770-879-4980, www.stonemountaincity.org; DeKalb County Police Department, 404-294-2519; East Precinct, 2484 Bruce St, 770-482-0300; http://web.co.dekalb.ga.us/dk_police; DeKalb County Sheriff's Office, 404-298-8145, www.dekalbsheriff.org
**Emergency Hospitals**: DeKalb Medical Center, 2701 N Decatur Rd, 404-501-1000, www.dekalbmedicalcenter.org
**Libraries**: Sue Kellogg, 952 Leon St, Stone Mountain, 770-413-2020; Hairston Crossing, 4911 Redan Rd, Stone Mountain, 404-508-7170; www.dekalb.public.lib.ga.us

*Lithonia*

**Public School Education**: DeKalb County Board of Education, 678-676-1200, www.dekalb.k12.ga.us

**Community Publications**: *CrossRoadsNews,* 404-284-1888; www.crossroads-news.com

**Community Resources**: City of Stone Mountain, 770-498-8984, www.stonemoun-taincity.org; Stone Mountain Village, www.stonemountainvillage.com; Stone Mountain Park, 770-498-5690, www.stonemountainpark.com; Stone Mountain Woman's Club, 5513 East Mountain St, 770-879-8771; DeKalb County Chamber of Commerce, 404-378-8000, www.dekalbchamber.org; DeKalb County Convention & Visitors Bureau, 770-492-5000, http://visitatlantasdekalbcounty.com; DeKalb History Center, 404-373-8287, www.dekalbhistory.org

**Public Transportation**: **MARTA**, 404-848-4711, www.itsmarta.com; **East-West Line station**: Indian Creek; for detailed bus routes visit www.itsmarta.com/bus-routes-by-route

## LITHONIA

Further south in DeKalb County is the City of **Lithonia**, another of the area's ethnically mixed, yet still somewhat rural, communities. It's also home to the upscale, Lionshead subdivision, a predominantly African-American neighborhood boasting large, newly built, traditional-style homes.

Established in the mid-1800s, this community began as a small settlement known as Cross Roads. Shortly after, the name was changed to Lithonia, a Greek word meaning "Rock Place." In just ten years, Lithonia was home to about 250 residents. Today Lithonia's population is just about 2,000.

Many choosing to live in Lithonia are looking to get away from the more crowded, intown neighborhoods and more heavily populated subdivisions. Here, residents enjoy nice homes on large lots at reasonable prices. Lithonia is home to many well-respected schools and churches, and a diverse ethnic mix. Local highways and interstates offer a reasonable commute to Downtown or south metro Atlanta.

It is important to note the area suffered a large number of foreclosures and subsequent depressed property values following the 2008 recession. The city has also struggled to maintain a stable local government, with ongoing political fights among elected and volunteer officials, and a high turnover of city staff. Hopefully Lithonia's officials will work more constructively for the city's best in coming years.

**Website**: http://georgia.gov/cities-counties/lithonia (at the time of publication, the city was going through some restructuring, which may impact its web address)

**Area Codes**: 770, 678

**ZIP Codes**: 30038, 30058

**Post Offices**: Lithonia Post Office, 3035 Stone Mountain St; Redan Post Office, 1544 Wellborn Rd; 800-275-8777, www.usps.com

**Police Precincts**: City of Lithonia Police Department, 6980 Main St, 770-482-4461; DeKalb County Police Department, 404-294-2519; East Precinct, 2484 Bruce St, 770-482-0300; http://web.co.dekalb.ga.us/dk_police; DeKalb County Sheriff's Office, 404-298-8145, www.dekalbsheriff.org

**Emergency Hospitals**: DeKalb Medical Center, 2701 N Decatur Rd, 404-501-1000, www.dekalbmedicalcenter.org, Hillandale DeKalb Medical Center, 2801 DeKalb Medical Pkwy, 404-501-8000, http://www.dekalbmedical.org/hillandale

**Libraries**: Lithonia-Davidson, 6821 Church St, 770-482-3820; Bruce Street, 2484 Bruce St, Lithonia, 770-482-0405; Salem-Panola, 5137 Salem Rd, Lithonia, 770-987-6900; www.dekalblibrary.org

**Public School Education**: DeKalb County Board of Education, 678-676-1200, www.dekalb.k12.ga.us

**Community Publications**: *CrossRoadsNews*, 404-284-1888, www.crossroads-news.com

**Community Resources**: City of Lithonia, 770-482-8136; DeKalb County Chamber of Commerce, 404-378-8000, www.dekalbchamber.org; DeKalb County Convention & Visitors Bureau, 770-492-5000, http://visitatlantasdekalbcounty.com; DeKalb History Center, 404-373-8287, www.dekalbhistory.org

**Public Transportation**: MARTA, 404-848-4711, www.itsmarta.com; for detailed bus routes visit www.itsmarta.com/bus-routes-by-route

## CHAMBLEE

Closer to the I-285 perimeter in DeKalb County is the community of **Chamblee** (pronounced SHAM-blee). As part of Atlanta's "International Corridor," this three-square-mile city, located northeast of Atlanta, has the most culturally diverse population in the State of Georgia. Families from Asia, India, Africa, Mexico, South America, Europe, and all parts of the United States now call Chamblee home.

Unlike the Chinatowns or a Little Italy in other US cities, in Chamblee you're likely to find a Mexican restaurant next to a Japanese grocery or Colombian bakery; a Chinese herb shop next to a Korean video store or an American fast food joint. And grocery stores like the popular International Farmers' Market or Atlanta Asian Foods operate in close proximity to American chain grocery stores such as Publix and Kroger.

But ethnic diversity is not the only thing Chamblee has to offer. In the heart of the historic business district is Chamblee's famous "Antique Row," the largest antique area in the South. Home to more than 150 dealers, the shops offer quality antiques and collectibles to fit any budget. Even if you don't want to buy anything, strolling along Antique Row is a great way to spend a Saturday afternoon. Parking is not usually a problem, but spaces are limited, so getting an early start is a good idea. And if you'd rather take advantage of Atlanta's transit system, you're in luck. The Chamblee MARTA station (on the Northeast rail line) is easily accessed.

Since 2000, Chamblee has worked hard to revitalize its downtown and overhaul its sometimes industrial image with more mixed-use developments and pedestrian friendly communal areas. With a nod to its beginnings (the downtown has been preserved as an early 20th century railroad community), the city's tagline is "A city on the right track." A number of new loft and townhouse developments have opened in the downtown area, as well as a newly constructed city hall. The city also renamed one its main thoroughfares, Peachtree Industrial Boulevard, to Peachtree Boulevard.

There are many quaint neighborhoods spreading out from Chamblee downtown: Huntley Hills, Sexton Park, and Keswick Village to name a few. Homes are priced in the low 200s and consist largely of split level ranches on large, shaded lots. Many neighborhoods also offer neighborhood swimming pools and tennis clubs.

One great selling point for these neighborhoods, and for Chamblee as a whole, is the area's public school system. Several nearby elementary schools are well respected and conveniently located. But the feather in Chamblee's educational cap has to be Chamblee High School. Ninety-nine percent of Chamblee High's seniors take the SATs, with an average score in the mid-500s in both math and verbal, and students here consistently rank among the top ten in test scores for the entire state.

For newcomers, especially those with young children, looking to live inside the perimeter, in a community close to I-285, the Perimeter Mall, and Buckhead, Chamblee is a good option.

**Website**: www.chambleega.com
**Area Codes**: 770, 678
**ZIP Codes**: 30341, 30366

*Chamblee*

**Post Offices**: Chamblee Post Office, 3545 Broad St; North Atlanta Carrier Facility, 1920 Dresden Dr NE; Embry Hills, 3579 Chamblee Tucker Rd; 800-275-8777, www.usps.com

**Police Precincts**: Chamblee Police Department, 3518 Broad St, 770-986-5005; DeKalb County Police Department, 404-294-2519; North Precinct, 4453 Ashford-Dunwoody Rd, 404-297-3950; http://web.co.dekalb.ga.us/dk_police; DeKalb County Sheriff's Office, 404-298-8145, www.dekalbsheriff.org

**Emergency Hospital**: Emory Dunwoody Medical Center, 4575 North Shallowford Rd, 770-454-2000; www.emorydunwoody.com

**Libraries**: Chamblee, 4115 Clairmont Rd, 770-936-1380; Embry Hills, 3733 Chamblee Tucker Rd, Chamblee, 770-270-8230; www.dekalb.public.lib.ga.us

**Public School Education**: DeKalb County Board of Education, 678-676-1200, www.dekalb.k12.ga.us

**Community Publications**: *North DeKalb Neighbor*, 770-454-9388; *DeKalb Neighbor*, www.neighbornewspapers.com

**Community Resources**: City of Chamblee, 770-986-5010, www.chambleega.com; Chamblee Antique Row, 770-455-4751, www.antiquerow.com; DeKalb Peachtree Airport, Clairmont Rd, Chamblee, 770-936-5440, www.pdkairport.com; DeKalb County Chamber of Commerce, 404-378-8000, www.dekalbchamberofcommerce.org; DeKalb County Convention & Visitors Bureau, 770-492-5000, www.visitatlantasdekalbcounty.org; DeKalb History Center, 404-373-8287, www.dekalbhistory.org

**Public Transportation**: **MARTA**, 404-848-4711, www.itsmarta.com; **Northeast Line stations**: Chamblee and Doraville; for detailed bus routes visit www.itsmarta.com/bus-routes-by-route

# DUNWOODY

The upscale city of **Dunwoody**, north of Chamblee, is a planned suburb originally based around Dunwoody Village, a commercial shopping complex. The neighborhoods surrounding Dunwoody Village are filled with large, traditional-style homes on tree-lined streets with culs-de-sac. The community gained its status of cityhood in 2008 and continues to stretch its municipal wings.

Due to the high price of single-family homes, most Dunwoody residents tend to be middle- to upper-middle-class families. Still, Dunwoody houses several gated apartment and townhome communities, making it more affordable and accessible to younger crowds, particularly aspiring executives and professionals.

Like neighboring Sandy Springs, which is linked to Dunwoody by Abernathy Road, this area has experienced phenomenal growth in recent years, making it one of the most desired, and most expensive, suburbs in metro Atlanta. In what was once untouched forest, now office parks and strip malls abound. Upscale restaurants are easy to find, as well as myriad coffee shops, bookstores, bakeries, and specialty boutiques. Yet, despite the extensive development, Dunwoody still has plenty of greenspace and one of the best nature centers in the area. Located on Roberts Drive, the Dunwoody Nature Center offers exhibits, classes, nature trails, and a small park. It's open year round, but it's best to call for hours, as they vary according to season.

As Lenox Mall and Phipps Plaza define the Buckhead community, so Perimeter Mall leaves an indelible mark on Dunwoody. Perimeter Mall and its surrounding sprawl are located just south of the Dunwoody Village neighborhoods. The upside of the mall—access to just about any type of store or restaurant you could need or imagine. The downside—an unending traffic nightmare only somewhat alleviated by public transportation and recent road improvements. In high rush hour traffic drivers can spend a good 30 minutes to an hour to move just a mile. Thank goodness for on-demand pod-casts, Pandora radio, and in-vehicle television for the kids!

Along with Perimeter Mall, Dunwoody is also home to an impressive list of businesses and corporations. Cox Communications, Intercontinental Hotel Group, Walden Security, Autotrader.com, and Porsche all call the city home. Also, *The Atlanta Journal-Constitution* moved its headquarters from Downtown to the area in 2010.

**Website**: www.dunwoodyga.gov
**Area Codes**: 404, 770
**ZIP Codes**: 30338, 30356, 30360
**Post Offices**: Dunwoody Post Office, 1551 Dunwoody Village Pkwy; Perimeter Station, 4707 Ashford Dunwoody Rd; 800-275-8777, www.usps.com

*Dunwoody*

**Police Precincts**: Dunwoody Police Department, 41 Perimeter Center East, Ste 100, 678-382-6900 www.dunwoodyga.gov/Departments/Dunwoody-Police-Department.aspx; DeKalb County Police Department, 404-294-2519, http://web.co.dekalb.ga.us/dk_police; DeKalb County Sheriff's Office, 404-298-8145, www.dekalbsheriff.org

**Emergency Hospitals**: Northside Hospital, 1000 Johnson Ferry Rd NE, 404-851-8000, www.northside.com; St. Joseph's Hospital, 5665 Peachtree Dunwoody Rd, 404-851-7001, www.stjosephsatlanta.org; Children's Healthcare of Atlanta, 1001 Johnson Ferry Rd NE, 404-256-5252, www.choa.org

**Library**: Dunwoody Branch, 5339 Chamblee-Dunwoody Rd, 770-512-4640, www.dekalb.public.lib.ga.us

**Public School Education**: DeKalb County Board of Education, 678-676-1200, www.dekalb.k12.ga.us

**Community Publications**: *Dunwoody Crier*, 770-451-4147, www.thecrier.net; *Dunwoody Neighbor*, 770-428-9411, http://neighbornewspapers.com

**Community Resources**: Dunwoody North Civic Association, www.dunwoodynorth.org; Dunwoody Homeowners Association, 770-817-8100, www.dunwoodyga.org; Dunwoody Nature Center, 770-394-3322, www.dunwoodynature.org; Perimeter Mall, 770-394-4270, www.perimetermall.com; DeKalb County Chamber of Commerce, 404-378-8000, www.dekalbchamber.org; DeKalb County Convention & Visitors Bureau, 770-492-5000, www.atlantasdekalb.org; DeKalb History Center, 404-373-8287, www.dekalbhistory.org

**Public Transportation**: **MARTA**, 404-848-4711, www.itsmarta.com; **Northeast Line station**: Dunwoody; for detailed bus routes visit www.itsmarta.com/bus-routes-by-route

**You might also want to consider the following DeKalb County communities:**

- **Doraville,** located northeast of Chamblee and on top of Atlanta's busy Spaghetti Junction (the crossing of I-285 with I-85 on the north side of the city). The city of 8,330 residents is known for its diversity and its former largest employer, General Motors, which operated a plant there for more than 50 years before announcing it would close the facility in 2005. Since the closure, the town has been busy looking to redefine itself, hoping someone will redevelop the plant. Doraville's upside—a large Asian community and a prime location near two major interstates, a rail line, MARTA, the Peachtree DeKalb airport, and Hartsfield International to the south. City of Doraville, 770-451-8745, www.doravillega.us
- **Tucker,** www.tuckerga.com, also on the northern ring of I-285, or the perimeter. With a population of 27,000, Tucker is a large community, with dense commercial and residential development throughout its 12 square miles. While Tucker is not one of the prettiest neighborhoods in Atlanta, it is considering cityhood and is also working with the Atlanta Regional Commission to improve quality of life for its residents through beautification projects, adding pedestrian-friendly sidewalks and trails, and revitalizing its downtown area. Tucker was given its own ZIP code in 2010—30084. If Tucker became a city, it would be one the largest in DeKalb County.
- **Clarkston,** a small town located in between Stone Mountain and Decatur. Clarkston is the headquarters of Georgia Perimeter College, the state's largest two-year college and third largest college. The city is also known for its diverse population, as it was a popular spot for international refugees to resettle in the 1990s. As a result, today Clarkston's high school has students from more than 50 different countries.

## COBB COUNTY

Like much of the area in and around metro Atlanta, Cobb County was once home to the Creek and Cherokee Indian nations. In 1832, after the state parceled out the land by lottery, settlers organized the Cobb County government and named their community after Thomas Willis Cobb, the illustrious politician who, during the course of his political career, served as a US Representative, a US Senator, and a Supreme Court Judge. Civil War fighting subsequently devastated the Cobb County area. However, by World War I, demand for the region's abundant agricultural products led to an economic growth that continues to this day. During the last three decades, Cobb has increased its population tremendously, reaching around 700,000 residents as of 2011.

Cobb County's booming economy, high standard of living, and safer streets lure many newcomers to the area. Numerous residents from other parts of metro Atlanta have chosen to relocate here as well. Once a bedroom community centered around Marietta and Smyrna, Cobb has grown into a suburban megaplex. One of the area's largest industrial employers, Lockheed Martin, employs roughly 7,000 workers at its Marietta plant. Twenty million square feet of office space, located at the intersection of I-75 and I-285 and dubbed the "Platinum Triangle," houses some of the nation's largest companies, including Home Depot, Sprint, and IBM.

The Cobb Galleria Centre and Cobb Energy Performing Arts Center surround south Cobb's shopping mall, Cumberland Mall. The Galleria offers a vast convention area, convertible arena, and stage seating for athletic events, concerts, and plays. The Cobb Energy Center includes a 2,700-seat state-of-the-art theater and a 10,000-square-foot ballroom, among other features. Cobb is also home to three of the Southeast's largest outdoor theme parks: Six Flags Over Georgia, White Water Park, and American Adventures Theme Park.

Cobb County offers numerous education options, both public and private. Its public school system is the second largest in the state, and many of its schools have won repeated excellence awards, including the National Blue Ribbon award. There are dozens of private schools and four colleges, Kennesaw State University, Chattahoochee Technical College, Life University, and Southern Polytechnic State University.

Cobb Community Transit offers residents public transportation through 17 bus routes. The transit system was established in July of 1989 as an alternative to MARTA. Also, Cobb County is considering constructing a light rail system.

## MARIETTA

The city of **Marietta** is the seat of Cobb County, its largest city, and with around 60,000 residents, one of the largest cities in metro Atlanta.

Named for the wife of Thomas Willis Cobb, Marietta was settled in 1833 and incorporated in 1852. The town has a rich Civil War history and boasts five nationally recognized historical districts. One district, Cherokee Street and Washington Avenue, exemplifies old southern charm with rows of antebellum and High Victorian–style houses on spacious lots with ample shade from lofty trees. The historic town square, in downtown Marietta, is home to Glover Park on the Square, a block of land donated in the mid-1800s by the city's first mayor; John H. Glover was a popular businessman and politician. The square has served generations of Cobb County consumers and residents with its shops and businesses and plays host to a variety of free concerts and events throughout the year.

Marietta is also boasts a vibrant cultural life. The Marietta-Cobb Museum of Art, built in the Greek Revival style in the 1930s, features a diverse program of exhibitions throughout the year. It is also the only local museum with a permanent exhibition of American art.

After sitting largely vacant since 1976, the historic Strand Theatre on Marietta's square reopened in 2009. The theater's resurrection is due largely to the nonprofit group Friends of the Strand, which raised $5 million in multiple

*Marietta*

campaigns between 2004 and 2007. Today the Strand hosts musical productions by the Atlanta Lyric Theatre, as well as classic movies, concerts, and private events.

The Marietta Museum of History is home to thousands of artifacts, including items from Marietta residents and businesses. And the Marietta Gone with the Wind Museum, also called "Scarlett on the Square," houses a collection of memorabilia related to both the book and the film.

You can find just about any price point in Marietta's many neighborhoods—from country club to urban living. Some estates or mansions are priced as high as $5 million. There are hundreds of family-oriented neighborhoods, with pools and community centers, where homes are priced from the $200,000 to $700,000s. Meanwhile there are plenty of apartments citywide and a variety of lofts in downtown Marietta. Buyers can expect their money to go further than inside the perimeter; lots tend to be more than generous, with homes to match.

**Website**: www.mariettaga.gov
**Area Code**: 770
**ZIP Codes**: 30008, 30060, 30062, 30064, 30065, 30066, 30067, 30068, 30090
**Post Offices**: Marietta, Main Post Office, 257 Lawrence St NE; Gresham Road Station, 1290 Gresham Rd; Cumberland Carrier, 1901 Terrell Mill Rd; Cumberland Mall, 1101 Cumberland Mall SE; Windy Hill, 3000 Windy Hill Rd; Mount Bethel, 4455 Lower Roswell Rd; East Cobb, 1395 East Cobb Dr; Sprayberry, 2886 Sandy Plains Rd; 800-275-8777, www.usps.com
**Police Precincts**: City of Marietta Police Department, 240 Lemon St, 770-794-5300, www.mariettaga.gov/city/police; Cobb County Police Department, 140 North Marietta Pkwy, 770-499-3900, www.cobbpolice.com
**Emergency Hospitals**: Wellstar Kennestone Hospital, 677 Church St, Marietta, 770-793-5000; Wellstar Windy Hill Hospital, 2540 Windy Hill Rd, Marietta, 770-644-1000; www.wellstar.org

**Libraries**: Central Headquarters, 266 Roswell St, Marietta, 770-528-2320; East Marietta, 2051 Lower Roswell Rd NE, 770-509-2711; Gritters, 880 Shaw Park Rd NE, Marietta, 770-528-2524; Hattie G. Wilson, 350 Lemon St NE, Marietta, 770-528-2526; Kemp Memorial, 4029 Due West Rd NW, Marietta, 770-528-2527; Merchant's Walk, 1315 Johnson Ferry Rd NE, Marietta, 770-509-2730; Mountain View, 3320 Sandy Plains Rd NE, Marietta, 770-509-2725; Sibley, 1539 S Cobb Dr SE, Marietta, 770-528-2520; Stratton, 1100 Powder Springs Rd SE, Marietta, 770-528-2522; West Cobb Regional, 1750 Dennis Kemp, Kennesaw, 770-528-4699; www.cobbcat.org

**Public School Education**: Marietta City Schools, 250 Howard St, 770-422-3500, www.marietta-city.org; Cobb County School System, 514 Glover St, 770-426-3300, www.cobb.k12.ga.us

**Community Publications**: *Marietta Daily Journal*, 770-428-9411, www.mdjonline.com; *The Bright Side*, http://brightsidenews.com

**Community Resources**: Marietta Welcome Center, Four Depot St, 770-429-1115; The Marietta Square, www.mariettasquare.com; Marietta-Cobb Museum of Art, 770-528-1444, www.mariettacobbartmuseum.org; Cobb County Chamber of Commerce, 770-980-9510, www.cobbchamber.org; Cobb Galleria Centre, 770-955-8000, www.cobbgalleria.com

**Public Transportation**: **Cobb Community Transit** (**CCT**) system, 770-427-4444, www.cobbdot.org/cct.htm; local and express routes throughout Cobb County; **Commuter Club**, 770-859-2331, www.commuterclub.com

## SMYRNA

The Southeast Cobb County community of **Smyrna**, originally an interdenominational religious camp and frontier village, is today an 11.4-square-mile city dominated by office towers, shopping malls, and vigorous commercial growth, although within this snarl of consumer and business traffic you will also find luxury apartment complexes and numerous condominiums.

One of the fastest growing areas in Cobb County, Smyrna is currently home to nearly 52,000 residents, many of them commuting into the City of Atlanta or working at nearby Lockheed Martin or IBM. Yet, despite continuous growth, city planners have been successful at preserving much of this community's charm. Nicknamed "the Jonquil City" for the yellow flowers that bloom here every spring, Smyrna is a pleasant and prosperous place to live. Smyrna's downtown area, "the Village Green," offers residents a mix of retail shops, a community center, and public library for residents. The library, the only independent city library in the state, offers over 55,000 books and other materials, as well as computers, a conference room, and an art gallery. The Village Green also hosts many local festivals and family events throughout the year and is home to Smyrna's city hall, as well as a number of charming homes.

*Smyrna*

Numerous mixed use developments under way in Smyrna stalled in 2008 with the recession. Since that time, developers have presented projects such as strip malls for the empty properties, but city officials have held out hoping for more forward-thinking projects as the economy rebounds. On a brighter note, the city has implemented some beautification projects on key corridors, such as Concord Road and Atlanta Road.

Newer homes in Smyrna range in price from the $300,000s to more than $1 million. Those looking for more spacious environs should consider the upper northwest corner of the county. This area has been less encroached upon by commercial development, and you can still find farmland and horse ranches.

**Website**: www.smyrnacity.com

**Area Code**: 770

**ZIP Codes**: 30080, 30081, 30082, 30339

**Post Offices**: Smyrna, 850 Windy Hill Rd; Ste 7, 3315 Lusk Dr SE; 4480-H, S Cobb Dr; 800-275-8777, www.usps.com

**Police Precincts**: City of Smyrna Police Department, 770-434-9481; Cobb County Police Department, 140 North Marietta Pkwy, 770-499-3900, www.cobbpolice.com

**Emergency Hospital**: Emory-Adventist Hospital, 3949 S Cobb Dr, Smyrna, 770-434-0710, www.emoryadventist.org/

**Libraries**: Lewis A. Ray, 4500 Oakdale Rd SE, Smyrna, 770-801-5335, www.cobbcat.org; Smyrna Public Library, 100 Village Green Cir, 770-431-2860, www.smyrna-library.com

**Public School Education**: Cobb County School System, 514 Glover St, 770-426-3300, www.cobb.k12.ga.us

**Community Publications**: *The Bright Side,* 770-423-9555, www.brightsidenews.com; *Marietta Daily Journal,* 770-428-9411, www.mdjonline.com

**Community Resources**: Smyrna Welcome Center, 2861 Atlanta Rd, 770-805-4277; Smyrna Museum, 770-431-2858, http://smyrnamuseum.com; Smyrna Community Development, 2190 Atlanta Rd SE, 770-319-5387; Smyrna Community Center, 200 Village Green Cir, 770-431-2842, http://www.smyrnacity.com; Cobb County Chamber of Commerce, 770-980-9510, www.cobbchamber.org

**Public Transportation: Cobb Community Transit (CCT)** system, 770-427-4444, http://dot.cobbcountyga.gov; **Commuter Club**, 770-859-2331, www.commuterclub.com

# VININGS

**Vinings** is a small parcel of land overlapping parts of Smyrna and unincorporated Cobb County. Throughout its history, Vinings has been a strategic gathering place: first for Creek and Cherokee Indians; then for settler Hardy Pace, who launched a prosperous ferry operation here in the 1830s; then for the Western & Atlantic Railroad, which established Vinings as a major crossroads; and finally for Union troops, who descended with General Sherman in 1864 and used Vinings' assets to their advantage when attacking Atlanta.

Today Vinings' abundant greenspace, high-end shopping options, and elegant charm make it a favorite among Atlantans who can afford its high price tag. Vinings is decidedly quieter than Buckhead, a quality it perhaps gains from its proximity to Atlanta's lazy Chattahoochee River. A number of its homes enjoy direct views of the "Hooch" from their homes.

Paces Ferry Road is Vinings' main road, and from it you'll find numerous traditional older homes and neighborhoods, as well as some new construction, and a few high-end townhouse communities. Also, for the younger crowd there are a handful of apartment complexes ranging from the bare-boned to the luxurious.

At the center of Vinings is Vinings Jubilee, a high-end outdoor shopping center that acts as the area's informal town square. Here you'll find plenty of stores, like Atlanta's favorite women's boutique Sandpiper, and restaurants where you can either sit outside and enjoy the fresh air, or cuddle up in a café or pub for a drink. Try Garrison's for the pub atmosphere, or SoHo for an evening date or power lunch. Also across the street is long-time favorite Vinings Inn, which offers an award-winning restaurant and lively neighborhood bar.

**Website**: www.viningsga.org
**Area Code**: 770
**ZIP Code**: 30339
**Post Offices**: Akers Mill, 2997 Cobb Pkwy; Cumberland Mall, 1101 Cumberland Mall SE; 800-275-8777, www.usps.com

*Vinings*

**Police Precinct**: Cobb County Police Department, 140 N Marietta Pkwy, 770-499-3900, www.cobbpolice.com

**Emergency Hospital**: Emory-Adventist Hospital, 3949 S Cobb Dr, Smyrna, 770-434-0710, www.emoryadventist.org

**Libraries**: Vinings, 4290 Paces Ferry Rd, 770-801-5330; Lewis A. Ray, 4500 Oakdale Rd SE, Smyrna, 770-801-5335; www.cobbcat.org

**Public School Education**: Cobb County School System, 514 Glover St, 770-426-3300, www.cobb.k12.ga.us

**Community Publications**: *The Bright Side,* 770-423-9555, www.brightsidenews.com

**Community Resources**: Vinings Estate Community Association, 655 Crescent Ridge Trail SE, 770-745-6615, www.viningsestates.com; Vinings Historical Preservation Society, 770-432-3343, www.vinings.org; The Vinings Club, 770-431-9166, www.theviningsclub.com; Cobb County Chamber of Commerce, 770-980-9510, www.cobbchamber.org

**Public Transportation**: **Cobb Community Transit** (**CCT**) system, 770-427-4444, http://dot.cobbcountyga.org; **Commuter Club**, 770-859-2331, www.commuterclub.com

## KENNESAW

Kennesaw is one of Atlanta's smaller towns, located on its north side in between Marietta and Acworth. Kennesaw's beginnings came from its proximity to the railroad, specifically Atlanta's Western Atlantic Railroad. The line through Cobb County was constructed in the 1830s, and during that time many workers set up shacks along the tracks in modern-day Kennesaw, which became known as the grand shanty. Due to this development, the town gained the name of "Big Shanty."

In the 1850s, the site was home to Camp McDonald, a major Confederate training camp during the Civil War. The war was hard on the people of Big Shanty, as the town saw a number of major battles, which ultimately ended in Union occupation, followed by the burning of much of the city when the Union soldiers left. It took a decade for the town to rebuild after the war, and in 1887, the city of Kennesaw was incorporated, gaining a mayor and city council. Over the next century different trades, including cotton, grew and diminished, until the city found its current niche as a family-friendly suburb of metro Atlanta. With plenty of shopping, dining, affordable housing, and proximity to historic sites and parks—such as Kennesaw Mountain, and the Southern Museum of Civil War and Locomotive History—Kennesaw is a great town for middle-income families. In fact, in 2007 the city was named one of the country's "10 Best Towns for Families" by *Family Circle Magazine,* due to its proximity to big-city opportunities, combined with suburban charm, affordable housing, good jobs, top-rated public schools, and an abundance of greenspace.

Also noteworthy, Kennesaw is home to Kennesaw State University, the state's third largest university, which has exceptional business, nursing, and education programs.

**Website**: www.kennesaw-ga.gov
**Area Code**: 770, 678
**ZIP Codes**: 30144, 30152, 30156, 30160
**Post Office**: Kennesaw, 2001 Duncan Dr, Kennesaw; Barrett Pkwy, 840 Ernest Barrett Pkwy Ste 572, Kennesaw; 800-275-8777, www.usps.com
**Police Precincts**: City of Kennesaw Police Department, 770-422-2505, www.kennesaw-ga.gov; Cobb County Police Department, 140 North Marietta Pkwy, 770-499-3900, www.cobbpolice.com
**Emergency Hospital**: Wellstar Kennestone Hospital, 677 Church St, Marietta, 770-793-5000; www.wellstar.org
**Library**: Kennesaw, 2250 Lewis St, Kennesaw, 770-528-2529; West Cobb Regional, 1750 Dennis Kemp Ln, Kennesaw, 770-528-4699; www.cobbcat.org
**Public School Education**: Cobb County School System, 514 Glover St, 770-426-3300, www.cobb.k12.ga.us
**Community Publications**: *Marietta Daily Journal,* 770-428-9411, www.mdjonline.com
**Community Resources**: Kennesaw City Hall, 2529 J.O. Stephenson Ave, Kennesaw, 770-424-8274, www.kennesaw-ga.gov; Kennesaw Business Association, www.kennesawbusiness.org; Kennesaw Mountain National Battlefield, www.nps.gov/kemo; Kennesaw Civil War Museum, www.southernmuseum.org; Rotary Club of North Cobb, www.clubrunner.ca/portal/Home; Cobb County Chamber of Commerce, 770-980-9510, www.cobbchamber.org
**Public Transportation**: **Cobb Community Transit** (CCT) system, 770-427-4444, www.cobbdot.org/cct.htm; **Commuter Club**, 770-859-2331, www.commuterclub.com

*Kennesaw*

## AUSTELL

Beginning as a rail town in 1880, when new rail lines were built from Atlanta to Birmingham, the City of **Austell** was incorporated in 1885 and named for the late General Alfred Austell, founder of the Atlanta National Bank. Today Austell is home to Six Flags Over Georgia, a popular amusement park and one of Atlanta's major tourist attractions. It's also home to the Lithia Springs Water Company and Sweetwater Creek State Park, a peaceful tract of wilderness featuring nature trails, fishing lakes, and a visitor's center.

Though long known as a hub of industry, Austell hasn't been so well known for its housing. This was changing at the turn of the 20th century, with development spilling over from growing Cobb County, but the 2008 recession stalled much of its growth. The area faced another setback when Sweetwater Creek flooded in 2009, destroying many homes and businesses. The flood, which affected all of Georgia, and in particular metro Atlanta residents, left an estimated $500 million in damage statewide, with the city's famous Hooch reaching 500-year levels. Residents in flood plains were the worst hit.

In the coming years Austell hopes to rebuild and grow as a quaint and affordable community for familiar or retirees.

**Website**: www.austellga.gov
**Area Code**: 770
**ZIP Codes**: 30106, 30168
**Post Office**: Austell, 2847 Veterans Memorial Highway; 800-275-8777, www.usps.com
**Police Precincts**: Austell Police Department, 770-944-4318, www.austellga.gov; Cobb County Police Department, 140 North Marietta Pkwy, 770-499-3900, www.cobbpolice.com

*Austell*

**Emergency Hospital**: Wellstar Cobb Hospital, 3950 Austell Rd, Austell, 770-732-4000, www.wellstar.org

**Library**: Sweetwater Valley, 5000 Austell-Powder Springs Rd, Austell, 770-819-3290, www.cobbcat.org

**Public School Education**: Cobb County School System, 514 Glover St, 770-426-3300, www.cobb.k12.ga.us

**Community Publications**: *Marietta Daily Journal,* 770-428-9411, www.mdjonline.com

**Community Resources**: Austell City Hall, 2716 Broad St SW, 770-944-4300, www.austellga.gov; Collar Community Center, 2625 Joe Jerkins Blvd, 770-944-4309, www.austellga.gov; Six Flags Over Georgia, 770-948-9290, www.sixflags.com/overgeorgia; Sweetwater Creek State Park, 770-732-5871, www.friendsofsweetwatercreek.org; Lithia Springs Water Company, 770-944-3880, www.lithiaspringswater.com; Cobb County Chamber of Commerce, 770-980-9510, www.cobbchamber.org

**Public Transportation**: **Cobb Community Transit (CCT)** system, 770-427-4444, www.cobbdot.org/cct.htm; **Commuter Club**, 770-859-2331, www.commuter-club.com

## ACWORTH

On the far north end of Cobb County, and reaching into both Cherokee and Bartow counties, is the city of Acworth. Like Smyrna, Kennesaw, and Austell, Acworth's beginnings come from its location on the Western & Atlantic Railroad. The town was known as Andersonville and then Northcutt Station in the 1850s, before it was officially incorporated in 1860, gaining its current name. The town was named by railroad engineer Joseph L. Gregg, after his home town in New Hampshire.

The town prospered up until the Civil War, when much of it was burned by Union General William Sherman. Acworth remained a small outpost of Atlanta until the 1990s, when it began to grow as a bedroom community. Today the city houses around 20,000 residents. Housing in the area is very affordable compared to communities closer to town, and residents commute to both Marietta and Downtown. Older neighborhoods include numerous ranch-style houses, popular in the 1960s, but there are multiple new developments with a range of home sizes and styles.

Downtown Acworth is full of historic ambiance and southern charm, as well as a mix of unique restaurants and shops. The city hosts a number of festivals here every year.

One of the greatest assets of Acworth is its proximity to Lake Allatoona, a reservoir that stretches more than 12,000 acres. Allatoona, a popular boating and camping destination for residents all over Atlanta, is also home to Acworth Beach, a section where white sand has been laid over Georgia's red clay so visitors can enjoy relaxing in the sun and swimming.

In 2011, Acworth's downtown hosted filming for the remake of the popular '80s movie *Footloose*. The remake included such big name actors as Dennis Quaid, Andie MacDowell, and Julianne Hough, among others, and obviously left many locals feeling very proud of their small town.

**Website**: www.acworth.org

**Area Code**: 770

**ZIP Codes**: 30103, 30102

**Post Office**: 4915 N Main St, Acworth, 770-966-8133; 4200 Mcever Industrial Dr, Acworth; 800-275-8777, www.usps.com

**Police Precincts**: Acworth Police Department, 440 Acworth Industrial Dr, 770-974-1232, www.acworth.org

**Emergency Hospital**: Wellstar Kennestone Hospital, 677 Church St, Marietta, 770-793-5000, www.wellstar.org/

**Library**: Acworth Library, 4569 Dallas St, Acworth, 770-917-5165

**Public School Education**: Cobb County School System, 514 Glover St, 770-426-3300, www.cobb.k12.ga.us

**Community Publications**: *Acworth Community Magazine*, 3459 Acworth Due West Rd Ste 121, 770-529-1516, http://acworthcm.com; *The Bright Side*, 770-423-9555, www.brightsidenews.com; *Marietta Daily Journal*, 770-428-9411, www.mdjonline.com; *Bartow Neighbor*, http://neighbornewspapers.com/

**Community Resources**: City of Acworth, www.acworth.org; Acworth Business Association, www.acworthbusiness.org; Lake Allatoona Preservation Authority, 678-801-4010, www.allatoona.org; N-Georgia, www.n-georgia.com; Cobb County Government, 770-528-1000, www.cobbcounty.org; Cobb County Chamber of Commerce, 770-980-9510, www.cobbchamber.org

*Acworth*

**Public Transportation**: **Cobb Community Transit** (**CCT**) system, 770-427-4444, www.cobbdot.org/cct.htm; **Commuter Club**, 770-859-2331, www.commuterclub.com

**In Cobb County, you might also want to consider:**

- **East Cobb,** a favorite for upper middle class families due to its family-friendly neighborhoods, strong school system, and many parks and recreational facilities. For Atlantans, East Cobb is synonymous with suburban family life. It is also the fastest growing part of Cobb County, as well as the most affluent. Around 200,000 people live in this area, and there are numerous shopping and dining options. Visit East Cobber to learn more, www.eastcobber.com.

## GWINNETT COUNTY

Driving north, away from Atlanta on I-85, is Gwinnett County, metro Atlanta's second most populous county after Fulton. Expect an international flare in beautiful Gwinnett; the county is the most ethnically and racially diverse community in both metro Atlanta and the Southeast.

Established in 1818, the 436-square-mile county was named for Button Gwinnett, one of Georgia's signers of the Declaration of Independence. Like many metro Atlanta counties, Gwinnett grew with the railroad lines that fueled its small towns' commerce. RH Allen Tannery in Buford was one of Gwinnett's earliest success stories; founded in 1868, the business grew to employ as many as 2,400 people during the 1930s Depression. In the 1950s, the county built Buford Dam, which provided residents with hydroelectric power, flood control, water supply, navigation, and recreational facilities.

The county's population boom began in the 1970s and only diminished somewhat during the 1990 and 2008 recessions. Its demographic shifted from largely white suburbanites to more than half non-white and a third non-English-speaking

*East Cobb*

began in the late 1990s. As of 2010, 820,869 residents called Gwinnett home, with projections of more than one million residents by 2030.

Gwinnett has faced some challenges due to its changing demographics and hard economic times. Since 2000, its poverty rate has doubled, and as of 2009 it passed Fulton County for highest number of foreclosures in metro Atlanta. Government officials have expressed concern over a 25% decrease in its tax index since 2008, which could impact resources like its school system.

Still, the community has excelled despite a changing population and tough economic times. In 2010 the Gwinnett County School System received the prestigious national Broad Prize from the Eli and Edythe Broad Foundation. The award, which honors large urban school systems that seek to narrow achievement gaps between income and ethnic groups, included a $1 million donation to provide qualifying high school students with college scholarships.

Employing around 20,000 people, Gwinnett's school system is the largest in the state and by far the largest employer in the county. Other large employers are its government and hospitals, followed by Walmart, Publix Super Markets, and the US Postal Service.

Gwinnett has plenty to offer shoppers. Gwinnett Place Mall boasts more than one million square feet of retail and dining, and the Mall of Georgia is the largest mall in the state. The latter houses more than 200 stores on three levels, as well as an 80-acre nature park, a 500-seat amphitheater, and a seven-story IMAX theater.

In addition to the plethora of shopping opportunities in Gwinnett County, there are numerous world-class venues that host cultural events year round. The Gwinnett Fine Arts Center, located next to the Gwinnett Civic and Cultural Center, boasts an exhibition hall, a ballroom, and a 1,200-seat theater, which has been the site of performances by the Gwinnett Ballet Company. And Gwinnett is also home to a world-class 12,000-seat arena, Gwinnett Arena, which is the largest of its kind in metro Atlanta, after Downtown's Philips Arena.

The county's natural recreational sites attract Atlanta nature lovers, who perform a reverse-commute on weekends, exchanging city streets for the incredible beauty of Georgia's forests and rivers. Lake Lanier Island, in Buford, has become the destination of choice for many residents looking for a quick getaway. The island is now home to two large luxury resorts with man-made beaches, golf courses, and a water park. It's one of north Georgia's most popular vacation spots during the warm weather months.

Gwinnett is also convenient for those attending or working at The University of Georgia in Athens. Due to the extension of Georgia Highway 316 in 2006, travel time to the college is only 25 minutes.

## LAWRENCEVILLE

Homebuyers enjoy a variety of options in Gwinnett's county seat of Lawrenceville. This busy city was chartered in December 1821, on the third anniversary of the birth of Gwinnett County, and named for Captain James Lawrence, a naval hero in the war of 1812. The first courthouse was built in 1824, and the first public school in 1826. Though the community suffered many human casualties during the Civil War, most of the town was left standing. In fact, Lawrenceville's historic courthouse was recently restored and is now listed in the National Register of Historic Places.

Today, Lawrenceville is home to around 28,000 people, with about half commuting into the city for work, and the other half working locally. Residents can enjoy dining, ambiance, and the arts at Lawrenceville's downtown square, which was revitalized in 2005. One project was a renovation of the Gwinnett Historic Courthouse, one of the most prominent buildings on the square. The courthouse houses the Gwinnett Historical Society and is a popular venue for weddings.

Downtown lofts and apartment were also added to the square, as well as Gwinnett's only professional theater, the Aurora Theater on East Pike Street.

Lawrenceville is also home to Georgia Gwinnett College, which opened in 2006. The liberal arts college offers students bachelor and associate degrees, as well as graduate programs, in conjunction with the University of Georgia and Georgia Perimeter College.

Home prices in Lawrenceville are very reasonable. You can expect to get land, square footage, and privacy for under $300,000. And, as in other metro Atlanta suburbs experiencing phenomenal growth, apartment complexes abound, offering an abundance of rental opportunities to those who want to live in the area but aren't ready to buy.

**Website**: www.lawrencevillega.org
**Area Codes**: 770, 678

*Lawrenceville*

**ZIP Codes**: 30042, 30044, 30045, 30046, 30049

**Post Offices**: Main Office, 121 E Crogan St; Lawrenceville, 35 Patterson Rd, 800-275-8777

**Police Precincts**: Lawrenceville Police Department, 770-339-2400, www.lawrencevillepd.com; Gwinnett County Police Department, 770-513-5000, www.gwinnettcounty.com; Gwinnett County Sheriff's Department, 770-822-3100, www.gwinnettcountysheriff.com

**Emergency Hospital**: Gwinnett Medical Center, 1000 Medical Center Blvd, Lawrenceville, 678-442-4321, www.gwinnettmedicalcenter.org

**Libraries**: Main Library, 1001 Lawrenceville Hwy, 770-822-4522; Five Forks Branch, 2780 Five Forks Trickum Rd, Lawrenceville, 770-978-5600; www.gwinnettpl.org

**Public School Education**: Gwinnett County School System, 770-963-8651, www.gwinnett.k12.ga.us

**Community Publications**: *Gwinnett Daily Post*, 770-963-9205, www.gwinnettdailypost.com

**Community Resources**: Lawrenceville Tourism and Trade Association, 678-226-2639, www.visitlawrenceville.com; Historic Downtown Lawrenceville, www.visitlawrenceville.com; Gwinnett County Chamber of Commerce, 770-232-3000, www.gwinnettchamber.org; Gwinnett Civic and Cultural Center, 6400 Sugarloaf Pkwy, 770-813-7501, www.gwinnettcenter.com

**Public Transportation**: **Gwinnett County Transit**, 770-822-5010, www.gwinnettcounty.com; local bus service throughout Gwinnett County

## NORCROSS

Located 20 miles northeast of Atlanta, the City of **Norcross** is a bustling community popular among businesses and families alike. What started as a small resort town for wealthy Atlantans in 1871 has grown into a highly industrial city of over

10,000 residents. Named for former Atlanta mayor Jonathan Norcross, this suburb is the second oldest in Gwinnett County and has managed to retain much of its old, southern charm, despite its growth in recent years.

Many turn-of-the-20th-century homes and commercial buildings can still be found here today, most of them lovingly preserved by residents who are proud of their community's history and intent on preserving it. There is even a 112-acre Historic District here, which encompasses a beautifully restored downtown square, 50 private residences, three church buildings, and a library. In fact, Norcross is the only Gwinnett County community to have a district listed in the US Register of Historic Places.

New housing in Norcross is similar to that in Lawrenceville and other Gwinnett County neighborhoods, with apartment complexes and carefully planned subdivisions dominating. In fact, because of the similarity between Gwinnett's communities, many Atlantans have trouble distinguishing where one Gwinnett city ends and another begins.

Nevertheless, Norcross is a popular community for families with young children, who like its comfortable, small-town feel and convenience to local highways. Interstate 85 runs right through Norcross, making it relatively easy to get into Atlanta and to other Gwinnett County communities. The downside is that, as in most north metro suburbs, traffic can be a nightmare during peak commute times, and Gwinnett's public transportation (which has only been operating since 2000) hasn't yet caught on here the way MARTA has in Atlanta's intown communities.

**Website**: www.norcrossga.net

**Area Codes**: 770, 678

**ZIP Codes**: 30071, 30092, 30093

**Post Offices**: Norcross, 265 Mitchell Rd; Peachtree Corners, 5600 Spalding Dr; Rockbridge Shopping Center, 4771 Britt Rd; 800-275-8777, www.usps.com

**Police Precincts**: Norcross Police Department, 770-448-2111, www.norcrossga. net; Gwinnett County Police Department, 770-513-5000, www.gwinnettcounty.com; Gwinnett County Sheriff's Department, 770-822-3100, www. gwinnettcountysheriff.com

**Emergency Hospitals**: Gwinnett Medical Center, 1000 Medical Center Blvd, Lawrenceville, 678-442-4321, www.gwinnettmedicalcenter.org

**Libraries**: Norcross, 6025 Buford Hwy, 770-448-4938; Peachtree Corners, 5570 Spalding Dr, 770-729-0931; www.gwinnettpl.org

**Public School Education**: Gwinnett County School System, 770-963-8651, www. gwinnett.k12.ga.us

**Community Publications**: *Gwinnett Daily Post*, 770-963-9205, www.gwinnettdailypost.com; *Gwinnett Citizen*, 770-963-3699, www.gwinnettcitizen.com

**Community Resources**: Norcross City Hall, 65 Lawrenceville St, 770-448-2122; Norcross Community Development, 770-448-4935, www.norcrossga.net; Nor-

*Norcross*

cross Youth Soccer, 770-840-7696, www.norcross-soccer.org; Gwinnett County Chamber of Commerce, 770-232-3000, www.gwinnettchamber.org; Gwinnett Civic and Cultural Center, 6400 Sugarloaf Pkwy, 770-813-7501, www.gwinnettcenter.com

**Public Transportation: Gwinnett County Transit**, 770-822-5010, www.gwinnettcounty.com; local bus service throughout Gwinnett County

**In Gwinnett County, you might also want to consider:**

- **Duluth,** the second largest city in Gwinnett County after Lawrenceville, which developed mainly with metro Atlanta's boom in the 1990s. Duluth has a beautiful downtown area, and is home to many of Gwinnett's biggest attractions, such as Gwinnett Place Mall, Gwinnett Civic and Cultural Center, the Arena at Gwinnett, Hudgens Center for the Arts, Red Clay Theater, and TCP Sugarloaf, a prestigious golf club located within the gated community at Sugarloaf Country Club. City of Duluth, www.duluthga.net.
- **Buford,** which lies on the northern end of Gwinnett County, bordering the southern tip of Lake Lanier. Still a small town, but with recent growth, its development has largely followed metro Atlanta. Buford has also benefited considerably from two large tourist draws, the Mall of Georgia and Lake Lanier. City of Buford, www.cityofbuford.com
- Other Gwinnett County neighborhoods worth looking into include the cities of **Lilburn,** www.cityoflilburn.com, and **Snellville**, www.snellville.org.

## CHEROKEE COUNTY

It's not hard to guess where Cherokee County got its name. The area was once the heart of the Cherokee Nation, and today is one of Atlanta and Georgia's fastest growing counties. Cherokee County lies directly north of Cobb County and is bisected by I-575 as it branches away from I-75 to head north into the Blue Ridge Mountains. Cherokee's proximity to two interstates allows its residents quick access to Marietta and Atlanta, which in turn has fueled the growth of shops, businesses, and housing developments all along their exits. Cherokee County, once considered rural and remote, now has a population nearing 215,000 and is becoming increasingly busy and cosmopolitan.

Cherokee's original county land covered more than 6,900 square miles of North Georgia and was established by the Georgia Legislature in 1831 while it still belonged to the Cherokee and Creek tribes. Despite a long struggle to keep their land, most of the remaining Indians from these native tribes were, by 1839, rounded up and forced to walk the infamous Trail of Tears to Oklahoma. With the natives gone, white settlers began populating the area. The Industrial Revolution helped provide jobs for them as mills were built to grind corn and process cotton. Discoveries of gold, copper, and marble also attracted many pioneers. During the Civil War, the county's residents united with such a strong, pro-Confederate position that General Sherman ordered much of the area burned in 1864. When the war was over, residents returned to Cherokee to rebuild and recover, and the county soon grew in importance.

During and after World War II, the population swelled, and cotton farming gave way to poultry production. The aerospace company Lockheed, a giant employer located in nearby Marietta, gave people more reason to settle in the area. Today many commute to Marietta, and even into the heart of Atlanta for work, and traffic jams on I-575 during rush hour are notorious. Cherokee offers residents many benefits—a beautiful landscape due to its proximity to the North Georgia mountains and inexpensive housing. The area has also been the fortunate recipient of many beautification grants and commercial developments, which will bring well-paying jobs and world class amenities to the area.

Residents of Cherokee County who commute into Atlanta have typically faced grueling commutes, but a project is under way that could improve conditions. The GDOT is in talks with state officials to build two optional, reversible toll lanes: one alongside I-75 from I-285 to I-575, and one reversible toll lane each along I-75 up to Hickory Grove Road and along I-575 up to Sixes Road.

## CANTON

From Cherokee County's tumultuous beginnings, five municipalities would emerge as centers of commerce and trade, each with its own identity. As the county seat, **Canton** became the center of government here. Situated on the banks of the Etowah River, from which it took its original name, this frontier settlement changed its name to Canton in 1834 when two town leaders envisioned it becoming the silk center of the West, simulating Canton in China. The Canton Cotton Mill (now completely redeveloped into loft apartments in the center of town) was established in 1899, employed over 1,000 people and put Canton on the map as word spread of its high-quality denim. Since the closing of the last two mills in 1981, Canton has transitioned nicely from mill town to a prosperous southern city.

Today the city is spread out into different sections (Canton is accessible from four exits off I-575), but downtown is the heart of the city, with its government buildings, refurbished theater, restaurants, and shops. Canton's downtown was redeveloped in 2005 as part of the "Streetscapes" program. Parking spaces were removed; sidewalks, lamp posts, lush landscaping, and intersection upgrades were added. Another bustling district lies along Riverstone Parkway, off exit 20 on I-575. The area offers plenty of entertainment and dining options for Canton residents, with architecturally pleasing strip malls, shops, restaurants, a movie theater, and other businesses. Housing, apartment, and hotel developments also surround the area.

Other noteworthy developments include the Etowah River Greenway Project, which added Heritage Park to the city. The park includes 90 acres of walking and biking trails, sports fields, and a natural amphitheater. In addition, Canton partnered with Metro Atlanta YMCA to build an $8 million community center, complete with indoor swimming pool, gymnasium, wellness center, and aerobics studio, which opened in 2008. Also, the Bluffs at Technology Park, the first stage of which opened in 2004, will be home to 15,000 high-tech jobs and a satellite campus for Chattahoochee Technical College when completed. And in 2007, the city completed work on an ambitious reservoir project, which provides 44 million gallons of water a day and is surrounded by 20 acres of public-use parkland.

New apartments, townhomes, and single-family home subdivisions are scattered throughout Canton. According to regional projections, the 22,000 residents today will reach 42,000 by 2025. Bridge Mill on Bells Ferry Road is perhaps the largest development. It offers a variety of dwellings, from condos to estate homes, an 18-hole golf course, and a 50-acre athletics club, including tennis courts, aquatic center and recreation clubhouse, jogging paths, playgrounds, and fitness center.

Another burgeoning area is along Highway 20 as it heads toward Forsyth County, where well-designed family subdivisions with a rural feel, and the services that support them, are popping up everywhere. Most have swimming pools, walking trails, tennis courts, and homeowner associations. A little to the south of Canton, the area along Sixes Road has also become known for large subdivisions and expensive homes.

The Cherokee Area Transportation System provides bus services to residents in Canton between the hours of 8 a.m. and 3 p.m. Visit its website for route information.

**Website**: www.canton-georgia.com
**Area Code**: 770, 678
**ZIP Codes**: 30114, 30115

*Canton*

**Post Offices**: The UPS Store, 6175 Hickory Flat Hwy #110, (770) 345-7151; Canton Branch, 2400 Riverstone Blvd; Holly Springs, 2631 Holly Springs Pkwy, (770) 345-6318; 800-275-8777, www.usps.com

**Police Precincts**: Canton Police Department, 770-720-4883, www.canton-georgia.com; Cherokee County Sheriff's Office, 678-493-4200, www.cherokeega-sheriff.org

**Emergency Hospital**: Northside Cherokee Hospital, Canton, 770-720-5100, www.northside.com

**Libraries**: Ball Ground Public Library, 435 Old Canton Rd, Canton, 770-479-3090; R.T. Jones Memorial Library, 116 Brown Industrial Pkwy, Canton, 770-479-3090; Hickory Flat Public Library, 2740 East Cherokee Dr, Canton, 770-345-7565; www.sequoyahregionallibrary.org

**Public School Education**: Cherokee County School System, 770-479-1871, www.cherokee.k12.ga.us

**Community Publications**: *Cherokee Ledger-News*, 770-928-0706, www.ledger-news.com, *Cherokee Tribune*, 770-479-1441, www.cherokeetribune.com

**Community Resources**: Canton City Information Line, 770-704-1526; City of Canton, www.canton-georgia.com; Historic Canton Theatre, 770-704-0755, www.cantontheatre.com; Cherokee County Chamber of Commerce, 770-345-0400, www.cherokeechamber.com; Cherokee County Georgia Online, www.cherokeega.com; Cherokee County Arts Center, 770-704-6244, www.cherokeearts.org

**Public Transportation: City of Canton Transit System**, 770-720-7674, www.canton-georgia.com/transportation.php; Cherokee Area Transportation System, http://cats.cherokeega.com

## WOODSTOCK

One of the largest communities in Cherokee County, with over 23,000 residents, **Woodstock** was chartered in 1897. Primarily a farming community, growing cotton and grains for the mills to the north, it also was home to some mineral mining. The Marietta and North Georgia Railroad came to Woodstock in 1879, bringing passengers and freight, but the area remained a sleepy settlement for many years. Not so anymore. Today the city of Woodstock is growing so fast that the road systems and utility companies can barely keep up. With more and more new businesses and professional services taking advantage of Woodstock's excellent location (where Highway 92 intersects I-575), the area has doubled in size in the last ten years.

The city has two distinct portions: historic downtown and Towne Lake. The former, with its brick-paved sidewalks and buildings dating back to 1879, has retained its old-South charm. Plus a rush of development in the mid-2000s added multiple new townhouse and loft developments, coupled with mixed-use space for hip retail or other business. The train depot is the focal point, with an active railway line cutting through the heart of the area. The city has an attractive mix of antique shops, tearooms, hair salons, gift shops, chiropractors, health spas, and more. The Visitors Center at Dean's Store offers information and directions. Woodstock City Park and Dupree Park are both nearby and offer relaxation, recreation, and other activities throughout the year. And Woodstock has a vibrant farmer's market that meets on Saturday mornings, often offering some festivities—family and child friendly—to go with the shopping.

Towne Lake, on the east side of Woodstock, is home to most of the area's neighborhoods. This area is characterized by enormous subdivision communities (such as Eagle Watch and The Arbors) of mainly large homes with homeowner associations and recreational facilities that line Towne Lake Parkway on both sides for miles. The area even has its own magazine, *The TowneLaker*, detailing news, people, and events. Two major golf clubs, Town Lake Hills and Eagle Watch, are professional standard. Servicing the thousands of residents, the district is surrounded by supermarkets, strip malls, specialty shops, restaurants, and businesses. But, as attractive as this area is to families, when commuters leave home on weekday mornings to make their way to work, they clog up the main arteries to the Interstate and cause huge traffic jams to the south.

Older subdivisions are spread out throughout the city and tend to contain smaller, less expensive homes on larger lots, and more greenery. Most of these do not have homeowner associations, and houses often need a little upgrading.

**Website**: www.woodstockga.gov
**Area Code**: 770, 678
**ZIP Codes**: 30188, 30189
**Post Office**: Woodstock, 225 Parkway 575; Woodstock 2, 3101 Parkbrooke Cir, 800-275-8777, www.usps.com

*Woodstock*

**Police Precincts**: Woodstock Police Department, 770-592-6030, www.wood-stockga.gov; Cherokee County Sheriff's Office, 678-493-4200, www.cherokeega-sheriff.org

**Emergency Hospitals**: Northside Hospital–Cherokee, Canton, 770-720-5100, www.northside.com; Piedmont Mountainside Hospital, Jasper, 706-692-2441, www.piedmontmountainsidehospital.org

**Libraries**: Woodstock Public Library, 7745 Main St, 770-926-5859; Rose Creek Public Library, 4476 Towne Lake Pkwy, Woodstock, 770-591-1491; www.sequoyahregionallibrary.org

**Public School Education**: Cherokee County School System, 770-479-1871, www.cherokee.k12.ga.us

**Community Publications**: *The TowneLaker*, 770-516-7105, www.townelaker.com; *Cherokee Tribune*, www.cheorokeetribune.com; *Cherokee Ledger*, 770-928-0706, www.ledgernews.com

**Community Resources**: Dean's Store, 8588 Main St, Woodstock, 770-924-0406; Woodstock City Park, 678-445-6518, www.woodstockga.gov; Woodstock Historic Train Depot, 770-592-6001, www.rockbarn.org/woodstockDepot.php; Cherokee County Chamber of Commerce, 770-345-0400, www.cherokeechamber.com; Cherokee County Georgia Online, www.cherokeega.com; Cherokee County Arts Center, 770-704-6244, www.cherokeearts.org

**In Cherokee County, you might also want to consider:**

- Three additional communities: **Holly Springs**, www.hollyspringsga.us; **Ball Ground**, 770-735-2123, www.cityofballground.com; and **Waleska**, 770-479-2912, www.cityofwaleska.com.

# ADDITIONAL COUNTIES

Of the following metro Atlanta counties, Clayton, Rockdale, and Henry are closest to Atlanta's inner-ring communities and offer the shortest commute into the city. However, it's important to note that all of these counties are included in the metro area because at least 25% of their residents work in Atlanta. So, while the daily commute may be long and tedious from most of these counties, many people have chosen to do it, despite the fact that most of them are 40 miles or more, and at least an hour and half drive from intown. If you are interested in one of these counties, you should also check out Xpress, www.xpressga.com, for information about its very popular express bus commuter lines to and from Atlanta. It's also important to note that some of these outer-ring counties use the "706" area code, which is long distance from Atlanta.

Regardless of location, each of the counties is home to several communities that may be of interest to newcomers who prefer a small-town lifestyle to the hustle and bustle of the city. For more information, check out the county websites listed below.

## NORTH METRO COUNTIES

**Bartow County**, www.bartowga.org
**Forsyth County**, www.forsythcounty.com
**Pickens County**, www.pickenscountyga.gov
**Dawson County**, www.dawsoncounty.org

## WEST METRO COUNTIES

**Paulding County**, www.paulding.gov
**Carroll County**, www.carrollcountyga.com
**Douglas County**, www.celebratedouglascounty.com
**Haralson County**, www.haralson.org

## SOUTH METRO COUNTIES

**Clayton County,** www.claytoncountyga.gov
**Coweta County**, www.coweta.ga.us
**Fayette County**, www.fayettecountyga.gov
**Henry County**, www.co.henry.ga.us
**Heard County**, www.heardcountyga.com
**Jasper County**, www.monticelloga.org
**Lamar County**, www.barnesville.org

**Meriwether County**, http://meriwethercountyga.us
**Pike County**, http://pikecounty.ga.gov
**Spalding County**, www.spaldingcounty.com

## EAST METRO COUNTIES

**Barrow County**, www.barrowga.org
**Butts County**, www.buttscounty.org
**Newton County**, www.co.newton.ga.us
**Rockdale County**, www.rockdalecounty.org
**Walton County**, www.waltoncountyga.org

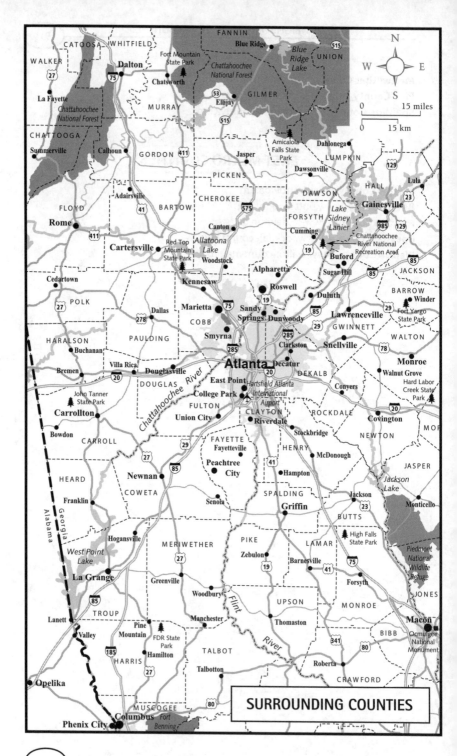

SURROUNDING COUNTIES

ATLANTA AND ITS SURROUNDING SUBURBS OFFER A WIDE VARIETY OF housing options made even wider by the still recovering real estate market. If there is a time to buy anywhere—including Atlanta—the time is now, when property values are lower than normal, and private home owners and developers alike are eager to wheel and deal. Residents can live the high life of Downtown in one of the city's many new high rises, or settle into a cozy craftsman in Virginia Highland. Choose a posh mansion with a yard and gate in Buckhead, a hip apartment/loft in Midtown, or any number of renovated or newly built homes in the many suburbs surrounding the city.

As for price, generally, the older, more prominent communities, like Buckhead and Virginia Highland, are the most expensive, while subdivisions farther away from Atlanta proper cost significantly less. For those hailing from a large US metropolitan area, prices here will probably seem comparable or even a bargain, particularly if you're coming from one of the coastal cities such as New York, Boston, Los Angeles, or San Francisco.

For newcomers looking for an urban living experience, there are any number of options sure to fit the bill. If you'd like a buffet of amenities to accompany your mortgage or rent, consider one of the city's many high-rise condominiums. Many are connected to shopping complexes, like the posh Twelve at Atlanta's intown retail development Atlantic Station. Amenities include such luxuries as an in-house theater, private lounge, spa, and gaming rooms, as well as dry cleaning and maid services, and of course easy access to three different MARTA stations.

For the more eccentric resident, Atlanta has numerous loft spaces both in town and throughout the suburbs. The intown lofts have been a popular choice for young students and professionals since the early 2000s, but many nearby cities such as Roswell, Decatur, Marietta, and Sandy Springs offer lofts overlooking their redeveloped downtown squares, or as part of new retail/residential developments.

Even the smaller cities such as Covington, Woodstock, Canton, and Acworth have added downtown loft living to bring new life to their squares.

Another housing trend is the ongoing regentrification of Atlanta's older communities, which has continued despite the slowdown in the real estate market. There buyers can purchase a home for a reasonable amount and spend the extra on renovations. If the market improves, you may see your home appreciate by more than $100,000 in just a few years. Some neighborhoods experiencing this trend are Kirkwood, East Point, and areas of East Atlanta.

Wherever you decide to live, factor in its proximity to your job or school. Hours spent each day on the highway will make the perfect four-bedroom, three-bathroom home with a nice yard and two-car garage a lot less appealing. Many people find that making do in a smaller house that is closer to their job is much more enjoyable.

If all else fails, you can always move into a nice apartment for now, and take your time looking for the right house. Metro Atlanta abounds with large, upscale apartment communities. Almost all offer such inviting amenities as swimming pools, gyms, and on-site dry cleaning; in fact, some are so nice that residents forego the home-buying quest altogether and opt for long-term apartment living.

## APARTMENT HUNTING

Apartment hunting in Atlanta takes time, energy, perseverance, and just a little bit of luck, but if you dedicate yourself to the task, you will find your ideal abode. The good news is that the hunt is difficult not because of a lack of options, but because of how many options there are. Moreover, as with all real estate right now, the buyer is in the driver's seat, so you can likely negotiate any lease down or at least get some perks, like the first month's rent free.

First, where you want to live will largely dictate what types of apartments are available. If you plan to stay intown or in Buckhead, you can choose high-rise living, which today is surprisingly affordable. If you prefer more charm than chic, consider one of the many townhome style rentals or complexes in Virginia Highland, Vinings, or Buckhead. These rentals feel more like a house and often include a backyard, which would allow you to have a pet.

As you move farther away from Downtown, apartment complexes become more uniform and less expensive. Most include those amenities largely expected by apartment dwellers—fitness center, pool, ample parking, clothes washer and dryer, and security in the form of a gate or similar system.

Apartment prices in Atlanta, by big city standards, used to be anywhere from reasonable to downright cheap. More recently, however, many residents have experienced a bit of sticker shock in regards to apartment rental prices. Over the last decade, rental prices in the metro area have increased by approximately 10%

to 15%. Skim the classifieds and you will see that the average price range for a one-bedroom apartment is $700 to $950; you can expect to pay anywhere from $950 to $1,500 for a two-bedroom, and between $1,500 to $2,500 for a three-bedroom. Of course, rents vary according to location and amenities. If you insist on living in one of the hot intown neighborhoods or making your home in an upscale apartment complex, you can expect to pay considerably more than you would if you chose a smaller, bare-bones complex or moved into one of the city's outer communities. Remember, good deals do exist in metro Atlanta, but you may need a little patience and persistence to find them.

In the suburbs, space is not generally a problem. Most apartments are roomy, especially compared to more densely populated cities. In parts of the greater metro area, you can rent a two-bedroom duplex with a front porch and spacious backyard for half of what you would pay for a studio in the Big Apple. In fact, porches—especially screened-in porches—are a great selling point in many dwellings. (Because of the intense summer heat, most older houses and apartment buildings were built with at least one screened-in porch.) Other types of apartments that are readily available throughout metro Atlanta are apartment complexes: groupings of identical apartment buildings enclosed by a fence and with a security gate to protect access to the complex. It's sort of like a little city, with a swimming pool, tennis courts, exercise facilities, and other conveniences all at your doorstep. Newcomers, in particular, may benefit from the many social opportunities available at a complex.

One advantage of living in a city composed of suburbs is that many rental houses are available. If you have a roommate, roommates, or a family, this might be your most pleasant and economical option. Many people who buy homes rent out a separate apartment within the house to help pay for their mortgage. Those with large old homes sometimes rent out their accompanying carriage houses to singles or couples.

When searching the classifieds for a place to live, you should learn the lingo and the euphemisms. A "1960s" building probably means that the apartment complex resembles a wing of a chain motel. In certain areas—Buckhead, Midtown, and a stretch on Briarcliff Road, to name a few—1960s apartment buildings are common. "On-street parking" means that the complex does not have its own parking lot. A "terrace apartment" is in the basement. If you see the same ad day after day, this may be an indication that the apartment building in question has a high tenant turnover rate, and that if you live there, you, too, might want to move out soon.

Apartment hunting in metro Atlanta can be competitive year-round, but is especially so in the late summer, when new college students flood the rental market. Get an early start if you are relying on the classifieds—apartments advertised in Creative Loafing are often already rented if you wait until afternoon to call. And keep in mind that when you're ready to view a rental property, it is common practice for the management staff to make a copy of your ID for their records before showing you the apartment. Below are some resources to help you find the perfect pad.

## NEWSPAPER CLASSIFIEDS

The major sources for print classified ads in metro Atlanta are as follows:

- *The Atlanta Journal-Constitution*, 404-526-5151, www.ajc.com; check the Sunday edition. This paper covers the entire metro Atlanta area. Also the *AJC* offers numerous resources online via ajchomefinder.com.
- *Creative Loafing*, 404-688-5623, www.creativeloafing.com; comes out every Wednesday. This free alternative weekly paper also covers the entire metro Atlanta area and is a great resource if you're looking for a roommate or a small home or apartment in a funky neighborhood. Many places listed in *CL* may not show up in the *AJC*.
- *Neighbor Newspapers, Inc.*, 770-795-3000, www.neighbornewspapers.com; includes most metro Atlanta counties and can be read in print or online.

You can also find a multitude of advertisements for apartment complexes in several free, full-color booklets, all of which can be found near the entrances of local supermarkets, malls, and video rental stores:

- *Apartment Blue Book*, 800-222-3651, www.apartmentfinder.com
- *Apartments For Rent*, 866-573-5928, www.forrent.com
- *Atlanta Apartment Guide*, 770-417-1717, www.apartmentguide.com

## ONLINE RENTAL SERVICES

There are now many online services offering listings of rental properties. Most are affiliated with local newspapers or rental agencies; some charge a nominal fee, some are free. Many sites post apartment listings only; others post home rentals as well, or help to match roommates. A few to consider:

- **AJC Homefinder**, www.ajchomefinder.com; free real estate service affiliated with the *Atlanta Journal-Constitution*; offers apartment, home, and roommate listings for the entire metro Atlanta area, including the outermost counties.
- **Apartment Ratings**, www.apartmentratings.com; not an apartment listing service, but rather a no-charge, nationwide rating service with residents posting assessments and reviews of the metro Atlanta apartments they've lived in (good or bad), for the benefit of others.
- **Apartment Selector**, www.aptselector.com; free online service offering detailed nationwide apartment listings, including listings from all areas of metro Atlanta.

- **Atlanta Rental Homes**, http://www.rentals.com/Georgia/Atlanta; free online service offering home, townhome, and condo listings from around the metro Atlanta area.
- **Craig's List**, http://atlanta.craigslist.org; the Atlanta component of this popular website posts listings for fee and no-fee apartment rentals, roommates, and sublets. A favorite resource among locals.
- **Creative Loafing Online**, www.creativeloafing.com; free online version of Atlanta's local, alternative newspaper; offers updated apartment, home, and roommate listings for the entire metro Atlanta area.
- **Lofts Atlanta**, www.lofts-atlanta.com; listings of Atlanta-area loft properties owned and managed by Aderhold Properties, Inc., available for no fee.
- **Move.com,** www.move.com; free nationwide apartment guide linked with flag-ship website realtor.com. Includes listings of available metro Atlanta units.
- **National Association of Realtors,** www.realtor.com; offers numerous detailed search features for free. Very cool interactive maps where you can search neigh-borhoods and simultaneously view specs like school system ratings.
- **Rent.com**, www.rent.com; a free online rental service with nationwide listings for apartments, homes, and roommates. Covers the metro Atlanta area.
- **Roommates.com**, www.roommates.com; online roommate matching service. Basic membership is free and includes general listings and searches. "Choice membership" offers advanced search and posting options, as well as the ability to receive messages from other members. A three-day trial costs $5.99.

## DIRECT ACTION

If you're tired of apartment shopping from the smudgy pages of the newspaper or the flickering screen of a computer monitor, get in your car and cruise around the neighborhood you want to live in. Just be sure to bring pencil, paper, and a cell phone so you can call on any places that catch your interest.

While you're in the neighborhood, stop by the local café or bookstore, where you might find a community bulletin board with "apartment for rent" or "room-mate wanted" notices. Ask the friendly people preparing your latte if they know of any apartments for rent in the area. A person's friend's cousin may have just vacated the perfect place ... you never know.

Finally, even if a building you are particularly fond of does not have a rental sign posted out front, call the manager anyway. Someone might be moving out, and you may just get yourself a great new place.

## APARTMENT SEARCH FIRMS

If you lack the time and energy to look for an apartment yourself, you can always try an apartment locator service. When you contact the apartment locator, you should first ask if there is a charge for the service. Fees vary, depending on the company. In some locations, the apartment owners pay the locator, and in others, the renters pay.

To find a successful match, your agent will ask you a series of detailed questions about apartment options. Consider your preferences beforehand so that you will be ready to answer. You should have an idea about which area of town you want to live in and how much rent you can afford to pay. Also, decide whether you want to live in an apartment complex managed by an on-site staff or whether you would prefer to deal with a landlord. Another question to consider is how much space and storage you will need in your new place; and let the agency know if you have pets, particularly a dog. Most of the apartment complexes in metro Atlanta accept pets, though some may have size limitations. Be sure you research this, or have the search firm check on this upfront.

In addition, you will probably want to make a list of the amenities that are necessary for your happiness and well-being. Some hardy individuals can live here without air-conditioning, but for most people in Atlanta it's a must. Do you want washer/dryer facilities in your apartment or on the premises, or do you mind lugging your washables to the laundromat so you can pay less in rent? Is it difficult to imagine living without a dishwasher or do you eschew modern conveniences? If you're moving to metro Atlanta from a colder climate, you might want to spend your summer weekends in the sun and treat yourself to a place with a pool.

Most apartment search firms serve the entire Atlanta area, and some have several offices. The following listed firms will help you find a unit that meets your needs, answer questions about the neighborhoods you're considering, and tour potential apartments with you. Check "Apartment Finding and Rental Services" in the Atlanta Yellow Pages for more options:

- **A&A Apartment Locators**, 770-594-1110, 866-237-1401, www.freeapartment-locators.com
- **Apartment Selector**, 770-552-9255, http://www.aptselector.com/atlanta
- **Promove**, 800-742-1883, www.promove.com

## REAL ESTATE FIRMS

Many local real estate brokers handle rental properties and are very knowledgeable about the neighborhoods or communities they represent. Additionally, they often have access to properties that aren't yet listed in the *AJC* or *Creative Loafing*. Some firms may charge the apartment hunter a nominal fee for using their leasing services, though most often the landlord pays this fee. Be sure to ask. Check the Atlanta Yellow Pages under "Real Estate" for a complete listing of real estate firms.

## CHECKING IT OUT

So, you've just moved to the city and you're desperate to find a place to call your own. You see an ad in the paper that sounds perfect, so you call to make an appointment and to meet the landlord and tour the place, only to have him tell you that there are ten other people who have already been by and are ready to sign the lease. What do you do? First, don't panic. Landlords have been known to use this tactic to pressure prospective tenants into taking a place that has been difficult to let, and in today's market, you are likely in the driver's seat, not the landlord or owner. When viewing units, take your time and examine the space to make sure it is exactly or close to exactly what you want. Never commit to an apartment with which you are not comfortable. When checking out prospective apartments, here are a few things keep in mind:

- Are the kitchen appliances clean and in working order? Do the stove's burners work? How about the oven? Is there enough counter and shelf space? Does it smell funny in the kitchen space—or anywhere else for that matter? Most Atlanta apartments and rental homes come furnished with refrigerator and stove, though the landlord is not required to provide them. Be sure to ask about this ahead of time, so you'll know exactly what you're getting.
- What is included in the rental price? Are you responsible for the monthly utilities or are they paid by the landlord? Again, find out so that you can budget accordingly. Generally, water and trash pickup are paid for by the landlord, though this may not always be the case.
- Does the apartment come with central air? If not, will you have a window unit for the hotter months? Summers in Atlanta can be nearly unbearable, with high temperatures and even higher humidity. All of the newer apartment complexes offer central air.
- Does the building allow pets? If so, what is the maximum size and weight? Are additional pet fees or deposits required? Are there places set aside outside for pets to walk or go off-leash?
- Are there any signs of pests or vermin? Even the nicest apartments can have bug problems, so be sure to ask, and find out what the landlord does in terms of pest control. Most of the newer apartment complexes provide monthly pest control for their tenants at no additional cost.
- Make sure you check all of the windows in the apartment. Do they open, close, and lock easily? Do they seem secure? Do the windows open onto a noisy or potentially dangerous area?
- Is there enough closet and storage space? Many intown apartments, especially the older ones, lack the closet space that the new complexes offer, though some may make up for that by offering additional storage space elsewhere in the building, like a basement or attic. Be sure to ask; you'll want to know that you'll have the space you need before signing the lease.

- If you're living with roommates, are there enough provisions, particularly bathrooms and closets, for everyone? Older Atlanta apartments typically offer only one bathroom; newer complexes and rental homes can have two or more, even in a two-bedroom unit.
- Are there enough electrical outlets for all your needs? Do the outlets work? Is the apartment wired for cable or DSL?
- How's the water pressure? You may want to run the faucets and shower, and flush the toilet to check. You can also ask how big the water tank is and whether or not it serves more than one unit.
- For safety reasons, make sure any home or apartment you're considering has a second exit and comes with working smoke or heat detectors. You may also want to ask whether fire extinguishers, carbon monoxide detectors, and/or fire alarms are included.
- Does the apartment come with a washer and dryer, or at least a washer/dryer hookup? If not, check if there are laundry facilities in the building or nearby.
- Do you feel comfortable in the neighborhood? Will you feel safe here at night? Is it too loud, particularly on weekend nights? Or does it feel too isolated? Is the street well lit?
- Is the building or apartment community convenient to public transportation and shopping? Have you considered your possible routes to work? How is traffic during rush hour along the routes you would take? In metro Atlanta, traffic is a big problem, so this is something to seriously consider before signing a lease.
- Whom do you contact in case of emergency?

*The Renters Handbook: Everything Your Landlord Doesn't Want You To* **Know** by Barney Fadal contains a more thorough renter's checklist for those interested in augmenting their own.

If it all passes muster, be prepared to stake your claim without delay!

## STAKING A CLAIM

When touring apartments, make sure you come prepared for the business of renting so that when you find the place you want you can act on it. Most likely you will need to fill out an application, which will require your bank account information, other credit information, and past rental references. A picture ID is usually required; the landlord will make a copy of it to keep with your application.

Credit checks are the norm when renting or buying and the fee is generally around $50. A check for that amount plus a security deposit will usually suffice in holding an apartment for you while you're awaiting approval. Keep in mind, though, that when applying for an apartment, you may also be asked to pay first and last month's rent up front, so be prepared. Ask ahead of time so that you know the total cost before you get too far into the paperwork. If it turns out your application is not approved, the deposit check will be returned to you minus the fee for the credit check.

## LEASES AND SECURITY DEPOSITS

Georgia law is not particularly tenant-friendly. When looking at leases and security deposits, the best advice is "buyer beware." Know what you're signing/understand the terms of the lease. And, unless you're desperate, if a rental situation seems difficult from the start, you should probably walk away and find something else.

### LEASES

In Georgia, a lease is a negotiable contract between the landlord and tenant. Leases run the gamut—from the standard residential forms used by most apartment complexes to documents drawn up by individual landlords. They are serious business and can vary greatly depending on the landlord. And there is no particular practice or condition that is considered illegal, except for "self-help eviction," meaning that a landlord must execute proper eviction procedures through the courts if he/she wants to evict a tenant.

Rental leases in Georgia are legal contracts and thus difficult to alter once both parties sign on the dotted line. With this in mind, be sure to find out as much as possible about the landlord and the apartment you are renting before signing the lease. Three items of common concern include apartment shares, pets, and sublets: If you plan to share your apartment with someone else, you'll both have to be on the lease; a "no pets" clause on the lease means no pets; and subletting is generally not allowed in metro Atlanta, so check with the landlord if this may be something you are interested in doing at a later date—or if you are investigating a sublet housing situation for yourself. It's better to be upfront about your requirements and the landlord's expectations in the beginning. If there are items in the lease that are not to your liking, negotiate changes before signing. For example, if you think your job might relocate you before your lease is up, you may want to ask your landlord to insert an early transfer clause in the lease. If an early transfer clause is not an option, you may be able to get a short-term or month-to-month lease for a slightly higher rental rate.

### SECURITY DEPOSITS

In Georgia, a landlord can charge whatever the market will bear for a security deposit; generally speaking, however, you can expect to be charged one month's rent or less. If you think an apartment's security deposit is too high, look elsewhere.

According to Georgia law, landlords must put your security deposit in an escrow account. They are not, however, required to place security deposits in an interest-bearing account, nor are they legally obligated to pay the tenant any interest earned. If you decide to move out once your lease is up, your landlord is required to return your deposit to you within thirty days of vacating the apartment—minus the cost of repairs for any damages beyond the usual wear and tear. However, he/she must inform you in writing within ten working days to explain the reasons for the deductions. If you do not receive a written explanation, or if your security deposit does not arrive within 30 days, you can file for its return in your city's magistrate court.

For more information regarding security deposits, use the state's free service, the Georgia Tenant Landlord Help Line at 404-463-1596 or 1-800-369-4706. The help line provides basic information on Georgia landlord tenant law and also publishes and distributes the handbook "Questions Frequently Asked by Landlords and Tenants." The handbook is available online at www.glsp.org, along with a host of other resources for new residents regarding Georgia law.

## TENANT RESOURCES

If you still have questions about tenants' rights in Georgia, or you want to lodge a complaint against a landlord, or if you have issue with your lease or your security deposit, try the following agencies:

- **Atlanta Legal Aid Society, Inc.**, 404-524-5811 (Atlanta); 404-377-0701 (DeKalb); 404-669-0233 (South Fulton/Clayton); 770-528-2565 (Cobb); 678-376-4545 (Gwinnett); www.atlantalegalaid.org
- **Georgia Department of Community Affairs, Affordable Housing Division,** http://www.dca.state.ga.us
- **Georgia Governor's Office of Consumer Affairs**, 404-651-8600 or 800-869-1123; http://consumer.ga.gov
- **Georgia Commission on Equal Opportunity, Fair Housing Division**, 404-656-7708, 800-473-OPEN, www.gceo.state.ga.us
- **Metro Atlanta Fair Housing Services**, 404-221-0147, 800-441-8393, www.metrofairhousing.com

## RENTER'S/HOMEOWNER'S INSURANCE

Once you've settled on a place to live, you will want to consider purchasing property insurance. Regardless of whether you're renting or buying your home, a good insurance policy should be a priority. It's especially important here in the South where damaging tornadoes and thunderstorms are common summertime occurrences.

A typical renter's insurance policy will cover damages to your belongings in cases of fire, theft, or water damage, though you may also have the option of additional coverage, including personal liability. The good news is that rental policies are fairly inexpensive. Depending on your possessions, you can expect to pay somewhere between $150 and $300 a year for coverage. That's a small price to pay for peace of mind, especially when you consider what it would cost to replace your possessions.

While renters in metro Atlanta have a choice in whether to purchase property insurance, buyers here typically do not. For most everyone dealing with a bank when buying a home, purchasing a homeowner's policy will undoubtedly be a necessary part of the process. Rates for homeowner's insurance vary depending on the value of your property and the estimated worth of your possessions. Most policies include coverage for personal liability, fire, water damage, theft, electrical problems, and more. Be sure to ask questions and go over the details of the policy with your insurance agent to make sure you have the coverage you'll need.

The ideal renter's or homeowner's policy will provide "replacement value" coverage. Unfortunately, most insurance companies no longer offer replacement value policies; instead, maximum coverage is 120% to 125% of the face value of your house and belongings.

For more information on renter's or homeowner's insurance in metro Atlanta, contact the **Georgia Insurance Commissioner's Office of Consumer Services**, 404-656-2070, 800-656-2298, http://oci.ga.gov/ConsumerService. You can also research insurance policies and compare quotes online at websites like **Insure.com**, www.insure.com, and **Insurance.com,** www.insurance.com.

To find an insurance agent in your neighborhood, check the local Yellow Pages, where offices are listed by county or community, or contact the following:

- **Allstate Insurance**, 866-621-6900, www.allstate.com; several offices throughout metro Atlanta
- **Country Financial**, 866-COUNTRY, www.countryfinancial.com; several offices throughout metro Atlanta
- **State Farm Insurance**, www.statefarm.com; several offices throughout metro Atlanta; local agent information (including toll free numbers and 24-hour service) can be located online by entering your ZIP code
- **Travelers**, 800-252-4633, www.travelers.com; several offices throughout metro Atlanta

## BUYING A HOME

Buying a home can be a complex, time-consuming, and stressful process. The resources and suggestions that follow can assist with the home-buying process.

The first thing you need to consider when buying a house is how much you can spend. Start with your gross monthly income, then tally up your monthly debt load: credit cards, car loans, personal debt, child support, alimony, etc. For revolving debt (like credit card debt), use your minimum monthly payment for the calculation. For the purposes of this calculation, ignore any debts you expect to have paid off entirely within six months' time. As a rule, your monthly housing costs shouldn't exceed 28% of your total monthly gross income, and your debt load shouldn't exceed 36% of it. That said, these days lenders might tailor the 28/36 ratio depending on your situation (assets, liability, job, credit history). When calculating your budget, don't forget to factor in closing costs, which may include insurance, appraisals, attorney's fees, loan fees, and transfer taxes. Fees normally range from 3% to 7% of the purchase price. Likewise, when figuring out your budget, be sure to factor in the additional monthly outgoes of homeowner's insurance, property taxes (tax deductible), utilities, condo fees, improvements, and maintenance.

Once you've figured out what you can afford to spend on a house, there will be other things to consider:

- How much space will you need? Are you single or married? Do you have children now or are you planning to have children in the future? What about pets? And will you need space for a home office?
- What kind of house do you want? While single-family homes are the most abundant option in metro Atlanta, condos and townhomes are popular as well. Are you looking for old or new? A vintage home can be an absolute gem once renovations have been made, but this is not always an easy or inexpensive task.
- What type of neighborhood will make you happy? Metro Atlanta offers great, intown neighborhoods, as well as numerous suburbs. Consider your proximity to work, shopping, and nightlife when determining where you'll buy. If you have children, you'll also want to check out the local school systems, nearby parks, crime rates, and traffic. And finally, take a look at property values throughout the city. Even if these factors aren't crucial to you personally, they are important, as they can affect the appreciation of your home and therefore the value of your investment.
- When looking at particular neighborhoods, pay attention to how quickly homes sell and whether or not there are significant gaps between asking price and sale price. Buying a home in an up-and-coming community can be a great investment, but keep in mind that not all up-and-coming areas come up.

## REAL ESTATE AGENTS

The Atlanta area has no shortage of agents and brokers, and because the city and surrounding suburbs cover such a large geographic area, many companies specialize in specific communities. To get a feel for metro Atlanta's neighborhoods and begin your home search, start with the **Neighborhoods** chapter of this book. Cruise the areas that you like and make a list of brokers working in that area for clues on who knows the local properties; almost all listed single-family homes and condos will have a sign in the yard. Also, be sure to ask around. Chances are someone you know or meet in Atlanta will have an opinion on a broker. Investigate the *Atlanta Journal-Constitution*'s Sunday classifieds, which contain a market area map, as well as other community newspapers (listed in the rental section of this chapter). The Atlanta Yellow Pages lists hundreds of real estate agents and brokers with an indication of the areas that they serve, and you can also use the resources available at **www.realtor.com**.

## PRE-QUALIFICATION/PRE-APPROVAL/CREDIT BUREAUS

Lenders suggest that you "pre-qualify" or, better still, get "pre-approved" for a loan. **Pre-qualification** is, in essence, an educated guess as to what you'll be able to afford for a loan. To be **pre-approved**, your loan officer will review your financial situation (by running a credit check, going over your proof of employment, savings, etc.) and then you will be given a letter documenting that the bank is willing to lend you a particular amount based on your proven financial situation. Pre-approval is a bit more labor-intensive for you and the lender, but sellers and real estate agents will take you more seriously if you show up with a pre-approval letter in hand.

For either pre-qualification or pre-approval of a loan, go to your lender with documentation of your financial history and a list of your debt load, and contact the three major credit bureaus (listed below) beforehand to make sure your credit history is accurate (visit www.annualcreditreport.com for online access to all three). It's best to get a copy of your credit report from each bureau, as each report may be different. You will need to provide your name, address, previous address, and social security number with your request. A credit report will list your credit activity for the past seven years, including your highest balance, current balance, and promptness or tardiness of payments. After seven years, the slate is wiped clean for any credit transgressions, except in the case of bankruptcy and foreclosure, which will appear on your record for 10 years. Your credit report will have a FICO (Fair Isaac and Company) score; typically, the higher your score, the easier it will be to get a loan.

If you discover any inaccuracies on your credit report, contact the service immediately and request that it be corrected. By law, credit bureaus must respond to your request within 30 days. If you have questions about your credit record, call Fannie Mae's nonprofit credit counseling service at 800-732-6643 before you apply for a mortgage. Be aware that too many credit record inquiries can lower your credit status.

The major **credit bureaus** are listed as follows and you can apply and often view your credit report online:

- **Experian**, www.experian.com, 888-397-3742
- **TransUnion**, www.transunion.com, 1-877-322-8228
- **Equifax**, www.equifax.com, 800-846-5279 or 866-322-3162

# FINANCING

Most buyers need a **mortgage** to pay for a house. A typical house mortgage is for either 15 or 30 years and consists of four parts, commonly referred to as "PITI" (principal, interest, taxes, and insurance). The **principal** is the flat sum of money that you borrowed from the lender to pay for the property. The larger the down payment, the less you will need to borrow to meet the total purchase price of your home. The lender charges **interest**, a percentage of the principal, as repayment for the use of the money that you've borrowed. (Points, each one equal to 1% of the amount you borrow for your mortgage, might also contribute to the interest.) Your community charges you **taxes** based on a percentage of your property value, which you'll continue paying even after your mortgage is paid off. The final component of PITI is house **insurance** against calamities such as fire, theft, and natural disasters. In many cases, people deposit funds into an escrow or trust account to cover insurance and taxes. Within three business days of receiving your loan application, your lender must give you a "good faith estimate" of how much your closing costs will be.

There are many loan programs available. Search the internet, newspapers, and books, and speak with financial planners, real estate agents, and mortgage brokers to find out what's best for you. Direct lenders (banks) and mortgage brokers are common places to go for a loan. A **direct lender** is an institution with a finite number of in-house loans, whose terms and conditions are controlled by the lender. A **mortgage broker**, on the other hand, is a middleman who shops around to various lenders and loan programs to find what's best for your needs. Because brokers shop around for the best interest rates, it's often worth paying their fee. To find a good local lender or mortgage broker you might call a real estate broker and ask for recommendations. They are usually more than happy to put you in touch with area lending institutions or mortgage brokers they've worked with in the past. Or contact the **Georgia Association of Mortgage Brokers**, 770-993-5507 or 770-698-0023, www.gamb.org.

In addition, a large number of lenders can be found by simply searching online, and many will find you a loan with a good rate over the phone. Lendingtree.com, Quickenloans.com and Bankrate.com are all good choices.

When educating yourself about mortgages, be sure to take the time to research institutions' loan costs and restrictions: interest rates, broker fees, points, prepayment penalties, loan term, application fees, credit report fees, and cost of appraisals.

## DOWN PAYMENT

Down payments vary. Some lenders have offered programs that require as little as 5% down or even zero down, but those days may be gone. If you are a first-time buyer, which is defined as someone who hasn't owned property within the past three years, you may qualify for state-backed programs that feature lower down payment requirements and below-market interest rates.

## MAKING AN OFFER, CONTINGENCIES, PURCHASE AND SALE (P&S) AGREEMENT

If you want your offer to be seriously considered, particularly in a tight market, be sure to offer a fair market price, include a statement of the source of your down payment, your pre-approval letter, and even a note to the seller about why/how much you want the house. Buyers offering cash, or with a pre-approval in hand, will be more attractive to the seller.

Common **contingencies** include an appraisal of the house that is satisfactory to the bank, financing (in cases where the buyer has not been pre-approved), a free and clear title, selling a current residence, and receiving a satisfactory inspection report of the property from a licensed inspector (see below). Some buyers put into their offer "on terms to be approved by the buyer's attorney."

The closing is just signing the paperwork that finalizes what you agreed to in your offer. If the seller agrees to your written offer, it becomes a binding sales contract, called a **purchase and sale (P&S) agreement**. If you default on this contract, you can lose your deposit money. If the seller defaults, you can sue him to force the sale to which he agreed in writing.

That said, after you make an offer, the buyer will accept it, reject it, or make a counter-offer, at which point you may accept, reject, or change the counter-offer, and so on. When both parties agree, it becomes a binding purchase agreement.

## INSPECTION

Choosing an inspector who is a member of the **American Society of Home Inspectors (ASHI)** will narrow the field of the many companies who offer inspection services; contact ASHI for recommendations or check with your real estate agent or broker, who will probably have several leads. The following organizations should be able to make referrals for more specialized testing of home environmental toxins such as mold, lead, asbestos, and radon, which are *not* covered in a standard home inspection:

- **American Society of Home Inspectors**, 800-743-ASHI, www.ashi.org
- **Georgia Association of Home Inspectors**, 770-952-7811, 800-521-5193, www.gahi.com
- **International Association of Certified Home Inspectors**, www.nachi.org

Should your inspector's report find that major repairs will be likely, you may be able to negotiate thousands of dollars off the purchase price. Or you might just decide to keep looking.

## CLOSING

Assuming the inspection goes well and/or all issues are resolved to your satisfaction, it is time for closing. At the closing, also known as "settlement" or "escrow," costs, such as transfer taxes, closing costs, legal fees, and adjustments are paid. This is a brief process in which the title to the property is transferred from seller to buyer; the seller gets his payment and you get the keys, and the closing agent officially records your loan.

## HOUSES AND CONDOS

Newcomers looking to buy a house, build a house, or invest in a condo should have no problems finding the right community. Like rental properties, home prices will vary depending on location. Generally, homes inside the perimeter, and particularly in Buckhead and Virginia Highland, will be most expensive, and homes farthest away from the perimeter, in surrounding suburbs, will be the least expensive. Metro Atlanta home prices can range from the mid $100,000s to the multi-millions. If you'd like to research average home prices based on neighborhood, check out the online version of the *AJC Homefinder*, www.ajchomefinder.com.

Single-family homes are, by far, the most common properties available. Your best bet is to drive through the neighborhoods you are interested in and see what's available. It's also a good idea to check out the real estate section of the *Atlanta Journal-Constitution's* Sunday edition, either online or in print. If possible, study it over the course of a few weeks to see which properties go the fastest and which are harder to sell. This may help in your negotiations when you are ready to make an offer on something.

Though not as prevalent as single-family homes, condos are another option in metro Atlanta. Most of the older, intown neighborhoods offer condos for sale, either in large renovated buildings, or sleek new complexes or high rises.

In Atlanta, a condo may be a single unit located in a building of many units, or a townhouse with a small deck or yard. In either case, the home will be yours, but the land and common areas will be community property, jointly owned by the condo association, of which you will be a member. As a member, you'll be required to pay monthly or quarterly dues to help cover basic community expenses like property maintenance and repairs, landscaping, and trash pickup. Membership fees may also be used to pay for maintenance and upkeep on any amenities your building offers, such as a hot tub, pool, or fitness center. It's a good idea to check out an association's financial reports upfront to get an idea of how often their fees have gone up, how much they typically increase, and what the funds are used for. At the same time, you will also want to get a list of the association's rules and regulations.

As owner of your individual unit, you will generally be allowed to make improvements to the space, rent it out, or resell it as you see fit, though this may not always be the case. Some associations are very strict about what is allowed on the premises. To avoid any surprises down the road, make sure you understand the rules before you buy.

## ADDITIONAL RESOURCES

### ONLINE—HOME LISTINGS

Most real estate agents offer home listings on their websites. For additional listings as well as real estate links, tips, and demographic information for metro Atlanta, you may also want to consider:

- **AJC Homefinder**, www.ajchomefinder.com
- **Atlanta Board of Realtors**, 404-250-0051, www.abr.org
- **HomeSeekers**, www.homeseekers.com
- **Listingbook,** www.listingbook.com
- **Move**, www.move.com
- **MSN Real Estate**, http://realestate.msn.com/
- **National Association of Realtors**, www.realtor.com
- **New Homes Atlanta**, www.newhomesatlanta.com
- **Owners.com**, www.owners.com
- **Yahoo! Real Estate**, http://homes.yahoo.com
- **ZipRealty**, www.ziprealty.com

### ONLINE—MORTGAGES

If basic information and current mortgage rates are what you're looking for, you may want to check out the following websites. These online mortgage service companies can explain the loan process to you, and provide updated rates and other useful information:

- **Bankrate.com**, www.bankrate.com; everything about mortgages and lending.
- **Fannie Mae**, www.fanniemae.com; loans for real estate purchases; dedicated to helping Americans achieve the dream of homeownership.
- **Freddie Mac**, www.freddiemac.com; provides information on low-cost loans, a home inspection kit, and tips to help avoid unfair lending practices.
- **Mortgage Bankers Association of Georgia**, www.gamb.org
- **Mint**, www.mint.com, offers numerous financial tools including mortgage calculators.

- **Interest.com**, www.interest.com; shop for mortgages and rates.
- **LendingTree**, www.lendingtree.com; request and compare loan offers online for free.
- **The Mortgage Professor**, www.mtgprofessor.com; demystifies and clarifies the confusing and often expensive world of mortgage brokers; helpfully written by an emeritus Wharton professor who answers questions (!); useful calculators.
- **Owners.com**, www.owners.com; all things mortgage and home sale related.
- **Quicken Loans**, www.quickenloans.com

## BUYING A HOME

Finally, aside from the selection of books you can pick up at your local bookstore or at an online bookseller, consider the following resources and publications:

- *100 Questions Every First Time Homebuyer Should Ask: With Answers from Top Brokers from Around the Country*, 2nd edition (Times Books), by Ilyce R. Glink
- *The 106 Common Mistakes Homebuyers Make (and How to Avoid Them)*, 3rd edition (Wiley), by Gary W. Eldred
- *The Co-Op Bible: Everything You Need to Know About Co-Ops and Condos: Getting In, Staying In, Surviving, Thriving* (Griffin Trade Paperback) by Sylvia Shapiro
- **Opening the Door to a Home of Your Own**: a pamphlet by Fannie Mae for first-time homebuyers. Call 800-834-3377 for a copy.
- **Score Card**; if you're particularly concerned about environmental toxins at your new property, check out www.scorecardgoodguide.com, a site sponsored by the Environmental Defense Fund.

B EFORE STARTING YOUR NEW LIFE IN METRO ATLANTA, YOU AND YOUR worldly possessions will have to get here. How difficult and expensive that will be depends on how much stuff you've accumulated, what your budget is, and where you're coming from.

## TRUCK RENTALS, COMMERCIAL FREIGHT CARRIERS, CONTAINER-BASED MOVERS, AND PORTABLE STORAGE

The first question you need to answer is: Should I move myself, or have someone else do it for me? If you'd rather do it yourself, you can just rent a vehicle and head for the open road. Look in the Yellow Pages under "Truck Rental" or "Moving," and then call around to compare prices. Below we list four national truck rental firms, their toll-free numbers, and their web addresses, but for the best information, you should call a local office. Note that most truck rental companies now offer "one-way" rentals (don't forget to ask whether they have a drop-off/return location in or near your destination), as well as packing accessories and storage facilities. Of course, these extras are not free, and if you're cost conscious, you may want to scavenge boxes in advance of your move or buy some directly from a box company. Those moving locally should check neighborhood **FedEx Office** locations, www.fedex.com, which frequently offer empty boxes in their self-serve area.

If you're planning on moving during the peak moving months (May through September), be sure to reserve your truck well in advance, at least a month ahead of when you'll need the vehicle. Remember, too, that the beginning of the month and Saturdays are extremely popular times to move. You may be able to get cheaper rates if you book a different day.

Once you're on the road, keep in mind that your rental truck may be a tempting target for thieves. If you must park it overnight or for an extended period (more than a couple of hours), try to find a safe place, preferably somewhere well-lit and easily observable by you, and do your best not to leave anything of particular value in the cab. Make sure the back door is locked and, if possible, use a steering wheel lock or other easy-to-purchase safety device.

- **Budget**, 800-527-0700, www. budget.com
- **Penske**, 888-996-5415, www.pensketruckrental.com
- **Ryder**,    800-BY-RYDER,    http://www.ryder.com/rental_home.shtml    (now    a Budget company, though still operating under the Ryder name)
- **U-Haul**, 800-GO-UHAUL, www.uhaul.com

Not sure if you want to drive the truck yourself? Commercial freight carriers, such as **U-PACK Moving**, 800-355-1696, www.upack.com, offer an in-between service; they'll deliver a 28-foot trailer to your home, you pack and load as much of it as you need, and then they'll drive the vehicle to your destination (often with some other freight filling up the empty space). However, if you have to share truck space with another customer, you may arrive far ahead of your boxes and furniture. Try to estimate your needs beforehand and ask for your load's expected arrival date. You can get an online estimate from some shippers, so you can compare notes.

Other companies will also deliver a container to your home. You pack and load it, and the carrier delivers the container to your destination. In some cases, this option can be cheaper than renting and driving your own truck, especially when you consider the cost of fuel. Also some of these companies offer storage as an extra option or part of the deal.

Here are a few of the largest container-based movers that serve metro Atlanta.

- **The Mobile Attic,** www.mobileattic.com
- **Smart Move,** www.gosmartmove.com
- **SmartBox Portable Storage,** http://smartboxusa.com
- **UPack,** www.upack.com

If you aren't moving an entire house and can't estimate how much truck space you'll need, keep in mind this general guideline: Two to three furnished rooms equal a 15-foot truck; four to five rooms, a 20-foot truck.

## MOVERS

### INTERSTATE

First, the good news: Moving can be affordable and problem-free. The bad news: If you're hiring a mover, the chances of it being so are dramatically reduced.

Probably the best way to find a mover is by **personal recommendation**. Absent a friend or relative who can recommend a trusted moving company, you can turn to what surveys show is the most popular method of finding a mover: the **Yellow Pages**. Then there's the **internet**; just type in "movers" on any of the major search engines and you'll be directed to dozens of more or less helpful moving-related sites.

In the past, **Consumer Reports**, www.consumerreports.org, has published useful information on moving. You might also ask a local realtor, who may be able to steer you towards a good mover, or at least tell you which ones to avoid. Members of the American Automobile Association have a valuable resource at hand in **AAA's Consumer Relocation Services**, which will assign the member a personal consultant to handle every detail of the move free of charge and which offers savings from discounts arranged with premier moving companies. For more information, call 800-839-MOVE, https://autoclubsouth.aaa.com.

*But beware!* Since 1995, when the federal government eliminated the Interstate Commerce Commission, the interstate moving business has degenerated into a wild and mostly unregulated industry with thousands of unhappy, ripped-off customers annually. In fact, there are so many reports of unscrupulous carriers that we no longer list movers in this book. Since states don't have the authority to regulate interstate movers and the federal government has been slow to respond, you are pretty much on your own when it comes to finding an honest, hassle-free mover. That's why we can't emphasize enough the importance of carefully researching and choosing who will move you.

To aid in your search for an **interstate mover**, we offer a few general recommendations. First, pay a visit to MovingScam.com, a website dedicated to improving consumer protections in the moving industry, and providing solid, impartial consumer education. Loaded with valuable articles, information and other resources (it even maintains a "Black List"), its message boards are staffed around the clock with experienced volunteers who answer moving-related questions promptly and at no cost to the consumer.

Second, check with the **US Department of Transportation's Federal Motor Carrier Safety Administration** (**FMCSA**) to see if your movers are properly licensed and insured (www.protectyourmove.org). The FMCSA's website publishes details about regulations governing professional moving companies together with news of recent criminal investigations and convictions. The site also contains tips on how to spot a rogue mover and offers links to local Better Business Bureaus, consumer protection agencies, state attorneys general, state moving associations, and the **FMCSA Safety Violation and Consumer Household Goods Complaint Hotline** (1-888-DOT-SAFT, 1888-368-7238, www.fmcsa.dot.gov/about). Don't expect much from this hotline, however. It is essentially just a database and you will only hear from the DOT if it looks at your complaint and determines that enforcement action is warranted. Georgia's consumer protection boards or attorneys general can be reached through the **Governor's Office of Consumer Affairs**, 404-651-8600, 800-869-1123, **consumer.georgia.gov**.

Assuming there is no negative information, you can move on to the next step: asking for references. Particularly important are references from customers who had moves similar to yours. If a moving company is unable or unwilling to provide references, eliminate it from your list. Unscrupulous movers have been known to give phony references who will sing their praises, so make sure you talk to more than one reference, and ask questions. If something feels fishy, it probably is. Another way to learn more about a prospective mover: ask them if they have a local office (they should) and then walk in and check it out in person.

Once you have at least three movers you feel reasonably comfortable with, it's time to ask for price quotes. These should always be free. Best is a binding "not-to-exceed" quote, in writing. This will require an on-site visual inspection of what you are shipping. If you have any doubts about a prospective mover, drop it from your list before inviting a stranger into your home to catalog your belongings.

Recent regulations by FMCSA require movers to supply several documents to consumers before executing a contract. These include a booklet titled *Your Rights and Responsibilities When You Move*; a concise and accurate written estimate of charges; a summary of the mover's arbitration program; the mover's customer complaint and inquiry handling procedure; and the mover's tariff, containing rates, rules, regulations, classifications, etc.

**Additional moving recommendations:**

- If someone recommends a mover to you, be sure to get names (the salesperson or estimator, the drivers, the loaders). To paraphrase the NRA, moving companies don't move people, people do. Likewise, if someone tells you they had a bad moving experience, note the name of the company and try to avoid it.
- Remember that price, while important, isn't everything, especially when you're entrusting all of your worldly possessions to strangers. Be sure to choose a mover you feel comfortable with. However, movers' rates in the state of Georgia are regulated and published in the Maximum Rate Tariff, which can be viewed at the PSC's website, www.psc.state.ga.us.
- Legitimate movers generally charge in one of two manners. For moves within 50 miles, they charge by the hour and number of workers required. For moves more than 50 miles, they charge by the weight of goods and total distance of the move. A licensed mover should give you a free estimate in writing.
- In general, ask questions, and if you're concerned about something, ask for an explanation in writing. If you change your mind about a mover once you've signed on the dotted line, write the company a letter explaining that you've changed your mind and that you won't be using its services. Better safe than sorry.
- Ask about insurance; the "basic" 60 cents per-pound, industry-standard coverage is not enough. If you have homeowner's or renter's insurance, check to see if it will cover your belongings during transit. If not, ask your insurer if you can add that coverage for your move. Otherwise, consider purchasing "full replacement" or "full value" coverage from the carrier for the estimated value of your shipment. Though it's the most expensive type of coverage offered, it's

probably worth it. Trucks get into accidents, they catch fire, they get stolen—if such insurance seems pricey to you, ask about a $250 or $500 deductible. This can reduce your cost substantially while still giving you more comprehensive protection in the event of a catastrophic loss.

- Whatever you do, do not mislead a salesperson about how much and what you are moving. And make sure you tell a prospective mover about how far they'll have to transport your stuff to and from the truck, as well as any stairs, driveways, obstacles or difficult vegetation, long paths or sidewalks, etc. The clearer you are with your movers, the better they will be able to serve you.

- Think about packing. If you plan to pack yourself, you can save a lot of money, **but if something is damaged because of your packing, you cannot file a claim for it.** On the other hand, if you hire a mover to do the packing, they may not treat your belongings as well as you will. They will certainly do it faster, that's for sure. Depending on the size of your move and whether or not you are packing yourself, you may need a lot of boxes, tape, and other packing materials. Mover boxes, while not cheap, are usually sturdy and the right size. Sometimes a mover will give a customer free used boxes. It doesn't hurt to ask. Also, *don't* wait to pack until the last minute. If you're doing the packing, give yourself at least a week to do the job; two or more is better. Be sure to ask the mover about any weight or size restrictions on boxes.

- You should transport any irreplaceable items such as jewelry, photographs, or key work documents personally. Do not put them in the moving van! For less precious items that you don't want to put in the moving truck, consider sending them via the US Postal Service or by UPS.

- Ask your mover what is not permitted in the truck: usually anything flammable or combustible, as well as certain types of valuables.

- Although movers will put numbered labels on your possessions, you should make a numbered list of every box and item that is going in the truck. Detail box contents and photograph anything of particular value. Once the truck arrives on the other end, you can check off every piece and know for sure what did (or did not) make it. In case of claims, this list can be invaluable. Even after the move, keep the list; it can be surprisingly useful.

- Movers are required to issue you a "bill of lading." Do not hire a mover who does not use them.

- Consider keeping a log of every expense you incur for your move, e.g., phone calls, trips to Atlanta, etc. In many instances, the IRS allows you to claim these types of expenses on your income tax. (See **Taxes,** below.)

- Be aware that during the busy season (May through September), demand can exceed supply, and moving may be more difficult and more expensive than during the rest of the year. If you must relocate during the peak moving months, call and book service well in advance of when you plan on moving—a month at least. If you can book service even more in advance, say four to six months early, you may be able to lock in a lower winter rate for your summer move.

- Listen to what the movers say; they are professionals and can give you expert advice about packing and preparing. Also, be ready for the truck on both ends—don't make them wait. Not only will it irritate your movers, but it may also cost you. Understand, too, that things can happen on the road that are beyond a carrier's control (weather, accidents, etc.), and your belongings may not get to you at the time or on the day promised.
- Treat your movers well, especially the ones loading your stuff on and off the truck. Offer to buy them lunch, and tip them if they do a good job.
- Before moving pets, attach a tag to your pet's collar with your new address and phone number in case your furry friend accidentally wanders off in the confusion of moving. Your pet should travel with you, and you should never plan on moving a pet inside a moving van.
- Be prepared to pay the full moving bill upon delivery. Cash or bank/cashier's check may be required. Some carriers will take VISA and MasterCard, but it is a good idea to get it in writing that you will be permitted to pay with a credit card since the delivering driver may not be aware of this and may demand cash. Unless you routinely keep thousands in greenbacks on you, you could have a problem getting your stuff off the truck.

## INTRASTATE AND LOCAL MOVERS

**The Georgia Public Service Commission** regulates the licensing, rates, and rules of the Household Goods Moving Industry within Georgia. They can be reached at 404-656-4501 or www.psc.state.ga.us. Most movers list their state license number in their advertisements, but if the number is not listed, or if you use a mover recommended by a friend or family member, be sure to ask for their license number up front.

For moves within Georgia, the PSC's regulations require all movers to provide each client with a written estimate before the move commences. The estimate should clearly state all decisions about what you want moved, what services will be included, the mover's liability for loss or damage, and an estimated price. In Georgia, three possible estimates are allowed: a "non-binding estimate," a "binding estimate," or, ideally, a "not-to-exceed price" estimate. Research these options ahead of time to ensure you're getting the estimate that works best for you. Once all of this is worked out, you'll be presented with an Agreement for Service form. The mover will have you sign this form before the move begins. And you'll want to be sure that the mover signs it as well.

## CONSUMER COMPLAINTS—MOVERS

If a **move goes badly**, and you blame the moving company, you should first file a written claim with the mover for loss or damage. If this gets you nowhere and it's an **intrastate** move, contact the **PSC**. They will typically suggest that you send them a letter of complaint, stating the following: the address of the point of origin and final destination; the nature of the complaint; all verbal and written correspondence with the carrier; and the course of action needed to resolve the issue. You will also be asked to enclose a copy of the estimate, the Bill of Lading, and any written correspondence between the carrier and yourself. For moves within the state of Georgia, the PSC has the authority to require the mover to resolve the claim within 90 days.

If your grievance is with an **interstate carrier**, your choices are unfortunately limited. Interstate moves are regulated by the **Federal Motor Carriers Safety Administration** (**FMCSA**), 888-368-7238, www.fmcsa.dot.gov/. While its role in the regulation of interstate carriers has historically been concerned with safety issues rather than consumer issues, the recent upsurge in unscrupulous movers and unhappy consumers has led the FMCSA to respond by issuing a set of rules "specifying how interstate household goods (HHG) carriers (movers) and brokers must assist their individual customers shipping household goods." According to its consumer page, carriers in violation of said rules can be fined, and repeat offenders may be barred from doing business. In terms of loss, however, "FMCSA does not have statutory authority to resolve loss and damage of consumer complaints, settle disputes against a mover, or obtain reimbursement for consumers seeking payment for specific charges. Consumers are responsible for resolving disputes involving these household goods matters." It is not able to represent you in an arbitration dispute to recover damages for lost or destroyed property, nor can it enforce a court judgment. If you have a grievance, your best bet is to file a complaint against the mover with the FMCSA and with the **Better Business Bureau**, www.bbb.org, in the state where the moving company is licensed, as well as with that state's attorney general or consumer protection office. To seek redress, hire an attorney.

## STORAGE WAREHOUSES

Storage facilities may be required when you have to ship your belongings before you've found an apartment, or if your new home is too small. If your mover maintains storage facilities in the metro area, as many do, you may opt to store with them. Some even offer one month's free storage. Otherwise, look in the Yellow Pages under "Storage," and then shop around for the best and most convenient deal. Below are a couple of major moving/storage companies. Listing here does *not* imply endorsement by First Books.

- **Door to Door Storage**, 888-366-7222, www.doortodoor.com, several locations throughout metro Atlanta, offering warehousing for cargo containers, which are delivered to you for packing, and are then picked up and transported back to the storage facilities.

- **Public Storage**, 800-447-8673, www.publicstorage.com, offers locations throughout metro Atlanta and the rest of the country for self-service storage, pickup service and storage, full-service moving, and/or local and long-distance truck rentals.

## SELF-STORAGE

The ability to rent anything from 5' x 5' rooms to storage rooms large enough to accommodate a car is a great boon to urban dwellers. Collectors, people with old clothes they can't bear to give away, and those with possessions that won't fit in their home or apartment all find mini-warehouses a solution to too-small living spaces.

Rates for space in metro Atlanta self-storage facilities are competitive. Expect to pay at least $40 per month for a basic 5' x 5' (25 square foot) climate-controlled unit, $72 per month for a 5' x 10' (50 square foot) space, and so on. Some offer free pickup; otherwise you or your mover delivers the goods. If you're looking for lower rates, inquire with the storage facility about move-in specials or other locations.

As you shop around, you'll probably want to check the facility for cleanliness and security. Does the building have sprinklers in case of fire? Does it have carts and hand trucks for moving in and out? Will you be billed monthly, or will the storage company automatically charge the bill to your credit card? Is the rental month to month or is there a minimum lease? Access should be 24-hour or nearly so. And, remember, some units are air conditioned, an asset if you plan to visit your locker in the summer, or if you are storing items that can be damaged by excessive heat or humidity.

Finally, a word of warning: Unless you no longer want your stored belongings, pay your storage bill and pay it on time. Storage companies may auction off the contents of delinquent customers' lockers.

Here are a few local self-storage companies. For additional options, check the Yellow Pages under "Storage." Or use the internet; a simple Google search brings up the most popular businesses, with customer reviews to boot.

- **City Storage**, 726 Ponce De Leon Pl NE, (404) 853-3303; national storage facility located in midtown  near Virginia Highland; lots of tools on their website for estimating the size and type of space you'll need.
- **Public Storage**, 800-447-8673, www.publicstorage.com; multiple locations throughout metro Atlanta, including Downtown, Alpharetta, Decatur, Lawrenceville, Marietta, Norcross, Roswell, Sandy Springs, Smyrna, and Stone Mountain.
- **U-Haul Self-Storage**, 800-GO-UHAUL, www.uhaul.com; has locations all over metro Atlanta, including College Park, Decatur, Doraville, Midtown, and Smyrna.

## CHILDREN

Studies show that moving, especially frequent moving, can be hard on children. According to an American Medical Association study, children who move often are more likely to suffer from such problems as depression, low self-esteem, and aggression. Often their academic performance suffers as well. Aside from not moving more than is necessary, there are a few things you can do to help your children through this stressful time:

- Talk about the move with your kids. Be honest but positive. Listen to their concerns and involve them in the moving process as much as you can.
- Make sure your children have their favorite possessions on the trip; don't pack "blankey" in the moving van.
- Make sure you have some social activities planned on the other end. Your children may feel lonely in your new home and such activities can ease the transition. If you move during the summer, you might consider finding a local day camp they can sign up for, as a way to make new friends. Check with the YWCA or YMCA, as well as places like Zoo Atlanta, Fernbank, and The Atlanta Botanical Gardens.
- Keep in touch with family and loved ones as much as possible. Photos and phone calls are important ways of maintaining links to the important people you have left behind.
- If your children are of school age, take the time to involve yourself in their new school and in their academic life. Don't let them fall through the cracks. Additionally, try to schedule your move during the summer, so that they can start their new school year at the beginning of the term.
- If possible, spend some time in the area you're moving to prior to the move, doing fun things like exploring the neighborhoods, visiting local playgrounds and parks, or checking out the malls with your teenagers. With any luck, they'll meet some other kids their own age.

For children ages 6–11, ***The Moving Book: A Kids' Survival Guide*** by Gabriel Davis is a wonderful gift, as is ***Moving Day*** by Ralph Fletcher, illustrated by Jennifer Emery. And for younger kids, ***Max's Moving Adventure: A Coloring Book for Kids on the Move*** by Danelle Till, illustrated by Joe Spooner, is a perfect gift. For general guidance, read ***Smart Moves: Your Guide Through the Emotional Maze of Relocation*** by Nadia Jensen, Audrey McCollum, and Stuart Copans.

## TAXES

If your move is work-related, some or all of your moving expenses may be tax-deductible—so you may want to keep those receipts. Though eligibility varies, depending, for example, on whether you have a job or are self-employed, generally, the cost of moving yourself, your family, and your belongings is tax deductible, even if you don't itemize. The criteria: in order to take the deduction, your move must be employment-related, your new job must be more than 50 miles away from your current residence, and you must be there for at least 39 weeks during the first 12 months after your arrival. If you take the deduction and then fail to meet the requirements, you will have to pay the IRS back, unless you were laid off through no fault of your own or transferred again by your employer. It's probably a good idea to consult a tax expert regarding IRS rules related to moving. However, if you're a confident soul, you can get a copy of IRS Form 3903 at www.irs.gov, and try figuring it out yourself!

## ADDITIONAL RELOCATION AND MOVING INFORMATION

- **American Car Transport**, www.americancartransport.com, can assist you if you need help moving your car.
- **Best Places**, www.bestplaces.net/city, compares quality of life and cost-of-living data of US cities.
- **Data Masters**, www.datamasters.com, provides basic community statistics by ZIP code.
- **Worldwide ERC (Employee Relocation Council)**, www.worldwideerc.org, is a professional organization offering members specialized reports on the relocation and moving industries.
- **First Books**, www.firstbooks.com, relocation resources and information on moving to Atlanta, Boston, Chicago, Los Angeles, Minneapolis–St. Paul, New York, Portland, the San Francisco Bay Area, Seattle, and Washington, DC, as well as London, England, and major cities in Texas and in China. Also publisher of the *Newcomer's Handbook® for Moving to and Living in the USA* as well as *The Pet-Moving Handbook*.
- *How to Survive A Move*, edited by Jamie Allen and Kazz Regelman, is a **Hundreds of Heads** guide (www.hundredsofheads.com). Divided into sections ranging from planning a move to packing tips, moving with kids, and worst moves ever, this easy-to-digest book provides the wisdom, dispensed mostly in single-paragraph bites, of hundreds of people who've lived through the experience.
- **Move**, www.move.com, provides numerous relocation resources, including a handy salary calculator that will compare the cost of living in US cities.
- *The How to Move Handbook* by Clyde and Shari Steiner is an excellent general guidebook.
- **The Riley Guide**, www.rileyguide.com/relocate.html, is an online moving and relocation clearinghouse. It offers lists of moving and relocation guides and

websites, as well as links to sites that cover cost-of-living demographics, real estate, school, and healthcare directories.

- **The United States Postal Service**, www.usps.com, offers helpful relocation information.

A S SOON AS YOU HAVE YOUR NEW ADDRESS, YOU WILL PROBABLY WANT to open a bank account. Read on for information about Atlanta banks and credit unions; credit cards; credit reports; city, state, and federal income taxes; and moving or starting a business.

## FINANCIAL INSTITUTIONS

Many banks in Atlanta maintain branch offices in numerous locations around the metropolitan area. In addition, these banks operate a multitude of ATMs for 24-hour banking convenience.

When shopping around for a bank, you can choose a giant conglomerate that operates in several states, or you can choose a locally run bank. Either way, you should compare bank services and fees to find the best deal for your financial needs. Some banks offer free checking under certain conditions, such as maintaining a minimum balance in your account. Some offer reduced monthly fees for people who bank mostly by ATM. And many banks offer special deals to new customers, such as a waiver of check fees or safe deposit rent. Though most people withdraw money from ATMs, many choose to execute other transactions, such as deposits, at the bank itself. Choosing a bank that has a branch in your neighborhood as well as one near your place of employment guarantees access to your bank during business hours. However, if you don't need a branch on every corner, you should look into a smaller bank that may be in your neighborhood. Local institutions may offer lower fees and friendlier service than their mega-bank competitors.

Due to recent changes in banking regulations, some of the old familiar names have merged with larger banks, and some who merged just a year or two ago are now in the second generation of name changes. Some of Atlanta's largest banks are listed below. These banks will not only administer your checking and savings accounts, but they can also help you with CDs, money market accounts, and other investment products such as mutual funds.

- **BB&T**, www.bbandt.com, 800-BANK-BBT
- **Bank of America**, www.bankofamerica.com, 800-900-9000
- **Citizens Trust Bank**, www.ctbconnect.com, 678-406-4000
- **SunTrust Bank**, www.suntrust.com, 800-SUNTRUST or 404-230-5555
- **Wells Fargo**, www.wellsfargo.com, 800-TO-WELLS

## CREDIT UNIONS

If membership in a credit union is an option, this may be the best place to go for your banking needs. Credit unions are typically run by a volunteer board and offer significantly lower service fees on savings and checking accounts, short-term loans, and credit cards. According to *American Banker*'s annual survey, credit unions continually rank high in customer satisfaction. Because credit unions limit membership based on set criteria, you'll need to investigate a few for a match. Organizations such as employers, unions, professional associations, churches, and schools (alumni associations) typically provide membership. The down side is that credit unions are usually unable to provide the wider variety of financial products and services, such as mutual funds, CDs, and other investment vehicles. Additionally, credit union members may find it difficult to get to their union's offices. Unlike large banks, most credit unions only have one or two locations, rather than branch offices throughout the city, which may be a problem if you don't live or work nearby.

For a complete list of local credit unions or information about them, you can visit the **Credit Unions National Association**, www.cuna.org, or the **National Credit Union Administration (NCUA)**, http://ncua.gov. Some of the larger credit unions in metro Atlanta are:

- **Atlanta Postal Credit Union**, 404-768-4126 or 800-849-8431, www.apcu.com; for Atlanta area postal workers
- **CDC Federal Credit Union**, 404-325-3270 or 800-245-9655, www.cdcfcu.com; for Centers for Disease Control employees
- **Delta Community Credit Union**, 404-715-4725 or 800-544-3328, www.delta-communitycu.com; originally a credit union for Delta Airline employees, but open to the public since 2007
- **Emory Alliance Credit Union**, 404-329-6415, www.emoryacu.com/; for employees of Emory Hospital, Emory University, and affiliated organizations
- **Georgia Federal Credit Union**, 770-493-4328 or 888-493-4328, www.gfcuonline.org/index.asp; originally for local school system and county employees, now open to the general public

## CHECKING ACCOUNTS

Most banks offer checking accounts in a variety of shapes and sizes, ranging from no-frills economy accounts with low maintenance fees and limited withdrawals, to flat fee accounts with unlimited transactions. Generally, though, if you maintain a certain minimum balance in your account, the bank will waive any service charges.

To set up a checking account, most banks require the address and phone number of your current employer; two signed pieces of identification such as a driver's license, credit card, or student ID; and a minimum start-up deposit. Some banks now also run a credit check on your social security number while you wait. If you have a bad credit record or a history of bouncing checks, you may not be allowed to open an account. Also, be aware that if you do open an account, there is usually a waiting period, from five to seven days, before you can access funds in that account.

## SAVINGS ACCOUNTS

Many people choose to open a savings account along with their checking account. And just as your bank offers you several checking options, it will probably offer you more than one savings plan from which to choose. If you have only short-term savings needs, you might choose an account that sets aside a small amount from your checking account each month and credits your savings. On the other hand, if you have a large sum of cash, you may want to open a savings account that gives you a higher interest rate in exchange for maintaining a minimum balance in your account. As with a checking account, employment information, identification, and a minimum start-up deposit will likely be required.

## CONSUMER COMPLAINTS—BANKING

Both the federal and state government regulate bank policies on discrimination, credit, anti-redlining, truth-in-lending, etc. If you have a problem with your bank, attempt to resolve the issue directly with the bank. Should you need to **file a formal complaint** against your financial institution, you can do so through the Board of Governors of the **Federal Reserve System, Division of Consumer and Community Affairs**. For specific information, call 888-851-1920 or go online to www.federalreserve.gov/econresdata/ccastaff.htm. You can also pursue the issue with the following agencies:

- Nationally chartered commercial banks go through the **US Comptroller of the Currency, Customer Assistance Group**, 1301 McKinney St, Ste 3710, Houston, TX 77010; 800-613-6743; www.occ.treas.gov.
- For **state-chartered banks**, contact the **Georgia Department of Banking and Finance**, 2990 Brandywine Rd, Atlanta, 770-986-1633, 888-986-1633, http://dbf.

georgia.gov. State-chartered banks that are members of the Federal Reserve System should contact the **Federal Reserve Bank of Atlanta**, 1000 Peachtree St NE, Atlanta, 404-498-8500, www.frbatlanta.org; or the **Federal Deposit Insurance Corporation** (**FDIC**), 877-ASK-FDIC, www.fdic.gov.

- Federally chartered credit unions; state-chartered credit unions with federal insurance: **National Credit Union Administration**, 9 Washington Sq, Washington Ave Ext, Albany, NY 12205, 518-862-7400, www.ncua.gov.

## CREDIT CARDS

The internet is a valuable resource when it comes to getting information about credit cards. A list of low-rate card issuers can be found online at **CreditCards. com**, **BankRate.com**, or **Consumer Action**, www.consumer-action.org.

For more information about a specific card, to request an application or to apply online, you can contact the following:

- **American Express**, 800-THE-CARD, www.americanexpress.com
- **Diner's Club**, 800-2-DINERS, www.dinersclubus.com
- **Discover Card**, 888-DISCOVER, www.discovercard.com
- **Visa** and **MasterCard** are available from banks and other financial service associations. Terms may vary widely, so shop around for the lowest interest rate and annual fees. Also, be sure to read the fine print. A card may offer a fabulous deal for six months and then charge an exorbitant rate after that—just when you've made all your Christmas purchases.
- **Department store credit cards** can be acquired at checkout counters and customer service desks. Most stores offer instant credit for those who qualify. Usually, you can get a discount on one day's purchase when you sign up for a department store credit card. Store charge accounts also offer advantages beyond credit, such as advance notice of sales, mail or phone orders, and free shipping.

## BANKING & CREDIT RESOURCES

For a list of articles about trends in banking and links to the Federal Trade Commission and other consumer protection agencies, visit the **Institute for Consumer Financial Education** website at www.financial-education-icfe.org. To look up current interest rates on deposits, go to www.bankrate.com.

If you're buying a car or boat, renovating your new fixer-upper, or sending the kids to college, be smart about how you shop for loans and do your research online first. Most major banks' loans have higher interest rates, although a few occasionally offer completive loans for current customers. Meanwhile, online loan calculators let you experiment with different payment plans and shop around.

There are several loan calculators on bankrate.com but you can look at other sites as well:

- **www.myfico.com**
- **www.411-loans.com**
- **Eloan**, www.eloan.com,
- **Financial Power Tools**, http://financialpowertools.com
- **Women's Financial Network**, http://wfn.com
- **The Motley Fool**, www.fool.com (an excellent place to learn about money, investing and banking. They offer online seminars, well-written articles, and an active discussion board.)

Obtain copies of your **credit report** from the three major credit bureaus at **www. annualcreditreport.com**. Avoid ordering your credit report more than once a year, though—suspiciously frequent requests could adversely affect your credit rating.

## TAXES

The **Georgia Department of Revenue (GDOR)**, 404-417-4477, https://etax.dor. ga.gov, is the principal tax collecting agency for the state. The Department, led by the Revenue Commissioner, is charged with the administration and enforcement of nearly all of the Georgia's tax laws, pertaining to everything from state income tax and sales tax, to ad valorem and property tax. The GDOR is headquartered at 1800 Century Center Boulevard NE, Atlanta, though several of their departments are located in other locations around town.

### SALES TAX

Georgia State Sales Tax is currently 4% (no sales tax on groceries), with each county or municipality having the power to levy additional sales taxes by popular vote. Added taxes are used for such local needs as building schools, improving local roads, and other special uses the county or city deems necessary. What follows is a sampling of metro area sales taxes, and how the tax funds are allocated:

- **City of Atlanta**: State sales tax plus 1% for MARTA, and 2% for special purpose
- **Fulton County**: State sales tax plus 1% for MARTA, 1% for local option, and 1% for education
- **DeKalb County**: State sales tax plus 1% for MARTA, 1% for homestead, and 1% for education
- **Cobb County**: State sales tax plus 1% for education, and 1% for special purpose
- **Gwinnett County**: State sales tax plus 1% for education, and 1% for special purpose

It's important to note that Georgia traditionally holds two tax-free days each year; generally one in late winter/early spring, and one again in the late summer, just in time for back-to-school shopping. Many items are sold minus sales tax during tax-free days, including clothing, shoes, computers, and school supplies. Certain water- and energy-efficient products under $1,500 are also sold tax-free. For more information about Georgia's tax-free days, including a complete list of goods that qualify for tax-free status and the upcoming tax-free day schedule, visit https://etax.dor.ga.gov.

## PROPERTY TAX

Georgia residents are required to pay property tax on any personal real estate (including their primary residence) or commercial property that they own in the state. This property tax is the primary source of revenue for local counties, cities, and public schools in Georgia. Each of the state's 159 counties, including the 28 counties that make up metro Atlanta, operates tax offices that assess and collect the tax. For more information on property tax collection in Georgia, contact the **GDOR's Property Tax Division**, 404-968-0707. You can also find county-by-county tax information, including contact information for your local tax commissioner, at the **GDOR's Contact Page**, https://etax.dor.ga.gov/doroff.aspx.

## MOTOR VEHICLE TAX

In addition to collecting property tax, it's also the responsibility of **GDOR's Property Tax Division** to value motor vehicles for taxation. To date, all Georgia residents who owned a car registered it with their county tax commissioner and paid an annual motor vehicle ad valorem tax. However, starting March 1, 2013, residents pay a one-time tax of 7% when they purchase a new or used vehicle. New residents are required to pay the tax on their vehicle but are allowed to spread the payments out over time. Current car owners will continue to pay the ad valorem tax until their vehicles are sold or junked. For more information about motor vehicle registration, tags, titles, and taxes, contact the state **Department of Driver Services**, 678-413-8400, www.dds.ga.gov, or the tax commissioner's office in your county.

## STATE INCOME TAX

The State of Georgia requires that income tax be withheld from wages paid to all resident and nonresident employees who work within the state. Residents are also required to pay state income tax on wages earned outside of Georgia, unless their employer has already withheld a state tax on them for another state. The deadline for filing a Georgia income tax return is April 15th. More information on Georgia's state income tax, as well as copies of Georgia's tax forms, is available at GDOR's website, http://www.etax.dor.ga.gov. Georgia tax forms are also available at most metro Atlanta post offices and public libraries.

## FEDERAL INCOME TAX

Federal Income Tax forms can be obtained by calling 800-TAX-FORM or by picking them up during tax season at any local post office or public library. If you need additional federal income tax information, the resources here can help:

- **IRS Tax Help Line**, 800-829-1040, www.irs.gov
- **Federal Teletax Information Line**, 800-829-4477
- **IRS Atlanta Office**, 401 W Peachtree St, NW, Atlanta, 404-338-7962, www.irs. gov

If you'd like someone else to prepare your tax return, professional tax services are listed in the Yellow Pages or online. Of the many firms listed, here are a few for consideration:

- **H & R Block**, 800-HR-BLOCK, www.hrblock.com; over 100 locations throughout metro Atlanta
- **Jackson Hewitt**, 800-234-1040, www.jacksonhewitt.com; over 100 locations in metro Atlanta
- **Townsend Income Tax & Accounting**, 770-433-0606, www.townsendtax.com; locally owned, with five offices throughout metro Atlanta

## ELECTRONIC INCOME TAX FILING

These days, many people are choosing to file their taxes electronically, by purchasing or downloading tax software, using an online tax service, or going through an accredited agency. According to the IRS, electronic filers receive their refunds in about half the time of mail filers; plus e-filing costs less and is more accurate than doing it the old-fashioned way. In fact, the IRS estimates that the recent trend in e-filing has reduced the error rate to less than 1%.

To research the many tax filing software options, go to your search engine and type in "tax software." **Intuit Turbo Tax**, http://turbotax.intuit.com, is just one of many that are available.

For more information on electronic filing, check out **IRS E-file**, www.irs.gov/efile. This site includes features such as convenient payment options or direct deposit for those expecting a return, and offers a list of software brands and internet sites that are capable of handling both federal and state returns.

If you'd like to file your Georgia State Income Tax online, visit the **GDOR's** website, www.etax.dor.ga.gov/Online_Services.aspx.

## STARTING OR MOVING A BUSINESS

If you are interested in starting a new business, or relocating your existing business to metro Atlanta, you may want to consider consulting an attorney who is familiar with the process and with the city itself. The following resources will give you an idea of how to get started, what to expect, and where to turn for information:

- **Metro Atlanta Chamber of Commerce, Business Recruitment Department**, 404-586-8446, www.metroatlantachamber.com; specializes in assisting companies who are planning a move into metro Atlanta, offering information on everything from commercial and residential real estate and employee training to local business taxes and incentives.
- **First Stop Business Information Center**, 404-656-7061, 800-656-4558, www.sos.state.ga.us/firststop/default.htm; a great source for the information and contacts necessary for doing business in Georgia. Here you'll find county contacts (where you will be required to go for your business license), state regulatory requirements, and informative articles on running a business.
- **Internal Revenue Service**, 800-829-1040, www.irs.gov; offers information on applying for an employer tax ID number.
- **US Small Business Administration**, 800-827-5722, www.sba.gov; provides information, aid, counseling, and assistance for those interested in starting and running a small business.

CONGRATULATIONS! YOU'VE FOUND A PLACE TO LIVE AND NOW IT'S JUST A matter of settling in before you'll start to feel like a true Atlantan. The crucial tasks of setting up your utilities, hooking up cable TV, getting online, registering your car, and signing up to vote are now at hand. Perhaps you'd also like to subscribe to the local paper, find a family doctor, and get a library card. Details follow.

## USEFUL APPS

The widespread use of the internet and smart phones has revolutionized the way people live and communicate and can be an incredible resource for newcomers. Take some time to research applications (apps) that will help you settle in and get around. Apple users can search's Apple's App Store, http://store.apple.com. Android users can search Amazon.com, Google's app store Android Market or Google Play at https://play.google.com/store/apps, and Archos Appslib at http://appslib.com, among other choices. Blackberry users can try the Blackberry App Store at http://appworld.blackberry.com or Crackberry Store at http://shop.crackberry.com. People using a Windows phone can try Windows Marketplace for Mobile at www.windowsphone.com/marketplace. You can search each store based on a specific need or simply search "Atlanta" or your local city, and you'll find a melee of useful apps. Here's a short list of apps to get you started:

- **YP Local Search and Gas Prices** app: The Yellow Pages go-to mobile app. Search more than 18 million businesses in a flash and find the best gas prices near you as an added bonus.
- **MARTA** app: Navigating Atlanta's public transit system MARTA just got easier. Download this app, available for Apple and other smart phones, to help you find the right rail or bus line to get you where you need to go.

- **Atlanta City Guide** app by Trip Advisor: A guide to Atlanta's restaurants, shops and attractions to help you make the most of your free time.
- **Atlanta Checker Cab** app: A no brainer if you use taxis regularly; this app lets you schedule an Atlanta Checker cab from your phone.
- **Atlanta Traffic** app from Silver Key: Research current traffic conditions in Atlanta, including wrecks, congestion, construction, and other pertinent information. Receive alerts on traffic jams or other delays.
- **Museums in Atlanta** app: This app helps you navigate Atlanta's many museums so you can add some culture to your life.
- **Meetup** app: Find local clubs or connect with people based on similar interests. You can join a group or create one, and manage your account with your Meetup app.
- **Yahoo! Weather** app: Check the weather for the week or weekend, or receive alerts for Atlanta's notorious thunderstorms and tornados.
- **Yelp** app: Search local businesses, restaurants, shops, and more with ample reviews and ratings.
- **Nextdoor** app: Here's an interesting app (you can also check out the website at www.nextdoor.com) that uses social media/networking to connect neighbors. Check out local neighborhoods and meet some of your neighbors before you decide on a house.
- **Mint** app: Mint offers a number of useful financial tools for your house hunt and more, such as a mortgage payment calculator.
- **Trulia, Zillow, Realtor** apps: Check out detailed information on homes for sale, your neighborhood, home values, foreclosures, school systems, crime, and more.
- **Crimemapping** app: Receive alerts for crimes in your area or check out the crime rates for different neighborhoods before you purchase a home.
- **Redbox** app: Find the nearest Redbox kiosk so you can rent that movie you were dying to see.
- **ZocDoc** app: Shop and book local doctors online or with your smart phone. View doctors' ratings, education, history, and more with useful filters such as language, sex and insurance plan.

## UTILITIES

Houses and apartments in metro Atlanta are equipped either solely with electricity or with a combination of electricity and gas. Even if you have an electric stove, you may still have a gas-powered water heater, so check the basement appliances or ask your landlord about your apartment's utilities.

# ELECTRICITY

If you are renting a house or apartment, your leasing agent or landlord will tell you which power company serves your new home. Some rentals include electric power with the monthly rent, though most do not, so it will be up to you to make arrangements with the power company to have the electricity turned on in your name.

For electric service in the City of Atlanta and much of Fulton, DeKalb, Cobb, and Gwinnett counties (especially the portions closer in to the city), contact **Georgia Power**, 888-660-5890, www.georgiapower.com. A $30 establishment fee will appear on your first bill, and an additional deposit (not exceeding $150) may be required if you are a new Georgia Power customer. Power will be turned on within 24 hours. If the power is already on when you move in, they will begin billing you after you put the account in your name. You may want to consider Georgia Power's Budget Billing Plan to soften the periodic shocks of peak electric bills throughout the year. The plan averages the power bills over a year into 12 equal payments. The good news is that if your service totals less than the estimated average at the end of the year you'll receive a refund. But, if it is more, the difference will be added to the monthly bills for the next year. Either way, Budget Billing helps you avoid $200 electric bills during the summer when temperatures soar and the air conditioner will be in high use.

Depending on your address, you may be serviced by a different power company. If in doubt, call Georgia Power, and they will be able to tell you which company to call.

Parts of DeKalb County are served by **Snapping Shoals EMC**, 770-786-3484, www.ssemc.com. This company is one of the Electric Membership Corporations originally established to offer power to rural areas of the state. Today they serve 95,000 residential and commercial customers in metro Atlanta and seven other counties southeast of the city. Membership is $10, and a $40 connection fee is required.

**Walton EMC**, 770-267-2505, www.waltonemc.com, and **Jackson EMC**, 800-462-3691, www.jacksonemc.com, both cover some parts of Gwinnett County as well other northeast Georgia counties. Each requires a $5 membership fee and $20 connection fee to establish service. Additional deposits may also be required, though the EMCs will sometimes accept a letter of credit from your previous electric company in lieu of this.

In addition to Georgia Power and the EMCs, Gwinnett County also receives power from several other sources, including the following municipalities: **City of Norcross**, 770-448-2122, www.norcrossga.net; **City of Buford**, 770-945-6761, www.cityofbuford.com; **City of Lawrenceville**, 770-963-2414, www.lawrencevillega.org. Minimal connection fees and deposits may be required by each.

Georgia Power (see above for phone number) serves most of Cobb County, including the cities of Austell, Marietta, and Smyrna. In some northeast and western portions of Cobb County, though, service is provided by **Cobb EMC**, 770-429-2100, www.cobbemc.com. Cobb EMC requires an establishment fee and credit check before establishing service. For electric service in the **City of Acworth** call 770-974-5233, www.acworth.org; service requires a deposit as well as a non-refundable application fee.

**Sawnee EMC**, 770-887-2363, www.sawnee.com, provides power to a limited number of Fulton County residents in the Alpharetta and Roswell areas, though most homes in these suburbs are served by Georgia Power. Sawnee EMC also covers additional north Georgia counties, including Forsyth, Dawson, and most of Cherokee. A $5 membership fee and $25 connection fee is required to establish service. Additional deposits (not to exceed $200) may also be required.

## NATURAL GAS

The state's natural gas deregulation in the late 1990s may have given Atlanta residents increased options in gas providers, but it also led to some confusion. Whom should you use? What are the differences between the providers? Are the rates basically the same or are some of the providers significantly less expensive than the others? Because of increased competition, many of the state's gas providers offer incentives to new customers, so be sure to ask when calling around. You will also want to inquire about the rate "per therm" and any additional charges that may appear on your bill. Some gas companies require an initial deposit as well as a contract and connection fee; others don't. Do your research ahead of time to make sure you're choosing the company that will best meet your needs. A few of the largest gas companies serving metro Atlanta are:

- **Atlanta Gas Light**, 800-427-5463, www.atlantagaslight.com
- **Georgia Natural Gas**, 877-850-6200, www.onlygng.com
- **Scana**, 877-467-2262, www.scana.com
- **Southern Company Gas**, 404-506-5000, www.southerncompanygas.com

Keep in mind that if you are renting an apartment in a large complex, the owner may have contracted with one of the gas companies to serve all of the apartments in that community, so your choice will be made for you. Remember to bring this up with the leasing agent before you move in.

For additional information about gas deregulation and providers in the State of Georgia, contact the **Georgia Public Service Commission**, 404-656-4501, www.psc.state.ga.us. They can explain deregulation, offer you a checklist of what to look for in a natural gas provider, and assist you if you have complaints.

## TELEPHONE

"We're not in Kansas anymore." That's an apt statement for someone looking to establish a phone line in their home today. Where just a decade ago residents could only use a telecommunications company or maybe a less reliable internet phone service, today there are many more options.

To begin, more and more people are forgoing a home line altogether in favor of cell phones. However, for families who want a phone line in their home there are many options. They can contact one of the telecommunications companies that serve metro Atlanta. The largest is **AT&T,** and they can be reached at 800-CALL-ATT, or www.att.com. See below for a list of other providers. All of the phone companies offer numerous plans and services such as call waiting, caller ID, voicemail, and call forwarding. A connection fee of around $50 is required for new service and will be included on your first month's bill. A credit check determines whether or not you'll be charged an additional deposit.

Another option for phone service is the local cable company Comcast, which offers phone service with its cable packages. The benefit of this service is that long distance is usually included for much less than you would pay a telecommunications company. Also, in the battle for customers, more and more companies are offering great rates for bundled service plans that include cable, internet, and phone service. See the section on cable providers for Comcast's information.

A final option for home phone service is an internet phone provider. Internet phone service, or voice-over IP (VoIP), has grown significantly in popularity and reliability in the last decade and there are plenty of providers to choose from. Most offer plans for unlimited local and long distance calling, plus voicemail and other services for as little as $10 a month. Some popular providers are Vonage, www.vonage.com, 866-243-4357; Phone Power, 886-60-POWER, www.phone-power.com; or ITP, 888-ITP-1110, www.itpvoip.com.

Other phone providers:

- **Alltel Wireless**, 800-255-8351, www.alltelwireless.com
- **MCI**, 888-MCI-LOCAL, www.mci.com

## LONG DISTANCE SERVICE PROVIDERS

When choosing a long distance service provider, be sure to do your research by phone or online. Carriers frequently advertise low per-minute rates, but make sure you read the fine print. If you have to pay a higher monthly fee to get the lower per-minute rate, and you don't make many long distance calls, it may make more sense for you to use a prepaid calling card or your cell phone for long distance, omitting the need for a long distance provider entirely. The major long distance carriers in metro Atlanta are:

- **AT&T**, 800-CALL-ATT, www.att.com
- **MCI**, 800-444-3333, www.mci.com
- **Sprint**, 800-877-4646, www.sprint.com
- **Verizon**, 800-343-2092, www.verizonwireless.com

If you are ever the victim of an unfair business practice, such as "slamming" (switching your long distance service without your consent), contact the **Department of Consumer Affairs** through the governor's office, 404-651-8600, 800-869-1123, http://consumer.georgia.gov. For more information on how to protect your family from consumer fraud, see the **Consumer Protection** section below.

## AREA CODES

Area code 404 covers Atlanta city limits, as well as most of Fulton County, most of DeKalb County, and a portion in the north of Clayton County. Area code 770 covers the surrounding suburbs, such as those in Gwinnett County, Cobb County, and most communities outside the I-285 perimeter. Area code 678 covers Alpharetta as well as other suburbs north of the perimeter. It is also the area code assigned to most new cell phone numbers established in metro Atlanta.

When dialing from the 404 area to the 770 or 678 area—or vice versa—dial only 10 digits: the area code plus the number. Do not dial a one or a zero before the number or you will reach a recorded message. Some programmable dialing systems automatically insert a "1" before dialing 10-digit numbers, so you should make sure your equipment will dial correctly.

## CELL PHONES

The Atlanta Yellow Pages devotes several pages to cell phone providers in the metro area. Because of competition, it's now possible to find a great service plan, with extra features, for relatively small fees. Be sure to ask what services are available when calling to establish your cell phone service. Also, if you need a new phone, this can be a great time to upgrade as most providers offer free or discounted phones for new customers. A few companies to consider are:

- **AT&T Wireless,** 800-CALL-ATT, www.att.com
- **Metro PCS**, 888-863-8768, www.metropcs.com
- **Sprint PCS**, 888-8-METRO8, www.sprint.com
- **T-Mobile**, 800-T-Mobile, www.t-mobile.com
- **Verizon Wireless**, 800-922-0204, www.verizonwireless.com

## INTERNET SERVICE PROVIDERS (ISPS)

Internet service in metro Atlanta varies from modem dial-up over your home phone line to cable modems and DSL. Dial-up provides you with the most basic of online services, typically just standard internet access and email, and is slow (the trade-off, of course, is that it is generally much less expensive than cable and DSL).

Most people prefer high-speed internet access, called a digital subscriber line (DSL). DSL runs on copper wires like those used for telephone service, but on a separate line. Unlike dial-up, a DSL connection is always on, so logging onto the internet is nearly instantaneous. Cable internet access is available from your local cable television provider. And, like DSL, the cable modem is "always on." However, there is a possibility that your access speed could be decreased if your neighbors also have cable access. Before you sign up for a cable modem, make sure you determine what speed is guaranteed. Cable modem and DSL availability varies according to the building or area you in which you reside.

As mentioned previously, consider getting your ISP from a company that already provides your phone or cable. The main benefit of this strategy is that you receive one bill each month, and often at a much lower rate than if you'd purchased the services separately. Currently, both Comcast and AT&T offer bundling packages in the Atlanta area. To find out whether your neighborhood is included, contact the providers directly.

For a complete listing of internet service providers in your area, check the Yellow Pages under "Internet Access Providers," or visit www.consumersearch. com or www.ispcompared.com to find and compare local plans. Also, a relatively young business, www.allconnect.com, offers free advice on how to bundle services and save money. In the meantime, here are a few metro Atlanta providers who offer dial-up access, cable modem, and/or DSL:

- **Verizon**, 800-922-0204, www.verizonwireless.com
- **AT&T Wireless,** 800-CALL-ATT, www.att.com
- **Comcast**, 800-COMCAST, www.comcast.com
- **Earthlink**, 800-EARTHLINK, www.earthlink.net
- **Net Zero**, 866-810-8092, www.netzero.net

Also, while you are waiting for your internet to be connected, find access at any number of local hot spots in metro Atlanta. Most service businesses and some government facilities—mostly libraries and schools—offer free wireless service. Also, you can find free hot spots by ZIP code at www.openwifispots.com

## WATER

Drinking water for the metro Atlanta area comes from the north, in the Georgia Mountains, travels south via the Chattahoochee River to Lake Lanier, and then farther south to collecting and processing plants closer to the city. The city's water department is Georgia's fourth largest utility and the third largest water system in the Southeast. It serves nearly two million customers in the metro areas of Fulton and DeKalb counties and sells water to many of the nearby municipalities, which, in turn, bill their residents through their own local water departments.

City officials tout the fact that Atlanta's water continues to meet or exceed national water standards established by the US Environmental Protection

Agency (EPA). Recent water quality reports for Metro Atlanta can be accessed online through the **City of Atlanta Bureau of Water**, www.atlantawatershed. org. For additional information about Georgia's water standards, or about metro Atlanta's water supply, contact **Clean Water Atlanta**, 404-529-9211, www. cleanwateratlanta.org, or the **City of Atlanta Department of Watershed Management**, 404-330-6081, www.atlantawatershed.org.

In most rental situations, the landlord will include water in the monthly rent, but remember to ask about this upfront. If you are responsible for your own water, a deposit, as well as a copy of your lease and a picture ID, will most likely be required to initiate service. When the bill arrives, expect to be charged for water consumption, plus a sewer fee, which is based on a portion of the water consumption. Though local water services are a value by national standards, it is a good idea to ask about the consumption history of the home or apartment you are considering. Once you move in, be sure to check periodically for toilets that run excessively, faucets with pesky drips, and outside hose bibs that leak. A toilet with an unchecked faulty valve can send your water bill up to the level of your monthly car payment. Or for homeowners, leaks in the pipes that run from the house to the main line can go unnoticed and double your monthly bill.

To establish service or to get more information about water service within the city limits, contact the **City of Atlanta Bureau of Water**, 404-658-6500, www. atlantawatershed.org. For water service outside the city, in DeKalb County, contact the **DeKalb County Water and Sewer Division**, 770-621-7200, www.dekalbwatershed.com; in North Fulton County, contact the **Fulton County Water & Sewer Billing Division**, 404-612-6830, https://waterbilling.fultoncountyga.gov; in Cobb County contact the **Cobb County Water System**, 770-423-1000, http://water.cobbcountyga.gov; Gwinnett County residents should contact the **Gwinnett County Department of Public Utilities**, 678-376-6800, www.gwinnettcounty.com.

## GARBAGE AND RECYCLING

Trash collection and recycling differ from neighborhood to neighborhood in the metro Atlanta area. The following section should provide you with enough information to help you figure out what works in your community. And remember, when in doubt, ask your leasing agent, landlord, or real estate broker to answer any questions you have concerning your new home, including trash collection and recycling procedures.

### TRASH REMOVAL

Apartment dwellers usually deposit household trash in a designated common container, a dumpster, within the apartment complex. It is then management's responsibility to have the container emptied on a regular basis, usually once or twice a week. Garbage fees are generally included in your monthly rent. If you are renting a house or duplex or purchasing a home or condominium, however, you will need to know which provider to call to begin trash pickup.

In the **City of Atlanta**, wheeled "Herby Curby" trash receptacles made of heavy-duty plastic are available to residents, and curbside trash pickup is provided once a week. Ask your neighbor or call 404-330-6333 to find out what day trash is collected in your neighborhood. The charge for sanitation service within the city limits is about $450 per year and is billed to the property owner every July. Also, the city of Atlanta will take just about anything, including appliances and yard debris. Just call before you put the items on the curb.

If you are renting, you should not receive a bill for trash pick-up. If the bill is sent to you by mistake, notify your landlord immediately so that he can pay it before the August 15th deadline. Otherwise, you may find yourself without trash pickup. If you'd like more information, contact the **City of Atlanta Bureau of Solid Waste, Sanitation Department**, www.atlantaga.gov, 404-330-3333.

- Unincorporated **Fulton County**, 404-730-4000, http://georgia.gov/cities-counties/fulton-county, uses private garbage haulers for residential service. Haulers must be registered with the county and satisfy various insurance and Environmental Protection Division (EPD) requirements. A list of approved private companies, along with their designated areas of service, can be obtained by contacting the county directly.
- **DeKalb County**, 404-294-2900, www.co.dekalb.ga.us, provides curbside pickup twice a week for household garbage, and once a week pickup for yard debris. Homeowners provide 20- to 30-gallon cans, and no special bags are required for household trash. Yard debris should be in paper bags and not mixed in with anything else. The charge for sanitation service in DeKalb County is generally about $200 per year; billed quarterly to the homeowner.
- The **City of Decatur**, which is in DeKalb County, has a unique plan, which is now being used by several other metro Atlanta cities. Called the "Pay As You Throw" program, it offers residents an incentive to recycle. The program requires an annual fee, billed in the spring, for collection of household garbage and yard trimmings. Residents must then purchase special garbage bags from local supermarkets and hardware stores. Trash will only be collected if it is contained in these bags, which range in price from 15 cents to $1, depending on size. Under this system, residents who recycle more or have less trash to dispose of will pay less than households with larger garbage amounts simply because they use fewer bags. Contact the **City of Decatur Sanitation Department**, 404-377-5571, www.decatur-ga.com, for more information.
- The **City of Austell**, part of Cobb County, uses the same plan as Decatur, with bags costing $1.50 and $2.75, depending on size. No additional charge is levied on residents. Residential trash pickup is Monday. For more information, contact the **Austell Solid Waste Division**, 770-944-4300, www.austellga.gov.

- The **City of Marietta** provides residential garbage collection twice a week, and solid waste and recycling collection once a week. All residents must display a city decal on their trash cans, which is mailed to homeowners once they establish service. The city requires that trash cans not exceed 32 gallons, or the homeowner will be charged an additional $10. For more information, including trash collection dates, contact the **Marietta Public Works and Sanitation Division**, 770-794-5581, www.mariettaga.gov.
- In **Smyrna**, residential trash is collected, curbside, twice a week. Days vary depending on your address. The charge for sanitation service in Smyrna is about $19.50 per month, billed monthly to the homeowner. For additional information, contact the **Smyrna Sanitation Department**, 770-319-5338, www.smyrnacity.com.
- Unincorporated **Cobb County** uses private haulers with the same insurance and registration requirements as Fulton County. For a complete list call 770-528-2500, or go online to www.cobbcountyga.gov.
- **Gwinnett County** employs private companies for residential trash pickup. For a current list of haulers and their requirements, contact **Gwinnett Clean and Beautiful**, 770-822-5187, www.gwinnettcb.org.

## RECYCLING

Most cities and communities in metro Atlanta have established recycling programs, either in the form of curbside pick-up or drop-off sites. You simply have to call and request a bin, which is usually picked up with your trash.

If you live outside the city limits and would like to know more about recycling in your neighborhood, contact the appropriate county office:

- **Fulton County**, 404-730-8097, www.fultoncountyga.gov
- **DeKalb County**, 404-294-2900, www.co.dekalb.ga.us
- **Cobb County**, 770-528-1135, http://cobbcountyga.gov
- **Gwinnett County**, 770-822-5187, www.gwinnettcounty.com

Additionally, several volunteer organizations in Atlanta and the surrounding communities also provide useful information about recycling efforts, as well as the location of recycling centers. For details, contact the agency nearest you:

- **Gwinnett Clean and Beautiful**, 770-822-5187, www.gwinnettcounty.com
- **Keep Atlanta Beautiful**, 404-249-5853, www.keepatlantabeautiful.org
- **Keep Cobb Beautiful**, 770-528-1135, http://kcb.cobbcountyga.gov
- **Keep DeKalb Beautiful**, 404-371-2654, www.keepdekalbbeautiful.org
- **Keep Georgia Beautiful**, www.keepgeorgiabeautiful.org, provides a list of local offices, by county, throughout the metro Atlanta area
- **Keep Marietta Beautiful**, 770-794-5606, www.mariettaga.gov

- **Keep Roswell Beautiful**, 770-594-6451, www.keeproswellbeautiful.org
- **Keep Sandy Springs/North Fulton Beautiful**, 770-551-7766, www.keepnorthfultonbeautiful.org
- **Keep Smyrna Beautiful**, 770-431-2863, www.smyrnacity.com
- **Keep South Fulton Beautiful**, 770-969-9324, www.ksfb.info

If you wish to dispose of household recyclables on your own, you can find a comprehensive listing of local recycling centers online at **Earth 911**, www.earth911.com. Just enter your ZIP code and you'll be directed to a page that lists centers for recycling paper, plastic, scrap metal, and more in your neighborhood. You can also find listings in the **Atlanta Yellow Pages**, under **Recycling Centers**.

## CONSUMER PROTECTION—UTILITIES COMPLAINTS

With the recent deregulation of local gas companies, various long distance providers vying for your business, and issues over what fees are possible for electric companies to charge when computing monthly billing, it is little wonder consumers are confused about their rights. If you have any questions or feel your rights as a consumer have been violated, the following consumer protection organizations should be able to help:

- If you have questions or complaints about your utility services and believe that your problems have gone unanswered by the individual company providers, contact the **Georgia Governor's Office of Consumer Affairs**, 404-651-8600, 800-869-1123, http://consumer.georgia.gov, or the **Office of the Attorney General of Georgia**, 404-656-3300, http://law.ga.gov. Both offices are responsible for protecting the rights of Georgia consumers and enforcing the state's consumer protection laws, including Georgia's Fair Business Practices Act.
- The **Georgia Public Service Commission** (**GPSC**), 404-656-4501, 800-282-5813, www.psc.state.ga.us, is another excellent source of information and assistance. As the official regulatory agency for utilities operating in Georgia, their job is to ensure that consumers receive safe, reliable and reasonably priced utility services from "financially viable and technically competent companies." The GPSC provides helpful tips for utilities customers, answers to frequently asked questions, and even an online link where consumers can file their complaints.
- For those seeking a more public forum for consumer complaints, WSB-TV and radio offers Georgia's best known and respected consumer rights guru, **Clark Howard**. His regular show airs complaints by consumers and offers connections between those with problems and those with the answers. Howard also writes a weekly column for the *Atlanta Journal-Constitution* newspaper and maintains a **Consumer Action Center** at 404-892-8227. Howard's persistence on behalf of consumers has prompted many to say, "If Clark can't help you, nobody can!"

## DRIVING IN GEORGIA

### DRIVER'S LICENSES, AUTOMOBILE REGISTRATION, AND STATE IDS

#### DRIVER'S LICENSES

If you have an out-of-state driver's license, Georgia law requires that you obtain a Georgia driver's license within 30 days. In order to meet new federal requirements under the Real ID Act, Georgia recently increased the number of required documents to get a driver's license. To purchase your license, bring your previous driver's license, your birth certificate or passport, your social security card and two proofs of Georgia residency (such as a utility bill or copy of your lease). You can purchase a 5-year license for $20 or an 8-year for $32. If your name is different than the one on your previous driver's license or ID, you will also be required to show official documentation of the name change (e.g., your marriage license or divorce papers). As far as testing requirements, new residents over 18 with a valid out-of-state license need only pass an eye exam to exchange the out-of-state license for a Georgia license. New residents under 18, or those whose out-of-state license has expired, must also pass the written road rules and sign tests, as well as the driving test.

For additional information regarding requirements and exam times, as well as a full listing of local exam offices, contact the **Department of Driver Services**, 678-413-8400, www.dds.ga.gov. Following is a short list of examination stations to get you started:

- **Atlanta**, 445 Capital Ave SE; open Monday–Friday, 7:30 a.m. to 6:30 p.m., Saturday 7:30 a.m. to 12 noon
- **Decatur**, 2801 Candler Rd, Ste 208; open Tuesday–Friday, 8 a.m. to 4:30 p.m., Saturday 7:30 a.m. to 12 noon
- **Sandy Springs**, 8610 Roswell Rd; open Tuesday–Friday, 7:30 a.m. to 6:30 p.m., Saturday 7:30 a.m. to 12 noon
- **Marietta**, 2800 Canton Rd, Piedmont Village Shopping Center; open Tuesday–Friday, 7:30 a.m. to 6:30 p.m., Saturday 7:30 a.m. to 12 noon
- **Lawrenceville**, 310 Hurricane Shoals Rd; open Tuesday–Saturday, 9 a.m. to 5 p.m., Saturday 7:30 a.m. to 12 noon

#### STATE IDS

State IDs can be obtained at any state driver's license exam office, with proof of residency. The cost is $20 for 5 years or $32 for 8 years. For more information visit any of the office locations listed above, go online to www.dds.ga.gov, or call 678-413-8400.

## AUTOMOBILE REGISTRATION

If you own a car, you must purchase Georgia tags within 30 days of establishing residency. You will need to bring your valid insurance card to register your car in Georgia. You are required by law to possess liability coverage.

In addition, you will also need your car's title, the name and address of lienholder or copy of lease agreement, current tag registration, vehicle mileage reading, and a valid, original certificate of emission (Fulton, DeKalb, Cobb, and Gwinnett counties require all gas-burning vehicles be checked for emission standards yearly). Have your car inspected at a state-designated inspection site (many gas stations provide this service); the cost is generally around $20.

Tag registration costs $20, and, in addition, you will also have to pay a 7% tax on the value of your vehicle. There are some exceptions to the car tax, such as if the car was made before 1985 or if you are a disabled veteran, you are exempt from paying the tax. To learn more about the car tax and calculate what how much you'll owe, visit www.newtitletax.com. Currently, new Georgia residents must pay 50% of the tax within 30 days of moving here and the remaining 50% within the next 12 months. The following County Tax Commissioner Tag Offices handle license tags and car registration:

- **Fulton County**, 404-730-4000, www.fultoncountytaxes.org; tag offices are open Monday–Friday. Office hours vary by location:
  - 141 Pryor St, Atlanta
  - 677 Fairburn Rd, Atlanta
  - 7741 Roswell Rd, NE, Atlanta
  - 5600 Stonewall Tell Rd, Atlanta
  - 2841 Greenbriar Pkwy, SW, Ste 106
  - 6500 Vernon Woods Dr, Sandy Springs
  - 3155 Royal Dr, Alpharetta
- **DeKalb County**, 404-298-4000, www.co.dekalb.ga.us/taxcommissioner; tag offices are open 8 a.m. to 4:30 p.m., Monday–Friday:
  - 1358 Dresden Dr, Atlanta
  - 4380 Memorial Dr, Decatur
  - 2389 Wesley Chapel Rd, Decatur
- **Cobb County**, 770-528-TAGS, www.cobbtax.org; tag offices are open 8:30 a.m. to 5 p.m., Monday–Friday:
  - 736 Whitlock Ave, Marietta
  - 700 South Cobb Dr, Marietta
  - 4400 Lower Roswell Rd, Marietta
  - 2930 Canton Hwy, Marietta
  - 4700 Austell Rd, Austell
  - 3858 Kemp Ridge Rd, Acworth

- **Gwinnett County**, 770-822-8818, https://ssl.gwinnetttaxcommissioner.com/; tag offices are open 8 a.m. to 6 p.m., Monday–Friday:
  - 75 Langley Drive, Lawrenceville
  - 750 South Perry, Lawrenceville
  - 5030 Georgia Belle Ct, Norcross
  - 6135 Peachtree Pkwy, Ste 201b, Norcross
  - 2845 Lenora Church Rd, Snellville
  - 2735 Mall of Georgia Blvd, Buford

For additional information about tag registration in metro Atlanta, or to find tag offices in counties other than the ones listed here, visit the **Department of Driver Services** website at www.dds.ga.gov.

## AUTOMOBILE SAFETY

Word to the wise on Georgia's drunk driving laws: The attitude here is "zero tolerance" for drunk driving. Local DUI limits are .04 for commercial drivers and .08 for non-commercial. If you are under the age of 21, .02 will get you arrested.

Georgia also has very strict seatbelt laws: It is permissible for an officer to stop a vehicle and cite the driver for a seatbelt violation only. Anyone in the front seat of a car must wear a seatbelt. Anyone 18 or younger in the front or back seat must wear a seatbelt. By definition, Georgia law means a shoulder strap and lap belt when the word seatbelt is used. Children age 7 and under must ride in a child safety-restraining seat suitable for their height, which must be installed according to manufacturer's recommendations. It is not permitted for an adult to hold a child or restrain both with one belt. For tips on properly installing car seats, or to stay up-to-date on child safety laws in Georgia, check www.safekids.org.

## AUTOMOBILE INSURANCE

Georgia is a tort state, which means that drivers here are financially responsible for any property damage and personal injury they cause during an auto accident. Therefore, Georgia drivers are legally required to carry automobile insurance— the minimum being liability coverage of 25/50/25. This means that, in the event of an accident, you're covered for $25,000 per person for injuries to the other party, up to $50,000 for all, and $25,000 for damage caused to the other party's property. However, keep in mind that these are only minimums, and most insurance agents will recommend higher levels of protection. Additionally, if your car is financed, your lienholder will most likely require that you carry comprehensive insurance coverage.

In addition to liability and comprehensive policies, most Georgia insurance companies also offer additional coverages, such as collision, medical, and uninsured motorist coverage. The uninsured motorist coverage, in particular, is worth considering, as it is designed to help cover the cost of your injuries and property damage should you be involved in an accident with an uninsured or underinsured driver.

For additional information on auto insurance within Georgia, contact the **Georgia Insurance Commission**, 404-656-2070, www.inscomm.state.ga.us.

The **Atlanta Yellow Pages** lists about 30 pages of insurance brokers and companies operating throughout the metro Atlanta area. All major national companies are represented, so chances are, if you already have auto insurance with a major provider, your transition to Atlanta will require only a phone call to your present company.

If you prefer to look up insurance companies and information online, the key words "Georgia Auto Insurance" bring up hundreds of websites, many offering free quotes, policy comparison, and state insurance information. You can also check **Insure.com**, www.insure.com, or **InsWeb**, www.insweb.com, for similar details. Direct site addresses for a few auto insurance companies are:

- **Allstate**, www.allstate.com
- **Geico**, www.geico.com
- **Liberty Mutual**, www.libertymutual.com
- **Progressive**, www.progressive.com
- **State Farm**, www.statefarm.com

## PURCHASING AN AUTOMOBILE

Metro Atlanta has a car dealer for almost any type of new or used vehicle you can imagine. The Atlanta Yellow Pages, in fact, offers 13 pages of dealership listings. The major dealerships run spots on local TV stations and advertise in all the Atlanta newspapers. Used cars are generally advertised in classified sections, and there are also several local magazines devoted to cars for sale by owners and dealers. You can find these in most bookstores, grocery stores, and convenience stores. There are also numerous ways to search for cars online either via Craigslist, atlanta.craigslist.org; Google; CarMax; www.carmax.com; or even eBay.

The experience of purchasing a car is both exciting and a hassle, and always a big expense. It pays to conduct research beforehand to determine the worth of the car you're thinking of purchasing. For used cars, check out the Kelley Blue Book site at www.kbb.com. To research dealer invoice prices for new cars, check www.autovantage.com. AAA offers a walk-in vehicle pricing report service to members and non-members for a nominal fee. Also, *Consumer Reports* offers a low-cost auto pricing information service, available via their website: www.consumerreports.org.

If you are looking at used cars, check out the **US Department of Transportation's Auto Safety Hotline**, 888-327-4236, www.safercar.gov, to get information about vehicle defects and recalls.

## CONSUMER PROTECTION—LEMON LAW

In 1990, Georgia state legislators passed the **Motor Vehicle Warranty Rights Act**, thereby establishing one of the country's most comprehensive "lemon laws." Georgia's law recognizes and states that the purchase of a new vehicle is a major one for consumers, and that buying a defective vehicle creates undue hardship on the consumer and could even be the cause of injury or death. As a result, automobile manufacturers are now legally required to repair any and all defects that affect the use, value, or safety of the vehicles they sell within the first 12 months or 12,000 miles (whichever comes first).

Georgia's lemon law also provides an easy complaint process for consumers who experience problems with newly purchased or leased vehicles that are registered in the state. If you're having continuous, recurring problems with your new car, and the automobile manufacturer fails to fix it after a "reasonable" number of repair attempts, you may request a state arbitration hearing. There, a panel of arbitrators will hear your complaint and decide whether or not you are eligible for a replacement vehicle or a full refund of the purchase price.

To find out more about the lemon law or to file a complaint, contact the **Georgia Governor's Office of Consumer Affairs**, 404-651-8600, 800-869-1123, http://consumer.georgia.gov.

# PARKING

Parking is generally not much of a problem in the suburbs that comprise most of the Atlanta metropolitan area. Almost anywhere you drive your car, you will have little trouble finding a place to park, with "difficult parking" defined as a one- or two-block walk to a restaurant. The true exceptions, however, are major malls on weekends, the airport, larger venues like **Aaron's Amphitheatre Lakewood,** and most places downtown. (The ever-popular alternative to driving is taking MARTA [see **Transportation** chapter]. A MARTA train will take you to all the downtown sports venues, and will whisk you straight to the airport. MARTA even has a stop at Lenox Square mall, if you want to go shopping without your car.) To avoid driving endlessly around an enormous mall parking lot, make your mall visits on weekday evenings when crowds are smaller.

## PARKING GARAGES AND LOTS

Suburban office complexes always have on-site parking for employees, most at no charge. If you work downtown, however, you will most likely be responsible for finding a space on your own. Many businesses have arrangements with parking garages close to the office. This is usually something discussed during the interview phase of a job search, since you may have to pay for your own parking. If you do have to pay, remember that you do have a few options. You can pay by the day and try to park in the least expensive lots whenever possible, or you can stick with the lot with which you feel most comfortable and buy a monthly parking pass. Most lots charge anywhere from $5 to $10 per day, but if a convention is in town and lots are filling up, the rates can go as high as $20 per day. With a monthly parking pass, your rate is secured regardless of what event may be taking place. For monthly parking passes, the best lots charge anywhere from $75 to $150. Parking on the periphery and walking a few blocks may get you the best deal—both financially and healthwise.

For downtown parking locations call a couple of the larger lot management companies. **AAA Parking**, 404-525-5959, www.aaaparkingonline.com; and **Central Parking System** at 404-525-9014, www.parking.com, are two of the bigger ones. Additional listings can be found in the Atlanta Yellow Pages under "Parking Facilities."

To avoid the hassle of finding parking downtown, remember that riding MARTA alleviates any need for parking worries. It's also much less expensive than paying for downtown parking. You can ride the rails (or the buses) one-way for a mere $2.50. MARTA also offers a monthly pass for $95 (or $68 for students), which offers unlimited access to the trains and buses for one low price. Schedules and routes for MARTA are available by calling 404-848-4711 or online at www.itsmarta.com. Park & Ride lots are strategically located all along the MARTA routes, and some lots even offer overnight parking for those headed to the airport. The transit system moves over 300,000 passengers daily and provides rail and interconnecting bus service throughout the city. If you are going to a sporting event, any downtown festival or concert, or to the airport, MARTA is the best choice. See **Transportation** for more information on MARTA.

## TOWED OR STOLEN AUTOMOBILES

Regardless of where you park in metro Atlanta, it pays to be aware of "No Parking" zones—even in parking lots. If you do park illegally and end up with a parking ticket you can expect to pay $25 to $50 for parking in a restricted area, at least $10 for overtime parking, and $60 to $100 for parking in a handicapped area. Your ticket will detail the citation and direct you on how to pay. Most fines are paid at 104 Trinity Street, Atlanta; call 404-658-6935 for more information.

Impound areas are clearly posted, so pay attention to the signs. If you are unlucky enough to have your car towed in the city due to a parking violation, call the **Atlanta Police Department, Impounded Vehicle Division**, 404-853-4330, for the location of the lot holding your vehicle. In areas outside the city limits, a sign will be posted on site identifying the towing company and a phone number to call. An impounded vehicle can cost as much as $200, and impound lots do not take checks. When you go to retrieve your car, make sure you have cash or credit card for the entire amount due, a photo ID, and proof that the vehicle is yours. A title, insurance policy, or registration receipt will suffice.

If it turns out your car has been **stolen**, rather than towed, you should call the police immediately. They will need your license and tag numbers, the car's year, make, model and color, and the vehicle's identification number. Most of this information can be found on your car title or insurance policy.

Unfortunately, many stolen cars end up stripped and sold for parts, so to have any hope of getting any of your "parts" back, you should mark your car's accessories in some way. For instance, if your car has a stereo, radar detector, or car phone, it's a good idea to write your driver's license number on them.

## BROADCAST AND PRINT MEDIA

### TELEVISION

Atlanta is the home of TBS, as well as cable stations CNN, AMC, TNT, and the Cartoon Network. Reception here without cable or satellite is pretty good for most of the major networks and the public broadcasting channels. However, if you are using an analog TV set, you'll need to purchase a digital-to-analog converter, due to the national analog switch-off that occurred in June 2009. For more information on the change from analog to digital TV, visit www.dtv.gov. Here is a list of Atlanta's major television stations:

### BROADCAST CHANNELS

| Channel 2 | WSB | **ABC**; www.wsbtv.com |
|---|---|---|
| Channel 5 | WAGA | **Fox**; www.fox5atlanta.com |
| Channel 8 | WGTV | **PBS (Georgia Public Television)**; www.gpb.org/gptv |
| Channel 11 | WXIA | **NBC**; www.11alive.com |
| Channel 14 | WPXA | **Ion**; www.iontelevision |
| Channel 17 | WPCH | **Peachtree TV**; www.tbs17.com |
| Channel 30 | WPBA | **PBS (Atlanta Public Television)**; www.wpba.org |
| Channel 34 | WUVG | **Univision**; www.univision.com |
| Channel 36 | WATL | **MyATLTV**; www.myatltv.com |
| Channel 46 | WGCL | **CBS**; www.wgcltv.com |
| Channel 57 | WATC | **Carolina Christian Broadcasting,** www.watc.tv |
| Channel 63 | WHSG | **Trinity Broadcasting Network**; www.tbn.com |
| Channel 69 | CW69 | **The CW**; http://cwatlantatv.com |

## CABLE TELEVISION

Cable TV service throughout all metro Atlanta counties is primarily offered by the following cable service providers. Which cable company serves you will depend on your address. For more information, or to find out which companies offer service in your neighborhood, contact the following:

- **Charter Communications**, 770-333-6400, www.charter.com, **AT&T**, 800-CALL-ATT, www.att.com, or **Comcast Cable**, 800-COMCAST, www.comcast. com; also offers internet service/bundling

## RADIO

Metro Atlanta offers diverse, high-quality radio programming. Here, you'll find everything from jazz to top 40, hard rock to Christian contemporary. In addition, the college stations in the area provide an eclectic mix of rap, alternative, ethnic, and spoken shows. However, if some of the stations listed below are no longer operating, don't be too surprised. The radio industry is highly competitive, meaning stations regularly change owners and formats every few years; below is a list of the city's top and longest standing stations. This is only a sample—the metro area boasts 75 stations—so for a full list, visit Radio Locator, www.radio-locator.com or www.ontheradio.net/metro/atlanta_ga.aspx.

Also, more and more people are forgoing regular radio and choosing to listen to music online or through their smart phones. Pandora Internet Radio, www.pandora.com, and Spotify, www.spotify.com, are two popular choices that offer tailor-made stations with few to no commercials. You can listen for free with some limitations or subscribe at low rates for broader listening options.

### FM DIAL

| | | |
|------|---------|------|
| 88.5 | WRAS | Georgia State University radio; diverse format, www2.gsu.edu |
| 89.3 | WRFG | blues, jazz, www.wrfg.org |
| 90.1 | WABE | Public Broadcasting Atlanta and NPR, www.wabe.org |
| 91.1 | WREK | Georgia Tech University radio; eclectic, www.wrek.org |
| 91.9 | WCLK | Clark Atlanta college radio; jazz, soul, www.wclk.com |
| 92.9 | WZGC | Dave FM; classic and current rock hits, www.929dave.fm |
| 94.1 | WSTR | Star 94; top 40, www.star94.com |
| 94.9 | WUBL | The Bull; country, www.bullatlanta.com |
| 95.5 | WSBB-FM | News Talk WSB 750/95.5 Radio; Atlanta's most popular talk radio station, www.wsbradio.com |
| 96.1 | WKLS | Power 96.1; top 40 hits, www.power961.com |

| 97.1 | WSVR | 97.1 The River; classic hits from the 70s and 80s, http://971theriver. com |
| 98.5 | WSB-FM | soft rock/adult contemporary, http://b985.com |
| 99.7 | WWWQ | Q100; top 40 hits, www.allthehitsq100.com |
| 100.5 | WNNX | ROCK 100.5; www.atlantasrockstation |
| 101.5 | WKHX | Kicks,;country hits, www.wkhx.com |
| 103.3 | WVEE | V-103—The People's Station; urban/R&B, www.v-103.com |
| 104.1 | WALR | Kiss 104.1; urban adult contemporary, www.kiss1041fm.com |
| 104.7 | WFSH | The Fish; contemporary Christian, www.thefishatlanta.com |

## AM DIAL

| 590 | WDWD | Radio Disney, http://radio.disney.go.com |
| 610 | WPLO | Hispanic, www.radiomex610atlanta.com |
| 640 | WGST | news and talk, www.wgst.com |
| 680 | WCNN | news, www.680thefan.com |
| 750 | WSB | talk radio, sports, Braves games, www.wsbradio.com |
| 790 | WQXI | sports talk, www790thezone.com |
| 970 | WNIV | Christian talk, www.wniv.com |

## NEWSPAPERS & MAGAZINES

Metro Atlanta is home to a wide variety of newspapers and periodicals. From Atlanta business, to Atlanta fashion, to neighborhood news and information, if you have a specific interest, there's sure to be a paper or magazine that covers it. Most of the magazines can be found at newsstands and bookstores throughout the city, and many of the papers can be picked up for free at area restaurants, or you can have them delivered straight to your door. For more information, call the numbers or visit the websites listed below:

## NEWSPAPERS

- *Alpharetta-Roswell Revue and News*, 319 N Main St, Alpharetta, 770-442-3278, www.northfulton.com; covers news and local interest for these two communities
- *Atlanta Intown*, 1280 W Peachtree St, Ste 220, Atlanta, 404-586-0002, www. atlantaintown.com; monthly newspaper offering community-focused news and real estate information to Atlanta's intown neighborhoods
- *Atlanta Daily World*, 145 Auburn Ave, Atlanta, 404-659-1110, www.atlantadailyworld.com; covers African-American news and entertainment

- **Atlanta Jewish Times**, 8300 Dunwoody Pl, Hightower Ct, 1, Ste 150, Atlanta, 404-564-4550, www.atlantajewishtimes.com; covers news of interest to Atlanta's Jewish community
- **The Atlanta Journal-Constitution**, 223 Perimeter Center Parkway, Dunwoody, 404-526-5151, www.ajc.com; metro Atlanta's main daily newspaper
- **Creative Loafing**, 750 Willoughby Way, Atlanta, 404-688-5623, www.creativeloafing.com; Atlanta's free weekly paper, highlighting news, events, and entertainment throughout the city
- **Gwinnett Daily Post**, 166 Highway 20 NE, Lawrenceville, 770-963-9205, www.gwinnettdailypost.com; provides news and local interest stories for and about Gwinnett County
- **Marietta Daily Journal/Neighbor Newspapers**, 580 Fairground St SE, Marietta, 770-428-9411, www.mdjonline.com; a main newspaper serving Marietta and Cobb County. Also offers several smaller, neighborhood editions specializing in local interest news and events.
- **The GA Voice—LGBT News**—1904 Monroe Dr NE, Atlanta, 404-815-6941, www.gavoice.com; metro Atlanta's premier gay and lesbian newspaper
- **Neighbor Newspapers,** 580 S. Fairground St., Marietta, 770-428-9411, www.neighbornewspapers.com; operated by the same company as the MDJ, you'll find Neighbor papers all over metro Atlanta offering local news with a focus on feel-good stories.

For a more complete listing of newspapers throughout the state of Georgia, check out the www.allyoucanread.com/atlanta-newspaper-ga or search Google or Wikipedia.

## MAGAZINES

- **Atlanta Magazine**, 260 Peachtree St, Ste 300, Atlanta, 404-527-5500, www.atlantamagazine.com; monthly publication with features on food, entertainment, arts, and travel, quarterly "Best in Atlanta" editions with reviews of schools, restaurants, medical offices, and more
- **Atlanta Parent**, 2346 Perimeter Park Dr, Chamblee, 770-454-7599, www.atlantaparent.com; family publication featuring resources and information for parents
- **Atlanta Tribune**, 875 Old Roswell Rd, Roswell, 770-587-0501, www.atlantatribune.com; monthly newsmagazine for metro Atlanta's African-American community
- **Atlanta Wine Report**, 2200 Parklake Dr, Atlanta, 678-382-0384, www.winereportonline.com; bi-monthly magazine for metro Atlanta wine enthusiasts
- **Georgia Trend**, 5880 Live Oak Pkwy, Norcross, 770-931-9410, www.georgiatrend.com; monthly publication covering Georgia news, business, and politics
- **Jezebel Magazine,** 3535 Piedmont Rd NE, #1200, Atlanta, 404-870-0123, www.jezebel.com

- *Modern Bridge Atlanta Magazine,* 3500 Piedmont Rd NE, Ste 505, Atlanta, 404-926-3512

## OFFICIAL DOCUMENTS

### VOTER REGISTRATION

You must register to vote in the county of your residence at least 30 days prior to an election. You can register either by mail or in person. You can register to vote at most local banks, colleges, city halls, and county offices. Also, in accordance with the motor voter law, you can register to vote when you obtain or renew your driver's license (see above section for locations). County voter registration offices can be accessed at the following locations:

- **Fulton County**: Control Office, 141 Pryor St, Ste 4085, Atlanta, 404-730-7072; South Annex, 5600 Stonewall Tell Rd, Room 218, College Park, 770-306-3050; North Annex, 7741 Roswell Rd NE, Room 222, Atlanta, 770-551-7675
- **DeKalb County**: 4380 Memorial Dr, Ste 300, Decatur, 404-298-4020
- **Cobb County**: 730 Whitlock Ave, Ste 400, Marietta, 770-528-2581
- **Gwinnett County**: 455 Grayson Hwy, Ste 200, Lawrenceville, 770-822-8787

For additional information about voter registration in Georgia or to find registrar offices in counties other than the ones listed above, contact the **Georgia Secretary of State, Elections Division**, 404-656-2871, 888-265-1115, www.sos.state. ga.us/elections.

If you'd like more information about local and national party affiliations, contact:

- **The Democratic Party of Georgia**, 678-278-2008, www.georgiademocrat.org
- **The Georgia Green Party**, 404-806-0480, www.georgiagreenparty.org
- **The League of Women Voters (Georgia)**, State Office, 678-547-0755, www. lwvga.org; Fulton County/Atlanta, 404-577-8683; DeKalb County, 404-321-0913; Cobb County/Marietta, 770-592-0625
- **The Libertarian Party of Georgia**, 404-888-9468, www.lpgeorgia.com
- **The Republican Party of Georgia**, 404-257-5559, www.gagop.org

### LIBRARY CARDS

Atlanta's central library is located downtown at One Margaret Mitchell Square. Other library branch addresses are listed in the **Neighborhoods** chapter of this book. All libraries within each county are interconnected, so if you check out a book at one location, you can return it to another branch in the same county. If you are looking for more obscure materials that public libraries may not have, check the area's university libraries. While you may not be able to obtain check-out privileges, you can still peruse materials on site. Also, take advantage of your library's online resources, where you can easily search for and reserve the media you need.

To obtain a library card in **Fulton County**, you'll need to bring one piece of identification such as a driver's license, and a recent piece of mail or a bill showing your address in Fulton County. For a library card in **DeKalb**, **Cobb**, and **Gwinnett Counties**, you need only bring one recent proof of residence in your particular county. A driver's license, rent receipt, utility bill, check, or postmarked piece of mail with your name and current address will do.

For more information on area libraries, see the **Literary Life** section in the **Cultural Life** chapter.

## PASSPORTS

If you're interested in getting a passport or renewing an old one, you have several options in metro Atlanta. Passport applications can be found online, as well as in most local post offices, libraries, courts, and county offices.

Depending on your needs, you may apply for a passport either in person or through the mail. However, you must apply for your passport in person if you are applying for the first time, your previous passport was lost or damaged, your previous passport was issued over 15 years ago and has expired, your name is different than it was on your last passport and you don't have legal proof of the change, or you are between the ages of 14 and 17 years old. Otherwise, you may apply through the mail. Either way, you should allow at least six weeks for processing.

Passport application forms are available through the **US Department of State**, **National Passport Information Center**, http://travel.state.gov/passport/passport_1738.html, or call them at 877-487-2778, TDD 888-874-7793, Monday–Friday, 8 a.m. to 8 p.m. Eastern Time. (General travel information and advisories are available at the Bureau of Consular Affairs' home page, www.travel.state.gov.) This government site provides answers to many questions re the passport application process, as well as pages of additional, helpful information—including a detailed listing of passport acceptance facilities throughout metro Atlanta.

When you apply for your passport, keep in mind you'll need not only to fill out the application form but also to provide the following: your social security number, proof of US citizenship and identity, and two passport photos. Acceptable documents proving your citizenship include a previous passport, certified birth certificate, consular report of birth abroad, naturalization certificate, or certificate of citizenship. Acceptable documents proving your identity include a previous passport, naturalization certificate, certificate of citizenship, or a current and valid ID (driver's license, state ID, military ID). Passport photos, two identical 2" x 2" photos, either black and white or color, are easily obtained at many local photo shops, AAA offices, or FedEx Office locations.

A new passport costs $165 for those over 16 years old and $105 for those under 16; renewals are $140. Allow six weeks for your completed passport to be processed. For expedited service, add $60; you can expect to receive your passport in two weeks. New applications for passports use form DS-11, and for minors under age 14 an additional consent form, DS-3053, is required. You will find the necessary forms at many post offices and libraries, at county court offices, or online at the State Bureau of Consular Affairs. You must appear in person to get your first passport; this includes minors. Most passport acceptance facilities accept payment for passport fees in the forms of check, money order, or bank draft made payable to the Department of State. (The facility's processing fees may be payable by debit or credit card.)

If you are in a hurry, Google "quick passport" and you'll find numerous companies that will expedite the process for you—some in just a week—but at a price. Expect to pay upwards of $300 when all the same-day shipping and other fees add up.

## FINDING A HEALTH CARE PROVIDER

If you have health insurance through one of the many HMO companies operating in Georgia, then choosing a physician is easy. Simply pick a doctor from your insurer's list of providers, or visit their website and access the information there. If you do not use an HMO provider, visit your insurance company's website for a list of affiliated doctors. You can also check out the nearly 100 pages of physician listings in the Atlanta Yellow Pages or consider one of Atlanta's favorite online directories, www.Kudzu.com, where businesses, including doctor's offices, are listed and reviewed by customers who have been there.

Also, a few of the many referral services that cover the Atlanta area are:

- **Atlanta Medical Center Physician Referral**, 404-265-3627, www.atlantamedcenter.com
- **Children's Healthcare of Atlanta**, 404-250-KIDS, www.choa.org
- **Emory Health Connection**, 404-778-7777, www.emoryhealthcare.org
- **Georgia Academy of Family Physicians**, 800-392-3841, www.gafp.org
- **Millennium Alternative Healthcare**, 770-390-0012, www.millennium-healthcare.com

Once you've narrowed your list of prospective physicians, you may want to research them further by utilizing the following online resources:

- **American Board of Medical Specialties**, 847-491-9091, www.abms.org; contact to see if your specialist is certified by the national board
- **Healthgrades**, 303-716-0041, www.healthgrades.com; purchase a complete report on your physician or healthcare facility for $10

- Georgia's **Composite State Board of Medical Examiners**, 404-656-3913, http://medicalboard.georgia.gov; verify that your physician is licensed to practice medicine and check for recent disciplinary actions. The CSBME is also the office to contact if you encounter problems with your healthcare provider or want to file a complaint.

## PETS

It is easy to be a dog or cat owner in metro Atlanta. Most apartment complexes and landlords allow for pets, though they may have size or weight limitations, and they will most definitely charge an additional pet deposit. Landlords that do not allow pets will usually state that restriction in their classified ads and on the "for rent" signs in front of the rental property. One of the great things about owning pets in metro Atlanta is that many of the homes here (both intown and in the suburbs) are set on nice-sized lots, offering plenty of outdoor space for pets.

There are few restrictions for pet owners in Atlanta, and the laws that are on the books aren't always strictly enforced. The main laws regarding pet ownership are highlighted below, though, of course, they may not be relevant to all counties in the metro area.

Also, it's important to keep in mind that this section deals primarily with laws and information pertaining to dogs and cats. If the pet you own, or are considering owning, is of the more exotic variety, you will definitely want to check in with the animal services department of the county in which you reside, as they will most likely have specific ordinances pertaining to the types of pets that are allowed and how they must be kept.

## LICENSING

The City of Atlanta and many of its surrounding counties require dogs and cats to be licensed. A rabies vaccination certificate from a vet or shelter must be presented, along with the appropriate license fee, upon application. In most cases, pet owners can apply by mail—ask the vet or shelter for an application, or download the application online from your local licensing agency's website. For more information on obtaining a pet license tag, contact the pet licensing office in your county:

- **Cherokee County Marshal's Office**, Animal Control, 678-493-6200, www.cherokeega.com
- **Cobb County Animal Control**, 770-499-4136, http://animalcontrol.cobbcountyga.gov/
- **DeKalb County Animal Control**, 404-294-2996, http://dekalbcountyanimalservices.com
- **Fulton County Animal Services**, 404-794-0358, www.bhvf.org

- **Gwinnett Animal Welfare and Enforcement**, 770-339-3200, www.gwin-nettcounty.com

## LEASH LAWS

All metro Atlanta counties have "running at large" ordinances in place, prohibiting pet owners from letting their dogs run loose. It is strongly recommended that dogs remain on-leash anytime they are out of their yards, particularly if you have them out in the traffic-heavy, retail areas around town. However, there is some leniency with this law, as well-behaved dogs that respond to voice commands are generally allowed to be off-leash, with their owners, in their neighborhoods without legal repercussions. As well, well-behaved dogs can often be found off-leash at most of the area's city and county parks, though it's important to reiterate that the City of Atlanta and most of the surrounding counties *do* have leash laws in place, restricting dogs from being off-leash on public property.

A handful of communities throughout metro Atlanta have developed neighborhood dog parks and dog runs—safe places for pets and their owners to spend time outdoors, running and playing without the leash:

- **DeKalb County's Mason Mill Park**, 404-371-2631, 1340 McConnell Dr Ste B, Decatur, www.co.dekalb.ga.us/parks/parks.htm; a half-acre dog park with high and low water fountains, a new fence, wood chips, benches, and pooper scoopers.
- **Cobb County Sweat Mountain Park,** 770-591-3155, 4346 Steinhauer Rd NE, Marietta, http://prca.cobbcountyga.gov, four-acre dog park offers areas for both small and large dogs.
- **Piedmont Park Off Leash Dog Park**, 404-875-7275, Piedmont Ave NE and 14th St, Atlanta, www.piedmontpark.org; 1.5 acres of leash-free greenspace, located at Monroe Dr and Park Dr. Open to the public.
- **Ronald Reagan Park**, www.gwinnettcounty.com, 2777 Five Forks Trickum Rd, Lawrenceville, 2 acres of fenced areas where pets can roam free with their owners.

In addition to area leash laws, all metro Atlanta counties have scoop-the-poop laws in place.

## VETERINARIANS

As a pet owner, you will want to have a vet lined up before you actually need one. Start by contacting the **Georgia Veterinary Medical Association**, 678-309-9800, www.gvma.net, for a list of accredited vets in your neighborhood. You may also want to check with pet-owning friends and neighbors, or visit local parks frequented by dog owners, to glean information on local vets. Choosing a vet, like choosing a physician, is a largely subjective thing. Beyond the cleanliness and friendliness of the establishment, both you and your pet will want to be comfortable with the vet you choose. You may also want to inquire to be sure your vet is available or covered after hours by an answering service.

In case of serious pet emergencies after-hours and on weekends, contact one of the following:

- **Animal Emergency Center of Sandy Springs**, 404-252-7881, www.aecsandysprings.com
- **Cobb Emergency Veterinary Clinic**, 770-424-9157, www.cobbevc.com
- **VCA DeKalb-Gwinnett Animal Emergency Hospital**, 770-491-0661, www.vcaspecialtyvets.com/dekalb-gwinnett
- **Georgia Veterinary Specialists**, 404-459-0903, www.gvsvets.com

## PET SERVICES

Dogs typically need to be walked at least three times a day, not a problem if you work from home or live with someone who is home during the day. Being social animals, they suffer more than cats from being left alone for long periods. You may want to consider the proposition that two dogs are not much more bother than one, and both are happier together than one alone. In any case, if you are away for more than eight hours a day, you will probably need a **dog walker**, a person who has your keys and who will come in and take your dog out for 15 to 60 minutes. While this can be expensive, you may find the happiness and well-being of your dog is more than worth the cost. To find a reliable dog walker, check with other dog owners and your vet for recommendations. Some of the better pet-care establishments keep a list of walkers whose credentials they can vouch for. Some dog walkers will also pet-sit when you are away, either staying in your home to care for your pets and plants or visiting three times a day to feed, water, play with, and walk your pet. The average going rate for pet sitting in metro Atlanta is currently about $16 a day for cats and $20 a day for dogs, though prices vary by neighborhoods.

In addition to dog walkers, metro Atlanta is now home to more than a few **"doggy daycares."** These facilities are designed to offer pet care and socialization opportunities for dogs that would otherwise be home alone all day. Most offer indoor and outdoor play areas, doggy lunch and/or snack, nap breaks, and more. Dogs are typically grouped according to size and temperament, and are generally required to have been spayed or neutered, and be up-to-date on vaccinations. Some include boarding, grooming, and dog training services as well. For listings and reviews, try the Yellow Pages, Google, Yahoo, Yelp, or Kudzu.com, a trusted local service search engine with reviews and referrals.

## ACQUIRING A PET

If you are interested in acquiring a pet once you've settled into your new home, there are plenty of places to look. You can check the *Atlanta Journal-Constitution*'s Sunday classifieds or the local paper in your neighborhood. Expect to find listings for a variety of pets—some of them free to a good home, and many of them pure-breds that will cost you anywhere from $50 to $2,000. Other great places to look are Craigslist, a local paper in your neighborhood, or a website dedicated to pets, like Petfinder.com, which connects you directly with breeders.

You may also want to consider pet adoption. Adoption fees are generally $60 for cats, $85 for dogs, and $15 or less for smaller pets such as rabbits and hamsters. Those fees typically include the cost of vaccinating, and spaying or neutering the pet. Most shelters require that you be at least 18 years old to adopt, and you must be able to show proof of age and current residence. If you rent rather than own your home, you must also bring in a copy of your lease indicating your landlord's pet policy.

All of the metro Atlanta counties run animal shelters and/or humane societies, and it's nearly impossible *not* to find a pet to fall in love with at one of them. You don't have to live in the county you adopt from, so it's a good idea to check out all of the local shelters to find the pet that will be just right for you. Adopting a pet is a big responsibility, so be sure you consider your lifestyle and your potential pet's temperament and needs before making a final decision.

To begin your search, check out the following shelters and humane societies; most of them offer photos, pet descriptions, and adoption information online for your convenience:

- **Atlanta Humane Society**, 404-875-5331, www.atlantahumane.org
- **Cherokee County Humane Society**, 770-592-8072, www.cchumanesociety.org
- **Cobb County Humane Society**, 770-428-LOST, www.humanecobb.org
- **PAWS Atlanta** (the **DeKalb County Humane Society**), 5287 Covington Hwy, Decatur, 770-593-1155, www.pawsatlanta.org
- **Fulton County Animal Shelter**, 404-794-0358, fultonanimalservices.com; permanent website under construction
- **Gwinnett County Humane Society**, 770-798-7711, www.gwinnetthumane.com

## CRIME AND SAFETY

As in any major urban area, crime occurs regularly in metro Atlanta. Atlanta's suburban sprawl has encouraged crimes in mall parking lots and wooded parks, and at out-of-the-way, dimly lit automated teller machines. Over the last ten years, there have been numerous reports of carjackings, robberies, and even abductions at these more remote locations. A good rule of thumb is never to walk alone at night, especially in Midtown, Downtown, and parts of south Atlanta. Remember to jog after dark only with a group of people, even in your own neighborhood. Avoid ATMs late at night, unless they are well lit and situated in a highly traveled area, such as a busy shopping center. And, at the mall, park in well-lit areas, pay close attention to your surroundings when you return to your car laden with packages, and if you feel uncomfortable walking out alone, request that someone from mall security escort you to your vehicle. Be aware that crimes frequently occur in covered mall parking lots, even in broad daylight.

In addition to parking lot crimes, Atlanta has been experiencing a rise in stolen cars, and car and home break-ins. Do your best to prevent these types of crimes by installing alarms on both your home and vehicle; keeping doors and windows locked at all times; and never leaving valuables in plain view in your car. It's also important, when you move into your new community, to check and see if there is a Neighborhood Watch program. It's a great way to meet your neighbors and a wonderful way to help protect your community. Being part of the Neighborhood Watch will also help keep you informed of any criminal activity that has occurred recently in the neighborhood. Neighborhood Watch programs can be official (with city-provided signs) or unofficial (with signs and organization provided by your block). To find out if there is a program in your neighborhood, or to set one up if there isn't, you can contact the **Atlanta Police Department Safe Neighborhood Task Force,** 404-853-7240, www.atlantapd.org. Or check out the police precincts in your area by calling the numbers listed after each neighborhood profile in the **Neighborhoods** chapter of this book.

## POLICE COMPLAINTS

If you have a complaint about a specific officer or the police force in your area, you will want to contact the city or county police departments directly at the main numbers below:

- **Atlanta Police Department**, 404-853-3434, www.atlantapd.org
- **Cherokee County Sheriff's Office**, 678-493-4200, www.cherokeega-sheriff.org
- **Cobb County Sheriff's Department**, 770-499-3900, www.cobbsheriff.org
- **DeKalb County Police Department**, 404-294-2519, http://web.co.dekalb. ga.us/dk_police
- **Fulton County Police Department**, 770-495-8738, www.fultonpolice.org
- **Gwinnett County Police Department**, 770-513-5000, www.gwinnettcounty.com
- **State Patrol Office**, 404-624-7000, http://dps.georgia.gov

If you feel you're not getting anywhere with your complaints against the local police department, you may also want to contact the national **Police Complaint Center**, www.policeabuse.com, an organization dedicated to investigating accusations of police misconduct, and assisting citizens in filing police complaints throughout the country.

N OW THAT YOU'VE FOUND A NEW HOME, AND HAVE TAKEN CARE OF the basics like getting electricity and water, you may want to take advantage of some of metro Atlanta's helpful services. Some of these services, including mail receiving/shipping and house cleaning, can make your life far simpler. Also here, you'll find services for people with disabilities, a section for immigrant newcomers, and a section on gay and lesbian life. Read on.

## DOMESTIC SERVICES

If you're interested in finding someone to help keep your house clean, ask your neighbors or co-workers for recommendations. Lots of singles and families use a cleaning service to simplify their busy schedules and keep their homes clean. You can also check Kudzu.com, Google, Yahoo, and Craigslist. Obviously, it's safer to go with a professional cleaning service, and there are plenty to choose from. If you do go with a private individual, do some research on them first to be sure they are trustworthy. Ask for references—if they are legit, they should have plenty.

- **Mighty Clean Home,** 678-439-9518, www.mightycleanhome.com
- **Completely Clean Atlanta,** 404-246-8141, www.atlantahousecleaningservice.com
- **The Maids,** 404-256-3200, www.themaids.com/144

## PEST CONTROL

Most apartment complexes handle periodic pest control for residents, so check your lease or ask your landlord about pest abatement in your building. Though metro Atlanta is not a tropical locale where you would expect major problems with pest control, the relatively warm winters and extended fall temperatures mean that bugs survive better here than in more northern climes. The most common pests are termites, ants, and small brown roaches that like to congregate around the kitchen. If you have pets, be diligent about flea control. A regular flea prevention and treatment from your local vet will not only keep your pet comfortable but also save you money on exterminating fees.

The Atlanta Yellow Pages lists over ten pages of pest control companies who will rid your house of everything from ants to squirrels. You can also search for a service online. Several of these companies will also trap larger animals and humanely relocate them outside the city. A few of the larger pest control companies include:

- **Chemical Technologies of Georgia**, metro Atlanta, 770-237-3244, www.gapestpro.com
- **Do-It-Yourself Pest Control**, metro Atlanta, 800-476-3368, www.doityourself-pestcontrol.com
- **Orkin Pest Control**, 866-953-2896, www.orkin.com
- **Peachtree Pest Control**, 855-PEACHTREE, www.peachtreepestcontrol.com
- **Terminix Pest Control**, 866-319-6147, www.terminix.com

A word on termite protection: If you are a homeowner or are house hunting, Georgia law requires termite inspection prior to selling and treatment if termites are found. For this reason, you may want to ask the pest control companies about a yearly contract, where you will receive annual inspections and minor treatments if needed. Also, if you are buying, ask about current termite bonds on your house, and whether they are transferable. In many cases they are, for a fee of course. But it's a wise investment. You don't want to move into a new home, only to find damage that could cost thousands of dollars after you move in.

## MAIL AND SHIPPING SERVICES

### MAIL DELIVERY

Atlanta is the hub for much of the mail delivery in the Southeast, so fast delivery is the norm. However, if you do have a problem with your postal delivery, you can contact the **Governor's Office of Consumer Affairs**, http://consumer.georgia.gov. For ZIP code information, contact the **United States Postal Service**, 800-275-8777, www.usps.com.

Atlanta's **Main Post Office**, 3900 Crown Road SW, Atlanta, 404-684-2308, is open 24 hours and handles the bulk of the mail processing in the city. Because of the large geographic area served, however, the postal system here is well covered by branches located throughout the entire metro area. The USPS 800 number and web address (listed above) or the Blue Pages of the phone book, "US Government, Postal Service," will guide you to the post office nearest you. You can also use the listings at the end of each neighborhood profile in the **Neighborhoods** section of this book or search online.

## JUNK MAIL

Junk mail will likely follow you to your new home, but there are a number of things you can do to fight the cycle. The **Direct Marketing Association** provides a wealth of information to consumers on its website www.dmaconsumers.org. The site covers how to get you and your family members' names off direct mailing, tele-marketing, email lists, and more. Many of these services can be performed online.

Also, the government offers consumers a "do not call" registry. Marketing agencies or businesses caught violating the list can be fined. The numbers are 888-382-1222 and TTY 866-290-4236, or visit the website www.donotcall.gov.

Also, the country's major credit bureaus share an opt-out line that allows you to reduce the volume of prescreened offers for credit and insurance that you receive. Call 1-888-5-OPTOUT (888-567-8688) or visit www.optoutprescreen.com to have your name removed from mailing lists that the credit bureaus sell to direct-mail marketers.

And if all else fails, the Georgia **Governor's Office of Consumer Affairs** web-site (listed above) offers information on decreasing your flow of junk mail.

## MAIL RECEIVING SERVICES

If you haven't yet settled at a permanent address, a number of companies will receive your mail for a fee. Renting a box at your neighborhood post office is a convenient option, and many metro Atlanta area post offices are being remodeled to provide after-hours access for mail retrieval. Also, many businesses offer full mail services, including mail forwarding and UPS delivery. The most common are UPS Store and FedEx, but you can search online or in the Yellow Pages for more options.

- **FedEx**, www.fedex.com/us, 800-488-3705
- **UPS Store**, www.theupsstore.com, 800-789-4623

## SHIPPING SERVICES

Most mail-receiving service centers will also ship your packages for you via one of the large national carriers. **Pak Mail Centers of America**, with numerous metro locations, will also custom pack and ship for you. Call 800-833-2821 for the loca-tion nearest you. Other major shipping companies to consider are:

- **UPS**, 800-742-5877, www.ups.com
- **FedEx**, 800-463-3339, www.fedex.com/us
- **US Postal Service**, 800-275-8777, www.usps.com

# CONSUMER PROTECTION

"Buyer beware" may be a cliché, but it is the best line of defense against fraud and consumer victimization. Sometimes, an unscrupulous business operator can hoodwink even the most cautious buyer. Here are some agencies that, depending on your concern, may be able to help you on your quest for justice:

- **Atlanta Bar Association**, metro Atlanta, 404-521-0781, www.atlantabar.org; can assist the public with locating attorneys who are qualified to handle all areas of law.
- **Atlanta Legal Aid Society**, Atlanta, 404-524-5811; Cobb, 770-528-2565; DeKalb, 404-377-0701; Gwinnett, 678-376-4545; South Fulton/Clayton, 404-669-0233, www.atlantalegalaid.org; represents metro Atlanta's low-income residents in civil legal cases, including those concerned with safe homes, education, protection against fraud and personal safety.
- **Better Business Bureau of Metropolitan Atlanta**, 404-766-0875, www.atlanta. bbb.org; handles complaints about local businesses, and will work as an intermediary to help resolve disputes. They can also provide helpful information on ethical business practices.
- **US Public Interest Research Group** (**USPIRG**), Georgia branch, 404-892-3573, www.georgiapirg.org; learn about important issues like where your tax dollars are going. They can also assist you with questions and child toy safety, health insurance for young adults, and how to avoid high bank fees.
- **WSB Consumer Action Center**, www.clarkhoward.com; answers consumer questions and complaints in association with the Clark Howard TV and radio show. You can also reach **Clark Howard** with consumer questions by calling 404-892-8227 (Monday–Friday, 1 p.m. to 3 p.m.), or by visiting his website. It's been said that if Howard, who also has a regular column in the *Atlanta Journal-Constitution*, can't help you, no one can.

The following are state and federal agencies worth considering:

- **Consumer Product Safety Commission**, 800-638-2772, www.cpsc.gov; this office works to inform and protect consumers from unreasonable risks of injury or death that could be caused by the more than 15,000 types of products currently under the agency's jurisdiction—including toys, cribs, power tools, cigarette lighters, household chemicals, and more.
- **Federal Trade Commission**, 877-FTC-HELP, www.ftc.gov/bcp/consumer.shtm; offers valuable information on consumers' rights, enforces a variety of consumer protection laws enacted by Congress, and works to protect consumers against unfair, deceptive, or fraudulent business practices.
- **Governor's Office of Consumer Affairs**, 404-651-8600, http://consumer. georgia.gov; enforces Georgia's Fair Business Practices Act, as well as other consumer protection laws—both civil and criminal.

- **Office of the Georgia Attorney General, Consumer Protection**, 404-656-3300, http://law.ga.gov; advises and represents all state agencies that protect the rights of Georgia consumers. This office has the authority to shut down loan sharks, fraudulent telemarketing schemes, sweepstakes scams, merchants that engage in price gouging during times of emergency, and other illegal practices aimed at Georgia citizens.
- **State Insurance Commissioner, Consumer Services**, 404-656-2070, http://www.inscomm.state.ga.us; this division of the Department of Insurance assists Georgia citizens who have questions or complaints about any phase of the insurance process, whether the insurance is for home, auto, health, or business. Consumer Services can also investigate and help mediate or resolve any disputes that Georgia consumers may have with their insurance company.

## SERVICES FOR PEOPLE WITH DISABILITIES

A number of organizations in metro Atlanta cater specifically to the needs of the disabled. For information about local resources, contact **disAbility Link**, 404-687-8890, www.disabilitylink.org. You can also contact **Friends of Disabled Adults and Children**, 770-491-9014, www.fodac.org, a local volunteer organization, offering important information and medical equipment to low-income, disabled residents throughout metro Atlanta. **The Shepherd Center**, 404-352-2020, www.shepherd.org, a medical, resource, therapy, and informational facility located at 2020 Peachtree Road NW, also offers a large outreach and assistance program for disabled citizens.

For those with hearing impairments, the **Georgia Council for the Hearing Impaired**, 404-292-5312, www.gachi.org, is a Decatur-based, community service organization that offers individual and family counseling as well as advocacy for the hearing-impaired throughout the metro area. The **Center for the Visually Impaired**, 404-875-9011, www.cviga.org, located at 739 West Peachtree Street NW, offers support and services for local blind and visually impaired individuals of all ages.

If you have a child with a disability, the **Georgia Learning Resources System** (**GLRS**), www.glrs.org, can help you find a program suited to his or her needs and provides referral information about services for disabled students, as well as workshops and specialized materials for parents, teachers, and others who work with children with disabilities. Georgia Learning Resources System (GLRS) is available in the **East Metro** area (including DeKalb, Fulton, Gwinnett, and Rockdale counties; as well as the cities of Buford and Decatur) at 678-676-2400, and in **West Metro** (including Clayton, Cobb, Douglas, and Forsyth counties; and the cities of Atlanta and Marietta) at 770-432-2404.

The **Atlanta Alliance on Developmental Disabilities**, 404-881-9777, www.aadd.org, is a primary service provider and support network for metro Atlanta children, adults, and families living with developmental disabilities. The AADD offers valuable information on public policy and legislation, recreational opportunities, health and wellness, and more.

## GETTING AROUND

Applications for handicapped parking permits are available through the **Georgia Department of Revenue,** www.etax.dor.ga.gov. Look online under "forms and manuals" for the downloadable form MV-9D. Along with the application, you must supply a notarized letter from your doctor, explaining why and for how long you will need the permit. If mailing in the application, you should expect to receive the permit within 7 to 10 days. You can also take the form to your local tag office, depending on your county of residence. For more information about parking permits, or to locate an exam office in your neighborhood, contact the GDOR at the phone number or web address above.

On **MARTA**, 404-848-4711, www.itsmarta.com, elderly and handicapped customers can ride trains and buses for half-price with a half-fare card. These cards can be obtained free of charge from the Five Points station or from the MARTA headquarters office, located at 2424 Piedmont Road across from Lindbergh Station. One hundred of MARTA's 150 bus routes and all of the rail stations now offer wheelchair accessibility. To find out if your neighborhood bus route has this convenience, contact MARTA at the number or web address above. If you'd like to request that your particular route become wheelchair accessible, call 404-848-5618. In addition to half-fare prices and wheelchair accessibility, MARTA also provides an **ADA Complementary Paratransit Service**, offering special lift-equipped vans on a curb-to-curb, shared ride basis, to eligible residents with disabilities who are unable to board, ride, or disembark from MARTA's regular buses or trains. Individuals who already have a MARTA ADA photo ID card may contact **MARTA's Paratransit Reservation Office**, 404-848-5826, www.itsmarta.com/howto/special/para.htm, to schedule a ride. The cost is $3.50 per one-way trip. For more information about MARTA's Paratransit Services, or to receive an application, call MARTA's Eligibility and Certification staff at 404-848-5389.

For private transportation within the metro area and to the airport, there are a number of special needs transportation companies operating much like a taxi service. A few to consider are: **Shuttle Service Atlanta**, 678-969-0007, www.valdmed.com; **Complete Medical Transportation**, 770-987-2798, www.completemedical.com; and **Georgia Medical Transportation**, 770-761-2322, www.gamedtransport.com. All these companies offer non-emergency transportation services for individuals or groups throughout metro Atlanta, catering largely to the disabled and elderly.

## COMMUNICATION

Free library services are available for the visually impaired and the physically disabled from the **Georgia Library for Accessible Services**, 1150 Murphy Avenue SW, Atlanta, 404-756-4619, www.georgialibraries.org/glass/. Patrons can get books in Braille or cartridge through the mail or in person; also the department recently added a download page for digital files.

To apply for service, contact the library and leave your name and address. They will mail you an application, which must be certified by your doctor. You may also download the application online via their website. Upon approval of your application, the library will mail you a cartridge player and a few titles. You can then select your own titles; the entire service, including the player, is free of charge. For more information about this library's services contact them at the number or web address above.

The **Georgia Relay Center** provides relay services for telephone calls to or from speech- or hearing-impaired telephone customers anywhere in the United States and internationally to English-speaking countries. The service is provided 24 hours a day, seven days a week. To contact the center go to www.georgiarelay. org or call 866-787-6710, or for TTY dial 7-1-1 and give Georgia Relay Assistance the previous number. For information on telecommunications equipment, contact the **Georgia Council for the Hearing Impaired**, 800-541-0710, www.gachi.org.

For sign language interpreting services, you may want to consider the **Georgia Interpreting Services Network**, 404-521-9100, 800-228-4992, www.gisn.org; or **Sign Language Interpreting Specialists**, 770-531-0700, TTY 770-287-9479, www. slisinc.com. You can also find additional sign language information and listings at the **Georgia Registry of Interpreters for the Deaf** website, www.garid.com.

## HOUSING

Most new apartment complexes have units dedicated to residents who require wheelchair access and other handicapped services. Any of the locator services listed in the **Finding a Place to Live** chapter should be able to assist you with an apartment search. For other housing choices, contact the **Disability Action Center of Georgia**, **disAbility Link**, 404-687-8890, www.disabilitylink.org.

## ADDITIONAL RESOURCES

Following is a list of resources, both governmental and nonprofit, that may be of use to those with special needs.

- **Southeastern Guide Dogs, Inc.**, www.guidedogs.org; offers information on guide dogs for the visually impaired and lists a number of resources by region and state

- **Epilepsy Foundation of Georgia,** Atlanta, 800-527-7105, www.epilepsyga.org
- **Down Syndrome Association of Atlanta**, 404-320-3233, www.dsaatl.org
- **Atlanta Area School for the Deaf**, 890 North Indian Creek Dr, Clarkston, 404-296-7101, www.aasdweb.com
- **The ALS Association of Georgia**, 1955 Cliff Valley Way, Atlanta, 404-636-9909, www.alsaga.org; provides information and support for individuals living with ALS (also known as Lou Gehrig's disease)
- **Americans With Disabilities Act, State of Georgia ADA Coordinator**, 404-657-9993 (TTY), 404-657-7313 (voice), http://ada.georgia.gov; can answer questions about the Americans with Disabilities Act
- **Shepherd Center Sports**, 404-367-1287, www.shepherd.org; provides information on joining local wheelchair sports teams
- **National Center on Physical Activity and Disability**, 800-900-8086, www.ncpad.org; offers free information for Americans with disabilities looking for an appropriate exercise plan

## IMMIGRANT NEWCOMERS

Atlanta has long considered itself the International City of the South; with more than 688,000 foreign-born residents from more than 32 countries settled into the area, it is a valid claim. Those new to metro Atlanta, and to the USA, may find the following listings helpful:

- **Celtic Atlanta**, a local organization that promotes all things Celtic; the website, www.celticatlanta.com, provides information on any number of Celtic topics or groups ranging from entertaining, to social, to educational
- **Center for Pan Asian Community Services, Inc.**, Doraville, 770-936-0969, www.icpacs.org; a private, nonprofit organization dedicated to providing comprehensive social and health services to metro Atlanta's pan-Asian community
- **The International Community School**, 404-499-8969, www.icsga.org; a private, multicultural and multilingual elementary school for refugee and immigrant school children in Atlanta; the school has locations in Decatur and Stone Mountain
- **The International Rescue Committee of Atlanta**, 404-292-7731, www.rescue.org/us-program/us-atlanta_old; a nonprofit, nonsectarian refugee resettlement agency dedicated to assisting refugees and their families from around the world as they resettle in the metro Atlanta area
- **Latin American Association**, 404-638-1800, www.thelaa.org; a nonprofit organization providing comprehensive transitional services and programs for Latino families in the metro Atlanta area
- **Metro Atlanta Indian American Community**, 770-436-3719, www.ipnatlanta.net; local organization providing information, events calendar and links to various Indian and South Asian groups and associations throughout metro Atlanta

- **The National Association of Chinese-Americans**, Atlanta, 770-394-6542, www.naca-atlanta.org; a nonprofit organization dedicated to promoting cultural, educational, scientific and business relationships between the Chinese community and local government, community, and business leaders
- **Polish American Chamber of Commerce of the Southeast United States**, Atlanta, 404-724-4500, www.pacc-south.com; promotes business and cultural ties between the USA, Poland, and other Central and Eastern European nations, through business programs and social forums
- **Refugee Women's Network, Inc.**, 404-299-0180, www.riwn.org; a nonprofit organization serving refugee and immigrant women through leadership training, education and advocacy.
- **Russian Atlanta.Net**, 404-592-8396, www.russianatlanta.net; an online resource providing the latest news on Russian culture, business and events in metro Atlanta

## CONSULATES

As testament to its international clout, Atlanta is home to more than 45 consulates and honorary consulates in metro Atlanta. The state offers a complete listing online at www.georgia.org/business-resources. You can also call for addresses or information at 404-962-4122. Also the Yellow Pages lists local consulates in its print edition and online at www.yellowpages.com.

## CITIZENSHIP AND IMMIGRATION SERVICES

**US Citizenship and Immigration Services (USCIS)** for metro Atlanta is located at 2150 Parklake Drive. In order to visit this office and speak with an officer you must make an appointment. The office's number is 800-375-5283 or go to www.uscis.gov for more information.

## IMMIGRATION RESOURCES

- **Bureau of Immigration and Customs Enforcement**, www.ice.gov
- **Customs and Border Protection**, www.cbp.gov
- **Department of Homeland Security**, www.dhs.gov; www.whitehouse.gov/deptofhomeland
- **General Government Questions**, 800-688-9889, www.usa.gov
- **Social Security Administration**, 800-772-1213, www.ssa.gov
- **US Bureau of Consular Affairs**, www.travel.state.gov
- **US Department of State, Visa Services**, http://travel.state.gov/visa/visa_1750.html
- **US Immigration Online—Green Cards, Visas, Government Forms**, http://www.uscis.gov/portal/site/uscis

## PUBLICATIONS

- *Newcomer's Handbook for Moving to and Living in the USA*, by Mike Livingston (First Books)

## MOVING PETS TO THE USA

- **Cosmopolitan Canine Carriers**, 800-243-9105, www.caninecarriers.com, has been shipping dogs and cats all over the world for over 30 years. Contact them directly with questions or concerns regarding air transportation arrangements, vaccinations, and quarantine times.
- *The Pet-Moving Handbook* (First Books) covers domestic and international moves, via car, airplane, ferry, etc. Primary focus is on cats and dogs.

# GAY, LESBIAN, BISEXUAL, AND TRANSGENDER LIFE

Atlanta has long been known as a city that embraces its large and incredibly diverse gay and lesbian community. In fact, the Atlanta City Council passed an ordinance prohibiting companies from discriminating on the basis of sexual orientation or domestic relationship status—this despite the fact that the state of Georgia overwhelmingly approved a constitutional ban on same-sex marriage that also includes civil unions and other partnership benefits. Though this unresolved issue has created conflict between the city government and the state legislature, and will most likely be argued both legally and politically for many years to come, the Atlanta ordinance is just one way the city has shown its support for the gay community.

According to a 2006 analysis conducted at UCLA, 12.8% of Atlanta's adult population identify themselves as gay, lesbian, or bisexual, giving Atlanta the third highest concentration, after San Francisco (15.4%) and Seattle (12.9%). Today most areas of the city are "gay-friendly," though you may still find that some neighborhoods are merely tolerant and choose to employ the "don't ask, don't tell" policy, and a handful of communities may be neither accepting nor tolerant. Unfortunately, this seems to be most true of the conservative neighborhoods that are furthest away from the heart of the city.

Metro Atlanta's artsy, intown communities, including Midtown, Decatur, Virginia Highland, and Candler Park, tend to be the most accepting of gays and lesbians. And it's here that you'll find a number of gay-owned, -operated, and -friendly businesses. Those residents who choose to live in the outer suburbs of, say, Lawrenceville, Norcross, Roswell, and Marietta, and are looking for a night out, generally travel into the city to take advantage of these fabulous bookstores, cafés, and nightclubs.

Some resources for gays and lesbians in metro Atlanta are:

- **Atlanta Gay and Lesbian Chamber of Commerce**, 404-377-4258, www.atlantagaychamber.org; local organization dedicated to the development and growth of businesses that support the gay, lesbian, bisexual, and transgender community
- **Atlanta Pride Committee**, 404-929-0071, www.atlantapride.org; the official committee of the Atlanta's annual Lesbian, Gay, Bisexual, Transgender Pride celebration
- **Atlanta Prime Timers**, www.primetimersww.com/atlanta; a nonpolitical, nonprofit, social group for mature gay and bisexual men and their friends
- **Black and White Men Together Atlanta**, 404-705-5300, www.bwmtatlanta.org; the Atlanta chapter of the national gay multicultural organization that hosts educational, political, cultural, and social activities
- **Gay Atlanta**, www.gayatlanta.com; a hub for news and entertainment geared toward the gay community
- **Gay Fathers of Atlanta**, 678-313-2832, www.gfoatlanta.org; local support group for gay men who are fathers or who want to be fathers
- **Gay & Lesbian Alliance Against Defamation (GLAAD), Southeastern Region**, www.glaad.org; office of the Southeastern monitor and response team, organized to monitor representations of the gay community
- **Kashi Atlanta**, 404-687-3353, www.kashiatlanta.org; an interfaith center for yoga, service, and community, offering GLBT-friendly yoga and meditation classes, counseling sessions, workshops, community service opportunities, and more
- **Parents, Families and Friends of Lesbians and Gays (PFLAG)**, 770-662-6475, www.pflagatl.org; local chapter of the national support organization for parents, families, and friends of gays and lesbians
- **Georgia Tech Pride Alliance**, 404-385-6554, http://pridealliance.gtorg.gatech.edu; the GLBT student organization of Georgia Tech University
- *Fenuxe Magazine,* 404-835-2016, www.fenuxe.com; popular gay and lesbian magazine covering style, entertainment, fashion, arts, events, and culture
- *The GA Voice,* 404-815-6941 www.thegavoice.com; a news outlet for Georgia's LGBT community
- *David Atlanta*, 404-418-8901, www.davidatlanta.com; metro Atlanta's premier gay newspaper
- **YouthPride Atlanta**, 404-521-9713, www.youthpride.org; offers confidential help, outreach, and support to young gays, lesbians, bisexuals, and transgenders throughout the metro area

This list is just a sampling of the organizations and groups that are available for metro Atlanta's gay and lesbian community. You may also want to check out *Creative Loafing's* **Gay and Lesbian listings** in their weekly "Happenings" section, www.creativeloafing.com, as well as "Gay and Lesbian Friendly Congregations" under "Places of Worship" and "Gay and Lesbian" under "Area Organizations" in the **Getting Involved** chapter.

A S IN MOST MAJOR US CITIES, FINDING AND AFFORDING A GOOD EDUcation from daycare to college can be both daunting and difficult. This chapter won't do the work for you, but it is a good place to start.

Georgia has a fine public education system, as well as numerous private schools and universities available to its residents. Also, for those unable to afford schooling, there are numerous state and federal programs that can either supplement or pay for tuition costs. Also, check out the myriad resources and groups aimed at helping people find the right fit—whether they are sending their child to school, sending their teenager to college, or looking to enroll in an adult continuing education program.

Please note: *Listing in this book is merely informational and is* **not** *an endorsement. When entrusting your child to strangers, always err on the side of safety and caution.*

## CHILDCARE

### DAYCARE

Metro Atlanta is home to hundreds of daycare facilities, some of which have waiting lists of a year or more. If you anticipate needing childcare, start your search as far in advance as possible. Daycare options in the metro area run the gamut: You can place your child in a privately owned national daycare center chain or a local facility; you can choose a nonprofit center run by a church, community group, or the city; you can bring your child to someone else's home; you can use your business's daycare service; or you can hire a nanny or au pair to come to your house.

Good advice when looking for childcare is to ask friends or co-workers with children if they have any recommendations. Your real estate agent or leasing agent could possibly provide suggestions as well. You may also want to check the

Atlanta Yellow Pages (print or online) or search engines such as Google, Yahoo, Yelp, or Kudzu.com under "Childcare Centers," "Childcare Service," or "Nanny Service." For a comprehensive list of daycare facilities in the Atlanta area, contact **Child Care Resource and Referral of Metro Atlanta**, 404-479-4233, a private, nonprofit, telephone referral service. Not only will they locate childcare centers in your area, they will also give you pertinent information, such as the school's registration charges, weekly rates, and student-to-teacher ratios. You can also visit them online at www.gaccrra.org, where you will also find information on childcare laws in Georgia, what to look for in a daycare facility, a listing of childcare centers throughout the state, useful links, and more. Or visit the state's agency in charge of regulating care for children ages 0 to 5, **Bright from the Start**, at www.decal.ga.gov. The agency offers residents a wealth of information on local daycare programs, including any history of complaints or offenses, and how they rated in yearly evaluations.

Following is a list of typical daycare options available in the metro Atlanta area:

- **Family Daycare Homes** are small facilities (up to six children) that operate in the home of the childcare provider. The care here is generally more individualized than what you may find in a larger facility, and prices tend to be much lower. Family daycare homes can be less structured than larger facilities and may not offer a daily curriculum for your child. Talking to the parents of other children that attend the daycare, as well as asking specific questions of the childcare provider regarding her childcare philosophy and daily routine, is a good idea.

- **Group Daycare Homes** are similar to family daycare homes in that they, too, operate in the provider's home. The difference, however, is that group daycare homes are licensed to care for a greater number of children. In Georgia, that number ranges from 7 to 18 children.

- **Childcare Centers** are what most people think of when they hear "daycare." Generally, these centers are larger and more structured than family daycare homes, and because of the number of employees and costly overhead needed to operate these facilities, prices tend to be much higher. Many of these centers are run like schools, with babies in one room, toddlers in another, preschool in yet another, and after-school students in another. A downside of childcare centers is that they often have a high teacher turnover rate, due to low pay. This can be difficult for your child if his/her favorite teacher suddenly leaves to take a more lucrative position elsewhere. When considering a childcare facility, it's important to ask about the teacher turnover rate, what incentives the school offers its employees to keep them on the job, whether or not any of the childcare workers are certified, and what type of curriculum will be offered to your child.

- **Montessori Childcare**, developed by Dr. Maria Montessori, who became Italy's first female physician in the early 1900s, is a method of childcare and teaching based on a child's individual needs and learning style. Creativity is encouraged at these centers, as well as the mixing of older children with younger children. While the overall structure here is loose compared to some other schools, the child's every experience, from water play to choosing a snack to helping to clean up, is embraced as a learning opportunity. There are several Montessori schools in metro Atlanta, some of which accept students from the age of 2 to 12 years; check the Atlanta Yellow Pages. For more information on the Montessori method, or to find local listings online, visit **Montessori Connections**, www.montessoriconnections.com.

- **Non-Traditional Options** refer to child development centers run out of neighborhood houses of worship, as well as employer-provided daycare and co-op daycare. To find a church-sponsored daycare center, your best bet is to call the churches in your area or look on Kudzu.com. You'll find many churches offering this service, even if you do not attend that church, though some offer only half-days or after-school programs.

And while it is not the norm, a growing number of employers in metro Atlanta are providing daycare on site for their employees. Be sure to ask your employer, or potential employer, whether it offers this benefit.

Co-op daycare is also becoming more mainstream, though not highly advertised. This option sells by word of mouth, so ask around to see if any of your friends or co-workers can recommend a co-op, or call the referral services listed above. Co-op daycare is an especially good option for parents who work part-time or have flexible schedules and can contribute the time necessary to make the co-op work. Though co-ops are run differently and according to the needs of each particular group, in a co-op situation you can expect to work a specified number of hours each week providing daycare at the center in exchange for daycare time for your own children. Such a scenario provides for greatly reduced daycare costs and the added perk of milling about with a bunch of little ones. If you have a job that requires you to work 50 hours a week or your employer won't give you time off to participate at the co-op, this option may not be for you.

## WHAT TO LOOK FOR IN DAYCARE

When visiting a prospective childcare center, ask the staff for the names and phone numbers of other parents using the center, and give them a call. Later, if you're still interested, make at least one unannounced visit to the facility. Also, make sure that the center is licensed by the state (in Georgia, that's Bright from the Start, mentioned above). Earning a state license involves strict health and safety requirements.

When viewing daycare centers, you may want to consider the following:

- How long has the school been in operation?
- Is the school licensed?

- Does the school receive funding from the state's "Georgia Lottery Pre-K" fund? (In some cases, facilities that receive state funds are held to stricter requirements than schools that do not.)
- Determine how many students are currently enrolled in the school and in your child's class and what the student-to-teacher ratio is.
- Are any of the teachers degreed or currently enrolled in child development classes?
- Does the school provide incentive for the teachers to become degreed or certified?
- Does the school run background checks on new employees to ensure that none have criminal records?
- What is the school's pupil and daycare provider turnover rate?
- How many of the teachers are currently child-CPR certified? (The state of Georgia requires that 50% of a facility's staff have up-to-date CPR certification.)
- What are the school's hours of operation?
- Are children provided with a hot, nutritious lunch each day? Ask for a sample week's lunch menu.
- How does the staff handle discipline?
- Will your child's teacher provide age-appropriate projects and activities throughout the day? Is there a set schedule or routine?
- How often are the children allowed to play outside?
- Is the outside play area safe? Be sure to investigate.
- Is your child's classroom child-proofed? Are dangerous items (like scissors or cleaning supplies) locked away or kept out of reach?
- How often are the classrooms cleaned? How often are the toys sanitized?
- What is the school's policy on sick children?

Once the questions have been asked, make sure you take your child to the school and let him/her meet the teacher and spend some time with you in the classroom. Often your child's impression of the daycare center is a great indication of whether or not it will be the right fit for your family.

## NANNIES

Hiring a nanny can be the most expensive daycare option, but it may also be the most rewarding for your family, if you can find the right person. The going rate for nannies in metro Atlanta is anywhere from $20,000 to $35,000 annually, depending on the nanny's experience and whether or not she (or he) will be receiving room and board.

To find a good match, nanny referral agencies are available and offer the benefit of prescreening applicants for you, but they will cost more than if you locate one yourself. If you are hiring a nanny without the help of an agency (see below), you'll want to do a background check, which can be done online. Go to any search engine and type in "employment screening." A host of companies are available to research criminal records, driving records, and credit information for you. Locally, you can check with **Safe Harbor Investigations**, www.safeharborinvestigations.

com, an Atlanta-based, full-service, private investigation agency specializing in background checks and detailed, pre-employment screenings. You can also check Kudzu.com and read reviews on this and other investigative services.

There are numerous ways to find a nanny for your child. You can go the old-fashioned route and check the *Atlanta Journal-Constitution*'s classified ads, especially the Sunday edition, the monthly *Atlanta Parent* magazine (see below), or even Craigslist, which has a long list of prospective nannies in its childcare section. However, there are a number of websites that specialize in nanny placement and are a great resource for parents. Most have already performed background checks on their nannies, and you can search for a nanny by skill set, age, background, language, or education. Some popular websites are **www.care.com/atlanta-nannies,** **https://atlanta.aplusnanniesinc.com**, and **www.nanny-quest.net**, but many more come up in any online search result. Search for "Nanny Service" or "Atlanta Nanny."

## NANNY REFERENCES

When you interview your prospective nanny, ask for references and follow up with them. Here are some questions to ask their former employer:

- Why did they hire the nanny in the first place?
- How long was the nanny in their service?
- How many children did the nanny care for at one time?
- What were the nanny's responsibilities?
- Did they ever have any problems with the nanny?
- Why did the nanny leave that job?
- Would they hire this person again?

## NANNY TAXES

For those hiring a nanny directly (not using a nanny agency) there are certain taxes you will be responsible for calculating, specifically social security and Medicare, and possibly unemployment. For help with such issues, check the **Nanitax** website, www.4nannytaxes.com, or call 800-NANITAX. Nanitax provides household payroll and employment tax preparation services. You can also check with the **IRS's** household employer page, www.irs.gov/taxtopics/tc756.html, which discusses taxes for household employees.

## AU PAIRS

If you land the right applicant, an au pair (typically, a young woman—18 to 25—from abroad who will take care of your child and do light housekeeping in exchange for room, board, and a weekly stipend) may be a better alternative than a nanny. However, an au pair will likely not have the extended experience of a professional nanny, usually works for only one year, and is required to enroll in an accredited post-secondary institution for not less than six semester hours of academic credit. The **US Department of State's Bureau of Educational and Cultural Affairs**, 202-647-4000, http://exchanges.state.gov, oversees and approves the organizations that offer this service in the USA. To find out more about hosting an au pair or to begin the hiring process, you may want to contact the following national agencies. Any of them can connect you with a local coordinator who will answer your questions and/or match up your family with the right au pair.

- **Au PairCare Inc.**, 800-4AUPAIR, www.aupaircare.com
- **Au Pair in America**, 800-928-7247, www.aupairinamerica.com
- **Au Pair USA InterExchange**, 800-AU-PAIRS, www.interexchange.org/aupair
- **Cultural Care Au Pair**, 800-333-6056, www.culturalcareaupair.com
- **EurAupair Intercultural Child Care Programs**, 949-494-5500, www.euraupair.com
- **Go Au Pair**, 888-AUPAIR1, www.goaupair.com

## BABYSITTING

Finding a dependable babysitter can be a daunting task, especially if you are new to a city. Once again, referrals from co-workers or friends are usually the best way to go, but if you don't know anyone with children, there are other options. Local YMCAs and YWCAs often have a list of teenage members who have either gone through their CPR program or who have volunteered as counselors for the Ys for after-school or summer camp programs. (Some locations may require you to become a Y member before being granted access to the list.) Contact the metro Atlanta **YMCA**, 404-588-9622, www.ymcaatlanta.org, and **YWCA**, 404-527-7575, www.ywcaatlanta.org, for further details. Other organizations that can assist you in locating a babysitter are nanny placement services (see above), your local house of worship, college job referral services, or campus employment offices.

At this writing, high school and college-age sitters can expect to earn between $8 and $15 per hour. Some of the more savvy ones may even charge you a minimum (e.g., $10 per hour with a three-hour minimum; however they also may lower the charge for hours when the child or children are asleep). If you use a nanny placement service, you should expect to pay more than you would for a neighborhood teenager.

## ONLINE RESOURCES—CHILDCARE

If you'd like to use the internet to find childcare services in the metro Atlanta area, whether it's a facility or an au pair you're looking for, the following sites may be of some use:

- **www.cremechildcare.com**, comprehensive information about Crème de la Crème childcare centers.
- **www.georgiadaycare.org**, a searchable database of over 2,000 daycare centers.
- **www.goddardpreschool.com**, information about the Goddard School daycare centers, as well as a listing of its three locations throughout Cobb County.
- **www.kehillatchaim.org/preschool.html**, information about Roswell's Temple Kehillat Chaim childcare facility.
- **www.primroseschools.com**, information about Primrose childcare centers, as well as a listing of all metro Atlanta locations.
- **www.qualitycareforchildren.org**, a childcare solutions referral service.

## PARENTING PUBLICATIONS

Metro Atlanta is home to *Atlanta Parent*, 770-454-7599, www.atlantaparent.com, an award-winning parenting magazine that provides information on raising children in Atlanta. In addition to its helpful articles, each issue of *Atlanta Parent* also offers a comprehensive list of area schools, daycares, party planners, fun things to do around town with the family, and a monthly special events calendar. This free magazine is published monthly and can be picked up at area bookstores, toy stores, and childcare centers.

## CHILD SAFETY

In metro Atlanta, the **Georgia Division of Public Health**, 404-657-2700, http://health.state.ga.us, works to ensure the safety, health, and welfare of children and families across the state. Additionally, each county's **Board of Health** has established programs that work to distribute information on child safety issues, such as detecting lead paint levels in older homes, immunization, and common childhood illnesses. Several metro Atlanta counties are listed below. (To find the Board of Health office in counties other than those listed here, check the county government listings in the blue pages of your Atlanta phone book or contact the county offices listed in the **Neighborhoods** chapter of this book.)

- **Cobb & Douglas County Public Health**, 770-514-2300, www.cobbanddouglaspublichealth.org
- **DeKalb County Board of Health**, 404-294-3700, www.dekalbhealth.net

- **Fulton County Department of Health and Wellness**, 404-730-1211, www.fultoncountyga.gov
- **Gwinnett County Department of Health and Human Services**, 770-822-8000, www.gwinnetthealth.com

Other child safety resources worth taking a look at are **Children's Healthcare of Atlanta**, www.choa.org, which includes a great deal of information on child safety, wellness basics, and injury prevention; **DeKalb County's Board of Health, Safe Kids Program**, 404-294-3700, www.dekalbhealth.net, which offers useful information on topics such as injury prevention, swimming pool safety, and carbon monoxide, as well as a downloadable home safety checklist; and the **National Safe Kids Campaign**, 202-662-0600, www.usa.safekids.org, which offers valuable child safety information as well as an online, searchable listing of each state's child safety laws.

If you are interested in taking emergency training classes, including infant and child CPR, contact the hospitals in your area, as most of them offer these classes periodically throughout the year. You may also want to consider your local YMCA, since they too offer CPR classes from time to time.

## LEAD POISONING

According to the EPA, lead is one of the most pervasive toxic substances in the country today. Lead in paint, which children ingest by eating paint chips or inhaling paint dust, can result in serious and permanent damage to the brain, kidneys, bones, nervous system, and red blood cells. Unfortunately, about 75% of houses and apartments built before 1978 in the USA contain lead paint. And houses built before 1960 may contain old lead paint with concentrations up to 50% lead by weight.

In Georgia, landlords, sellers, and renovators are required to provide information on lead-based paint and lead-based paint hazards before the sale or lease of a private home or apartment built before 1978. Properties not included in the law are zero-bedroom dwellings (such as lofts and efficiencies), short-term or vacation rentals, housing for the elderly and the handicapped (unless children live there), and foreclosure sales. The **Georgia Department of Natural Resources, Environmental Protection Division**, 404-657-5947, www.georgiaepd.com, is the office in charge of creating and enforcing environmental safety rules based on Georgia statutes, including those dealing with lead-based paint hazards and their abatement (through containment, replacement, or removal). They are also in charge of providing certification and licensing for all state lead inspectors and assessors, and anyone conducting lead training programs. If you have questions or complaints regarding a home lead inspection or if you would like to find a certified inspector in your area, this is the office to contact.

For additional information about lead poisoning and prevention, including screening guidelines for children, contact the **Georgia Health Homes and Lead Poisoning Prevention Program**, 404-463-3754, www.health.state.ga.us/programs/lead, or the **National Lead Information Center**, 800-424-LEAD, www.epa.gov/lead.

## SCHOOLS

The following information may be useful as you search for the best schooling option for your children.

## PARENT RESOURCES

There are a number of resources available for parents, both locally and nationally. A quick Google search will bring up a number of websites that list schools and include user reviews. However, for a more thorough approach, below are some trusted sources to point you in the right direction:

- **American Association for Gifted Children**, 919-783-6152, www.aagc.org; information on gifted children and their education
- **Educational Resources Information Center**, 800-538-3742, www.eric.ed.gov; federally funded, national information system that provides information about a broad range of education issues
- **The Association of Boarding Schools**, 202-966-8705, 800-541-5908, www.boardingschools.com; comprehensive directory of boarding schools
- *Atlanta Parent Magazine*, 770-454-7599, www.atlantaparent.com; a city parenting magazine that often lists private schools, highlights the top public schools, and features editorials on local education issues
- **Coordinated Campaign for Learning Disabilities**, www.ldonline.org; information on all types of learning disabilities
- **Governor's Office of Student Achievement**, 404-256-4050, www.gaosa.org/FindASchool.aspx; search statistics for all of Georgia's school system with an easy map; categories include accountability, testing scores, demographics and more
- **The National Association of Independent Schools** (**NAIS**), 202-973-9700, www.nais.org; a detailed guide to selecting a non-public school that also provides a nationwide database of schools and parenting resources
- **National PTA (Parent Teacher Association)**, 800-307-4782, www.pta.org
- **School Match**, 614-890-1573, www.schoolmatch.com; a private organization offering one-page summary statistics on area high schools or lists of the top 15 schools (public or private) in your area that best meet your requirements
- **US Department of Education**, 800-872-5327, www.ed.gov; provides a wide variety of education information pertaining to both public and private schools;

for local information call 404-463-1172, or visit www.schooldatadirect.org and click on Georgia

# PUBLIC SCHOOLS

Metro Atlanta is home to a number of nationally recognized public schools. Whether you live within the city limits or in one of Atlanta's growing suburbs, you are bound to find an elementary, middle, or high school in your district that can provide a safe, educationally stimulating environment for your child. The key is to do your research ahead of time, find out as much as you can about your county's individual schools, and try to find one that would be the best fit for your family. Following is some basic information on the various school districts around Atlanta.

All of the school districts in metro Atlanta are experiencing record growth as more and more newcomers move to the area. This increase in population has led to overcrowding in many classrooms. School boards have tried to keep up with the boom by adding mobile classrooms (i.e., trailers) to area schools; to help with the school travel crunch, "staggered" or "varying" schedules have been suggested (where some students attend school from 8 a.m. to 3 p.m., while others attend from 8:45 a.m. to 3:45 p.m.); and by offering parents the option of sending their children to other, less-crowded schools within their county, when space is available. State and local school superintendents are also working to ensure that metro Atlanta schools are staffed accordingly. Today the average student-to-teacher ratio in each Atlanta area district is about 18:1.

In addition to the overcrowding issue, Atlanta-area parents are also dealing with changes to the school schedules in each county. Instead of operating on the typical September through June schedule, metro Atlanta schools now begin the school year by mid-August. Despite some complaining from parents that the early start dates interfere with vacation plans, not to mention the complaints from children, education officials at both state and local levels believe the early start dates are necessary in order to ensure that students have enough time to prepare for their annual standardized tests.

Families moving to Georgia and planning to enroll children in the public school system should research online or over the phone the county or city school system where they will be residing for registration specifics. Typically, registration is held in the spring, and procedures vary from school system to school system. Regardless of your county of residence, you will be required to show the following:

- Records or transcripts from your child's previous school (if applicable)
- Your child's social security number (or a signed statement from the parent declining to provide the number)
- Proof of residency

- An official document (like a birth certificate) showing proof of the child's age (Georgia requires that all children between the ages of 6 and 16 be enrolled in a public, private, or homeschool program)
- Certification of eye, ear, and dental examinations
- A current certificate of immunization for measles, rubella, tetanus, diphtheria, polio, mumps, whooping cough, varicella (chickenpox), and hepatitis B (or a signed medical exemption authorized by a medical doctor; or a sworn affidavit from the parents stating that immunization conflicts with their religious beliefs)

For more detailed information on education in Georgia, visit the **Georgia Department of Education** website at www.doe.k12.ga.us. Or contact metro Atlanta's city and county school districts directly. Phone numbers and web addresses for some are listed below; others can be found in the Government Blue Pages of the Atlanta Business phone book.

## ATLANTA CITY SCHOOLS

Public school students living within the Atlanta city limits, regardless of county, will attend an **Atlanta City School**. District maps can help you figure out which schools serve each neighborhood and can be found online at www.atlanta.k12.ga.us.

There are currently over 54,000 students enrolled in Atlanta's 50 elementary, 15 middle, 13 charter, and 21 high schools. A few of the system's standout schools include **Mary Lin Elementary School**, located in Candler Park, **Willis Sutton Middle School**, located in Buckhead, and **Grady High School**, located near Downtown. Mary Lin boasts strong parental involvement, a curriculum that combines core skills with arts-based education, and a diverse student body, all of which makes it one of the most popular neighborhood elementary schools in the city. Willis Sutton offers excellent academic and extracurricular opportunities, including a respected jazz band and concert orchestra program, national and international field trips, and math and science clubs. Willis Sutton also allows students to earn up to three high school credits while attending the school. Grady High School is home to *The Southerner*, an award-winning student newspaper, recently named one of the best high school papers in the country. Grady is also home to several state and nationally recognized academic teams, including a winning Mock Trial Team and Debate Team.

In addition, the City of Atlanta school system is home to seven not-for-profit charter schools, including **Charles R. Drew Charter School**, the **Neighborhood Charter School, Inc.**, and **Tech High School**. Each boasts strong parental involvement, academic excellence, and innovative educational ideas. Charles R. Drew students, for example, attend an extra hour of school each day, and an extra 20 days of school each year. And, under Drew's technology program, all students receive a computer for their home beginning in third grade.

It's important to note the Atlanta school system went through quite a scandal between 2009 and 2011. After test scores at some schools rose dramatically, local news hounds took notice and began an investigation. Scrutiny from the press led to a state investigation, which found 178 teachers or staff guilty of correcting students' tests to improve their scores. Atlanta Mayor Kasim Reed called the scandal a dark day for the city, and parents and residents felt betrayed and angry. The good news is the staff was replaced and new efforts were taken to prevent future cheating.

For more information on Atlanta City Schools, contact the **Atlanta City School Board**, 404-827-8599, www.atlanta.k12.ga.us.

## COBB COUNTY SCHOOLS

The **Cobb County** school system is the second largest in Georgia and among the largest in the USA. It is one of the fastest growing districts in the state, with an annual student population of more than 107,000 and approximately 2,500 new students enrolling each year. To pay for this tremendous growth, Cobb County residents rely on a 1% sales tax for education (SPLOST). The money collected provides funding to build new schools and renovate nearly all of the other school facilities in the county.

In Cobb County, there are 67 elementary schools, 25 middle schools, and 16 high schools; they all operate on a semester schedule, meaning that the 180-day school year is divided into two 90-day segments, with a break in between, rather than the typical system of three 60-day quarters. Proponents believe this allows for more uninterrupted instructional time for students, leading to better retention of the subjects that are covered.

Parental involvement is well documented in the Cobb County School System, which may account for the students' high test scores and numerous honors. For instance, several of the district's Parent Teacher Associations have won national awards for excellence and successful programs, participation, and fundraising. Moreover, in order to further raise funds to support the schools, many PTAs have also started school foundation clubs strictly committed to fundraising. The clubs target local and national businesses and non-profits, as well as residents. The combination of these funds with SPLOST funds means that Cobb schools come with perks you'd expect to see in top private schools, such as Promethium boards in classes starting in Kindergarten, computers in every classroom, laptops for all teachers, and multiple college-level courses and extracurricular activities.

Music lovers will also be pleased with the award-winning band programs available in Cobb. The Lassiter High School Band, The Trojans, is considered one of the best in the country. The band has received multiple national awards over the last 20 years and played at events such as the Macy's Thanksgiving Parade and the Tournament of Roses Parade. In 2012 the district added a new state-of-the-art 1,000-seat performing arts center, dubbed the Lassiter Concert Hall.

For more information on Cobb County schools, contact the **Cobb County Board of Education**, 770-426-3300, www.cobb.k12.ga.us.

## DEKALB COUNTY SCHOOLS

The **DeKalb County** school system, with over 100,000 students enrolled annually, is one of Georgia's best and brightest. The 83 elementary, 20 middle, and 22 high schools here have received more state and national honors than any other district in Georgia. A few shining examples are:

- **Austin Elementary School** in Dunwoody, which consistently ranks among the top ten highest-scoring elementary schools in the state on nationally standardized tests. This school also offers foreign language classes, a chess club, and more.
- **Avondale High School** has boasted two Governor's Honors students, an MLK Essay Award winner, as well as winners of National Council of Teachers of English Achievement awards and numerous state and national literary awards. It was also one of seven schools in the USA, and the only Georgia school, selected to represent the USA at the International GLOBE Conference in Helsinki, Finland.
- **Chamblee High School** perennially ranks among the highest in SAT scores at public schools in the state, boasts an award-winning band, choir, student newspaper, and yearbook, and has been awarded the Siemens Award for Science, Math and Technology. In 2006 the school also won first place in the State Science Symposium, was a Governor's Cup Regional Winner, and We the People State Champions. A consistent 85% of the school's graduating class qualifies for the HOPE (statewide, merit-based) Scholarship each year.

While these examples of student achievement clearly point to a strong school system, DeKalb County schools also offer something else: diversity. As mentioned in previous chapters, DeKalb County is one of the most diverse counties in the USA, with residents from across the country and from around the world settling here. **Cross Keys High School** in North Druid Hills, historically, has maintained the most culturally diverse student population in the state, with students from 65 countries, speaking over 75 different languages, enrolled. For more information on DeKalb County schools, contact the **DeKalb County Board of Education**, 678-676-1200, www.dekalb.k12.ga.us.

## FULTON COUNTY SCHOOLS

The **Fulton County** school system serves all of Fulton County outside of the Atlanta City limits. Like DeKalb County schools, Fulton County schools have also received a fair amount of local and national recognition over the last decade. In the past, as many as five of Fulton County's schools have been ranked as Georgia Schools of Excellence, and one was named a National Blue Ribbon School. More than 80% of Fulton County graduates go on to some form of higher education. And this school district was one of four in the USA to receive a Gold Medallion from the National School Public Relations Association in the late 1990s.

Top schools here include **Alpharetta Elementary School**, which offers students both a mentoring program and "The Eagles Nest," an outdoor classroom featuring an amphitheater, pond, and certified wildlife habitat; **Camp Creek Middle School**, the birthplace of the school system's After Three Club, an after-school program offering a variety of free activities to Fulton County middle school students, and home to several enrichment programs, including The Writers Workshop, Math Club, Chess Club, and Junior Beta Club; and **North Springs High School**, which boasts the an impressive Arts & Science Magnet Program. The program allows students to participate in either one or both of the components, through a variety of challenging opportunities focusing on the areas of math, science, drama, dance, technology, and visual art.

All 53 elementary, 18 middle, and 12 high schools that make up Fulton County's schools currently operate on a semester school calendar, rather than the typical quarter system. Student population in Fulton County schools is lower than the populations of other area school systems, with just over 75,000 enrolled annually. For more information on Fulton County schools, contact the **Fulton County Board of Education**, 404-768-3600, www.fultonschools.org.

## GWINNETT COUNTY SCHOOLS

The **Gwinnett County** school system is the most heavily populated in metro Atlanta and is one of the fastest growing in the USA. Approximately 161,000 students are enrolled annually, with an increase of approximately 4,000 new students per year. Currently, there are 77 elementary schools, 26 middle schools, 19 high schools serving the district, plus 4 charter schools and 7 additional facilities.

Gwinnett County public school educators are consistently recognized for outstanding achievements by national organizations including the President's Award for Excellence in Math and Science Teaching, the National School Library of the Year award, the National Middle School Teaching Team awards, and recently, the Broad Award for Excellence in Urban Education. Gwinnett County boasts both Georgia Schools of Excellence and National Schools of Excellence, and the school system's academic teams consistently win regional and state academic competitions in science, math, and problem solving. Almost 90% of Gwinnett County high school students continue their education after graduation.

Innovative schools here include **Peachtree Elementary**, which offers a variety of fun events for students and their families throughout the year, including an "International Block Party," celebrating diversity through traditional dances, songs, stories, and food from around the world; and **Central Gwinnett High School**, which is a state School of Excellence and offers college-level classes in Language Composition, Literature, Calculus, Statistics, World History, Economics, Chemistry, and more. In addition, Central Gwinnett High is home to at least 40 more extracurricular clubs and programs, including athletic teams, a Drama Club, and Thespian Society. If you'd like to find out more about Gwinnett County schools, contact the **Gwinnett County Board of Education**, 770-963-8651, www.gwinnett.k12.ga.us.

## PRIVATE AND PAROCHIAL SCHOOLS

If you are dissatisfied with your school district or looking for something the public system doesn't offer, you should consider one of Atlanta's many private or parochial schools. Simply Google "Private Schools Atlanta" and you'll find a host of discussions, news articles, and websites to get you started. Also, talk to people you know who have children in private schools or who have lived in Atlanta for a while and know the landscape. Or ask your realtor; many have lists by community with contact information and tuition costs.

One good bit of advice when looking for a private school is to consider location, reputation, and the needs of your child. For a complete list of schools, check Atlanta Yellow Pages under "Schools—Private" in print or online, or try websites like www.greatschools.org or http://private-schools.findthebest.com. Also, some local publications, such as *Atlanta Magazine* and the *Atlanta Business Chronicle*, review local private schools in special sections or editions each year. Look online or call the publication to purchase a recent copy. Plus, the *Atlanta Journal-Constitution* keeps an online section devoted to schools in Atlanta at http://schools.ajchomefinder.com.

Here are some more useful websites:

- **Private School Review**, www.privateschoolreview.com, links to over 30,000 private schools in the US, includes a complete list of Atlanta schools
- **School Digger**, www.schooldigger.com, a website listing private schools with contact information, plus rankings and reviews
- **Atlanta Private Schools Directory**, www.privateschoolsdirectory.com, a directory of private, Christian, Catholic, and charter schools in metro Atlanta and North Georgia
- **KnowAtlanta's Premier Relocation Guide**, www.knowatlanta.com/education, provides information on metro Atlanta's schools, including resources for public and private schools, colleges, universities, and daycare

## HOMESCHOOLING

Georgia's state laws regarding homeschooling are relatively simple and easy to follow. Basically, all Georgia children between the ages of 6 and 16 are required to enroll in a public, private, or homeschool program. Therefore, homeschoolers must submit a Letter of Intent to their county school system each September (or no later than 30 days after beginning a homeschool program), for each child. They must also submit monthly attendance forms for each child, showing that they are receiving a home education equal to four and a half hours per day for 180 days during a 12-month period. Official forms can be found at the Georgia **Home Education Information Resource (HEIR)** website, www.heir.org. There, you will also find more detailed information on Georgia homeschool laws, current updates on proposed changes to Georgia's homeschool legislation, and links to various homeschool groups and organizations around the state.

A great many children are being homeschooled in the Atlanta area, and those numbers are on an upward trend. Some parents simply want more control over their children's education; others want private school perks with a lower price tag. A number of new schools have opened, offering part-time educational support for homeschoolers, and some parents teach their children together and take turns leading the class. This lightens the overall burden of full-time homeschooling and improves the available curriculum.

Also, thanks to the internet and the commitment of parents, there are numerous resources for parents looking to homeschool their children. A few to consider are (some may have a religious affiliation):

- **Atlanta Alternative Education Network**, www.aaengroup.com; local homeschooling group serving metro Atlanta through classes, park days, field trips, and more
- **Communities of Home Educators for Christ**, www.chec-ga.org; Christian-based homeschooling group serving Cobb and Paulding counties
- **Georgia Home Education Association**, 770-461-3657, www.ghea.org; great online resource for homeschooling in Georgia, including lists of homeschool activities and local groups, information on state laws, tips for new homeschoolers, and more
- **LEADhomeschool**, www.leadhomeschool.org; an all-inclusive, Decatur-based homeschooling group serving Atlanta area homeschoolers through weekly park days and classes, monthly parent support meetings, and field trips

## HIGHER EDUCATION

Metro Atlanta is home to the largest concentration of colleges and universities in the southeast United States, including trade schools, two-year colleges, traditional four-year universities, ongoing education, law school, medical school, and so on. Also, thanks to technology, getting your credits has never been more flexible with almost all schools offering some online or flexible hours for students. For a list of schools in metro Atlanta check out the Atlanta Yellow Pages in print or online under "Schools." In the meantime, here is a list of some of the oldest or largest:

- **Agnes Scott College**, 141 E College Ave, Decatur, 404-471-6000, 800-868-8602, www.agnesscott.edu; is an independent national liberal arts college for women, located in a national Historic District in Decatur. Founded in 1889, Agnes Scott is affiliated with the Presbyterian Church (USA) and is consistently ranked one of the best women's colleges in the nation by publications such as *The Princeton Review, Kaplan/Newsweek College Catalogue* and *The Fiske Guide to Colleges.* Approximately 1,000 students attend Agnes Scott, with more than 90% residing in college residence halls or apartments.
- **Atlanta University Center,** www.aucenter.edu; is a consortium of four individual institutions, making it the largest predominantly African-American educational complex in the world. Members of the AUC are:
  - **Clark Atlanta University**, 223 James P. Brawley Dr, Atlanta, 404-880-8000, www.cau.edu; a comprehensive, urban coeducational institution offering both undergraduate and graduate courses. Founded in 1988 by the merging of Atlanta University, one of the oldest African-American universities in the nation, and Clark College, a respected liberal arts college, Clark Atlanta University is now home to approximately 4,000 students representing more than 50 different countries and nearly every state in the USA.
  - **Morehouse College**, 830 Westview Dr SW, Atlanta, 404-681-2800, www.morehouse.edu; the nation's only historically black private liberal arts college for men. Founded in 1867, Morehouse College now enrolls approximately 3,000 students each year and confers bachelor's degrees to more African-American men than any other school in the USA.
  - **Morehouse School of Medicine**, 720 Westview Dr SW, Atlanta, 404-752-1500, www.msm.edu; a four-year, degree-granting medical institution, established in 1975. Originally a two-year educational program in basic medical sciences at Morehouse College, Morehouse School of Medicine became an independent institution in 1981. The first class of M.D.'s trained at Morehouse graduated in May 1985. Today there are approximately 290 medical students enrolled at the school.
  - **Spelman College**, 350 Spelman Ln SW, Atlanta, 404-681-3643, www.spelman.edu; a predominantly residential, private, historically Black, liberal arts college for women. Founded in 1881, Spelman consistently ranks among the best liberal arts colleges according to *US News & World Report* and is home to more than 2,100 students from 41 states and 15 foreign countries.
- **Emory University**, 1380 S Oxford Rd NE, Atlanta, 404-727-6123, www.emory.edu; is noted nationally for its many fine programs and departments, as well as its most prominent lecturer and faculty member, former President Jimmy Carter. Emory University offers nine major academic divisions, numerous centers for advanced study, and a host of affiliated institutions, including Oxford College, a two-year undergraduate division located in Oxford, Georgia. There are currently over 14,000 students enrolled at Emory, representing all regions of the USA and 100 foreign nations.

- **Georgia Institute of Technology**, 225 North Ave NW, 404-894-2000, www. gatech.edu; founded in 1888, Georgia Tech is consistently ranked among the top ten universities in the USA by *US News & World Report* and *Money* magazine. Known for its schools of engineering, science, business management, and architecture, this university enrolls approximately 21,000 students each year. Georgia Tech's placement center is also one of the nation's most successful: At each graduation, over 50% of students receiving their diplomas have already been hired for a job or accepted into graduate school.
- **Georgia Perimeter College**, 678-891-2805, www.gpc.edu; is a non-residential unit of the University System of Georgia, with campuses throughout the metro area. Established in 1964, the school now offers more than 40 undergraduate credit and non-credit programs, specializing in liberal arts associate degrees, technical degrees, and professional preparation. The 26,000 students enrolled each year are seeking to complete associate's degrees, transfer to senior colleges or universities, or prepare for entry into careers.
- **Georgia Gwinnett College**, 1000 University Center Ln, Lawrenceville, 678-407-5000, www.ggc.edu; founded in 2006, it was the first four-year college established in Georgia in 100 years and the nation's first four-year college created in the 21st century. It offers 12 degrees in 40 areas of study and has broken ground on a $30 million Allied Health and Science facility, which is expected to open in time for the 2014 fall semester.
- **Georgia State University**, 33 Gilmore St, SE, Atlanta, 404-651-2000, www.gsu. edu; features six academic colleges, including a respected law department, and is the second largest institution in the University System of Georgia. Georgia State, nicknamed the "concrete campus" because of its location in downtown Atlanta, offers 52 undergraduate and graduate degree programs in more than 60 fields of study to approximately 32,000 students annually. About 25% of the student body is made up of graduate students.
- **The Interdenominational Theological Center**, 700 Martin Luther King Jr Dr, Atlanta, 404-527-7700, www.itc.edu; an ecumenical, graduate professional school of theology. Chartered in 1958, the ITC now consists of six seminaries, including the Gammon Theological Seminary, the Turner Theological Seminary, the Johnson C. Smith Theological Seminary, the Morehouse School of Religion, the Phillips School of Theology, and the Charles H. Mason Theological Seminary.
- **Mercer University**, Cecil B. Davis Campus, 3001 University Dr, Atlanta, 678-547-6000, www.mercer.edu; offers programs in 20 diverse fields of study, including liberal arts, business, and medicine. Founded in 1833 in Penfield, Georgia, and later moved to Macon (where the school's main campus is located), Mercer University is home to approximately 8,000 students, 2,600 of whom attend the Cecil B. Davis Campus in Atlanta. The Cecil B. Davis Campus is home to the Graduate and Professional Center, as well as its newest academic unit, the James and Carolyn McAfee School of Theology.

- **Oglethorpe University**, 4484 Peachtree Rd NE, Atlanta, 404-261-1441, 800-428-4484, www.oglethorpe.edu; is an independent, coeducational liberal arts institution of approximately 1,000 students. Chartered by the state in 1835, Oglethorpe opened in 1838 and then closed again in 1862 due to the Civil War. The school was rechartered in 1913 and opened at its current location in Brookhaven in 1915. Oglethorpe University is home to the Georgia Shakespeare Festival, a not-for-profit repertory theatre that offers Shakespearean productions throughout the year. Call 404-264-0020 or visit www.gashakespeare.org for tickets/show information.
- **Savannah College of Art and Design**, 1600 Peachtree St NE, Atlanta, 404-253-2700, www.scad.edu; opened its doors in Atlanta in 2005, and quickly expanded in 2006 by acquiring the Atlanta College of Art, a 100-year-old art school. SCAD is the only accredited four-year art college in the USA to share a campus with a noted museum, theater company, and symphony orchestra. The second location of its Savannah parent, SCAD as a whole offers 20 degree programs, along with other certificate programs and individual courses, and currently instructs 10,400 full-time students with a 16:1 student-to-faculty ratio.

TYPICAL OF OTHER LARGE METROPOLITAN AREAS, ATLANTA IS A LAND of malls, superstores, and shopping districts. It is likely that wherever you choose to live in metro Atlanta, you will be an easy drive from at least one shopping mall or district.

## SHOPPING DISTRICTS

If Atlanta has a quintessential shopping district, **Buckhead** is it. This is where you'll find two of the city's most popular malls—Lenox Square Mall and Phipps Plaza, as well as an assortment of galleries, specialty shops, and upscale boutiques. Prices here seem astronomical, compared to what you'll find in other areas of the city; however, this is most likely the only place you'll be able to find that breathtaking Versace gown or locally designed fine jewelry. Don't be intimidated by Buckhead's high-class reputation; shopping here can be a great adventure, and bargains abound, particularly during the changing seasons' clearance sales. Numerous Buckhead boutiques line Peachtree, Roswell, West Paces Ferry, and Piedmont Roads, not to mention those in development winding from its numerous side streets. And don't forget Pharr Road or Buckhead Avenue, which boast some of the most interesting and affordable of Buckhead's retail establishments, such as non-profit art studio **Work of Our Hands**, 404-504-9912, www.workofhands.com, and resale children's boutique **Sweet Repeats**, www.sweetrepeatsatlanta.com, 404-261-7519.

**Virginia Highland** offers stylish clothing, antiques, cards, flowers, and other delights in one-of-a-kind boutiques that mix funky with upscale. Shops in Virginia Highland line three non-consecutive blocks along North Highland Avenue. Start your tour just before the intersection of North Highland and Virginia Avenue and head south. On weekends especially, you may have to pay $5 to $10 to park in one of the pay lots located throughout the neighborhood (or you can try parking on one of the side streets radiating off of North Highland—watching for the posted no-parking zones). Top off the day with a visit to **Murphy's** (at the intersection of North Highland and Virginia Avenue), 404-872-0904, www.murphys-atlanta-restaurant.com, a popular neighborhood restaurant offering brunch, lunch, and dinner, as well as a full dessert menu, specialty coffee, and wine.

The **Little Five Points** (**L5P**) area is for the young and cool. Come here to rifle through vintage clothing, buy a kite, get your navel pierced, or browse some of Atlanta's best music stores. Shopping starts on Moreland Avenue with the **Junkman's Daughter**, 404-577-3188 (a popular L5P destination offering funky clothing, kitschy household items, and more), and **The Vortex Bar and Grill**, 404-688-1828, www.thevortexbarandgrill.com, and continues around the bend on Euclid Avenue and beyond.

The city of **Decatur**, like Virginia Highland, abounds with small, independently owned boutiques, cafés and restaurants, and more. Because downtown Decatur is a true town square, you'll want to park your car and head out on foot. (Your best bet for parking is to find one of the metered spaces along East Ponce de Leon or one of the side streets, which can be a challenge on weekends.) Popular shops include the **Squash Blossom** clothing boutique, 404-373-1864, www.squashblossomboutique.com, on East Court Street; **The Little Shop of Stories**, an adorable children's book store off East Court Square, (404) 373-6300, www.littleshopofstories.com; and **Mingei World Arts**, 404-371-0101, www.mingeiworldarts.com, on Church Street. And, if you find yourself hungry, nothing beats an inexpensive, gourmet taco from **Taqueria del Sol**, 404-377-7668, www.taqueriadelsol.com.

## SHOPPING MALLS

The delight of mall shopping for many is the efficiency and comfort it offers; a shopper can bring a list of diverse items and find them all at one convenient (and air conditioned) location. And malls here run the gamut in size and quality—Phipps Plaza, for example, is modeled after an elegant, Georgian mansion, with its interior boasting brass fixtures, fine woodwork, and marble floors. Meanwhile, many newer developments are open air malls that combine residential and retail properties. Atlanta's recent addition, Atlantic Station, offers shopping, a major movie theater, a five-star hotel, high-rise condos, and numerous chic restaurants. Here are some of Atlanta's biggest malls:

- **Atlantic Station**, 171 17th St, Ste 1650, Atlanta, 404-876-2616, www.atlanticstation.com
- **The Avenue** outdoor malls, 877-THE-AVENUE, www.shoptheavenue.com, **East Cobb**, 4475 Roswell Rd, Marietta; **Webb Gin**, 1350 Scenic Hwy, Ste 356, Snellville; **West Cobb**, 3625 Dallas Hwy, Ste 470, Marietta; **Forsyth,** 410 Peachtree Pkwy, Cumming

- **Cumberland Mall**, I-75 at Cobb Pkwy, Atlanta, 770-435-2206, www.cumberlandmall.com
- **Sugarloaf Mills**, 5900 Sugarloaf Pkwy, Lawrenceville, 678-847-5000, www.simon.com/mall/sugarloaf-mills
- **Galleria Specialty Mall**, One Galleria Pkwy NW, Marietta, 770-989-5100, www.galleriaspecialtymall.com
- **Gwinnett Place Mall**, 2100 Pleasant Hill Rd, Duluth, 770-476-5160, www.shopgwinnettplacemall.com
- **Lenox Square**, 3393 Peachtree Rd NE, Atlanta, 404-233-6767, www.simon.com/mall/lenox-square
- **Mall at Stonecrest**, 2929 Turner Hill Rd, Lithonia, 678-526-8955, www.mallatstonecrest.com
- **Mall of Georgia**, 3333 Buford Dr, Buford, 678-482-8788, www.simon.com/mall/mall-of-georgia
- **North DeKalb Mall**, 2050 Lawrenceville Hwy, Decatur, 404-320-7960, www.northdekalbmall.com
- **Northlake Mall**, 4800 Briarcliff Rd NE, Tucker, 770-938-3564, www.shopnorthlake.com
- **North Point Mall**, GA 400 at Haynes Bridge Rd exit, Alpharetta, 770-740-9273, www.northpointmall.com
- **Perimeter Mall**, Ashford-Dunwoody Rd, Atlanta, 770-394-4270, www.perimetermall.com
- **Phipps Plaza**, 3500 Peachtree Rd NE, Atlanta, 404-262-0992, www.simon.com/mall/phipps-plaza
- **The Gallery at South DeKalb**, 2801 Candler Rd, Decatur, 404-241-2431, www.southdekalbmall.com
- **Southlake Mall**, 1000 Southlake Mall Dr, Morrow, 770-961-1050, www.southlakemall.com
- **Town Center Mall**, 400 Ernest W. Barrett Pkwy, Kennesaw, 770-424-9486, www.simon.com/mall/town-center
- **Underground Atlanta**, 50 Alabama St SW, Atlanta, 404-523-2311, www.underground-atlanta.com

## OUTLET MALLS

- **Chelsea Premium Outlets**, 800 Hwy 400 South, Dawsonville, 706-216-3609, www.premiumoutlets.com; this outlet mall is located about 45 minutes north of Atlanta, up Georgia 400, and is enormous, making it impossible to visit all of the stores in one day. Shops here include Off Fifth (the Saks Fifth Avenue outlet store), a Williams-Sonoma outlet, Crate and Barrel outlet, Gap outlet, Banana Republic outlet, various shoe and toy stores, and more. The mall also offers designer specialty shops—from Calvin Klein to BCBG to Adrienne Vittadini—for shoppers who want designer fashion at discount prices.

- **Tanger Factory Outlets**, I-85 north to exit 52, 800 Steven B. Tanger Blvd, Commerce, 706-335-3354, www.tangeroutlet.com; located about an hour north of Atlanta on Interstate 85. Shops here include a Polo Ralph Lauren factory outlet, a Brooks Brothers outlet, J Crew, Tommy Hilfiger outlet, Carter's, and the very popular Nike Factory Store.

## DEPARTMENT STORES

- **Belk**, 800-669-6550, www.belk.com; a leading retail department store with locations throughout metro Atlanta, primarily in its major malls.
- **Bloomingdales**, 404-495-2800, 770-901-5200, www.bloomingdales.com; located at Lenox Square and Perimeter Mall; an upscale national department store chain that got its start in New York's Lower East Side in the 1860s. Personal shoppers or interior designers are available.
- **Dillard's**, 1-800-345-5273, www.dillards.com, well-known department store brand with stores across the state and five in Atlanta. To find your nearest location, visit the website.
- **J.C. Penney**, 800-322-1189, www.jcpenney.com; multiple locations throughout metro Atlanta, chock full of all the usual department store stuff for your home and you.
- **Macy's**, 877-493-9207, www.macys.com; multiple locations in metro Atlanta, including Lenox Square, South DeKalb, and Cumberland Mall. Macy's is a solid, mid-range store with a large variety of items for the home, gifts, clothing, makeup, perfume, shoes, wedding registry, etc.
- **Neiman Marcus**, 800-555-5077, www.neimanmarcus.com; located at Lenox Square, this posh department store offers an elegant collection of home goods, clothing, shoes, beauty items, gifts, shoes, etc., from the best designers. Come here for Manolo Blahnik shoes, Prada bags, Dolce & Gabbana dresses, and more.
- **Saks Fifth Avenue**, 877-551-7257; www.saksfifthavenue.com; located at Phipps Plaza. Another of the nation's finest department stores, Saks has a large selection of upscale goods and incredible sales at end of season.
- **Sears**, 800-349-4358, www.sears.com; several locations throughout metro Atlanta, including Southlake, Cumberland, and Northlake Mall. The original department store, Sears is *the* place for appliances—refrigerators, lawnmowers, toolkits, washers and dryers, etc. And don't forget the automotive centers.

## DISCOUNT DEPARTMENT STORES

- **Kmart**, 866-562-7848, www.kmart.com; nine locations throughout the metro Atlanta area
- **Kohl's**, 866-887-8884, www.kohls.com; ten locations throughout the metro Atlanta area

- **Loehmann's**, www.loehmanns.com; locations at 2480 Briarcliff Rd, 404-633-4156, and 120 Perimeter Place, 770-391-9389
- **Marshall's**, 888-MARSHALLS, www.marshalls.com; locations throughout metro Atlanta, including Buckhead, Sandy Springs, Alpharetta, Lithonia, and Smyrna
- **Target**, 800-440-0680, www.target.com; many locations in metro Atlanta, including several Super Target stores
- **Walmart**, 800-925-6278, www.walmart.com; throughout metro Atlanta, including Dunwoody, Tucker, Marietta, and Roswell

## HOUSEHOLD SHOPPING

Once you've found your dream home, furnishings may be in order. From appliances to rugs, lamps, beds and bedding, or wallpaper, the following resources will get you started.

### APPLIANCES/ELECTRONICS/CAMERAS/COMPUTERS

The Atlanta Yellow Pages lists numerous authorized appliance and electronics dealers and stores in its print edition and online. In the Sunday edition of the *Atlanta Journal-Constitution* you can find pullout advertisements for all the major stores in the city; for computer dealers in particular, check the "Personal Technology" section. Also search Google, Yelp, Bing, or other search engines for stores near you, or forgo the trip and order what you need online and have it shipped and/or delivered. In the meantime, here are a few to get you started:

- **Apex Supply Company**, 404-262-0562, www.apexsupply.com; three showrooms in metro Atlanta, including Buckhead, Marietta, and Alpharetta
- **Best Buy**, 888-BEST-BUY, www.bestbuy.com; locations throughout metro Atlanta
- **Home Depot**, 800-553-3199, www.homedepot.com; locations throughout metro Atlanta
- **Howard Payne Company**, 3583-D Chamblee Tucker Rd, Chamblee, 770-451-0136, www.howardpayne.com; family-owned and -operated kitchen appliance store
- **Lowe's**, 800-445-6937, www.lowes.com; throughout metro Atlanta
- **MicroCenter**, Marietta, 770-859-1540, Duluth, 770-689-2540, www.microcenter.com; computer and electronic equipment
- **Office Depot**, 888-GO-DEPOT, www.officedepot.com; locations throughout metro Atlanta
- **Radio Shack**, 800-843-7422, www.radioshack.com; locations throughout metro Atlanta
- **Staples**, 800-378-2753, www.staples.com; locations throughout metro Atlanta

## BEDS, BEDDING & BATH

- **Bed, Bath and Beyond**, 800-GO-BEYOND, www.bedbathandbeyond.com; locations throughout metro Atlanta
- **Bed Down**, 504 Amsterdam Ave NE, Atlanta, 404-872-3696, www.beddown.com; specializes in luxurious designer linens, beds, and gorgeous bedroom collections
- **The Great Futon Port**, 6576 Dawson Blvd, Norcross, 770-448-4388, www.thegreatfutonport.com; sells futons, frames, and other home furnishings
- **Home Goods**, 800-888-0776, www.homegoods.com; specializes in designer furnishings at discount prices, locations throughout metro Atlanta
- **Mattress Barn**, 1240 Old Chattahoochee Ave, Atlanta, 404-351-6760
- **Mattress Firm**, 800-MAT-FIRM; www.mattressfirm.com; several locations in metro Atlanta
- **World Market**, 877-WORLD-MARKET, www.worldmarket.com; carries home goods and gifts with a global flair, store locations throughout metro Atlanta and Georgia

## CARPETS & RUGS

- **Allan Arthur Oriental Rugs**, 196 14th St NW Ste A, Atlanta, 404-607-1007, 800-686-7030, www.cyberrug.com
- **Atlanta Carpet Masters**, 1105 Parkside Ln, Woodstock, 404-306-3000, http://atlantacarpetmasters.com
- **Bell Carpet Galleries**, 6223 Roswell Rd, Atlanta, 404-255-2431, www.bellcarpetgalleries.com
- **Buckhead Yamin's Oriental Rugs**, 3252 Peachtree Rd, Atlanta, 404-231-1727, http://yamins.com
- **Carpet Depot**, www.carpet-depot.com; six locations in and around metro Atlanta, visit the website to find the one nearest you
- **Dalton Carpets**, 800-544-5334, www.daltoncarpets.com; multiple locations in and around metro Atlanta
- **Floor & Décor**, 877-675-0002, www.flooranddecoroutlets.com; five locations in metro Atlanta
- **Oriental Designer Rugs**, 1250-B Menlo Drive NW, Atlanta, 404-367-0001, www.orientaldesignerrug.com

## FURNITURE

To view a lot of furniture in a short time, take I-85 to the Jimmy Carter Boulevard exit. On Dawson Boulevard (the service road on the east side of I-85) is a long row of giant furniture showrooms showcasing a variety of styles of furniture in a wide range of prices. Also, try some online searches with Google, Yelp, Bing or a similar engine for local furniture stores. Here are a few other options:

- **American Signature Furniture**, 3535 Peachtree Rd NE, Ste 300, Lenox Market Pl, Atlanta, 678-538-0910, www.asfurniture.com; multiple locations throughout metro Atlanta
- **Ashley Furniture**, 678-990-4663, www.ashleyfurniture.com; four locations in metro Atlanta
- **Bassett Furniture**, 120 Perimeter Center West, Ste 400 Atlanta, 678-731-9706, www.bassettfurniture.com
- **Crate and Barrel**, 800-967-6696, www.crateandbarrel.com; two locations in metro Atlanta
- **Ethan Allen**, 888-EAHELP1, www.ethanallen.com; four locations in metro Atlanta
- **Huff Furniture**, 3178 Peachtree Rd, Atlanta, 404-261-7636; www.hufffurniture.com
- **Rooms To Go**, 888-709-5380, www.roomstogo.com; locations throughout metro Atlanta
- **Woodstock Outlet**, 100 Robin Rd, 6250 GA-92, Acworth, 678-255-1000, www.woodstockoutlet.com; family-owned and operated furniture store specializing in designer brands and discounted prices

## HOUSEWARES

- **Bed, Bath and Beyond**, see above
- **Crate and Barrel**, see above
- **Pier One Imports**, 800-245-4595, www.pier1.com; throughout metro Atlanta
- **Pottery Barn**, 888-779-5176, www.potterybarn.com; locations throughout metro Atlanta, including Lenox Square, Northpoint Mall, and the Mall of Georgia
- **Williams-Sonoma**, 877-812-6235, www.williamssonoma.com; locations throughout metro Atlanta, including a Williams-Sonoma Clearance Center at the North Georgia Premium Outlet Mall

## LAMPS & LIGHTING

- **Aaron's Lamp & Shade Center**, 3220 Cobb Pkwy, Marietta, 770-952-9459, http://aaronslampatlanta.com
- **Lamp Arts, Inc.**, 1465-A Howell Mill Rd, Atlanta, 404-352-5211, www.lampartsinc.com
- **Lux Lighting**, 770-476-4028, www.luxlightingltd.com; four locations in metro Atlanta
- **Sunlighting Lamp and Shade Center**, 4990 Roswell Rd NE, Atlanta, 404-257-0043, www.sunlightinglamps.com/
- **Vinings Lighting**, 631 North Main St, Ste 104, 770-801-9600, http://store.viningslightingonline.com

## HARDWARE/PAINTS/WALLPAPER/GARDEN CENTERS

Atlanta is the corporate headquarters of Home Depot, a national chain of home improvement warehouses ready to supply you with just about anything you would ever need to fix up your home or apartment. Bring your imagination and a comfortable pair of shoes; you might spend all day there. Below is contact information for **Home Depot**, **Lowe's**, and local **Ace** and **True Value** stores:

- **ACE Hardware**, 866-290-5334, www.acehardware.com; locations throughout metro Atlanta
- **Home Depot**, 800-553-3199, www.homedepot.com; locations throughout metro Atlanta
- **Lowe's Home Improvement Warehouse**, 800-445-6937, www.lowes.com; locations throughout metro Atlanta
- **True Value**, 773-695-5000, www.truevalue.com; locations throughout the metro Atlanta area

# SECONDHAND SHOPPING

If you're someone who enjoys rack-rummaging at thrift stores and looking for treasures at various flea markets and antique shops, then you'll like metro Atlanta—home to hundreds of secondhand stores, antique centers, and indoor flea markets. And because of the mild weather here throughout most of year, outdoor flea markets are abundant as well.

## ANTIQUE STORES & AUCTIONS

The undeniable antique capital of metro Atlanta (and some say the South) is **Antique Row**, 404-606-3367, www.antiquerow.com, in Chamblee, located along Peachtree Road, between Chamblee-Dunwoody Road and North Peachtree. Dealers here sell crafts, toys, jewelry, furniture, and a wide variety of collectibles. And with over 15 stores, comprising 500,000 square feet of antiques and collectibles, Antique Row attracts shoppers from all over the state. Well-known establishments, such as **Biggar Antiques**, 770-451-2541, www.biggarantiques. com, a cool and kitschy shop selling everything from antique signs and furniture to 1950s kitchenware; **China and Crystal Matchers, Inc.**, 800-286-1107, www. chinaandcrystal.com, a company specializing in helping people replace missing or broken items in their discontinued china and crystal patterns; and **Eugenia's**, 770-458-1677, www.eugeniaantiquehardware.com, a family-owned, hardware store, carrying authentic antique hardware for the home—no reproductions— are located here. When visiting Antique Row, your best bet is to park and walk. A walking map is available online at the Antique Row website.

If it's Southern antiques and country furniture you're looking for, try **Stone Mountain Village**, 770-938-1200, www.stonemountainvillage.com, located just outside of Georgia's Stone Mountain Park. Many of the stores here are housed in charming historic buildings and feature everything from collectibles and furniture to jewelry and hand-made gifts by Georgia artisans. Some of the more popular spots here are **Stone Mountain Old Post Office Antique Mall**, 770-465-4318, www.stonemountainantiquemall.com, a Civil War museum and memorabilia shop with over 30 dealers, and ART Station, 770-469-1105, www.artstation.org, a local theater that offers both year round productions and a range of classes (pottery, drawing, theater, dance) for all ages.

If upscale, high-design antiques are more your taste, and you've got the budget to support that, you will probably want to check out the shops at **Miami Circle**, www.buckhead.org/miamicircle, in Buckhead. Located just off Piedmont Road, a few blocks north of the Lindbergh MARTA station, this little antique and design district is now home to over 60 shops, including **Mandarin Antiques**, 404-467-1727, www.mandarinantiquesinc.com, the largest Chinese antiques importer in the Southeast, and **Frances Aronson Fine Art**, 404-949-9975, www.francesaronsonfineart.com, a gallery specializing in 19th and early 20th century French and American fine art. Miami Circle is also home to **Eclipse di Luna**, 404-846-0449, www.eclipsediluna.com, a deliciously funky restaurant and tapas bar, perfect for a quick lunch when you've had enough shopping.

In Marietta, the **Historic Shopping Square**, www.mariettasquare.com, features beautifully restored buildings and warehouses that are now home to nearly 20 collectibles and antiques shops. While here, be sure to visit **Mountain Mercantile**, 770-429-1663, www.mountainmercantile.com, a cozy shop that sells everything from Primitive, Victorian, and American Country art to books, albums, and gift items. You'll also want to check out **King's Row Antiques**, 770-919-7877, www.kingsrowantiques.com, a 3,200-square-foot shop featuring quality, solid-wood, antique furniture and home accessories, and the **Church Street Market**, 770-499-9393, a gourmet shop specializing in native Georgia food products, herb baskets, fresh cut garden flowers, heirloom vegetable and flower seeds, and more. To get to the square, take I-75 North from Atlanta to GA 120 West and exit on Marietta Parkway.

To find other antique shops in your neighborhood, check out the Atlanta Yellow Pages under "Antiques" in print or online. Or search online with Google, Yahoo, or Yelp, or visit **Atlanta Antique Dealers at** www.atlantaantiquedealers.com.

## FLEA MARKETS

Regardless of where you live in metro Atlanta, there is bound to be a flea market of some sort nearby. Most are fairly large and offer just about anything you can imagine. Others are smaller and may specialize in things like antiques and home furnishings. Some of the larger flea markets are listed below, but be sure to check the Atlanta Yellow Pages or search online for more comprehensive listings, and *Creative Loafing* and the *AJC* for weekly updates.

- **Buford Highway Flea Market**, 5000 Buford Hwy, Chamblee, 770-452-7140, www.bufordhighwayfleamarket.com; open weekends
- **Flat Creek Flea Market**, 3084 Hwy 78, Loganville, 770-466-4223; call for hours
- **Flea Emporium**, 9740 Main St, Woodstock, 770-592-1177; open daily
- **Georgia Antique Center & Market**, 6624 Dawson Blvd NE Expressway, Norcross, 404-446-9292; open weekends
- **Glenwood Flea Market**, 3900 Glenwood Rd, Decatur, 404-284-9139; call for hours
- **Lake Acworth Antique Flea Market** 4375 Cobb Pkwy NW, Acworth, 770-974-9856; open weekends
- **New South Atlanta Flea Market**, 8160 Tara Blvd, Jonesboro, 770-603-9944; call for hours
- **Peachtree Peddler's Flea Market**, 155 Mill Rd, McDonough, 770-914-2269, www.peachtreepeddlers.com; open weekends
- **Pride of Dixie Antique Market**, North Atlanta Trade Center, Norcross, 770-279-9899; open 4th weekend of every month
- **Roswell Antique Mall and Flea Market**, 700 Holcomb Bridge Rd, Roswell, 770-993-7200; open seven days a week
- **Scott Antiques Market**, Atlanta Expo Center, Atlanta, 770-569-4112, www.scottantiquemarket.com; open the second weekend of every month

## THRIFT & VINTAGE SHOPS

Not only can you find some really cool, inexpensive stuff at thrift stores, but local charities and organizations often benefit from the proceeds. What could be better than shopping for a cause, and saving a little money? The following are some of the most popular and well-stocked thrift stores in metro Atlanta. Keep in mind, they're all generally busiest on the weekends, and most put out their new items on Tuesdays. Knowing the store's schedule can help you get a jump on other shoppers who may be looking for the same special item you are.

- **Alexis' Suitcase**, 7878 Roswell Rd, Sandy Springs, 770-390-0010, www.alexis-suitcase.com
- **America's Thrift Store**, 3344 Canton Hwy, Marietta, 770-423-0094; 7055-C Highway 85, Riverdale, 770-996-5900, www.americasthrift.com
- **Goodwill Thrift Stores**, www.goodwill.org; locations throughout metro Atlanta; search Google for your closest store
- **Last Chance Thrift Store**, 5488 Peachtree Industrial Blvd, Chamblee, 770-452-656; 61709 Church St, Decatur, 404-296-1711; 900 Thornton Rd, Lithia Springs, 770-948-4492, www.lastchancethriftstore.com

- **St. Vincent de Paul Thrift Store**, locations throughout metro Atlanta, visit www.svdpatl.org to find the one nearest you
- **Salvation Army Thrift Store,** 746 Marietta St NW, 404-523-6214
- **Cathedral of Saint Phillip Thrift House**, 1837 Piedmont Ave, Atlanta, 404-876-5440
- **Value Village Thrift Store**, 1899 Metropolitan Pkwy SW, 770-840-7283, www.valuevillage.com

## FOOD

Metro Atlanta is home to a healthy offering of supermarkets, warehouse shopping, farmers' markets, and health food and specialty stores. Have fun stocking your kitchen with all your favorites!

### SUPERMARKETS

The major grocery store chains in the Atlanta area are **Kroger**, **Publix**, and **Whole Foods**.

- **Kroger**, 866-221-4141, www.kroger.com; known as a 24-hour, one-stop shop in Atlanta, with most of its 50+ locations providing pharmacy services, film developing, banking, cafés, and health food departments, in addition to grocery items. Some stores even have gas stations in the parking lot, offering lower gas prices to Kroger Plus members.
- **Publix**, 800-242-1227, www.publix.com; offers a wide selection of produce and grocery items, banking and pharmacy services at most locations, and publishes a free monthly health-food guide, *Greenwise*. Their Publix Apron's program, designed to inspire customers to discover the joys of cooking through in-store demonstrations and cooking classes, recipe cards, and meal-planning assistance, is popular.
- **Whole Foods**, 512-477-4455, www.wholefoods.com; this Texas-based natural foods supermarket debuted in Atlanta in the late 1990s in the Emory area, and two more were quickly added in Midtown and Sandy Springs. Whole Foods then went on to purchase the popular Atlanta-based Harry's Farmers Markets. Today there are six Whole Foods/Harry's locations throughout the metro Atlanta area, offering organic meats, produce, and dairy items, fresh food cafés, kosher bakeries, sushi, and more.

### WAREHOUSE SHOPPING

In metro Atlanta, there are three chain stores (each with several locations) that offer residents the warehouse shopping experience for a membership fee. Whether you are in the market for jumbo cans of corn or cases of paper towels, these stores are sure to meet all your bulk shopping needs.

- **BJ's Wholesale Club**, 800-BJs-CLUB, www.bjs.com; locations throughout metro Atlanta
- **Costco Wholesale**, 800-220-6000, www.costco.com; locations throughout metro Atlanta
- **Sam's Club**, 888-746-7726, www.samsclub.com; locations throughout metro Atlanta

## FARMERS' MARKETS

If you are looking for the freshest food or a greater variety than your local grocery store, visit one of Atlanta's numerous farmers' markets. The metro area has many large permanent markets—some indoors and some outdoors. Plus many markets open on the weekend near town centers. To browse markets in your area consider visiting www.pickyourown.org, a great resource for finding markets.

**DeKalb Farmers' Market** is an immense indoor market with an amazing and often inexpensive array of produce, not to mention cheeses, meats, seafood, coffee, and other exotic foods from around the world. The market also has its own restaurant/buffet where you can enjoy a huge variety of fresh, tasty foods on the spot or to go. **Whole Foods/Harry's Farmers Markets** tend to attract an upscale clientele, with beautiful produce, cheeses, and organic meats, but expect higher prices to match.

Other popular markets include the **Atlanta State Farmers' Market** in Forest Park and the many outdoor, neighborhood "tailgate" markets scattered throughout the city, particularly between June and October. Following is a listing of the best-known and established markets in and around metro Atlanta:

- **Atlanta State Farmers' Market**, 16 Forest Pkwy, Forest Park, 404-675-1782, agr. georgia.gov; 150-acre, open-air market, open year-round
- **DeKalb Farmers' Market**, 3000 E Ponce De Leon Ave, Decatur, 404-377-6400, www.dekalbfarmersmarket.com; open daily, year round from 9 a.m. to 9 p.m.
- **Decatur Farmers Market**, 163 Clairmont Ave in the Bank of America parking lot, www.decaturfarmersmarket.com; weekly, outdoor farmers' market, open Wednesdays 4 p.m. to 7 p.m., year round
- **Dunwoody Green Market**, 4681 Ashford Dunwoody Rd, Dunwoody, 770-214-8531, www.localharvest.org/dunwoody; outdoor market, open Wednesdays, 8 a.m. to 12 noon, May through November
- **Green Market at Piedmont Park**, 1071 Piedmont Ave, Atlanta, 404-875-7275, www.piedmontpark.org; open-air market, open Saturdays, 9 a.m. to 1 p.m., through May 3 through December 13
- **Harry's/Whole Foods Farmers Market**, Roswell, 770-664-6300; Marietta, 770-578-4400; www.wholefoods.com; local market, owned and operated by Whole Foods, open daily, year round, call each location for hours and specials

- **Morningside Farmers' Market**, 1393 North Highland Ave, Atlanta, 404-444-9902, www.morningsidemarket.com; outdoor market, located in the parking lot next to Horizon Restaurant, open Saturdays 8 a.m. to 11:30 a.m., year round

## HEALTH FOOD STORES

There is no shortage of health food stores, natural food grocers, and vegetarian cafés in metro Atlanta. For a complete list, check the Atlanta Yellow Pages under "Health and Diet Food Products." Some of the most popular include:

- **ABC Natural Food Outlet**, 4003 Memorial Dr, Decatur, 404-299-1191; natural foods, health and book store
- **The Good Earth**, 211 Pharr Rd, Atlanta, 404-266-2929; natural foods store and café
- **Life Grocery & Café**, 1453 Roswell Rd, Marietta, 770-977-9583, www.lifegrocery.com; natural foods co-op, open to the public
- **Mother Nature's Market**, 3853 Lawrenceville Hwy, Tucker, 770-491-0970, www.mymothernatures.com; natural foods market and health shop
- **Nuts 'N Berries**, 4274 Peachtree Rd, Atlanta, 404-237-6829, www.nutsnberries.com; natural foods and supplement store with deli and juice bar
- **Rainbow Grocery**, 2118 North Decatur Rd, Decatur, 404-636-5553, www.rainbowgrocery.com; all-vegetarian, health food market
- **Return to Eden**, 2335 Cheshire Bridge Rd, Atlanta, 404-320-EDEN, www.return2eden1.com; family-owned, all vegetarian, health food supermarket
- **Sevananda Food Co-Op**, 467 Moreland Ave NE, Atlanta, 404-681-2831, www.sevananda.com; organic food co-op, open to the public
- **Whole Foods**, Atlanta, 404-634-7800; www.wholefoods.com; natural foods supermarket, with several locations in metro Atlanta

## MAKE-AND-TAKE MEAL ASSEMBLY

An option that might be more of a bargain than you'd expect is **make-and-take meal assembly**, where the store does the prep and all you do is the assembly. A couple of the more popular companies, both with multiple Atlanta-area locations, follow. You can also go to the Easy Meal Prep Association's website, www.easymealprep.com, for updated lists and locations.

- **Dream Dinners**, www.dreamdinners.com
- **The Dinner AFare,** www.thedinnerafare.com

## FOOD TRUCKS

- Another fun meal option that's gained popularity in Atlanta is Food Trucks. Food trucks are exactly what they sound like—trucks that move throughout the city selling food. The variety of types of food trucks is endless, similar to the wide variety of restaurants in Atlanta. You'll find food trucks along Peachtree Street, Virginia Highland Ave, and a number of other metro thoroughfares. To find a food truck near you, visit www.roaminghunger.com.

- Not everyone has embraced the food trucks boom in Atlanta. Many municipalities and restaurant owners say the trucks take business from local merchants, while not paying the taxes that brick and mortar businesses pay. **The Atlanta Street and Food Truck Coalition** is working against the stigma, and to reverse ordinances that prohibit food trucks, www.atlantastreetfood.com.

- In the meantime, some trucks have taken to pooling their resources and opening parks where they can cluster and sell their goods. **The Atlanta Food Truck Park** is located off I-75 just south of downtown Atlanta at 1850 Howell Mill Road. The park houses dozens of food trucks, which you can research on their website, www.atlantafoodtruckpark.com. The park also hosts events, such as a movie night for families and live music on weekend nights.

## ETHNIC DISTRICTS

Metro Atlanta's diverse ethnic populations are generally concentrated in specific areas throughout the city, and it's in these communities that you will find the largest number of ethnic specialty stores. For example, those in the market for Asian products should head over to Buford Highway and New Peachtree Road, near DeKalb Peachtree Airport in Chamblee. Here, you'll find authentic Asian restaurants, strip malls and grocery stores, as well as the **Chinese Community Center**, 770-454-9167. Some of the most popular spots for dining, shopping, and socializing in this part of town include **Chinatown Square**, 770-458-6660, www.atlantachinatown.com; Hong Kong BQ, 770-451-7277; the **Dinho Supermarket**, 770-452-6907; and the **Great Wall Gift Store**, 770-457-8886, to name just a few. You'll also find that many of the ethnic grocers in this area carry hard-to-find Indian, Mexican, and Japanese ingredients as well. To find out more about Asian shopping and dining, check out **US Asian Business Council** online, www.usasean.org.

The North Druid Hills and Toco Hills communities are both home to a large Indian and Pakistani population. In these neighborhoods, where North Druid Hills intersects with Briarcliff Road, LaVista Road, Clairmont Road, and then Lawrenceville Highway, you'll find a great selection of Indian clothing stores, food markets, and restaurants. Some of the most popular shops and restaurants here include **Madras Saravana Bhavan**, 404-636-4400, www.saravanabhavan.com, considered by many to be the best South Indian restaurant in town; **Texas Sari Sapne**, 404-633-7274; and **Al-Huda Groceries**, 678-205-5252, http://alhudagroceries.com. For more information about Indian shopping and dining in Atlanta, visit any number of the websites devoted to Indian culture in Atlanta, including **www.atlantaindia.us** and **www.atlantaindians.com**.

Though the intown neighborhoods, particularly in DeKalb County, boast the largest international population, it's not uncommon to find authentic ethnic restaurants, shops, and grocery stores scattered throughout metro Atlanta. In recent years, Gwinnett County, in particular, has attracted a large number of Asian and Indian residents, many of whom have opened businesses along Jimmy Carter Boulevard, including **Ladlee Sarees**, 770-798-9707; **Spices House**, 678-969-9797; and **Ashiana** restaurant, 770-446-8081, www.theashiana.com. Jimmy Carter Boulevard is also home to the **Global Mall**, www.amsglobalmall.com, a 220,000-square-foot shopping center full of Indian and Asian restaurants, movie rental stores, clothing boutiques, and more.

Back along Buford Highway, towards the intersection of Buford Highway and Clairmont Road, many from the Hispanic community shop at the **Plaza Fiesta**, 404-982-9138, www.plazafiesta.net, a 380,000-square-foot shopping center, billing itself as "*the* shopping center for the Latin family." Plaza Fiesta prides itself on offering warm and friendly service, authentic Mexican- and Latin-American restaurants, and nearly 200 shops and kiosks, selling "a great variety of items not easily found anywhere else in the US." For more information about the Hispanic community in metro Atlanta, go online to **Atlanta Latino**, www.atlantalatino.com.

**W**ELCOME TO THE ARTS! WHETHER IT'S HIGH-CALIBER PERFOR-
mances in music, dance, or theater, or a tour of the visual arts you're
wanting, it's all here. As the center for culture and arts in the Southeast,
Atlanta is particularly proud of the Woodruff Arts Center, which houses several
of the area's fine arts institutions, including the internationally acclaimed Atlanta
Symphony Orchestra, the Alliance Theatre Company, and the High Museum of
Art. Theatrical performances, from touring Broadway shows and Shakespearean
drama to traditional ballet performances and classical opera, are readily available
in the metro region. And, if your taste is more suited toward student lab productions, puppet shows, or off-the-beaten-path theater productions, such as *Hamlet,
The Musical*, you will be certain to find a venue that suits you. Local museums
exhibit a wide assortment of visual arts—African-American, ancient, folk, and
high Renaissance, to name a few, and area galleries are a great place to browse for
funky local talent. Local music establishments host a variety of touring and local
acts, from jazz, blues, acoustic, and punk to big band and reggae. And, finally,
Atlanta has a thriving literary and intellectual community, which hosts lecture
series, author readings, and book signings.

To take advantage and enjoy metro Atlanta's diverse cultural offerings,
refer to the *AJC* (or its online arm, www.accessatlanta.com), which publishes a
"Weekend" section every Friday alerting readers to the goings-on about town. You
can also sign up to receive weekend email alerts. In addition, the weekly *Creative
Loafing* is an excellent source of information on artistic endeavors of all kinds:
Check its articles, reviews, and event listings in the "Happenings" section of the
paper or online. Also, Atlanta On the Cheap, www.atlantaonthecheap.com, is a
great resource for local arts, shopping and entertainment, plus how to save on
tickets or take advantage of free events. Also, the following contacts can point you
in the right direction for art events:

- **Arts at Emory**, 404-727-6187, www.emory.edu/arts; information on current and upcoming art, theater, and musical events sponsored by Emory University
- **Atlanta.net**, www.atlanta.net; a website developed by the city of Atlanta in coordination with multiple public and private partners to show visitors and locals all there is to do in the city of Atlanta
- **Atlanta Symphony Orchestra**, 404-733-4949, www.atlantasymphony.org; updated information on current and upcoming ASO concerts and events

## TICKETS

Tickets for most major events and performances can be purchased at the venue box office or at any **Ticketmaster** location. You can also charge by phone with Ticketmaster at 404-249-6400 or visit www.ticketmaster.com. **Empire Tickets** (formerly Ticketline) specializes in hard-to-get tickets. Contact them at 404-255-2020, www.empiretickets.com, for more information. It's usually a good idea to get tickets as far in advance as possible because many shows, concerts, exhibits, and events sell out quickly. When calling ahead, make sure you have your credit card ready and be prepared to pay service charges, usually between $5 and $10 per ticket. If you prefer to avoid the service charges, buy your tickets directly from the box office (cash or credit card only).

## PERFORMANCE VENUES: CONCERT HALLS, STADIUMS, AND ARENAS

The following concert venues are the largest in metro Atlanta. They play host to a variety of concerts each year—from rock, to country, to classical, and everything in between. When big-name acts and national and international performers come to town, these are the places they play, though you may also catch some of the better-known local bands here as well. For information about upcoming shows, ticket prices, and seating, contact each venue directly.

- **Boisfeuillet Jones Atlanta Civic Center**, 395 Piedmont Ave, 404-523-6275, www.atlantaciviccenter.com
- **Chastain Park Amphitheater**, 4469 Stella Dr NW, Atlanta, 404-233-2227, www.classicchastain.com
- **Center Stage Atlanta**, 1374 W Peachtree St, 404-885-1365, http://www.center-stage-atlanta.com/
- **The Fox Theatre**, 660 Peachtree St, Atlanta, 404-881-2100, www.foxtheatre.org
- **The Georgia Dome**, One Georgia Dome Dr, Atlanta, 404-223-9200, www.gadome.com
- **Georgia State University Concert Hall**, 404-651-4636, www.music.gsu.edu/events.aspx

- **The Gwinnett County Civic Center Arena**, 6400 Sugarloaf Pkwy, Duluth, 770-813-7500 or 800-224-6422, www.gwinnettcenter.com
- **Aaron's Amphitheatre**, 2002 Lakewood Way, Atlanta, 404-443-5000, www.lakewoodamphitheatre.org
- **Philips Arena**, One Philips Dr, Atlanta 404-878-3000, www.philipsarena.com
- **Rialto Center for the Performing Arts**, 80 Forsyth St at Luckie St, Atlanta, 404-651-1234, www.rialtocenter.org
- **Spivey Hall**, 5900 N Lee St, Clayton State University, Morrow, 770-961-3683, www.spiveyhall.org
- **Variety Playhouse**, 1099 Euclid Ave, Atlanta, 404-524-7354, www.variety-playhouse.com
- **Woodruff Arts Center** at 1293 Peachtree St, Atlanta, 404-733-5000, www.woodruffcenter.org.

## PERFORMING ARTS

## PROFESSIONAL MUSIC—SYMPHONIC, CHORAL, OPERA, CHAMBER

### ATLANTA SYMPHONY ORCHESTRA

Debuting in 1945 as the Atlanta Youth Symphony, and then changing its name in 1947, the Atlanta Symphony Orchestra (ASO), www.atlantasymphony.org, is one of the youngest American orchestras to achieve international prominence. The ASO is also part of the Robert W. Woodruff Arts Center, which includes the **Alliance Theatre Company**, the **High Museum of Art**, and the **Savannah College of Art and Design**. The ASO is particularly proud of its 15 Grammy Awards, earned from over 40 recordings. The ASO plays its regular season in Symphony Hall, located in the **Woodruff Arts Center**.

The regular symphony season runs from September through May, but the ASO stays busy throughout the year, giving over 200 performances in all. During the regular season, you can choose from 24 Classical Master Season programs, a Saturday Matinee Series entitled "Four @ 2:00," a Family Concert Series, or a series of Champagne and Coffee concerts featuring popular classics. During the summer months the ASO offers SummerFest, a casual series of concerts centered on a particular composer or theme, which take place in Symphony Hall. You can also attend the ASO's Classic Chastain and Country Chastain summer concerts, which are held at the **Chastain Park Amphitheatre**, 4469 Stella Drive NW in Atlanta. (Visit www.classicchastain.org for more information.) In addition, the symphony puts on a series of free outdoor concerts in Atlanta's city parks, which attract thousands of people with blankets and picnics.

In addition, in May of 2008, the ASO debuted at the **Verizon Wireless Amphitheater at Encore Park**, www.vzwamp.com, 404-733-5010, in Alpharetta. The 12,000-seat state-of-the-art amphitheater is the ASO's official outdoor venue, and hosts numerous other concerts and events throughout the year.

You can purchase **ASO tickets** several ways:

- **By phone**: To charge tickets by phone, call 404-733-4800 for full or partial season subscriptions, 404-733-5000 for individual tickets, or 404-733-4848 for group rates. There is an additional fee for this service.
- **In person**: Purchase tickets at the box office at the Woodruff Arts Center. Box office hours are 10 a.m. to 8 p.m., Monday–Friday and noon to 8 p.m., Saturday and Sunday.
- **Rush tickets** are available for every Thursday night performance of the Master Season Program. You can pay $15 at the box office for whatever remaining seats they have. They sell the tickets starting at 5 p.m. the afternoon of the performance.
- **Sneak preview open rehearsals**: For a few season concerts each year you can see the program for only $10 general admission. These rehearsals typically occur in the mornings. Call the box office, 404-733-5000, for information.

## ATLANTA SYMPHONY ORCHESTRA CHORUS AND CHAMBER CHORUS

The ASO Chorus was established under the musical direction of Robert Shaw during the 1967–68 orchestra season. Today the ASO Chorus is made up of 200 singers that perform with the Atlanta Symphony Orchestra, and the Chamber Chorus is made up of a select group of approximately 60 vocalists that perform both with the Atlanta Symphony Orchestra and independently.

For more information on the ASO Chorus and Chamber Chorus, call 404-733-4876, or visit them online at www.asochorus.org.

## ATLANTA SYMPHONY BRASS QUINTET

This quintet, the oldest chamber ensemble in Atlanta, has developed an international reputation by touring Denmark and Norway and playing for such dignitaries as Prince Charles of England. The Atlanta Brass Quintet offers a varied repertoire, from Baroque music to theatrical pieces, performing regularly at Kennesaw State University, www.kennesaw.edu, and throughout the USA. Call 404-875-TUBA or visit www.atlantabrass.com for more information.

## ATLANTA LYRIC THEATRE

The Atlanta Lyric Theatre (formerly the Savoyards Light Opera) performs several fully staged, professional light operas and a handful of smaller, alternative musical theatre productions each year. For more information, contact them at 114 N Park Square, Marietta, 404-377-9948, www.atlantalyrictheatre.com.

## ATLANTA OPERA

Since the late 19th century, the City of Atlanta has been home to an assortment of opera companies. The present-day Atlanta Opera has been in existence since 1985, when it changed its name from the Atlanta Civic Opera and appointed William Fred Scott as Artistic Director. Today this nationally acclaimed company offers four main stage productions each season. Recent shows have included Beethoven's *Fidelio*, *La Bohème*, *Aida*, and Gershwin's *Porgy and Bess*. Opera performances take place three times a year at the Cobb Energy Performing Arts Center. For ticket information or to be added to the Atlanta Opera's mailing list, call 404-881-8801, or go online to www.atlantaopera.org.

# COMMUNITY MUSIC—SYMPHONIC, CHAMBER

Many local musicians are keeping the community-based orchestra tradition alive in metro Atlanta. The following list is just a sampling of local community orchestras.

## ALPHARETTA CITY BAND

The Alpharetta City Band is a traditional community band made up of amateur adult and high school–aged musicians. They play a variety of music ranging from marches to big band jazz. Performances are held at various locations throughout north metro Atlanta. Contact them at 770-475-9684, www.alpharettaband.com, for more details.

## ATLANTA CONCERT BAND

The Atlanta Concert Band performs free to the general public at various locations throughout metro Atlanta or at special events. Funded by donations and the Fulton County Board of Commissioners, this North Atlanta community band provides an outlet for adult musicians to maintain and improve their musical skills and talents. Contact them at 404-237-9711, http://www.atlantaconcertband.org, for more information.

## ATLANTA WIND SYMPHONY

The Atlanta Wind Symphony, established in 1979, is composed of adult musicians ranging in experience from professional to hobbyist. The AWS Master Concert Series is made up of five core events and is performed annually at the **Roswell Cultural Arts Center**, 770-594-6232, www.roswellgov.com. They also play various outdoor venues and special events throughout the year. Call 770-641-1260, or visit them online at www.atlantawindsymphony.org for more information.

## EMORY COMMUNITY BRASS ENSEMBLE

The Emory Community Brass Ensemble is a 20-piece community ensemble composed of students, semi-professionals, and amateur adult musicians. Rehearsals are held weekly in the Schwartz Center for Performing Arts on the Emory University Campus, and concerts are held in that same building at the Cherry Logan Emerson Concert Hall. The musical director is Michael Moore, Principal Tuba of the Atlanta Symphony Orchestra and professor of tuba and euphonium at Emory. Call 404-875-TUBA for more information.

# DANCE PERFORMANCES—BALLET, JAZZ, MODERN

## ATLANTA BALLET

The Atlanta Ballet is the longest continuously running ballet in the country. Started in 1929 at the Fox Theatre, the ballet was originally called the Dorothy Alexander Concert Group after its founder. The ballet's regular season shows are still held at the **Fox Theater** in Downtown, as well as at the **Cobb Energy Performing Arts Center** in Cobb County. The Atlanta ballet performs five or six ballets each season, including classical productions like *Romeo and Juliet* and *Swan Lake*, alongside modern and innovative pieces such as *Moulin Rouge: The Ballet* and *Dracula*. The company has also collaborated with two Grammy-nominated performances: *Shed Your Skin*, performed with the Indigo Girls, and *big*, performed with the help of Antwan "Big Boi" Patton from Outkast. For schedule and season ticket information, contact the box office at 404-892-3303, or visit the Atlanta Ballet online at www.atlantaballet.com. Individual tickets can be purchased through TicketMaster, 404-249-6400, www.ticketmaster.com.

## BALLETHNIC DANCE COMPANY

The Ballethnic Dance Company, 2587 Cheney Street, East Point, 404-762-1416, www.ballethnic.org, which celebrated its 20th season in 2010, is a premier dance company, renowned for its mixing of rhythms of African dance with the precise techniques of classical ballet. The company performs various original pieces throughout the year, including their annual *Urban Nutcracker*.

## BEACON DANCE COMPANY

The Beacon Dance Company, headquartered in the **Beacon Hill Arts Center**, 1361 Chalmette Drive, Atlanta, is a contemporary dance troupe that regularly performs at various venues throughout metro Atlanta. For more information, call 404-377-2929 or go online to www.beacondance.org.

## THEATER—PROFESSIONAL AND COMMUNITY

Metro Atlanta doesn't technically have a theater district, but it does have a theater scene. **Atlanta Coalition of Performing Arts** is a nonprofit alliance of metro Atlanta's performing arts organizations and professionals. The group consists of 170 partner and associate organizations from over a dozen greater Atlanta counties, 404-873-1185, www.atlantaperforms.com. The group produces a wide variety of shows in various neighborhood locales. Though you will find expensive visiting Broadway productions in a few theaters, for the most part, Atlanta's theater scene offers a variety of smaller, more affordable productions.

- **Actor's Express**, 887 West Marietta St NW, Atlanta, 404-875-1606, www.actors-express.com; box office 404-607-7469
- **Alliance Theatre Company**, Woodruff Arts Center, 1280 Peachtree St NE, Atlanta, 404-733-5000, www.alliancetheatre.org
- **Atlanta Shakespeare Company**, 499 Peachtree St NE, Atlanta, 404-874-9219, www.shakespearetavern.com
- **Aurora Theatre Company**, 128 Pike St, Lawrenceville, 678-226-6222, www.auroratheatre.org
- **Georgia Ensemble Theatre**, Roswell Cultural Arts Center, 770-641-1260, www.get.org
- **Georgia Tech Theatre for the Arts**, 349 Ferst Dr NW, Atlanta, 404-894-9600, www.ferstcenter.gatech.edu
- **Horizon Theatre Company**, 1083 Austin Ave NE, Atlanta, 404-584-7450, www.horizontheatre.com
- **Onstage Atlanta**, N Decatur Rd, Atlanta, 404-872-8427, www.onstageatlanta.com; box office 404-897-1802
- **Push Push Theater**, 121 New St, Decatur, 404-377-6332, www.pushpushtheater.com
- **Seven Stages**, 1105 Euclid Ave NE, Atlanta, 404-523-7647, www.7stages.org
- **Stage Door Players**, 5339 Chamblee Dunwoody Rd, Dunwoody, 770-396-1726, http://www.stagedoorplayers.net

- **Theater Emory**, Emory University, Atlanta, 404-727-6187, www.theater.emory.edu
- **Theatrical Outfit**, 84 Luckie St, Atlanta, 678-528-1500, www.theatricaloutfit.org
- **Whole World Theatre**, 1214 Spring St, Atlanta, 404-817-0880, www.whole-worldtheatre.com

# FILM

Metro Atlanta is home to a few really good, alternative movie houses. If you are interested in foreign films, art house flicks, documentaries, or classic B-movies, the theaters below will probably have what you are looking for. If you're looking for mainstream, Hollywood movies, refer to the Atlanta Yellow Pages under "Theaters" for general multi-screen movie complexes.

- **Cinefest at Georgia State University** is well known for bringing wacky, obscure, and arty films to Atlanta film buffs. To contact Cinefest, call 404-413-1798, or visit them online at www.cinefestfilmtheatre.com.
- Various departments at **Emory University** regularly sponsor film series at White Hall and the Harland Cinema that are open to the public. Contact 404-727-5050, http://arts.emory.edu, for more information.
- **Fernbank Museum of Natural History IMAX Theatre**, 767 Clifton Rd NE, Atlanta, 404-370-0019, www.fernbank.edu.
- The **High Museum** hosts film series in the Hill Auditorium throughout the year. Contact them at 404-733-4570 or www.high.org for details.
- **LeFont Theater Sandy Springs**, Parkside Shopping Plaza, Sandy Springs, 404-255-0100, www.lefonttheaters.com.
- **Tara Cinema**, 2345 Cheshire Bridge Rd NE, 404-634-6288.

## FILM FESTIVALS

- **Atlanta Film and Video Festival** (runs through April), various locations throughout Atlanta, 404-352-4225, www.atlantafilmfestival.com; showcases the innovative animation, documentary, experimental, and student works by local, national, and international video and filmmakers. Highlights include screenings of work, educational seminars, guest speakers, and contests.
- **Summer Film Series**, Fox Theatre, Atlanta, 404-881-2100, www.foxtheatre.org; each summer the Fox Theatre hosts a series of films, which may include recently released movies, family-oriented movies, and classic films. The schedule changes annually, so be sure to contact the theater for more information.
- **Festival League,** 1132 Virginia Ave NE, Atlanta, started in 2002, the league operates numerous festivals in the Atlanta area, all meant to offer the public something different from Hollywood blockbusters. Ongoing festivals include Atlanta Horror Fest, Montezuma International Film Festival, Atlanta Under-

ground Film Festival, Docufest, and Animation Attack! For showtimes or information on submissions, visit www.festivalleague.com.

# MUSIC—CONTEMPORARY

Metro Atlanta has a thriving and diverse local music scene. Foremost, Atlanta is known as the South's capital of hip-hop due to the successes of countless urban and R&B artists, such as Ludacris, Toni Braxton, TLC, Outcast, Ciara, Usher, Cee Lo Green, and more. However, its tastes and talents hardly stop there. Whether you enjoy rock, jazz, county, or classical, the city has something for everyone. Find your fair share of alternative musicians, such as the Indigo Girls and R.E.M., or some southern rock like the Black Crowes in midtown or north Atlanta. Grammy award–winning group The Zac Brown Band started out as regulars around Kennesaw and Woodstock, and there are always plenty of jazz and blues bars in Virginia Highlands and midtown. To find local music acts and venues, check out Yelp, AccessAtlanta. com, or *Creative Loafing*'s website, www.creativeloafing.com. In the meantime, the following venues are a good place to start.

## BARS AND NIGHTCLUBS

Atlanta's nightclub and bar scene is vast, vibrant, and diverse. Venues range from laid back live music over drinks in cozy atmospheres, to typical sports bars, to chic theme bars like Buckhead's **Havana Club**, to light-pulsing, bass-pounding night-clubs. Moreover, Atlanta's suburbs, which traditionally housed few nightclubs, have added their own mix. Downtown areas in Roswell, Marietta, Woodstock, and Alpharetta have chains like **Taco Mac**, plus local pubs or clubs. And a few larger establishments like **Wild Bills** in Duluth attract singles or couples in their 20s for music and dancing.

## COOL HANG-OUTS

- **Manuel's Tavern**, 602 N Highland Ave, 404-525-3447, www.manuelstavern. com, called the grandfather of Atlanta's nightclub scene, the bar dates back to the 1950s—and its unique history is evident in its ample pictures and memorabilia. Manuel's has served many a celebrity and famous politician, as it's been the favorite watering hole of locals for decades—but it still offers some of the fastest service in town and lots of great activities, like a regular trivia contest and a comedy troupe the first Saturday of every month.
- **The Tavern at Phipps,** 3500 Peachtree Rd, Phipps Plaza, Atlanta, 404-814-9640, www.thetavernphipps.com, located in Atlanta's exclusive mall, Phipps Plaza, The Tavern offers patrons a chic but casual place to relax and enjoy great food and drinks. Great patio overlooking Peachtree St; occasional live entertainment.

## ALTERNATIVE, ROCK, HIP-HOP

- **Darkhorse Tavern**, 816 N Highland Ave, Atlanta, 404-873-3607, www.darkhorseatlanta.com
- **Masquerade**, 695 North Ave NE, Atlanta, 404-577-8178, www.masqueradeatlanta.com
- **Smith's Olde Bar**, 1578 Piedmont Ave, Atlanta, 404-875-1522, www.smitholdebar.com
- **The Tabernacle**, 152 Luckie St, 404-659-9022, www.tabernacleatl.com

## BLUES

- **Blind Willie's**, 828 North Highland Ave, Atlanta, 404-873-2583, www.blindwilliesblues.com
- **Fatt Matt's Rib Shack**, 1811 Piedmont Ave NE, Atlanta, 404-607-1622, www.fatmattsribshack.com
- **Darwin's Burgers and Blues**, 1598 Roswell Rd, Marietta, 770-578-6872, www.darwinsburgers.com

## FOLK, COUNTRY, ACOUSTIC

- **Eddie's Attic**, 515 N McDonough St, Decatur, 404-377-4976, www.eddiesattic.com
- **Trackside Tavern**, 313 E College Ave, Decatur, 404-378-0504, www.tracksidetavern.com
- **Wild Bills**, 2075 Market St, Duluth, 678-473-1000, www.wildbillsatlanta.com

## IRISH

- **Fado Irish Pub**, 273 Buckhead Ave, Atlanta, 404-841-0066, www:fadoirishpub.com/Atlanta
- **Johnnie MacCracken's**, 15 Atlanta St, Marietta, 678-290-6641, www.johnniemaccrackens.com
- **Limerick Junction**, 822 N Highland Ave, Atlanta, 404-874-7147, www.limerickjunctionpub.com
- **Old Blind Dog Irish Pub**, 12650 Crabapple Rd, 678-624-1090, www.oldblinddog.com

## NIGHTCLUBS

- **Johnny's Hideaway**, 3771 Roswell Rd, 404-233-8086, www.johnnyshideaway.com
- **Opera Nightclub**, 1150B Peachtree Rd, Atlanta, 404-874-0428, www.operaatlanta.com

- **Sanctuary**, 3209 Paces Ferry Rd, Atlanta, 404-262-1377, www.sanctuarynight-club.com
- **Tongue & Groove**, 565 Main St NE, Atlanta, 404-261-2325, www.tongueand-grooveonline.com

## R&B, JAZZ

- **Cafe 290**, 290 Hilderbrand Dr NE, Atlanta, 404-256-3942, www.cafe290atlanta.com
- **Sambuca Jazz Café**, 3102 Piedmont Rd, 404-237-5299, www.sambucarestau-rant.com

## REGGAE

- **The Royal Peacock**, 186 Auburn Ave, Atlanta, 404-584-2522
- **Club 426**, 5694 Memorial Dr, Stone Mountain, 404-297-9910, http://club426at-lanta.com

# VISUAL ARTS AND SCIENCES

## ART MUSEUMS

- **Atlanta International Museum of Art and Design,** Peachtree Center, Marquis II Tower, 285 Peachtree Center Ave, Atlanta, 404-688-2467, www.museumofde-sign.org; hosts multicultural folk art, ethnographic, and design exhibitions. Free admission, but a donation is appreciated.
- **The High Museum of Art**, 1280 Peachtree St NE, Atlanta, 404-733-4400, www.high.org; designed by Richard Meier, this museum houses an extensive perma-nent collection of decorative art, 19th-century American paintings, and modern art. Admission costs are $19.50 for adults, $16.50 for seniors or students, $12 for children 6 to 17 years of age, free for children under 6, and free for Fulton County residents for the permanent exhibits, but a donation is appreciated.
- **Hammonds House Galleries and Resource Center of African American Art**, 503 Peeples St, Atlanta, 404-612-0500, www.hammondshouse.org; showcases African-American art, including works by Romare Bearden, and an extensive Haitian art collection.
- **High Museum of Art at Georgia Pacific Center**, 30 John Wesley Dobbs Ave NE, Atlanta, 404-577-6940, www.high.org; hosts folk art, photography, and trav-eling exhibitions. Admission is free, but a donation is appreciated.
- **Michael C. Carlos Museum**, Emory University, 571 South Kilgo St, Atlanta, 404-727-4282, http://carlos.emory.edu; hosts a large collection of ancient art of the Mediterranean and Americas. Free admission, but $3 donation is appreciated.

- **Oglethorpe University Museum**, 4484 Peachtree Rd NE, 404-364-8555, http://museum.oglethorpe.edu; hosts original exhibits of mythological art. Free admission.

If you want to get out of the museum setting and see some art in its natural habitat, consider Reverend Howard Finster's **Paradise Gardens** in Pennville, Georgia, about an hour-and-a-half drive north of Atlanta. Finster is famous for his album covers (Talking Heads and R.E.M., among others), painted Coca-Cola bottles, and his preaching. Though Reverend Finster passed away in 2001, the trip to Paradise Gardens is worth the drive, and you can buy a Finster without the exorbitant gallery mark-up. For more information, call 706-857-5791, or check out www.finster.com.

To find out more about Atlanta's fine and decorative art scene, check out **Arts in Atlanta**, www.artsatl.com. This site includes a calendar of exhibit openings, maps, and more.

## HISTORY AND CULTURAL MUSEUMS

- **African-American Panoramic Experience-APEX**, 135 Auburn Ave NE, Atlanta, 404-523-2739, www.apexmuseum.org; presents American history from an African-American perspective.
- **Atlanta Cyclorama**, Grant Park, Georgia Ave and (800) Cherokee Ave SE, Atlanta, 404-658-7625, http://atlantacyclorama.org; 360-degree diorama depicting Civil War battles in Atlanta.
- **Atlanta History Center**, 130 W Paces Ferry Rd NW, Atlanta, 404-814-4000, www.atlantahistorycenter.com; both permanent and temporary exhibits highlighting various aspects of Atlanta's history.
- **Herndon Home**, 587 University Plaza NW, Atlanta, 404-581-9813; the historic home of Alonzo Herndon, an ex-slave who became one of the foremost African-American businessmen of his era. The museum offers tours, exhibits, special events, and more. Admission is free, but donations are appreciated.
- **Jimmy Carter Library and Museum**, 441 Freedom Pkwy, Atlanta, 404-865-7100, www.jimmycarterlibrary.gov; the Presidential Library of former US President Jimmy Carter. The Carter Center (as it's known) offers museum tours, lectures, special events, and more. Admission is $7 for adults and free for children under 16 years old.
- **The Margaret Mitchell House**, 990 Peachtree St, Atlanta, 404-249-7015, www.margaretmitchellhouse.com; the historic home of *Gone With the Wind* author Margaret Mitchell and birthplace of this classic American novel. The museum highlights Mitchell's life both before and after the book, as well as the making of the movie, which premiered in Atlanta in 1939. Admission ranges from $13 for adults to $8.50 for children aged 4 to 12.
- **The Martin Luther King, Jr., Birth Home Museum**, 450 Auburn Ave NE, Atlanta, 404-331-5190, www.nps.gov/malu; admission is free to this birthplace of civil rights activist, Dr. Martin Luther King, Jr.

- **The Martin Luther King, Jr., Center for Nonviolent Social Change**, 449 Auburn Ave NE, Atlanta, 404-526-8900, www.thekingcenter.org; admission is free, though a donation is appreciated.
- **Omenala-Griot Afrocentric Teaching Museum**, 337 Dargan Pl, Atlanta, 404-755-8403; general admission is free.
- **Road to Tara Museum**, 104 North Main St, Jonesboro, 770-478-4800, www. visitscarlett.com; another *Gone With the Wind* museum, featuring original film props, costume reproductions, a foreign edition library, photo gallery, and more. The museum is open Monday through Saturday.
- **Southeastern Railway Museum**, 3966 Buford Hwy, Duluth, 770-476-2013, www.srmduluth.org; Georgia's official transportation history museum featuring Pullman cars, classic steam locomotives, and more. During spring, summer, and fall, the museum is open Thursdays, Fridays, and Saturdays. During the winter, they're open on Saturdays only. Call for times and admission prices.
- **The William Breman Jewish Heritage Museum**, 1440 Spring St, Atlanta, 678-222-3700, www.thebreman.org; a museum dedicated to collecting, preserving, interpreting, and teaching about Jewish history, particularly the Holocaust and the experience of Jews in Georgia.

## SCIENCE MUSEUMS

- **Fernbank Museum of Natural History**, 767 Clifton Rd NE, Atlanta, 404-929-6300, www.fernbank.edu; a beautiful, natural history museum featuring permanent exhibits such as "A Walk Through Time in Georgia" and traveling exhibits such as "Ends of the Earth" and "Penguins of the Antarctic." Fernbank is also home to an interactive science room, an IMAX theatre, café, and more. This is a popular destination for adults and children. Call for admission prices.
- **Fernbank Science Center**, 156 Heaton Park Dr NE, Atlanta, 678-874-7102, www.fernbank.edu; features an observatory, planetarium, library, and exhibit hall. Admission to the Library and Exhibit Hall is free, and visitors will see a variety of floor exhibits, interactive models, and a real Apollo space capsule. The Observatory is also free, but is only open on Thursday and Friday nights from 8 p.m. to 10:30 p.m. when the weather is clear. Admission to the planetarium is $7 for adults and $5 for students and seniors.

## CULTURE FOR KIDS

Cultural opportunities for children abound in metro Atlanta. From children's museums and nature centers to a world-class zoo, you'll find it all here. In addition, many of the regular museums and theatres offer children's programs on a monthly basis. Be sure to check out museum websites, or look in the weekend edition of the *Atlanta Journal-Constitution* for event announcements and schedules.

## MUSEUMS

Most of the above-listed museums are as good for youngsters as for adults. Some even offer special kid-friendly events or shows geared toward children. Contact the above museums for details. A few specialty museums, many designed with the child in mind, include:

- **Fernbank Museum of Natural History**, see above
- **Fernbank Science Center**, see above
- **Georgia Aquarium**, 225 Baker St, Atlanta, 404-581-4000, www.georgiaaquarium.org; the Georgia Aquarium holds eight million gallons of fresh and saltwater marine life, making it the largest of its kind in the world. Wildly popular, the aquarium offers numerous programs for both children and adults, including educational classes, a summer camp for kids, a 4D theater, a chance to swim with marine life, and sleep-overs (yes, sleep-overs!) where you are treated to a behind-the-scenes tour and light dinner before sleeping in front of your tank of choice. Costs of each package vary, and special prices are available if you purchase an annual membership.
- **Imagine It! The Children's Museum of Atlanta**, 275 Centennial Olympic Park Dr NW, Atlanta, 404-659-KIDS, www.childrensmuseumatlanta.org; recommended for children aged 2 through 8, and their accompanying adults.
- **Southeastern Railway Museum**, 3966 Buford Hwy, Duluth, 770-476-2013, www.srmduluth.org; for railroad lovers of all ages. Admission is $8 for adults, $5 for children, and includes a train ride.
- **The World of Coca-Cola**, 121 Baker St, Atlanta, 404-676-5151, www.worldofcoca-cola.com; learn the history of Coca-Cola, see Coke artifacts from around the world, and sample dozens of domestic and international drinks from the soft drink giant.

## OUTDOOR

- **The Atlanta Botanical Garden**, 1345 Piedmont Ave NE, Atlanta, 404-876-5859, www.atlantabotanicalgarden.org; in addition to the regular gardens (which are often a draw for children of all ages), the Atlanta Botanical Garden also offers a fantastic, whimsical children's garden. The Children's Garden features a variety of plants, flowers, and trees, an open fountain perfect for playing in during Atlanta's hottest months, slides, waterfalls, and more.
- **Chattahoochee Nature Center**, 9135 Willeo Rd, Roswell, 770-992-2055, www.chattnaturecenter.com; popular nature center offers a variety of fun programs

for children of all ages. There are also gardens, picnic areas, an aviary, a Discovery Center, and more ... all alongside the Chattahoochee River.

- **Dunwoody Nature Center**, 5343 Roberts Dr, Dunwoody, 770-394-3322, www. dunwoodynature.org; kids can enjoy up close animal encounters, an annual Butterfly Festival, a wetlands boardwalk, and more. Dunwoody Nature Center also offers spring break and summer Day Camps, as well as weekly tours and hikes along their main trail, which leads past a meadow, to peaceful Wildcat Creek.
- **Six Flags Over Georgia,** 7561 Six Flags Pkwy, Austell, 770-948-9290, www.sixflags.com/parks/overgeorgia; this world-class amusement park features over 100 family rides and thrill rides, as well as Skull Island, a one-acre family water play area with six water slides and a gigantic water play structure. In addition to its regular shows, the park also hosts numerous special events, such as a Christian music festival, a kids' festival, and a Halloween-themed fright festival.
- **Stone Mountain Park**, Highway 78, Stone Mountain, 770-498-5702, www. stonemountainpark.com; part outdoor getaway and part theme park. Kids will probably be most drawn to the theme park aspect. Here you'll find the Great Barn, an 1870s-era barn that's been renovated and filled with four floors of rope nets for climbing, mazes to explore, and super slides that whisk you from the ceiling to the floor. The park is also home to a skylift, which takes visitors to the top of the mountain, an antebellum plantation and farmyard, two three-story-high treehouses (one for boys, one for girls) with over three dozen interactive activities, numerous restaurants and gift shops, and much, much more.
- **Zoo Atlanta**, Grant Park, 800 Cherokee Ave SE, Atlanta, 404-624-5000, www. zooatlanta.org; home to a variety of animals, housed in outdoor, natural habitats. It's also home to a train, which takes you on a short tour of the zoo, a carousel, a playground, a petting zoo, and more.

## THEATER

- **Young Audiences Woodruff Arts Center**, 1280 Peachtree St, Atlanta, 404-733-4660, www.yawac.org
- **ART Station**, 5384 Manor Dr, Stone Mountain, 770-469-1105, www.artstation. org; contemporary arts center and theatre, located in downtown Stone Mountain
- **Aurora Theatre**, **Leaps and Bounds**, 128 Pike St, Lawrenceville, 678-264-6222, www.auroratheatre.com
- **Center for Puppetry Arts**, 1404 Spring St, Atlanta, 404-873-3391, www.puppet.org
- **Dad's Garage**, 280 Elizabeth St, Atlanta, 404-523-3141, www.dadsgarage.com; theater company and improv group
- **Georgia Ensemble Theatre**, Roswell Cultural Arts Center, 950 Forrest St, Roswell, 770-641-1260, www.get.org
- **Horizon Theatre Company**, 1083 Austin Ave, Atlanta, 404-523-1477, www.horizontheatre.com

- **Kudzu Playhouse Main Stage & Family Theater,** 10743 Alpharetta Hwy, Roswell; **Kudzu Sprouts Theater**, 608 Holcomb Bridge Rd, Roswell, 770-594-1020, www.kudzuplayhouse.org
- **Stage Door Players**, 5339 Chamblee Dunwoody Rd, Dunwoody, 770-396-1726
- **The Strand Theatre**, 117 North Park Square, Marietta, 770-293-0080, www.earlsmithstrand.org
- **Theatre in the Square**, 11 Whitlock Ave, Marietta, 770-422-8369, www.theatre-inthesquare.com

## OTHER

- **Hobbit Hall Children's Bookstore–Story and Crafts**, 120 Bulloch Ave, Roswell, 770-587-0907; special events, story time, arts and crafts, and more; check online for current schedule. Admission is free.
- **Redwall Art Studio**, 1428 Ponce de Leon Ave NE, Atlanta, 404-371-9383, www.redwallstudio.org; ongoing hands-on art classes for children and adults of all ages.
- **Spruill Center for the Arts, Education Center**, 5339 Chamblee Dunwoody Rd, Atlanta, 770-394-3447, www.spruillarts.org/education_center.htm; call for class and events schedule, and pricing.

# LITERARY LIFE

## BOOKSTORES

Metro Atlanta is home to a wide selection of bookstores. Whether you prefer an independent bookseller or a large chain store, you're sure to find what you're looking for somewhere in the city. Below is a listing of some of your options, including literary workshops and groups.

## CHAIN BOOKSELLERS

- **Barnes & Noble**, 800-843-2665, www.barnesandnoble.com; several locations throughout metro Atlanta
- **Berean Christian Store**, 441 Cleveland Ave SW, Atlanta, 404-767-7514, www.berean.com; one location
- **Lifeway Christian Bookstores,** numerous locations in metro Atlanta, 800-448-8032, www.lifewaystores.com; chain of Christian book stores operated by Lifeway Christian Resources of the Southern Baptist Convention

## INDEPENDENT BOOKSELLERS

- **A Capella Books**, 208 Haralson Ave NE, Atlanta, 404-681-5128; bookstore specializing in out-of-print titles, first editions, fine literature, and books on culture and the arts
- **CHARIS Books and More, Feminist Bookstore**, 1189 Euclid Ave NE, 404-524-0304, www.charisbooksandmore.com; the South's oldest independent feminist bookstore
- **Eagle Eye Book Shop,** 2076 N Decatur Rd, Decatur, 404-486-0307, eagleeyebooks.com; used and new books, hosts a writers' group
- **Engineer's Bookstore**, 748 Marietta St NW, Atlanta, 404-221-1669, www.engr-bookstore.com; the largest technical bookstore in the Southeast
- **Hoot Owl Attic Metaphysical Bookstore**, 185 Allen Rd NE, Sandy Springs, 404-303-1030, www.hooty.com; popular metaphysical shop specializing in books, candles, and more
- **Phoenix & Dragon Bookstore**, 5531 Roswell Rd, Sandy Springs, 404-255-5207, www.phoenixanddragon.com; Atlanta's largest, oldest and most well-known metaphysical bookstore
- **Tall Tales Book Shop**, 2105 LaVista Rd, Atlanta, 404-636-2498; small shop specializing in both wide-release titles and smaller market books, including a nice-sized children's section

## LITERARY WORKSHOPS AND GROUPS

There are several literary groups in metro Atlanta. Whether you're interested in joining a book club or would like to workshop with other struggling writers, you're bound to find a group to fit your needs. Below you'll find just a sampling of what's out there. For more options, check out *Creative Loafing*'s "Happenings" section, under "Literature."

- *Atlanta Review*, www.atlantareview.com, an independent international poetry journal with links to activities in the Atlanta area
- **Atlanta Writers Club,** www.atlantawritersclub.org, gathers at the Dunwoody campus of Georgia Perimeter College; for a list of meetings visit the website; highlights include lectures by the state's poet laureate and University of Georgia professor, Dr. David Bottoms, among other famous authors
- **Georgia Writers Association, Inc.,** 1000 Chastain Rd, Kennesaw, 770-420-4736, http://georgiawriter.org; a non-profit organization committed to encouraging and strengthening the writing skills of those in both creative and business circles; links to classes, workshops, and lectures
- **Village Writers Group**, www.villagewritersgroup.com, meets the first Tuesday of each month (except July and August) at Eagle Eye Books at 2076 North Decatur Rd. The group is open to anyone interested in writing.

# LIBRARIES

Metro Atlanta is home to a number of excellent libraries—from your neighborhood's city or county branches, to the handful of historical libraries, to the many college and university libraries around town. Below is contact information for many of the main branches of metro Atlanta's public libraries, as well as information on other libraries open to the public. Most of them offer monthly book clubs, special literary events, family activities, and more. See also the Libraries listings under each neighborhood in the **Neighborhoods** chapter.

## PUBLIC LIBRARIES

- **Fulton County Central Library**, One Margaret Mitchell Sq, NW, 404-730-1700, www.afpls.org
- **DeKalb County Central Library**, 215 Sycamore St, Decatur, 404-370-3070, www.dekalblibrary.org
- **Cobb County Central Library**, 266 Roswell St, Marietta, 770-528-2320, www.cobbcat.org
- **Gwinnett County Central Library**, 1001 Lawrenceville Hwy, 770-822-4522, www.gwinnettpl.org
- **City of Smyrna Public Library**, 100 Village Green Cir, Smyrna, 770-431-2860

## HISTORICAL LIBRARIES

- **Atlanta History Center (Archives)**, 130 W Paces Ferry Rd NE, Atlanta, 404-814-4000, www.atlantahistorycenter.com; one of the Southeast's largest history museums, with a full research library and archives that serve more than 10,000 patrons each year
- **Auburn Avenue Research Library of African American Culture and History**, 101 Auburn Ave NE, Atlanta, 404-730-4001, www.af.public.lib.ga.us; part of the Atlanta Fulton County library system, this research branch specializes in texts and events highlighting African-American culture and history
- **City of Roswell Archives and Research Library**, 770-594-6405, www.roswellgov.com; this research library, housed in the Roswell Cultural Arts Center, is open Monday–Thursday, from 1 p.m. to 4:30 p.m., and features text and archives highlighting local history and preservation efforts
- **Jimmy Carter Library and Museum**, 441 Freedom Pkwy NE, Atlanta, 404-865-7100, www.jimmycarterlibrary.gov; presidential library of former US President Jimmy Carter

## COLLEGE AND UNIVERSITY LIBRARIES

- **Agnes Scott College Campus Library**, 141 E College Ave, Decatur, 404-471-6339, http://library.agnesscott.edu
- **Clark Atlanta University Campus Library**, James P. Brawley Dr and Fair St, Atlanta, 404-880-8697, www.cau.edu
- **Georgia Institute of Technology Campus Library**, 225 North Ave NW, Atlanta, 404-894-4529, www.library.gatech.edu
- **Georgia Perimeter College, Decatur Campus Library**, 3251 Panthersville Rd, Decatur, 404-244-5026; **Dunwoody Campus Library**, 2101 Womack Rd, Dunwoody, 770-551-3046; **Lawrenceville Campus Library**, 1301 Atkinson Rd, Lawrenceville, 770-339-2279; www.gpc.edu/library
- **Georgia State University, Pullen Library**, 100 Decatur St, Atlanta, 404-651-2422; **Law Library**, 100 Decatur St, Atlanta, 404-651-2767; www.library.gsu.edu
- **Mercer University Campus Library**, 3001 Mercer University Dr, Atlanta, 770-986-3282, http://libraries.mercer.edu

# LECTURES

Many Atlanta area universities and colleges sponsor lecture series, as do public libraries, bookstores, and churches. **Emory University**, 404-727-6397, www.emory.edu; **Georgia State University**, 404-651-1777, www.gsu.edu; and **Georgia Tech**, 404-894-2000, www.gatech.edu, are good places to start. The best place to learn about the weekly lecture scene is to consult *Creative Loafing*; under the "Happenings" section is a "Lectures and Seminars" column, which will direct you to lectures on everything from Jungian philosophy to personal charisma. Popular hosts to visiting lecturers include:

- **The Art Institute of Atlanta**, 770-394-8300, www.artinstitutes.edu/atlanta; offers art seminars and courses
- **Atlanta Botanical Garden**, 404-876-5859, www.atlantabotanicalgarden.org; provides interested participants with an ongoing series of workshops, seminars, and lectures about gardening and horticulture
- **The Buckhead Library**, 404-814-3500, www.afpls.org; often hosts lectures on a wide variety of subjects
- **Fernbank Science Center**, 404-378-4311, www.fernbank.edu; offers various lecture series on scientific topics, such as astronomy, geology, and biology
- **High Museum**, 404-733-4400, www.high.org; sponsors numerous lectures in the Hill Auditorium by artists and scholars specializing in the visual arts
- **Theosophical Society**, 404-943-9469, www.theosophical.org; holds public lectures every Sunday at 3 p.m. (except holidays) at 275 Carpenter Dr, Ste 305, Sandy Springs

HOST OF THE 1994 AND 1999 SUPER BOWLS AND THE 1996 OLYMPIC Games, Atlanta has made a name for itself as an international sports center. Warm weather, beautiful parks with winding trails, and state-of-the-art sports facilities make the city an ideal place to engage in sporting activities, and it is home to several professional sports teams, abundant college athletics, and countless participant sports. So, if you're looking to work up a sweat yourself or watch others do it, metro Atlanta offers plenty of opportunities.

To find out more about metro Atlanta area health clubs, exercise trends, and sports teams, check out **Atlanta Sports and Fitness** magazine, 404-870-0123, www.asfmagazine.com. This publication features news and information on what's hot in Atlanta sports and fitness.

## PROFESSIONAL SPORTS

### AUTO RACING

The **Atlanta Motor Speedway**, located 30 miles south of Atlanta off I-75 in Hampton, is home to yearly NASCAR races. For more information, call 770-946-4211, or check them out online at www.atlantamotorspeedway.com.

For additional racing events, try **Road Atlanta**, 800-849-RACE, www.roadatlanta.com, in Braselton off I-85 North.

### BASEBALL

Atlanta is a city that loves baseball, thanks in part to the superb efforts of its hometown team, the **Atlanta Braves**. With an amazing record of Division titles, World Series appearances, and a 1995 World Series victory, the Braves are considered by many to be one of the top teams in the history of professional baseball. The Braves play at **Turner Field**, situated near the intersection of I-20 and the Downtown Connector, next to where the old Atlanta–Fulton County Stadium once stood. Built for the opening ceremonies and track and field events of the 1996 Olympic Games, Turner Field is the latest in a wave of boutique ballparks that offer fans gourmet food, arcade games, and children's areas. Turner Field, named for former Braves' owner Ted Turner, even has a Braves' museum showcasing memorabilia from the team. Baseball season runs from April to September; however, to keep fans engaged, the team often organizes post-season events.

You can buy a season pass directly from the Braves, www.atlantabraves.com, or individual tickets through **TicketMaster**, 404-249-6400, www.ticketmaster. com, or any number of other ticket brokers online. Just search "Buy Braves Tickets" and go from there. Ticket prices range from $10 to $150 and are usually available, particularly at the beginning of the season. For information on season tickets, call 404-577-9100. For information on Turner Field tours, call 404-614-2311. For general information about the Atlanta Braves or Turner Field, go to http://atlanta. braves.mlb.com.

Parking downtown is always a hassle, even in the best of circumstances, and sporting events only complicate matters. The best way to get to the stadium is by MARTA, which offers a stadium shuttle service from both the West End and Five Points stations (see the **Transportation** chapter for specifics). The stadium is also located a relatively short walk from the Georgia State station.

## BASKETBALL

**Philips Arena**, 404-878-3000, www.philipsarena.com, located downtown at One Philips Drive, across from the World Congress Center and CNN Center, is home to the NBA's **Atlanta Hawks**. The regular basketball season starts in November and lasts until the end of April. Individual tickets are available online or by phone from TicketMaster, 404-249-6400, www.ticketmaster.com, and at TicketMaster locations throughout metro Atlanta. For general information and season tickets, contact the Hawks at 404-827-DUNK (3865) or 866-715-1500, www.nba.com/ hawks. Tickets go for anywhere from $15 (upper level bleachers) to $500 (court-side and center).

Parking near Philips Arena is limited, so your best bet may be MARTA: The Georgia Dome/World Congress Center station will take you right to the door of the arena.

The WNBA's **Atlanta Dream,** 877-977-7729, www.wnba.com/dream, also play in Philips Arena, May through September.

## FOOTBALL

The **Atlanta Falcons** fight it out at the **Georgia Dome**, 404-223-4636, www.gadome.com, located at One Georgia Dome Drive, next to the World Congress Center, on the side opposite Philips Arena. At capacity the dome holds 71,500 spectators, and fans are fond of saying there's not a bad seat in the house.

Individual tickets are available starting in August. Purchase them at the Dome ticket office or through TicketMaster, 404-249-6400, www.ticketmaster.com. You can also order them by mail by writing the Atlanta Falcons Ticket Office, One Georgia Dome Drive, Atlanta, GA 30313. For more information about the Atlanta Falcons, check out www.atlantafalcons.com. For general information and season tickets, call 404-223-8000. Dome seats go for $25 to $50 each, depending on seat location. Football season runs from August through December.

Catching a MARTA train is your best bet for a relatively hassle-free trip to the Dome. Parking nearby is almost a guaranteed nightmare. Both the Georgia Dome/World Congress station and the Vine City station are located conveniently near the stadium. Also, you can take a MARTA shuttle from downtown parking lots and from the Garnett station as well.

## GOLF

In nearby Augusta, just two hours east of Atlanta, you can attend the annual **Masters Tournament,** which is held at the **Augusta National Golf Club** every April. For more information, including ticket prices and availability, visit them online at www.masters.com, or call 706-667-6000.

## TENNIS

The **Infinite Energy Atlanta Slam** is just one of the many tennis tournaments you can find in metro Atlanta. The event is held in December at the Gwinnett Area, www.gwinnettcenter.com. You can purchase tournament tickets, which range between $100 and $175, from TicketMaster, 404-249-6400, www.ticketmaster.com.

# COLLEGE SPORTS

College sports often incite as much enthusiasm as professional tournaments. Rowdy fans of the Georgia Tech Yellow Jackets frequently crowd bars to cheer on their team, especially when archrivals the Georgia Bulldogs are the opponent. If you follow the college sports scene, here is some information about Atlanta area college athletic programs:

- **Georgia State** has a 17-sport, Division One athletics program, including a football team, men's and women's basketball teams, a softball team, a golf team, and more. Contact 404-651-3166, www.gsu.edu, for schedule and ticket information.
- **Georgia Tech**'s basketball and football teams attract many devoted supporters and garner most of the attention for this school's athletic department. But Tech is also home to a baseball team, softball team, swim teams, and more. For information call 404-894-5447, www.ramblinwreck.collegesports.com.
- **Emory University** and **Oglethorpe University** teams compete in Division Three sports. Call 404-727-6547 or visit www.emory.edu for details about Emory's athletic department, and 404-364-8422, www.oglethorpe.edu for information on sports at Oglethorpe.
- **Clark Atlanta University**, 404-880-8126, www.cau.edu; **Morehouse College**, 404-215-2669, www.morehouse.edu; and **Morris Brown College**, 404-220-0270, www.morrisbrown.edu, also compete against each other in most of the major sports.

In addition, the Georgia Dome hosts the **Chick-fil-A Bowl** college football game annually. Contact 404-586-8500, www.chick-fil-abowl.com, for more information.

## OTHER SPECTATOR SPORTING EVENTS

Every Fourth of July, hordes of metro Atlanta spectators line the sidewalks of Peachtree Street early in the morning to watch runners participate in the **Peachtree Road Race**. Cocktails and jam boxes in hand, supporters yell, play the theme from *Chariots of Fire*, and offer spirited high-fives while they cheer on the thousands of runners in this gargantuan 10K race. **The Atlanta Track Club**, 404-231-9064, www.atlantatrackclub.org, sponsors the event, and all you have to do to watch is find your spot along the course and join in the merriment.

The **Atlanta Steeplechase** takes place each spring in Cumming, Georgia, complete with candelabras, strawberries, and champagne. To buy tickets for this equestrian racing event, contact 404-237-7436, www.atlantasteeplechase.org, or write to the Atlanta Steeplechase, 3160 Northside Parkway NW, Atlanta, GA 30327.

## PARTICIPANT SPORTS AND ACTIVITIES

### PARKS AND RECREATION DEPARTMENTS

Joining an amateur sports team is an effective and fun way to meet new friends and get a workout at the same time. Neighborhood parks and recreation departments offer adult and child leagues in many sports, including baseball, softball, and basketball. Contact the one nearest you to investigate your options:

- **Atlanta City Parks and Recreation**, 404-817-6766, www.atlantaga.gov
- **Alpharetta Parks and Recreation**, 678-297-6100, www.alpharetta.ga.us
- **Chamblee Parks and Recreation**, 770-986-5016, www.chambleega.com
- **Cherokee County Recreation and Parks Authority**, 770-924-7768, www.crpa.net
- **Cobb County Parks and Recreation**, 770-528-8800, prca.cobbcountyga.gov
- **Decatur Recreation Department**, 404-377-0494, www.decaturparks.com
- **DeKalb County Parks and Recreation**, 404-371-2631, www.co.dekalb.ga.us/parks
- **Duluth Parks and Recreation**, 770-623-2781, 770-814-6981, www.duluthmn.gov/parks
- **Fulton County Parks and Recreation**, 404-730-6200, www.fultoncountyga.gov
- **Gwinnett County Parks and Recreation**, 770-822-8840, www.gwinnettcounty.com
- **Marietta Parks and Recreation**, 770-794-5601, www.mariettaga.gov
- **Roswell Recreation and Parks**, 770-641-3705, www.roswellgov.com
- **Smyrna Parks and Recreation**, 770-431-2842, www.symrnacity.com
- **Stone Mountain Recreation Department**, 770-498-2414, www.stonemountainpark.com

Another way to join an amateur team is through your place of work. Corporate sponsorship of amateur sports teams is a popular metro Atlanta practice. Check with your employer about current team sponsorship or organize one yourself if no team exists. Many businesses don't mind footing the bill when team playing on the field translates into professional team playing in the office. Also, consider finding a team online. Meetup.com is one of a number of websites committed to connecting people of similar interests in the metro area. Search under what sport and area you are interested in and see what you find.

## BASEBALL/SOFTBALL

If you're looking to join a team and play scheduled games throughout the season, call the **Atlanta Men's Senior Baseball League**, 770-785-2588, www.atlantamsbl.com. They will be able to give you detailed information on trying out, practices, games, and more. You can also call the **parks and recreation department** in your community (see phone numbers above) for a complete listing of adult and youth baseball and softball teams. Or pick up your glove and head to **Piedmont Park**, 404-875-7275, www.piedmontpark.org, with some friends—you'll probably meet others who are there for the same reason and you'll have a game going in no time.

## BASKETBALL

**Run N' Shoot Athletic Center**, 1959 Metropolitan Pkwy, 404-762-6222, offers seven indoor basketball courts with freshly painted hardwood floors, and computers that keep track of play time, so those in line for a court know exactly how long they'll have to wait. The center is open 24 hours a day. Admission is $6 per person per day, with no membership fees.

Another popular indoor basketball spot is the **YMCA** gymnasium (several locations throughout metro Atlanta, contact 404-588-9622, www.ymcaatlanta. org, for the location nearest you). Most Ys offer open court time periodically throughout the day and may require a membership fee, so be sure to call first for schedules and pricing.

## BICYCLING

Numerous clubs and organizations in Atlanta support bicyclists—organizing rides and events alike. The **Southern Bicycle League (SBL)**, 770-594-8350, www. bikesbl.org, is a volunteer organization designed to support recreational cycling. The **Atlanta Bicycle Coalition**, 404-881-1112, www.atlantabike.org, promotes bicycle transportation and use, including advocacy and rider education, and keeps a list of social riding clubs. And Atlanta Bicycle Chic is a blog that captures bikers of all kinds on Atlanta streets (an entertaining website if anything!): http:// atlantabicyclechic.blogspot.com.

There are many places to bike in Atlanta. **Piedmont Park**, 404-875-7275, www.piedmontpark.org, is a popular choice, as long as you don't mind sharing the paths with runners and rollerbladers. You can rent bikes across from the park at **Skate Escape**, 404-892-1292, www.skateescape.com. The **Freedom Parkway**, a road that connects the Downtown Connector to Ponce de Leon and Moreland Avenue, has bike paths that wind around the Carter Presidential Center and through Candler Park. **The Silver Comet Trail** is popular for its length and lack of cars, www.silvercometga.com, and bike rentals are also available at **Stone Mountain Park**, 770-498-5690, www.stonemountainpark.com. Robert E. Lee Boulevard makes a five-mile circle around the park and is very popular with cyclists.

A few other bicycling clubs to consider are:

- **Bicycle Club of Atlanta**, 770-496-1908, www.bicyclegeorgia.com/gaclubs
- **Bike Alpharetta**, http://bikealpharetta.org
- **Gwinnett Touring Club**, 770-476-7975, www.gtcbike.org
- **North Atlanta Riding Club**, http://bikearc.com/
- **Southern Off-Road Bicycle Association**, 770-565-1795, www.sorba.org

Even though metro Atlanta does not enforce a strict helmet law, it's always a good idea to protect yourself when you ride.

## BOATING/SAILING/WINDSURFING

Pools are not the only way to escape the Atlanta summer heat. You can pass a splendid lazy summer afternoon cooling off while floating down the

Chattahoochee River. Rent a raft, canoe, or inner tube anytime between Memorial Day weekend and Labor Day weekend, and enjoy the ride. The Johnson Ferry Unit of the **Chattahoochee River National Recreation Area**, www.nps.gov/chat (located across from the intersection of Riverside Drive and Johnson Ferry Road), is the most popular put-in point on the river. Be sure to contact the Recreation Area's **Visitor Station**, 1978 Island Ford Parkway, 678-538-1200, for raft rental information and more. Or contact the **City of Roswell Recreation Department**, 770-641-3705, www.roswellgov.com.

A great spot for sailing, boating, and water fun is **Lake Lanier**, www.lakelanierislands.com, less than an hour's drive northeast of Atlanta. You can sun on a man-made beach, ride down the rapids in the water park, swim in the lake, or rent a boat from Lake Lanier's **Harbor Landing**, 770-932-7255. Sailing enthusiasts can join the **Lake Lanier Sailing Club**, 770-967-6441, www.llsc.com, to meet other sailors and take advantage of charter cruises and boat rentals. The club also offers sailing lessons for adults and juniors.

If boating interests you, contact one of the following organizations. This may be a great way to meet people with similar interests, and get your feet wet!

- **Atlanta Yacht Club**, www.atlantayachtclub.org, in Lake Allatoona, sponsors sailing and sailboat racing activities for adults and families
- **Atlanta Rowing Club**, 770-993-1879, www.atlantarow.org
- **Atlanta Boardsailing Club**, 404-237-1431, http://windsurfatlanta.org
- **Atlanta Whitewater Club**, 800-231-6058, www.atlantawhitewater.com
- **Georgia Canoeing Association**, 770-421-9729, www.georgiapaddle.com
- **Lanier Canoe and Kayak Club**, 770-287-7888, www.lckc.org

## BOWLING

If you're looking for a sport you can practice year-round, bowling may be it. There are several popular bowling alleys in the metro Atlanta area, and most of them offer bowling league play if you're interested in joining a team. A few to consider are:

- **AMF Bowling Centers**: Marietta Lanes, 565 Cobb Pkwy, Marietta, 770-427-4696; Woodstock Lanes, 108 Woodstock Blvd, Woodstock, 770-926-2200; Snellville Lanes, 2350 Ronald Reagan Pkwy, Snellville, 770-972-5300
- **Brunswick Bowling Centers**: Azalea Lanes, 2750 Austell Rd SW, Marietta, 770-435-2120; Cedar Creek Lanes, 2749 Delk Rd, Marietta, 770-988-8813; Gwinnett Lanes, 3835 Highway 29, Lawrenceville, 770-925-2000; Norcross Lanes, 6345 Spalding Dr, Norcross, 770-840-8200; Roswell Lanes, 785 Old Roswell Rd, Roswell, 770-998-9437; 775 Cobb Place Blvd, Kennesaw, 770-427-7679; www.brunswickbowling.com
- **Funtime Bowl**, 3285 Buford Hwy NE, Atlanta, 404-636-7548, www.funtime-bowl.com

- **Suburban Lanes**, 2619 N Decatur Rd, Decatur, 404-373-2514, www.atlantasu-burbanlanes.org
- **Tucker Bowling Center**, 4365 Cowan Rd, Tucker, 770-938-7171

## CHESS

There are several good chess clubs and centers in metro Atlanta. For a complete listing and for more information on chess in Georgia, check out the **Georgia Chess Association**, www.georgiachess.org. You may also want to consider the following:

- **Atlanta Chess and Game Center**, 3155 E Ponce de Leon Ave, Scottdale, 404-377-4400, www.atlantachessclub.com; offers rated tournaments and a large selection of chess books and equipment
- **Championship Chess**, 3565 Evans Rd, Doraville, 770-939-4596, www.championshipchess.net/
- **Kids Chess**, 2501 E Piedmont Rd, Ste 160, 770-575-5802, www.kidschess.com; offers after-school chess and tournaments for children

## DANCE

If you'd like to learn a new dance, join a dance club, or be invited to members-only social dances, the following resources may be useful:

- **Atlanta Ballroom Dance Club**, www.atlantaballroomdance.org, holds monthly dances at the Knights of Columbus Hall, 2620 Buford Hwy; also offers Wednesday night dance lessons for beginning and intermediate dancers of all ages.
- **Atlanta Swing Era Dance Association**, 160 Legion Dr, Smyrna, www.aseda.org, is a nonprofit organization that sponsors monthly community dances, workshops, dance events, lessons, and more.
- **Atlanta Tango**, 404-376-6732, www.atlantatango.com, offers weekly classes, events and community dances at various locations around town.
- **Awalim Dance Company**, 404-297-9343, www.awalim.com, offers traditional, middle-eastern dance classes at Several Dancers Core in Decatur, 519 N McDonough St, and performances at various locations throughout metro Atlanta.
- **Metro Atlanta Square Dancers Association**, 770-445-7035, www.masda.net, is a network of square dancers across the state. The association can provide you with a schedule of upcoming events and classes, as well as offer an introduction to other folks interested in this art form.
- **The Royal Scottish Country Dance Society**, 770-242-3889, www.rscds-atlanta.org is the Atlanta branch of this national organization.

Many of the local **YMCA**, 404-588-9622, www.ymcaatlanta.org, and **YWCA**, 404-527-7575, www.ywcaatlanta.org, branches also offer dance classes for adults and children. Contact your neighborhood branch directly for schedule and pricing information.

## FENCING

For information on fencing in metro Atlanta, including locations for classes, summer camps, and local tournaments, contact the **Atlanta Fencers Club**, 404-762-7666, www.atlantafencersclub.com.

## FISHING

It's fairly simple to get a fishing license in metro Atlanta. All you need is a photo ID, proof of residency (such as a signed lease or recent utility bill), and $9. Once you have those things, just head over to the fishing section of your local sporting goods or discount department store. There, you'll be able to purchase a license in less time than it takes to bait a hook. A few stores to consider for fishing equipment and licenses are listed below.

- **Dick's Sporting Goods**, 877-846-9997, www.dickssportinggoods.com; formerly Galyans, eight locations in metro Atlanta
- **REI–Recreational Equipment**, 800-426-4840, www.rei.com; four locations in metro Atlanta
- **The Sports Authority**, www.sportsauthority.com; locations throughout metro Atlanta
- **Kmart**, 866-562-7848, www.kmart.com; five locations in metro Atlanta
- **Walmart**, 800-925-6278 www.walmart.com; locations throughout metro Atlanta

It's also possible to purchase your fishing license directly from the **Department of Natural Resources, License Unit**, over the phone by calling 888-748-6887, or online at www.georgiawildlife.com. There is, however, an additional service charge of $3.95 per license for either of those options. For more information on obtaining a fishing license in Georgia, call the **Fishing License Information Line**, 770-414-3333.

Once you have your license, you'll probably want to know where to go for good fishing. Some of the small lakes in metro Atlanta's parks are open for fishing. To find out if there's one close to you, call the **Parks and Recreation Department** in your neighborhood (see numbers above). For statewide fishing information, contact the **Georgia State Natural Resources Department, Fishing Information Line**, 770-918-6418, www.georgiawildlife.com.

## FRISBEE

Though some may think a Frisbee is just something to toss around the park after they've finished their picnic lunch, many people consider disc golf to be a serious (yet fun!) sport. If you'd like to learn more or just find out where you can go to be a spectator or to participate, contact the **Atlanta Disc Golf Organization**, www.discgolfatlanta.com.

Also, Ultimate Frisbee, often referred to as simply Ultimate, is popular at many area colleges including Kennesaw State University, Georgia State University, and Emory University, among others. For more information about intramural games or schedules, visit the school's website under their athletics departments.

## GOLF

Local parks and recreation departments operate a number of golf courses. Call the one convenient to your neighborhood for fees and reservations. For a list of additional public golf courses and private golf clubs, consult your Yellow Pages.

- **City of Atlanta**: *9-Hole Golf Course:* Candler Park Golf Course–Candler Park, 585 Candler Park Dr NE, 404-371-1260, http://candlerpark.americangolf.com; *18-Hole Golf Courses:* Alfred Tup Holmes Golf Course, 2300 Wilson Dr SW, 404-753-6158; Bobby Jones Golf Course, 384 Woodward Way NW, 404-355-1009; Browns Mill Golf Course, 480 Cleveland Ave SE, 404-366-3573; North Fulton Golf Course, 216 West Wieuca Rd NE, 404-255-0723; www.atlantaga.gov
- **DeKalb County**: Mystery Valley Golf Course, 6100 Shadow Rock Dr, Lithonia, 770-469-6913, www.mysteryvalley.com; Sugar Creek Golf Course, 2706 Bouldercrest Rd SE, Atlanta, 404-241-7671; www.sugarcreekgolfcourse.com
- **Cobb County**: Cobblestone Golf Course, 4200 Nance Rd, Acworth, 770-917-5151, www.cobblestonegolf.com; Legacy Links Golf Course, 1825 Windy Hill Rd, Marietta, 770-434-6331, www.legacyfoxcreek.com
- **Cherokee County**: BridgeMill Athletic Club, 1190 Bridge Mill Ave, Canton, 770-345-5500, www.bridgemillathleticclub.com; Woodmont Golf Club, 3105 Gaddis Rd, Canton, 770-345-9260, www.woodmontgolfclub.com; Cherokee Golf Center, Highway 92 and I-575, Woodstock, 770-924-2062; Eagle Watch Golf Course, 3055 Eagle Watch Dr, Woodstock, 770-591-1000, www.cantongategolf.com/eaglewatch; Towne Lake Hills Golf Club, 1003 Towne Lake Hills East, Woodstock, 770-592-9969; www.townelakehillsgc.com
- **Gwinnett County**: Bear's Best, 5342 Aldeburgh Dr, Suwanee, 678-714-2582; Heritage Golf Club, 4445 Britt Rd, Norcross, 770-493-4653, www.heritagegc.com; St. Marlo Golf Club, 7755 St. Marlo Country Club Pkwy, Duluth, 770-495-7725, www.stmarlo.com; Collins Hill Golf Club, 585 Camp Perrin Rd, Lawrenceville, 770-822-5400, www.collinshillgolf.com

- There are also several **golf clubs and organizations** (both amateur and professional) in the metro Atlanta area. A few to consider:
- **Amateur Golf League of Atlanta**, 404-467-4853, www.agatour.com
- **Atlanta Junior Golf Association**, 770-850-9040, www.atlantajuniorgolf.org
- **American Singles Golf Association**, Atlanta Chapter, 770-785-2669, http://atlantasinglesgolf.com
- **Executive Women's Golf League**, Atlanta, 770-984-7617, www.ewgatlanta.com
- **Georgia State Golf Association**, 770-955-4272, www.gsga.org

## HIKING

Aside from the many miles of trails in area parks, there are countless scenic places to hike within a 90-minute drive of the city. Especially enticing to many Atlantans are the **North Georgia Mountains**, home to quaint southern towns and various state parks. In the **Chattahoochee National Forest**, Springer Mountain is the southern starting point of the Appalachian Trail, which winds for 2,050 miles through the eastern United States. An eight-mile trail meanders through **Amicalola Falls State Park**, located 50 miles north of Atlanta; its falls are some of the highest in the United States. The **Tallulah Gorge State Park** offers hiking and wildflower trails leading to the spectacular gorge that measures 1000 feet in depth. For more information about hiking trails in and around metro Atlanta, see the **Greenspace** and **Quick Getaways** chapters of this book. To learn more about Georgia's State Parks, contact the **State Parks and Historic Sites Information Office**, 404-656-3530, www.gastateparks.org.

If you'd like to meet others interested in hiking, or learn more information about area trails, consider the following organizations:

- **Atlanta Outdoor Club**, www.atlantaoutdoorclub.com
- **Benton MacKaye Trail Association**, www.bmta.org
- **Kennesaw Mountain Trail Club**, www.kennesawmountaintrailclub.org
- **Pine Mountain Trail Association**, www.pinemountaintrail.org
- **Sierra Club**, http://georgia.sierraclub.org

## HOCKEY

The **Atlanta Amateur Hockey League**, www.atlantahockey.org, organizes matches for metro Atlanta's league teams, which play at the **Marietta Ice Center**, 4880 Lower Roswell Rd, 770-509-5067, www.mariettaicecenter.com. The Ice Center also offers hockey lessons for children and adults, as does the **Alpharetta Family Skate Center**, 770-649-6600, www.coolerathletics.com. Call for schedule and pricing. You may also want to contact the **Southern Amateur Hockey Association**, 404-816-3303, www.sahaonline.org; and the **Metro Atlanta Street Hockey**

**Association**, 770-840-6952, www.mashahockey.com, for more information on teams, leagues, classes, and events for all ages in your area.

## HORSEBACK RIDING

Numerous metro Atlanta stables offer horseback riding lessons, rent and sell horses, and board horses. Here are just a few:

- **Chastain Horse Park**, 4371 Powers Ferry Rd NW, Atlanta, 404-252-4244, www.chastainhorsepark.org
- **East Cobb Stables**, 1649 Johnson Ferry Rd, Marietta, 678-560-9154, www.eastcobbstables.com
- **Vogt Riding Academy**, 1084 Houston Mill Rd NE, Atlanta, 404-321-9506, www.vogtridingacademy.com
- **Wills Park Equestrian Center**, Alpharetta, 678-297-6120, www.alpharetta.ga.us

## ICE SKATING

Though Atlanta's temperatures are pretty moderate year round, you can still hone your ice skating skills at the city's few indoor rinks. The **Atlanta Iceforum**, 2300 Satellite Boulevard, Duluth, 770-813-1010, and the **IceForum at Town Center**, 3061 Busbee Parkway, Kennesaw, 770-218-1010, www.iceforum.com, offer public skating, birthday packages, private lessons, rentals, and more. **The Marietta Ice Center**, 4880 Lower Roswell Road NE, Marietta, 770-509-5067, www.themicice.com, offers hockey leagues, lessons, private parties, public skating, and more. All three rinks provide a full-service pro shop and daycare packages.

For a limited time each winter (usually just December and January), skaters can enjoy an outdoor rink hosted by either Centennial Olympic Park or The World of Coca-Cola (the facilities alternate each year). For additional information on hours of operation, admission prices, skate rentals, and more, contact **Centennial Olympic Park** at 404-223-4412, www.centennialpark.com, or **The World of Coca-Cola** at 404-676-5151, www.worldofcoca-cola.com

## IN-LINE/ROLLER SKATING/SKATEBOARDING

If in-line skating is your thing, you will find many fellow enthusiasts in metro Atlanta. One of the most popular spots to show off your skills and whiz down paved trails is **Piedmont Park**, 404-875-7275, www.piedmontpark.org. You can rent or buy blades right across the park at **Skate Escape**, 1086 Piedmont Avenue NE, 404-892-1292, www.skateescape.com.

If you'd like to skate with others, participate in races, or just get more information on the best places to skate, contact the **Atlanta Peachtree Road Rollers**, 404-806-7251, www.aprr.org.

If a few lessons are needed before heading out on your own, you may want to consider **Bohemian Skate School**, 404-377-5811, www.bohemianskateschool. com; or the **Starlite Skating Center**, 770-474-7655, www.starliteskatingcenter. com. Both places have certified instructors that can help get you rolling.

And if you're a skateboarder, there are many parks and facilities where you can practice your moves. **Skatepark of Atlanta**, 5900 Sugarloaf Parkway, Suite 325, Lawrenceville, 678-847-0115, www.woodwardskateparks.net, has a huge facility with courses and ramps for all levels and ages, and a summer camp for those wanting some serious instruction. Also check out **Action Skate Park**, 5225 Deerlake Drive, Alpharetta, 770-889-5675; **Factory Skate Park,** 140 Werz Industrial Drive, Newnan, 770-683-7588, http://newnanfactoryskatepark.com; and **Empire Skate Park,** 3540 Highway 78 W # A, Snellville, 770-466-7110.

## LACROSSE

There are several local amateur lacrosse clubs and associations. To find out more about the sport, local teams, and events, contact any of the following organizations:

- **Atlanta Youth Lacrosse Association**, www.metroatlantalax.com/
- **Baggataway Lacrosse**, 770-777-9331, www.baggatawaylacrosseschool.com
- **Trojan Youth Lacrosse**, www.trojanyouthlacrosse.com
- **Georgia Lacrosse Foundation**, www.lacrossegeorgia.com
- **Thunder Lacrosse**, www.thunderlacrosse.org

## RACQUET SPORTS—TENNIS AND SQUASH

The **Atlanta Lawn Tennis Association** (**ALTA**), with over 70,000 members, is the largest organization of its kind in the United States. It offers league matches for men, women, juniors, and wheelchair players; leagues are divided according to levels of expertise. Contact 770-399-5788, www.altatennis.org for more information.

The **parks and recreation department** in your area operates a multitude of public tennis centers where you can play without paying a fee. Here's a list of the major tennis centers:

### CITY OF ATLANTA

- **Bitsy Grant Tennis Center**, 2125 Northside Dr NW, 404- 609-7193, http://bitsytennis.com
- **Chastain Park Tennis Center**, 110 West Wieuca Rd NE, 404-255-3210
- **Sharon J. Lester Tennis Center**, Park Dr NE, 404-872-1507, www.utstennis.com/sharon

## FULTON COUNTY

- **North Fulton Tennis Center**, 500 Abernathy Rd NE, Sandy Springs, 404-303-6182
- **South Fulton Tennis Center**, 5645 Mason Rd, College Park, 770-969-2200

## DEKALB COUNTY

- **Blackburn Tennis Center**, 3501 Ashford Dunwoody Rd NE, Atlanta, 770-451-1061, www.blackburntenniscenter.net
- **DeKalb Tennis Center**, 1400 McConnell Dr, Decatur, 404-325-2520, http://dekalbtenniscenter.com
- **Sugar Creek Tennis Center**, 2706 Bouldercrest Rd SE, Atlanta, 404-243-7149, http://sugarcreektenniscenter.com

## COBB COUNTY

- **Fair Oaks Tennis Center**, 1460 Brandon Dr SW, Marietta, 770-528-8480
- **Harrison Tennis Center**, 2650 Shallowford Rd NE, Marietta, 770-591-3150
- **Kennworth Tennis Center**, 3900 S Main St NE, Acworth, 770-528-8800
- **Sweetwater Tennis Center**, 2447 Clay Rd SW, Austell, 770-819-3221

## GWINNETT COUNTY

- **Hudlow Tennis Center**, 2051 Old Rockbridge Rd, Norcross, 770-417-2210
- **Mountain Park Tennis Center**, 5050 Five Forks Trickum Rd, Lilburn, 770-564-4651, http://mprctennis.com
- **Pleasant Hill Tennis Center**, 3620 Pleasant Hill Rd NW, Duluth, 770-417-2210, http://phtennisclub.org
- **Rhodes Jordan Park**, 100 E. Crogan St, Norcross, 770-417-2210

## ROCK CLIMBING

If you're interested in rock climbing and backpacking courses, try the **Providence Outdoor Recreation Center**, 13440 Providence Park Drive, Alpharetta, 770-740-2419. All-day and overnight courses introduce participants to the basics. **Atlanta Rocks**, www.atlantarocks.com, offers indoor rock climbing classes, camps, and more at two locations: **Intown**, 1019-A Collier Road, Atlanta, 404-351-3009, and **Perimeter**, 4411-A Bankers Circle, Atlanta, 770-242-7625.

If you'd like to learn more about rock climbing in Georgia, or if you'd like to meet other enthusiasts, contact the **Atlanta Climbing Club**, 404-237-4021, www.atlantaclimbingclub.org.

## RUGBY

Diehard rugby enthusiasts can scrum with the **Atlanta Renegades Rugby Club**, 770-483-6793, www.atlantarenegades.com; the **High Country Rugby and Social Club**, www.highcountryrugby.com; or the **Atlanta Harlequins Women's Rugby Club**, 770-908-1526, http://atlantaharlequins.com.

## RUNNING

Because the weather is rarely cold here, runners hit the paths year round. On any given day, at most hours of the day or night, you can find at least one or two joggers huffing and puffing down the road; on a sunny spring or fall weekend afternoon, runners are out in force on neighborhood streets and in parks all over the city. There are countless opportunities in the greater Atlanta area to run in various races or just for fun.

The **Atlanta Track Club**, 404-231-9064, www.atlantatrackclub.org, one of the largest running clubs in the country, sponsors over 20 races a year, including the popular Thanksgiving morning marathon and half-marathon. Its biggest event is the Peachtree Road Race, an incredibly well attended 10K on the Fourth of July. It attracts 60,000 amateur and professional runners and wheelchair racers each year. Watch for entry blanks in the paper and act fast. For such a large race, it fills up quickly. Also sign up for the ATC's email newsletters and alerts for updates on local races.

There are dozens of runners clubs in metro Atlanta—for every neighborhood or demographic you can find a group—it's just a matter of doing your research. Check out **Run Georgia's** website, www.rungeorgia.com. Remember, it's not always safe to run alone, even in the daytime, so you may want to contact the organizations above to find running partners and a list of safe routes in your area.

## SKIING

There are no slopes nearby, but there is an **Atlanta Ski Club** that sponsors local activities as well as ski trips around the world. For more information, call 404-303-1460, or visit www.atlantaskiclub.org.

## SOCCER

If soccer is your game, consider contacting the **Georgia State Soccer Association**, 770-452-0505, www.georgiasoccer.org, or the **Atlanta Youth Soccer Association**, 404-248-9333, www.aysa.net, for information about the numerous leagues, teams, and soccer programs in the metro Atlanta area. Or you may want to contact the organizations listed below:

- **The Atlanta Cup (Youth Tournament)**, 770-452-0505, www.soccerincollege.com
- **Cobb Futbol Club**, 678-594-5041, www.cobbfc.org
- **Georgia Adult Co-ed Soccer League**, 770-428-0364, www.gacsl.addr.com
- **Greater Atlanta Women's Soccer Association**, www.gawsa.org
- **Gwinnett Soccer Association**, 770-925-4106, www.gsasoccer.com
- **Fayette County Youth Club**, www.fcysl.org

## SWIMMING

The nearest ocean is close to a three-hour drive from metro Atlanta, but there's no shortage of places to go swimming. Most neighborhoods (especially in the suburbs) have a local or club pool, and there are numerous county or private pools you can join for a reasonable amount. It's certainly worth joining a club or pool if you enjoy swimming or have children because Atlanta's summers are long and hot—and a local pool is a great way to get exercise and relax with family or friends.

The **City of Atlanta**, www.atlantaga.gov, offers 18 outdoor aquatics facilities that operate only in the summertime. For a complete listing, see the blue pages Atlanta City Government section of your phone book. Here are a few of the more popular **outdoor pools**:

- **Candler Park Pool**, 1500 McLendon Ave NE, 404-373-4349
- **Chastain Park Pool**, 235 West Wieuca Rd NW, 404-255-0863, www.chastain-parkac.org
- **Garden Hills Pool**, 4058 E Brookhaven Dr NE, 404-848-7220, gardenhillspool.org
- **Grant Park Pool**, 625 Park Ave SE, 404-622-3041, www.grantparkpool.org
- **Piedmont Park Pool**, 1085 Piedmont Ave NE, 404-892-0117

Atlanta also operates four **indoor aquatic facilities**:

- **M.L. King**, 582 Connally St NE, 404-802-5415
- **Adamsville**, 3201 MLK Jr Dr, 404-505-3181
- **Southeast Atlanta**, 365 Cleveland Ave SE, 404-624-0774
- **Washington Park**, 102 Ollie St NW, 404-658-1436

### COBB COUNTY, WWW.COBBCOUNTY.ORG
- **Central Aquatic Center**, 520 Fairground St SE, Marietta, 770-528-8465
- **Mountain View Aquatic Center**, 2650 Gordy Pkwy, Marietta, 770-509-4925
- **Powder Springs Pool**, (outdoor) 3899 Brownsville Rd, Powder Springs, 770-439-3615
- **Sewell Park Pool**, (outdoor) 2055 Lower Roswell Rd, Marietta, 770-509-2741
- **South Cobb Aquatic Center**, 875 Six Flags Dr, Austell, 770-739-3180
- **West Cobb Aquatic Center**, 3675 MacLand Rd, Powder Springs, 770-222-6700

## DEKALB COUNTY

- **DeKalb County Aquatics Department,** 678-937-8925, www.co.dekalb.ga.us/ parks/aqua.htm, has six pool/aquatic centers in DeKalb

## GWINNETT COUNTY, WWW.GWINNETTCOUNTY.COM

- **Best Friend Park Pool**, 6224 Jimmy Carter Blvd, Norcross, 770-417-2202
- **Bethesda Park Aquatic Center**, 225 Bethesda Church Rd, Lawrenceville, 678.277.0880
- **Bogan Park Aquatic Center**, 2723 N Bogan Rd, Buford, 678.277.0853
- **Collins Hill Aquatic Center**, 2200 Collins Hill Rd, Lawrenceville, 770-237-5647
- **Dacula Park Pool**, 205 Dacula Rd, Dacula, 770-822-5410
- **Lenora Park Pool**, 4515 Lenora Church Rd, Snellville, 770-982-5309
- **Mountain Park Pool**, 5050 Five Forks Trickum Rd, Lilburn, 678.277.0870
- **Rhodes Jordan Park Pool**, 100 East Crogan St, Lawrenceville, 678.277.0892
- **West Gwinnett Park Aquatic Center,** 4488 Peachtree Industrial Blvd, Norcross, 678.407.8801

## SOUTH FULTON COUNTY

- **Welcome All Park Pool**, 4255 Will Lee Rd, College Park, 404-762-4058, www. fultoncountyga.gov

## OTHER SWIMMING VENUES

There are also several metro Atlanta **swim clubs** to consider, including:

- **Chattahoochee Gold Masters**, 770-591-4135, www.goldswim.com
- **Dynamo Swim Club**, 770-457-7946, www.dynamoswimclub.com
- **Dynamo Masters Swim Club**, 770-457-7946, www.dynamomasters.com
- **Swim Atlanta Masters**: Roswell, 770-992-1778; and Sugarloaf, 678-442-7946; Johns Creek, 770-622-1735; www.swimatlantamasters.com

And finally, **White Water Park**, 250 N Marietta Parkway, Marietta, 770-948-9290, www.sixflags.com/parks/whitewater, offers 40 acres of water activities, including water slides, wave pools and a toddler pool, so it's fun for the whole family. For those who don't mind a short drive to Buford, Georgia—about 40 miles north of Atlanta—there's always **Lake Lanier Islands**, 6950 Holiday Road, Buford, 770-932-7200, www.lakelanierislands.com, which offers a man-made beach, boat and jet-ski rentals, resort, and a water park.

## VOLLEYBALL

For information on volleyball in metro Atlanta, including teams, schedules, workshops, open play, and more, contact **North Atlanta Volleyball Club**, http://northatlantavolleyball.com. You may also want to check out **Atlanta Volleyball**, www.atlantavolleyball.net, for a listing of local adult and junior leagues, college teams, and **TCA Atlanta Volleyball Club**, also for juniors, 404-919-9167 http://atlanta.tcavolleyball.com.

## YOGA

Yoga has become increasingly popular in metro Atlanta over the last decade, though several schools and organizations have been here since the 1970s. Keep in mind, there are several different styles of yoga, though they all share a common lineage. No style is better than another; it's simply a matter of personal preference. **Ashtanga Yoga** (also called Power Yoga) is very rigorous; participants jump from one posture to another, building strength, flexibility, and stamina. If you are a beginner or haven't worked out in a while, you may want to steer clear of this one. **Kripalu Yoga** is a gentle form of yoga that emphasizes pranayama (proper breathing), alignment, coordinating breath and movement, and working within the limits of each individual's flexibility and strength. It's very popular with beginning students. **Iyengar Yoga** (named for legendary teacher B.K.S. Iyengar) is one of the most popular styles of yoga in the world. Iyengar teachers stress the importance of the precise alignment of postures. Props are often used to assist beginners who may not be able to complete an asana (pose). **Viniyoga**, in the tradition of renowned yoga teacher T.K.V. Desikachar, is a form of flow yoga that can be gentle for beginners yet becomes more strenuous as you advance. Teachers of this yoga style will generally adapt the asanas to fit each practitioner, so you can work at your own pace. And, finally, **Classical Yoga**, a system based in ancient yogic philosophy, incorporates varying degrees of breathwork, asana, meditation, mudra, and mantras, and emphasizes *seva*, or selfless service as an integral part of one's personal practice.

For more complete information on yoga and its various branches, try ***Yoga Journal***, www.yogajournal.com, a bi-monthly publication, and ***Yoga Basics***, www.yogabasics.com, a popular yoga website. You should also talk to someone at the school or schools you are interested in attending to find out more about the type of yoga they teach before signing up. Yoga can be a wonderful physical and mental workout, if you find the style that works best for you.

Today, there are a number of really good schools in the area, and yoga classes can even be found at your local **YMCA**. A few established schools to consider are:

- **Atlanta Yoga at the King Plow Arts Center**, 887 West Marietta Ste N-105, Atlanta, 404-273-4388, www.atlantayoga.com; offers classes in Ashtanga yoga

- **Decatur Hot Yoga**, 431 W Ponce de Leon Ave, 404-377-4899, www.deca-turhotyoga.com; Bikram-style classes and more
- **Kashi Atlanta**, 1681 McLendon Ave, Atlanta, 404-687-3353, www.kashiatlanta. org; classical yoga, meditation, and more
- **Metamorphosis Yoga Center**, 2931A North Druid Hills Rd NE, Atlanta, 404-633-8484; Kripalu-style yoga and Phoenix Rising Yoga Therapy
- **Peachtree Yoga Center**, 6050 Sandy Springs Cir, Sandy Springs, 404-847-9642, http://peactreeyoga.com; offers a variety of classes, including Kripalu and Ashtanga
- **The Pierce Program**, 1164 North Highland Ave NE, Atlanta, 404-875-7110, www. pierceyoga.com; offers Viniyoga classes in the tradition of T.K.V. Desikachar
- **Stillwater Yoga Studio**, 931 Monroe Dr, Atlanta, 404-874-7813, www.stillyoga. com; offers classes in Iyengar yoga.
- **YMCA**, 404-588-9622, www.ymcaatlanta.org; various locations throughout metro Atlanta

## HEALTH CLUBS, GYMS, AND YMCAS

Health clubs are a way of life in metro Atlanta among the young and fit-ness-minded. Deciding which one to join can be rather overwhelming, but many clubs offer free or inexpensive introductory memberships as an incentive to try them out. The following is only a partial list of your many options. Consult the Atlanta Yellow Pages for more.

- **Buckhead Athletic Club**, 3343 Peachtree Rd NE, Atlanta, 404-442-2600, http://cityclubofbuckhead.com
- **Curves**, www.curvesinternational.com; locations throughout metro Atlanta
- **DeKalb Medical Center**, 2665 N Decatur Rd, Decatur, 404-501-2222, www. dekalbmedicalcenter.org
- **Gold's Gym**, www.goldsgym.com; locations throughout metro Atlanta
- **Lifetime Fitness**, 855-430-5433, www.lifetimefitness.com; six locations in metro Atlanta
- **LA Fitness**, 949-255-7200, www.lafitness.com; locations throughout metro Atlanta
- **Northpark 400 Health Club**, 1000 Abernathy Rd NE, Sandy Springs, 770-668-2220, www.northparktowncenter.com
- **Peachtree Center Athletic Club**, 227 Courtland St NE, Atlanta, 404-523-3833, www.peachtreeac.com
- **Midtown Athletic Club at Windy Hill**, 135 Interstate North Pkwy, Atlanta, 770-953-1100
- **YMCA**, 404-588-9622, www.ymcaatlanta.com; several locations throughout metro Atlanta

## SPORT AND SOCIAL CLUBS

In addition to the many social organizations specific to a particular sport (see listings above), metro Atlanta is also home to several clubs geared towards fitness-minded people in general. Two to consider are **Atlanta Club Sport**, 404-257-3355, www.usclubsport.com, and the **Adventure Club**, www.adventureclub.com. Contacting these organizations may be a great way to meet people who share similar interests and learn more about sports and fitness opportunities throughout the city.

ATLANTA IS A CITY RENOWNED FOR ITS BEAUTIFUL TREES AND LUSH urban landscape. It's a city that takes pride in its parks and reveres its trees, so much so that in 1985 a group of residents formed Trees Atlanta, 404-522-4097, www.treesatlanta.org, a volunteer organization dedicated to planting and preserving trees throughout the city. Every spring, when the dogwood trees bloom and colorful azaleas blanket the roadsides, metro Atlanta feels like a garden paradise. As a resident of this blooming oasis, you too can enjoy the wide variety of indigenous and non-native trees and flowers in the numerous parks and gardens that blanket the city.

All of metro Atlanta's neighborhoods boast their own small green gems—modest but beautiful parks that welcome nearby residents. There are so many, in fact, throughout the metro Atlanta area, it's impossible to list them all here. However, one such Atlanta park, known as the **Duck Pond**, is a lovely expanse of greenspace located in the middle of Buckhead's Garden Hills district. Another well-loved neighborhood park is **Murphy-Candler Park** in Dunwoody, a sprawling, 135-acre park featuring nature trails, a beautiful lake (with ducks and fish), a playground, picnic tables, and more.

Regardless of which part of town you're in, be sure to take time to explore your new community and its area greenspaces and pocket parks; you may discover an unexpected jewel of your own and get to know some of your new neighbors in the process. An organization you might find helpful is the **Garden Club of Georgia**, http://gardenclub.uga.edu, which includes 16,000 members and more than 550 individual garden clubs. Actively welcoming newcomers, they share gardening tips, exchange plants, and learn about floral and landscape design as well as environmental issues.

While most of the suburban parks offer a number of amenities including picnic tables, playgrounds, and acres of greenspace, it's the impressive City of Atlanta parks that draw the largest crowds. Intowners and suburbanites alike frequent these intown parks regularly throughout the warm weather months, enjoying the sunshine and open space, as well as the many festivals that are held in Atlanta's parks each year.

Below you'll find an overview of and contact information for metro Atlanta's largest and most popular greenspaces. For a listing of parks in your community, check the Parks and Recreation Department of the county in which you reside (listed later, under **City Parks**).

## CITY PARKS

Atlanta's largest and best-known park is **Piedmont Park**, 404-875-7275, www. piedmontpark.org, located in Midtown at Piedmont Avenue and 14th Street. Originally part of the Gentleman's Riding Club, the land was purchased by the city government in 1904 for use as a public park. A four-mile jogging trail snakes through the grounds, which house a tennis center, athletic fields, and Playscapes (an unusual children's playground designed by sculptor Isamu Noguchi). The park is a favorite locale for joggers, rollerbladers, cyclists, families, and picnickers who enjoy exploring the trails around lovely Lake Clara Meer.

Numerous events take place in Piedmont Park throughout the year, including the **Atlanta Arts Festival**, which attracts artists from all over the state; **The Peachtree Road Race**, which begins and ends at the park every July 4th; and free Sunday evening, summertime concerts by the **Atlanta Symphony Orchestra**. Piedmont Park also plays host to the always-popular **Dogwood Festival**, 404-329-0501, www.dogwood.org, every April, and its well-tended fields are the locale of choice for several local softball leagues. Contact the park to learn more about upcoming events and field use.

Piedmont Park is also home to the **Atlanta Botanical Garden** (**ABG**), 404-876-5859, www.atlantabotanicalgarden.org, a private, nonprofit facility designed to educate the public, support horticulture research, and display a wide variety of plant life. The entrance to the Atlanta Botanical Garden is located at the north end of the park on Piedmont Avenue, and it includes the Storza Woods, a 15-acre hardwood forest with trails, the Dorothy Chapman Fuqua Conservatory, and landscaped gardens that spread across 15 acres. In the 16,000-square-foot glass-covered Conservatory is a fabulous array of tropical, desert, and endangered species; the outdoor gardens display over 3,000 plants, including a rose garden, vegetable and herb gardens, a fragrance garden for the blind, and a Japanese garden. Green-thumb enthusiasts can take advantage of the ABG's extensive **Sheffield Botanical Library** and can also call the **Garden's Plant Hotline**, 404-888-GROW, with any gardening questions. The botanical garden includes a $3 million orchid house and a whimsical children's garden replete with fountains, a butterfly pavilion, a treehouse, and a number of hands-on exhibits and activities. Also in 2010, the garden doubled its greenspace, while adding to and modernizing its facilities. Most notably, the ABG added a new visitor center and 600-foot-long canopy walk.

At Atlanta Avenue and Boulevard, in the heart of the neighborhood that shares its name, lies Atlanta's oldest park, **Grant Park**, home to lofty shade trees, numerous pavilions, and enticing paved paths. In addition, Grant Park is home to **Zoo Atlanta**, 404-624-5600, www.zooatlanta.org, and the **Atlanta Cyclorama**, 404-658-7625, http://atlantacyclorama.org, a fifty-foot circular painting of the Battle of Atlanta. And amateur sports teams utilize its athletic facilities throughout the year. Annual events include September's **Grant Park Tour of Homes**, 404-215-9955, www.grantpark.org/tour, through the surrounding Victorian neighborhood, as well as the **Christmas Candlelight Tour**, which takes place in December.

In the heart of the Emory University campus, just off the main entrance at Clifton Road, lies **Lullwater Estate Park**, the beautifully maintained residential grounds belonging to the university's president. A hidden treasure, this 185-acre park features a paved trail leading around the Tudor Revival style house and several miles of dirt trails winding around the lake. Lullwater is a popular destination with Emory students and faculty and with local residents.

Six miles east of the downtown area, in the stately Druid Hills neighborhood, it is a real treat to wander through **Fernbank Forest**, a 65-acre old growth forest. A two-mile-long trail winds through the dense woods, and signs marking the area's vegetation educate the interested observer. If you want to relax in the midst of the forest, you can take a seat at one of several rest areas; mobility-impaired visitors can enjoy the forest's wonders by using the paved "easy effort" trail located near the gatehouse. The forest is located on the grounds of the **Fernbank Science Center**, 678-874-7102, http://fsc.fernbank.edu, which houses a planetarium, an observatory, and an exhibition hall. Visitors may also view a greenhouse and the Cator Woolford Memorial Gardens. Finally, the **Fernbank Museum of Natural History**, 404-929-6300, www.fernbankmuseum.org, with its IMAX Theater and science exhibits, is situated on adjoining land.

**Chastain Park**, 404-237-2177, eight miles north of Downtown, just off of Roswell Road, is a city-run, 320-acre park that's home to a tennis center, swimming pool, riding stables, public golf course, art gallery, and much more. The park is really an all-purpose sporting and recreation extravaganza. Joggers, walkers, and rollerbladers crowd the 3½-mile jogging trail, and cyclists can join in organized rides throughout the park. Amateur sports enthusiasts play year round on Chastain's many athletic fields, while families and kids make use of the playground and many picnic areas. In addition, the park's **Chastain Park Amphitheater**, 404-233-2227, www.atlantaconcerts.com/chastain.html, accommodates over 6,000 people, and hosts various outdoor concerts and performances throughout the year.

For more information on Atlanta's many city parks, contact the **Bureau of Parks** for Atlanta, 404-546-6813, www.atlantaga.gov.

For more information on parks in your community, contact your local **Parks and Recreation Department**:

- **Alpharetta Parks and Recreation**, 678-297-6100, www.alpharetta.ga.us
- **Chamblee Parks and Recreation**, 770-986-5016, www.chambleega.com
- **Cobb County Parks and Recreation**, 770-528-8800, prca.cobbcountyga.gov
- **Decatur Recreation Department**, 404-377-0494, www.decaturparks.com
- **DeKalb County Parks and Recreation**, 404-371-2631, www.co.dekalb.ga.us
- **Duluth Parks and Recreation**, 770-623-2781, www.duluthga.com
- **Fulton County Parks and Recreation**, 404-730-6200, www.fultoncountyga.gov
- **Gwinnett County Parks and Recreation,** 770-822-8840, www.gwinnettcounty.com
- **Marietta Parks and Recreation**, 770-794-5601, www.mariettaga.gov
- **Roswell Recreation and Parks**, 770-641-3705, www.roswellgov.com
- **Smyrna Parks and Recreation**, 770-431-2842, www.symrnacity.com
- **Stone Mountain Recreation Department**, 770-498-2414, www.stonemountaincity.org

## CHATTAHOOCHEE NATURE CENTER

In addition to the city parks mentioned above, the privately owned, not-for-profit **Chattahoochee Nature Center**, 770-992-2055, www.chattnaturecenter.org, is also one of metro Atlanta's most popular greenspace destinations. Located about 17 miles north of Downtown, it is a wonderful place to hike, explore, and be environmentally educated. The center contains two nature trails, which allow hikers to experience the Chattahoochee's ecosystem firsthand. The Woodland Trails lead past Kingfisher Pond into forestland populated by indigenous birds and animals. One branch of the trail passes the remains of a pioneer cabin and a cemetery, while another offers an assortment of seasonal wildflowers. The Wetland Trail meanders through the Redwing Marshland on the banks of the Chattahoochee River, where beavers and other marsh creatures make their homes. The center also hosts a wide variety of educational programs for visitors of all ages.

## STATE PARKS

If you want to bicycle or jog along scenic paved roads, all in sight of the world's largest chunk of exposed granite, visit **Stone Mountain Park**, 770-498-5600, just 16 miles due east of Atlanta. A must for hikers, this 2,300-acre park contains numerous trails that twist and turn around three picturesque lakes and up the mountain itself. Whether you're looking for a five-mile hike around the mountain or an easy stroll through the woods, you'll find it here. Many choose to walk up the mountain and ride the skylift back down, but you can reverse the trip. Either way, take time to relish the mountain's man-made miracle—the world's largest statue, a 90-foot-tall carving of Robert E. Lee, Stonewall Jackson, and Jefferson Davis on horseback—as well as its natural wonders. Trail maps are available at park information desks. The park also features lakefront beaches, a golf course, a scenic railroad, restaurants, a paddlewheel riverboat, a petting zoo, family-friendly attractions, including an indoor playground called "The Great Barn," and a reconstructed antebellum plantation. A small fee is charged per car to enter the park and access the public picnic areas, nature trails, and playgrounds. And there are additional charges for guests who want full access to the park's attractions. One-day passes can be purchased at the front gate. Annual parking and visitor passes are available as well.

Like nearby Stone Mountain, Panola Mountain is a mass of exposed granite. But unlike Stone Mountain Park, a definite tourist mecca, **Panola Mountain State Conservation Park**, 770-389-7801, www.gastateparks.org/info/panolamt, is 600 acres of virtually untouched hilly forestland. Situated 18 miles southeast of the city, this day-use park is a Registered National Landmark, designed to preserve and showcase the mountain environs in their natural state. Guided tours of the mountain take place each weekend, and visitors can explore the area adjacent to the mountain on two marked trails. The park also offers wildflower walks in the spring and fall as well as other educational programs.

For a more comprehensive list of Georgia's state parks, see the **Quick Getaways** chapter of this book, or contact **Georgia State Parks and Historic Sites**, 404-656-2770, 800-864-7275, www.georgiastateparks.org.

## NATIONAL PARKS

The **Chattahoochee River National Recreation Area**, 678-538-1200, www.nps.gov/chat, which contains over 70 miles of trails along the banks of the river north of Atlanta, extending from Standing Peachtree Creek all the way to Lake Lanier, should not be missed. Established in 1978 as part of the National Parks system, the Recreation Area is made up of several land units where visitors can fish, hike, and raft. The Johnson Ferry Unit provides a put-in point for commercial rafting and canoe trips, as well as guided tours of its numerous trails. Along the river's shores in the Palisades West Unit, people flock to fish and to view the rafters floating by. At the Cochran Shoals Unit, fitness buffs take to the 3.1-mile fitness trail. Cochran Shoals is also a popular haunt for cyclists and joggers. The Recreation Area is home to a spectacular array of landscapes, including zones of pristine Appalachian old-growth forests, steep outcroppings of rock, river channels and creeks, and flood plains. Hiking, whether you want an easy jaunt or a strenuous trek, is especially recommended in the fall, when temperatures cool and the leaves offer striking color contrasts.

If you'd like to combine your back-to-nature activities with an educational exploration of a Civil War battlefield, just head 19 miles northwest of downtown Atlanta on I-75 to the **Kennesaw Mountain National Battlefield Park**, 770-427-4686, www.nps.gov/kemo. Designed to commemorate and tell the story of the

Atlanta Campaign and the Battle of Kennesaw Mountain, this 2,884-acre National Battlefield Park has over 16 miles of hiking trails that snake through the country-side. Whether you choose to make the entire 16-mile loop around the mountain or take an abbreviated hike, you can see remains of Confederate fortifications and some exquisite scenery along the way. There is no entrance fee.

For more information on Georgia's National Parks, see the **Quick Getaways** chapter of this book, or contact the **National Park Service**, 800-365-2267, www.nps.gov.

F OR THOSE MOVING TO ATLANTA FROM THE NORTH, THE OBVIOUS GOOD news is that the area boasts relatively mild weather most of the year, allowing for nearly 12 months of outdoor recreation. Its plant hardiness zone is 8a.

**Springtime** temperatures in metro Atlanta generally hover in the mid-60s to mid-70s from March to May, but don't be surprised if you wake up one April morning to find the mercury has dropped to 40 degrees. In spring, Atlanta temperatures can fluctuate wildly, from frosty one day to the mid-80s the next, so it's probably a good idea to wait until the middle of May to pack away your winter wardrobe. The fluctuating springtime temperatures sometimes cause severe weather situations to develop. Thunderstorms and tornadoes usually occur during this time of year, and while devastating funnel clouds rarely touch down in the metro Atlanta area, tornado activity here is a real possibility. In mid-March 2008, for instance, tornadoes plowed through several parts of downtown Atlanta, causing severe damage to skyscrapers, businesses, and homes. The tornadoes damaged such landmarks as the Georgia Dome and the CNN Center.

In addition to the threat of tornadoes and thunderstorms, springtime in metro Atlanta also brings **pollen**. Lots of pollen. And you'll find it everywhere. The pollen can be so heavy that it covers everything in sight—cars, outdoor furniture, the ground—and many Atlanta residents get regular allergy shots or take over-the-counter antihistamines rather than face a month or two of sneezing and watery eyes. For pollen count updates, watch your local news; area weather forecasters devote a significant chunk of their on-air time to pollen counts and lists of other allergens affecting the city. These reports can help you decide whether to limit your outdoor time on days when the pollen counts are highest. Also check out www.atlantaallergy.com or www.weather.com for pollen updates.

While tornadoes and pollen counts seem to get the most media coverage, Atlanta's biggest weather story may actually be the sweltering heat and unbearable humidity of **summer**. Because the north Georgia mountains block cooler air from the north and hold in moisture from the Gulf Coast, not to mention the heat and pollution generated by urban environs, summer temperatures often soar to the upper 90s or even higher, with a whopping 90% humidity. Most Atlanta homes and apartments now offer central air conditioning (or, at the very least, window units), though some hardy souls still manage to survive the sticky heat with nothing more than a few good electric fans. Fortunately, the stifling summer spells are often interrupted by cooling, afternoon thundershowers, so Atlanta residents are given some relief as the temperatures drop to the lower 90s.

**Fall** is probably Atlanta's most predictable season weather-wise. Temperatures this time of year are normally in the upper 60s, though the mercury has been known to hit 80 degrees throughout the month of September. The first freeze generally doesn't occur until early November. Autumn is an especially pleasant season in Atlanta, since mild temperatures allow residents to spend more time outside enjoying the changing colors.

Temperatures during the **winter** months are more variable. Often, stretches of mild, cool weather (or "sweater weather" as many locals call it) will alternate with winter cold spells. The high humidity in Atlanta during the summer months contributes to a damp cold winter from December to February, with at least one day of snow or ice. Atlanta's snowfall is generally less than 4 inches (see statistics below), but, unfortunately, that's usually enough to throw the city into chaos. When snow falls in Atlanta, the schools and most businesses close, while news reports warn people to stay off the roads. All this hoopla over an inch or two of the white stuff usually makes transplanted northerners groan with disbelief, though many are happy to have an extra day off work.

Since the fall of 2007, metro Atlanta, along with most of the southeastern United States, has been in a severe drought. The result has been widespread watering restrictions and sometimes bans for residents and businesses, as water levels at the area's largest water supplies, Lake Lanier and Lake Allatoona, have fallen to record low levels. In fact, the city has not seen such drought conditions in more than 75 years, according to the US Army Corps of Engineers. As a result, more Atlantans have taken to serious water conservation, using rain barrels to save water for their gardens and lawns, and buying toilets or shower heads that use less water. To stay informed on the drought condition in the Southeast, visit www.atlantawatershed.org/drought.

## METRO ATLANTA WEATHER STATISTICS

According to the National Weather Service, on average, Atlanta experiences clear skies 28% of the time; partly cloudy 33% of the time; and cloudy skies 39% of the time, with an annual average rainfall of 48–50 inches, and snowfall of 2–4 inches.

The following represent average daily low and high temperatures for each month, but don't let these averages fool you—as mentioned above, summertime temperatures can soar to the upper 90s, while winter temperatures often drop below freezing: **January** 35–51° F; **February** 36–54° F; **March** 43–62° F; **April** 51–71° F; **May** 60–79° F; **June** 67–86° F; **July** 70–87° F; **August** 69–86° F; **September** 64–82° F; **October** 54–72° F; **November** 43–61° F; **December** 37–52° F.

If you'd like more information on Atlanta's weather, including current conditions and weekly forecasts, visit the **National Weather Service** website, www.nws.noaa.gov, or **The Weather Channel**, www.weather.com.

## AIR POLLUTION

In Atlanta, air pollution is one of the city's biggest challenges. During the hot summer months (May to September), emissions from cars and other sources mix with sunlight and the city's heat to form ground level ozone, or smog. This toxic gas is a serious public health problem that causes respiratory problems, chest pain, shortness of breath, and sore throats. It may even lead to permanent lung damage. In the past, the Atlanta Regional Commission reported that the Environmental Protection Agency (EPA) has categorized metro Atlanta as a "Serious Non-Attainment" area for ground level ozone, meaning that Atlanta and its surrounding communities consistently exceeded the federal air quality standard of 0.12 parts per million. Following a great deal of work by local media, government, and organizations, in February of 2013 the EPA announced plans to redesignate metro Atlanta area to Attainment status, based on satisfactory air quality monitoring data for the 2008 through 2010. The EPA also indicated that Atlanta has continued to meet the Attainment standard since 2010.

Atlanta's air quality problem gets a lot of media attention during peak months, so residents are kept informed. Local newspapers, television, and radio stations report air quality levels daily as part of their weather reports, and do an excellent job of explaining what these levels mean. There are also several "clean air" organizations in metro Atlanta that lobby for stricter emissions testing, help to educate the public on ground level ozone, and offer helpful tips on improving Atlanta's air quality. To find out more, contact **Georgia's Clean Air Force**, www.cleanairforce.com, 800-449-2471; the **Metro Atlanta Clean Air Campaign**, www.cleanaircampaign.org, 877-CLEANAIR; and the **Atlanta Regional Commission**, www.atlantaregional.com, 404-463-3100. If you'd like up-to-the-minute ozone reports, the EPA provides real-time data at their **AIRNOW** website, www.airnow.gov.

## INSECTS

Insects are a major issue here in the South. Mosquitoes are the most prevalent flying pest in the metro area, and are particularly bothersome after an especially wet winter. Those venturing outside from April through October may find themselves besieged by these blood-sucking creatures. Your best bet is to invest in a good insect repellent and wear it faithfully if you plan on enjoying Atlanta's beautiful weather. Also, home owners can treat their yards for mosquitos by placing repellent in key areas and making sure there is no standing water for the bugs to breed in.

Aside from being plain pesky, mosquitoes are a health issue because of **West Nile virus**, which causes an infection similar to encephalitis. Although the virus most commonly plagues birds and horses, it is possible for a person bitten by a mosquito carrying West Nile to become infected. According to the Centers for Disease Control, approximately 80% of people who are infected with WNV will not show any symptoms. For the other 20%, the most common symptoms are fever, headache, muscle weakness, body aches, swollen lymph glands, and rashes. Those suffering a more severe case may also have a high fever, neck stiffness, stupor, disorientation, coma, tremors, convulsions, paralysis, and encephalitis. Between 3% and 15% of those with visible infection may die, particularly young children, the elderly, and those with compromised immune systems. Unfortunately, there's not yet a vaccine or specific treatment for the virus. The best prevention is to avoid going out for prolonged periods at night, particularly to woodsy or swampy areas, to wear bug spray, and to make sure you have screens on your windows. For more information on this issue, contact the **Centers for Disease Control**, 404-639-3311, www.cdc.gov.

In addition to mosquitoes, bees and ticks can pose challenges to the city's nature lovers. Bees are attracted to metro Atlanta's many flowers, and can be a major nuisance to anyone trying to enjoy a picnic or a day in the park. Ticks, on the other hand, aren't as troublesome unless you live (or play) in heavily wooded areas or own pets that run around outside. With regard to ticks, your best bet is to slather on the insect repellent when you plan on spending time in the woods, and then do a tick check on yourself and your pet once you head back inside. The biggest concern here is with the deer tick, which transmits Lyme disease.

Y OU'VE FOUND A PLACE TO LIVE, UNPACKED, AND GOTTEN SETTLED into your new home. Now it's time to get involved in the community. This chapter lists a variety of options for community involvement, from joining organizations, to volunteering, to finding a place of worship.

## MEETING PEOPLE

Moving to a new area is always intimidating. New residents are in full "adapt" mode, and making friends may be the last thing on your mind until you are ready to blow off some steam over the weekend or find someone who can join you for that movie, play, or concert. Atlantans are typically very friendly people; it's that southern hospitality thing that's bred into locals and often passed on to transplants. If you're in the suburbs, your neighbors will likely come over to meet you after you move in; if they don't, don't be afraid to introduce yourself when you run into each other. Contact people you already know in the area—old high school or college friends, any family, or former colleagues—and branch out from there.

Since Atlanta is so spread out, consider what type of social life you want when choosing your home. You might want to pick a place near a downtown area or major park; with easy access to seasonal festivals and activities, you can mingle and meet new friends. Research local clubs—fitness, sports, cooking, music, volunteering—whatever your interests, and get involved. Check your local paper or periodicals; look online at Meetup.com or Yelp.com, or Google "Atlanta Social Clubs" to find multiple resources. Subscribe to event emails such as Access Atlanta, www.accessatlanta.com, or Atlanta on the Cheap, www.atlantaonthecheap.com, for a list of events in your area.

Then get out and circulate, and follow up by adding new friends to Facebook, Twitter, or LinkedIn to stay connected.

## ALUMNI GROUPS

Most colleges and universities have alumni groups in Atlanta that host social and networking events for former students. Check with the alumni or development office at your alma mater about alumni groups in your area. Be sure your old school has your current contact information, so they can let you know about any upcoming alumni events planned in your area. Armed with an alumni directory, you might consider initiating an event yourself and inviting fellow alumni in your area.

## BUSINESS GROUPS

People (especially those who are single and in their 20s or 30s) often make important social connections at work, at informal gatherings of co-workers. But depending on your field, you might want to consider joining a professional networking group, since these organizations frequently schedule social events for members. Check out **Atlanta Event**, 678-508-5975 www.atlantaevent.com/networkgroups.htm, an incredible resource that lists hundreds of groups for every location, trade, and demographic, including their contact information. If you're working from home, seek out groups that organize social and networking events for freelancers. You can check LinkedIn or Meetup.com, or your local trade group for freelancing events.

## THE OUTDOORS

Atlanta is an incredible location for outdoor enthusiasts. Its countless parks, rivers, mountains and lakes, combined with its mostly pleasant year-round weather make outdoor living easy and enjoyable. Whether you're looking to enjoy its lakes, lounge in its parks, or hike its historic mountains—you'll find ample friends to join you. For sports enthusiasts, check the **Sports and Recreation** chapter of this book, or try a specific search online such as "North Atlanta Cyclists" or "Midtown Basketball." For other outdoor clubs, search Google, Meetup.com, or Facebook with similar specifics, such as "Bird Watching Atlanta." Also, the Atlanta Outdoor Club, www.atlantaoutdoorclub.com, organizes everything from hiking, to biking, to canoe trips all over and around metro Atlanta.

## PARENTS' GROUPS AND SCHOOL FUNCTIONS

If you are moving to the city with kids, you have a social advantage, at least in terms of meeting other parents. Atlanta parents with very young children can network through a number of clubs and groups. Atlanta Parent, www.atlantaparent. com, is a go-to guide for parents in Atlanta, and Atlanta Moms, www.atlantamoms. com, connects moms for playdates and other activities. Google parent clubs in your specific neighborhood, or check Meetup.com or Facebook. Once your children are school age, you'll have plenty of opportunities to meet and chat up other parents at school functions or waiting at school or the bus stop. Public schools, in particular, depend upon the help of parent volunteers—if you advertise your willingness to help out, you'll get a flood of invitations.

## POLITICAL GROUPS

Connecting with people who share your political beliefs is a great way to make new friends. There are plenty of active organizations and many host regular socials or outings, as well as the expected volunteer work associated with political clubs. For a full list of options, check the section on "Area Organizations," or Google your specific interest: "Buckhead Democrats," "Cobb Republicans," "Young Libertarians," etc.

## RELIGIOUS GROUPS

Atlanta is right in the middle of a section of the country called "The Bible Belt," and if you move to town, you will quickly realize why. While the term technically refers to its early Christian heritage, today churches of every religion, denomination, or sect abound. Most offer a host of activities for residents wherever they are in life—from students, to singles, to families, to seniors. Also, the larger churches can be a great place to meet people and network through church-organized activities—sports, studies, trips, socials—where you can make new friends. Check the Places of Worship section later in this chapter for an extensive list. Also, search Google or Yelp, or try www.usachurch.com for Christian denominations, www.masjidomar. org/atlantaMasajid.php for Islamic mosques; www.gaychurch.org/Find_a_Church for churches friendly to the LGBT community; or www.jewishatlanta.org, to name a few.

## SPECIAL INTERESTS

Join a poker league, meet up with fellow chess players, confer with other beading enthusiasts, or practice your conversational Russian—start searching and you'll find there's a group for nearly every interest. Trying searching Meetup.com, which lists scheduled gathering of various groups in your area. Type in your ZIP code and the subjects you're interested in, and you'll be rewarded with a wealth of options. A few places to start:

- **Atlanta Convention & Visitors Bureau "Insider Blog,"** http://atlinsider.atlanta. net/blogs/bloggers.aspx; while you would expect to find a wealth of information about local events at the ACVB website, they also offer a great insider's page with more than a dozen blogs. Expect to find a wealth of information to help you navigate the social scene.

- **AtlantaontheCheap.com** compiles a useful list of deals from discount vendors such as Groupon.com, HalfoffDepot.com, LivingSocial.com, and more. Check out the "Atlanta Daily Deals" section for any number of fun events where you can either take new friends or make them.

- **Localtweeps** (http://localtweeps.com/about) is an opt-in ZIP code level means of connecting local like-minded individuals—whether their interests are social or commercial. Members may use it to promote specific events and tweet-ups throughout a targeted ZIP code.

- **The Atlanta Fandom Guide,** http://atlfandom.wordpress.com, a surprisingly thorough and entertaining resource for sci-fi and fantasy lovers who want to connect and catch local events.

- For newcomers with a literary bent, **libraries and bookstores** around the city sponsor book groups that anyone can join.

## VOLUNTEERING

Giving back to the community is a rewarding experience. Whether you are skilled at building houses, caring for the elderly, tutoring underprivileged children, or canvassing neighborhoods (having bilingual skills in any of these areas can be particularly useful), you can find a volunteer project that suits your talents and beliefs. Helping out in your new community is also a great way to meet people, and it can make the transition to an unfamiliar place less stressful. In the chapter of this book entitled **An Atlanta Year**, you'll find listings of festivals and events occurring each month that rely on an army of volunteers to run smoothly. Choose one that appeals to you and sign up.

### VOLUNTEER PLACEMENT SERVICES

The following organizations coordinate much of metro Atlanta's volunteer activity. Contact them directly if you want to volunteer but aren't sure where. They'll send you where help is needed most. Or contact **Volunteer Match**, www.volunteer-match.org, a national volunteer placement service.

- **Hands on Atlanta**, 600 Means St, Atlanta, 404-979-2800, www.handsonatlanta.org
- **The United Way of Metropolitan Atlanta**, 100 Edgewood Ave NE, Atlanta, 404-614-1000, www.unitedwayatlanta.org

## OTHER CONNECTIONS

- **Check bulletin boards or websites** at your office, church, neighborhood grocery store, laundries, and school.

# GENERAL AREAS FOR INVOLVEMENT

## THE HUNGRY AND THE HOMELESS

Scores of volunteers concern themselves with shelter for Atlanta's homeless. Jobs include monitoring and organizing the shelters; providing legal help; ministering to psychiatric, medical, and social needs; raising money; manning phones; and caring for children in the shelters. Many people solicit, organize, cook, and serve food to the destitute at sites throughout Atlanta. Still others deliver meals to the homeless and the homebound.

## CHILDREN

If involvement with children is especially appealing, you can tutor in and out of schools, be a big brother or sister, teach music and sports in shelters or at local community centers, run activities in the parks, entertain children in hospitals, and accompany kids on weekend outings. Schools, libraries, community associations, hospitals, and other facilities providing activities and guidance for children are all worth exploring.

## HOSPITALS

The need for volunteers in hospitals is manifold: From interpreters to admitting and nursing aides, many volunteers are required. Assistants in crisis medical areas—emergency rooms, intensive care units, and the like—may be an option if you have the skills, as are volunteers to work with victims of sexual abuse. If you just want to be helpful, you might assist in food delivery or work in the gift shop.

## THE DISABLED AND THE ELDERLY

You can read to the blind, help teach the deaf, work to prevent birth defects, and help the retarded and developmentally disabled, among others. You can also make regular visits to the homebound elderly, bring hot meals to their homes, and teach everything from nutrition to arts and crafts in senior centers and nursing homes.

## EXTREME CARE SITUATIONS

Helping with suicide prevention, Alzheimer's and AIDS patients, rape victims, and abused children is a special category demanding a high level of commitment—not to mention emotional reserves and in many cases, special skills.

## THE CULTURE SCENE

Museums and cultural centers are always in need of volunteers to lead tours or lend a hand in any number of ways. Libraries, theater groups, and ballet companies have plenty of tasks that need to be done. Fundraising efforts also require many volunteers to stuff envelopes and/or make phone calls. The Public Broadcasting Service (PBS) is a good example. Its large volunteer staff raises money for its stations through extensive on-air fundraising campaigns that include collecting pledges.

## THE COMMUNITY

Work in your neighborhood. You can help out at the local school, neighborhood block association, nursing home, settlement house, or animal shelter.

# AREA ORGANIZATIONS

If you were involved in a volunteer effort before you moved, or if you already know the specific cause that sparks your interest, you can call the following organizations and inquire about donating your time.

## AIDS

- **AID Atlanta**, 1438 West Peachtree St, Ste 100, Atlanta, 404-870-7700, www. aidatlanta.org
- **AIDS Education/Services for Minorities**, 2140 Martin Luther King Dr, Atlanta, 404-691-8880, www.naesm.org
- **Project Open Hand Atlanta**, 176 Ottley Dr NE, Atlanta, 404-872-8089, www. projectopenhand.org

## ALCOHOL AND DRUGS

- **Atlanta Harm Reduction Center**, 1561 McLendon Ave NE, Atlanta, 404-526-9222, www.atlantaharmreduction.org
- **Council on Alcohol and Drugs**, 6045 Atlantic Blvd, Norcross, 770-239-7442, www.livedrugfree.org

## ANIMALS

- **Atlanta Humane Society**, 981 Howell Mill Rd, Atlanta, 404-875-5331, www.atlantahumane.org
- **Cherokee County Humane Society**, 770-928-5115, www.cchumanesociety.org
- **Cobb County Humane Society**, 770-428-5678, www.humanecobb.com
- **Gwinnett County Humane Society**, 770-798-7711, www.gwinnetthumane.com
- **PAWS Atlanta** (the **DeKalb County Humane Society**), 5287 Covington Hwy, Decatur, 770-593-1155, www.pawsatlanta.org
- **Zoo Atlanta**, 800 Cherokee Ave, Atlanta, 404-624-5600, www.zooatlanta.org

## CHILDREN

- **Big Brothers–Big Sisters of Metro Atlanta**, 100 Edgewood Ave, Ste 710, Atlanta, 404-601-7000, www.bbbsatl.org
- **Boys and Girls Club of Metro Atlanta**, 100 Edgewood Ave, Ste 700, Atlanta, 404-527-7100, www.bgcma.org
- **Children's Wish Foundation**, 8615 Roswell Rd, Atlanta, 770-393-9474, www.childrenswish.org
- **Families First**, 1105 W Peachtree St NE, Atlanta, 404-853-2800, www.families-first.org
- **Georgia Council of Child Abuse**, 1375 Peachtree St, Atlanta, 404-870-6565, www.georigafamily.org
- **Quality Care for Children**, 50 Executive Park South, Ste 5015, Atlanta, 404-479-4200, www.qualitycareforchildren.org

## CULTURE AND THE ARTS

- **African-American Panoramic Experience-APEX**, 135 Auburn Ave NE, Atlanta, 404-523-2739, www.apexmuseum.org
- **Atlanta Ballet**, 1400 W Peachtree St NW, Atlanta, 404-873-5811, www.atlanta-ballet.com
- **Atlanta Cyclorama**, 800 Cherokee Ave SE, Atlanta, 404-658-7625, http://atlantacyclorama.org
- **Atlanta History Center**, 130 W Paces Ferry Rd NW, Atlanta, 404-814-4000, www.atlantahistorycenter.com
- **Atlanta Symphony Orchestra Volunteer Ushers**, 404-733-4899, www.atlantasymphony.org
- **Fernbank Museum of Natural History**, 767 Clifton Rd NE, Atlanta, 404-929-6300, www.fernbankmuseum.org
- **The Fox Theatre**, 660 Peachtree St, Atlanta, 404-881-2100, www.foxtheatre.org
- **Hammonds House Galleries/Resource Center of African American Art**, 503 Peeples St, Atlanta, 404-752-8730, www.hammondshouse.org

- **High Museum of Art**, 1280 Peachtree St NE, Atlanta, 404-733-4400, www.high.org
- **Historic Rhodes Hall**, 1516 Peachtree St NW, Atlanta, 404-885-7800, www.georgiatrust.org
- **Jimmy Carter Library and Museum**, 441 Freedom Pkwy, Atlanta, 404-865-7100, www.jimmycarterlibrary.gov
- **Margaret Mitchell House**, 990 Peachtree St NE, Atlanta, 404-249-7015, www.margaretmitchellhouse.com
- **Martin Luther King Historical Site**, 449 Auburn Ave NE, Atlanta, 404-526-8900, www.nps.gov/malu
- **Rialto Center for the Performing Arts**, 80 Forsyth St at Luckie St, Atlanta, 404-651-1234, www.rialtocenter.org
- **The William Breman Jewish Heritage Museum**, 1440 Spring St, Atlanta, 678-222-3700, www.thebreman.org

## DISABLED ASSISTANCE

- **American Foundation for the Blind, National Literacy Center**, 100 Peachtree St, Ste 620, Atlanta, 404-525-2303, www.afb.org
- **Center for the Visually Impaired**, 739 W Peachtree St NW, Atlanta, 404-875-9011, www.cviga.org
- **Compeer Atlanta**, 1903 N Druid Hills Rd, Atlanta, 678-686-5918, www.compeeratlanta.org
- **Creative Community Services**, 4487 Park Dr, Ste A, Norcross, 770-469-6226, www.ccsgeorgia.org
- **The Disability Action Center of Georgia**, 755 Commerce Dr, Decatur, 404-687-8890, www.disabilitylink.org
- **Georgia Council for the Hearing Impaired**, 4151 Memorial Dr, Ste 103-B, Decatur, 404-292-5312, www.gachi.org

## ENVIRONMENT

- **Earthshare for Georgia**, 1447 Peachtree St, Ste 214, Atlanta, 404-873-3173, www.earthsharega.org
- **Environmental Community Action**, 250 Georgia Ave, SE, Atlanta, 404-584-6499, www.eco-act.org
- **Georgia Conservancy**, 817 W Peachtree St, Atlanta, 404-876-2900, www.georgiaconservancy.org
- **Georgia Forest Watch**, 706-635-TREE, www.gafw.org
- **Georgia Public Interest Research Group**, 741 Piedmont Ave, Atlanta, 404-892-3405, www.georgiapirg.org
- **Georgia Sierra Club**, metro Atlanta, 404-607-1262, http://georgia.sierraclub.org

- **Southern Environmental Law Center**, 127 Peachtree St, Atlanta, 404-521-9909, www.southernenvironment.org

## GAY & LESBIAN

- **Atlanta Lambda Community Center**, 828 W Peachtree St NW, Atlanta, 404-881-1985
- **Atlanta Pride Committee**, 20 Executive Park West, Atlanta, 404-929-0071, http://atlantapride.org
- **The Rainbow Center**, 4549 Chamblee Dunwoody Rd, Atlanta, 770-677-9471, www.therainbowcenter.org
- **YouthPride Atlanta**, 1017 Edgewood Ave, Atlanta, Decatur, 404-521-9713 and 24-hour help line is 404-521-9711, www.youthpride.org

## HEALTH & HOSPITALS

- **American Cancer Society**, 250 Williams St, Atlanta, 404-315-1123, www.cancer.org
- **American Lung Association of Georgia**, 2452 Spring Rd, Smyrna, 770-434-5864, www.long.org
- **DeKalb Medical Center**, 2701 N Decatur Rd, Decatur, 404-501-1000, www.dekalbmedical.org
- **Northside Hospital**, 1000 Johnson Ferry Rd NE, 404-851-8000, www.northside.com
- **Piedmont Hospital**, 1968 Peachtree Rd NW, Atlanta, 404-605-5000, www.piedmonthospital.org
- **Atlanta Medical Center**, 1170 Cleveland Ave, East Point, 404-466-1170, www.atlantamedcenter.com
- **United Cerebral Palsy of Greater Atlanta**, 3300 Northeast Expressway, Atlanta, 770-676-2000, www.ucpga.org

## HISTORICAL RESTORATION

- **Historic Oakland Foundation**, 248 Oakland Ave SE, Atlanta, 404-688-2107, www.oaklandcemetery.com

## HOMELESS

- **Atlanta Center for Self Sufficiency**, 75 Peachtree Place NW, Atlanta, 404-874-8001, http://atlantacss.org/
- **Atlanta Union Mission**, numerous shelters serving men, women, and children in the Atlanta area, for men's services, 404-350-1300, for women and children, 404-532-1929, www.atlantamission.org

- **Georgia Law Center for the Homeless**, 100 Edgewood Ave, Atlanta, 404-681-0680, www.galawcenter.org
- **Homeless Task Force**, 363 Georgia Ave SE, Atlanta, 404-589-9495

## HUMAN SERVICES

- **American Red Cross**, there are four district offices in Atlanta, while the Red Cross's headquarters is located at 1955 Monroe Dr NE, Atlanta, 404-876-3302. Visit the Red Cross website to find the location nearest you: www.redcrossatlanta.org
- **Atlanta Urban League**, 100 Edgewood Ave NE, Ste 600, Atlanta, 404-659-1150, www.atlul.org
- **Catholic Charities Atlanta**, 5238 Peachtree Rd, Chamblee, 770-429-2369, www.catholiccharitiesatlanta.org
- **Compeer Atlanta**, 1903 N Druid Hills Rd, Atlanta, 678-686-5918, www.compeeratlanta.org
- **Creative Community Services**, 4487 Park Dr, Ste A, Norcross, 770-469-6226, www.ccsgeorgia.org
- **Families First**, 1105 W Peachtree St NE, Atlanta, 404-853-2800, www.familiesfirst.org
- **Habitat for Humanity**, 519 Memorial Dr SE, Atlanta, 404-223-5180, www.habitat.org
- **Jewish Family & Career Services**, 4549 Chamblee Dunwoody Rd, Atlanta, 770-677-9300, www.jfcs-atlanta.org

## HUNGER

- **Atlanta Community Food Bank**, 732 Joseph E. Lowery Blvd, Atlanta, 404-892-FEED, www.acfb.org
- **Feed the Hungry Foundation,** 1440 Dutch Valley Pl, Atlanta, 770-980-1550, www.feedthehungryfoundation.com
- **Food Not Bombs**, 770 Ormewood Ave SE, Atlanta, 404-622-5859, www.foodnotbombs.net
- **Kashi Atlanta**, 1681 McLendon Ave, Atlanta, 404-687-3353, www.kashiatlanta.org/service.htm

## INTERNATIONAL

- **Amnesty International USA**, 730 Peachtree St NE, Ste 1060, Atlanta, 404-876-5661, www.amnestyusa.org
- **American Red Cross**, 1955 Monroe Dr NE, Atlanta, 404-876-3302, www.redcrossatlanta.org

- **Georgia Peace Coalition**, P.O. Box 133016, Atlanta, 30333, 404-522-4500, www. georgiapeace.org

## LEGAL—CIVIL RIGHTS

- **American Civil Liberties Union of Georgia**, 70 Fairlie St, Ste 340, Atlanta, 404-523-5398, www.acluga.org
- **Martin Luther King Jr. Center for Nonviolent Social Change**, 449 Auburn Ave NE, Atlanta, 404-526-8900, www.thekingcenter.com
- **The Southern Center for Human Rights**, 83 Poplar St NW, Atlanta, 404-688-1202, www.schr.org

## LITERACY

- **Literacy Volunteers of America**, 246 Sycamore St, Decatur, 404-377-READ, www.lvama.org

## POLITICS—ELECTORAL

- **The Democratic Party of Georgia**, 404-870-8201, www.democraticpartyof-georgia.org/
- **The Georgia Green Party**, 404-806-0480, http://georgiagreenparty.org
- **The League of Women Voters (Georgia)**, State Office, 678-547-0755, www. lwvga.org; Fulton County, 404-577-8683; DeKalb County, 404-321-0913; Cobb County/Marietta, 770-592-0625
- **The Libertarian Party of Georgia**, 1776 Peachtree St, Atlanta, 404-888-9468, www.lpgeorgia.com
- **Buckhead Republicans,** P.O. Box 14907, Atlanta, www.buckheadyr.org
- **The Republican Party of Georgia**, 404-257-5559, www.gagop.org
- **Young Democrats of Georgia**, www.georgiayds.org

## SENIOR SERVICES

- **American Association of Retired Persons**, 999 Peachtree St NE, Atlanta, 404-881-0292, www.aarp.org/ga
- **Central Fulton Senior Services**, 236 Forsyth St SW, Ste 201, Atlanta, 404-818-8001
- **Compeer Atlanta**, 1903 N Druid Hills Rd, Atlanta, 678-686-5918, www.com-peeratlanta.org
- **Creative Community Services**, 4487 Park Dr, Ste A, Norcross, 770-469-6226,www.ccsgeorgia.org

- **Senior Citizens Law Project**, 151 Spring St, Atlanta, 404-524-5811, www.atlantalegalaid.org
- **Senior Citizen Services**, 1705 Commerce Dr NW, Atlanta, 404-351-3889, www.scsatl.org

## WOMEN'S SERVICES

- **Atlanta Day Shelter for Women,** 655 Ethel St NW, Atlanta, 404-876-5286, http://atlantadayshelter.org
- **Atlanta Women's Foundation**, 50 Hurt Plaza SE, Ste 401, Atlanta, 404-577-5000, www.atlantawomen.org
- **DeKalb Rape Crisis Center**, 204 Church St, Decatur, 404-377-1429, www.dekalbrapecrisiscenter.org
- **Feminist Women's Health Center**, 1924 Cliff Valley Way NE, Atlanta, 404-728-7900, www.feministcenter.org
- **Georgia Advocates for Battered Women & Children**, 250 Georgia Ave SE, Ste 308, Atlanta, 404-524-3847
- **Spark Reproductive Justice Now**, P.O. Box 8551, Atlanta, 404-532-0022, www.sparkrj.org
- **Grady Hospital Rape Crisis Center**, 80 Jesse Hill Jr Dr SE, Atlanta, 404-616-4861, www.gradyhealth.org
- **Healthy Mothers Healthy Babies of Georgia**, 2300 Henderson Mill Rd, Ste 410, Tucker, 770-451-0020, www.hmhbga.org
- **Women's Resource Center to End Domestic Violence**, P.O. Box 171, Decatur, 404-370-7670, www.wrcdv.org

## YOUTH

- **Atlanta Children's Shelter**, 607 Peachtree St, Atlanta, 404-892-3713, http://acsatl.org
- **Big Brothers-Big Sisters of Metro Atlanta**, 100 Edgewood Ave, Ste 710, Atlanta, 404-601-7000, www.bbbsatl.org
- **Boys and Girls Club of Metro Atlanta**, 100 Edgewood Ave, Ste 700, Atlanta, 404-527-7100, www.bgcma.org
- **Center for Children and Young Adults/Open Gate**, 2221 Austell Rd, Marietta, 770-333-9447, www.umbrellaweb.org
- **Southwest YMCA Youth Outreach**, 100 Edgewood Ave, NE, Atlanta, 404-588-YMCA, www.ymcaatlanta.org

## PLACES OF WORSHIP

A recent visitor to Atlanta remarked that there seemed to be a church on every street corner. While this may be a slight exaggeration, metro Atlanta does offer a multitude of opportunities for prayer, spiritual retreats, and religious communities of all kinds. The city's diverse racial and ethnic population is echoed in a wide assortment of houses of worship. For a more complete listing of the over 2,000 organized places of worship in Atlanta, check the Yellow Pages.

### BAHÁ'Í

Although Bahá'í houses of worship may differ from one another in architectural styles, they are often stunning and are recognizable by their nine sides and central dome, which symbolize "the diversity of the human race and its essential oneness." To find out more about the Bahá'í religion, visit its main website, www.bahai.org. To find out more about Atlanta's Bahá'í community, check out www.atlantabahai.org.

- **Atlanta Bahá'í Center**, 379 Edgewood Ave SE, Atlanta, 404-688-0208, www.atlantabahai.org
- **The Bahá'í Center of Alpharetta**, 10690 Jones Bridge Rd, Alpharetta, 800-22UNITE
- **Bahá'í Unity Center**, 2370 Wesley Chapel Rd, Decatur, 770-981-0097, www.bahaiunitycenter.org
- **North Gwinnett Bahá'í House**, 5621 Little Mill Rd, Buford, 770-932-8399

### BUDDHIST

Buddhism dates back over two millennia, and today over 350 million around the world consider themselves Buddhists. There are many different sub-traditions, including **Zen**, **Tibetan**, **Tantric** (**Vajrayana**), and **Mahayana**. An informative online resource for Buddhism is www.buddhanet.net; for more information on the Buddhist community in Atlanta, visit the Atlanta Buddhist Directory, http://atlantabuddhism.mm.st.

- **Atlanta Soto Zen Center**, 1167 C/D Zonolite Place, Atlanta, 404-532-0040, www.aszc.org
- **Dorje Ling Buddhist Center**, 3253 Shallowford Rd, Chamblee, 770-451-7715, www.jonang.org
- **Drepung Loseling Institute**, 1781 Dresden Dr, Atlanta, 404-982-0051, www.drepung.org
- **Georgia Buddhist Vihara**, 3153 Miller Road, Lithonia, 770-987-8442, www.gbvihara.org

- **Rameshori Buddhist Center**, 6860 Peachtree-Dunwoody Rd, Sandy Springs, (770) 913-0260, www.meditationforeveryone.org

# CHRISTIAN

## AFRICAN METHODIST EPISCOPAL AND EPISCOPAL ZION

If you'd like to find out more about the AME or Episcopal Zion church, visit www. ame-today.com. To find an AME church in your neighborhood, check out the AME links page at www.ame-today.com/links/index.shtml, or visit www.amechurch. com. You may also want to investigate the following:

- **Allen Temple AME Church**, 1625 Simpson Rd NW, Atlanta, 404-794-3316, http://allentempleame.org
- **Big Bethel AME Church**, 220 Auburn Ave NE, Atlanta, 404-827-9707, www.big-bethelame.org
- **St. Paul AME Church**, 821 Third St, Stone Mountain, 770-469-4995, http://st-paul-ame.org
- **St. Philip AME Church**, 240 Candler Rd SE, Atlanta, 404-371-0749, www.saint-philip.org
- **Turner Monumental**, 66 Howard St NE, Atlanta, 404-378-5970

## ANGLICAN/EPISCOPAL

The Episcopal and Anglican churches are both descended from the Church of England. The Episcopal Church took root in America as early as 1607, with the first permanent English settlement in Jamestown, Virginia. There are plenty of Episcopal and Anglican churches in metro Atlanta. To find one in your neighborhood, check the Atlanta Yellow Pages, or consider the listings below. To learn more about the **Episcopal Church of the US**, visit them online at www.episcopalchurch.org; for information on the **Anglican Church** worldwide, go to http://anglicansonline.org.

- **All Saints Episcopal Church**, 634 W Peachtree St NW, Atlanta, 404-881-0835, www.allsaintsatlanta.org
- **Holy Comforter Episcopal Church**, 737 Woodland Ave, Atlanta, 404-627-6510, https://holycomforter.episcopalatlanta.org
- **The Church of Our Saviour**, 1068 N Highland Ave, Atlanta, 404-872-4169, https://oursaviour.episcopalatlanta.org

## APOSTOLIC

The Apostolic Church of America consists of approximately 90 congregations throughout the United States, Japan, Mexico, and Canada. The church also conducts services on many college campuses, and is in engaged in missionary and humanitarian work throughout the world. For more information about the Apostolic Church, visit their website, www.apostolicchristian.org. To find a church in your neighborhood, check the Atlanta Yellow Pages, or consider the following:

- **Apostolic Christian Church of Atlanta**, 6225 Campbellton Rd, Fairburn, 770-306-1113
- **Apostolic Faith Church**, 629 James P. Brawley Dr NW, Atlanta, 404-524-1861, http://apostolicfaithchurchatlanta.com
- **Greater Christ Temple Holiness Church**, 914 Cherokee Ave SE, Atlanta, 404-622-9723, www.greaterchrist.org

## ASSEMBLY OF GOD

Assemblies of God are the largest Pentecostal denomination of the Protestant church in the USA. Their homepage, http://ag.org/top, is informative and provides a complete directory of its churches nationwide. A few to consider in metro Atlanta are:

- **Cavalry Assembly of God**, 5067 Chamblee Dunwoody Rd, Dunwoody, 770-393-2197
- **Celebration Church**, 7373 Covington Hwy, Lithonia, 770-482-7770
- **Roswell Assembly of God**, 11440 Crabapple Rd, Roswell, 770-993-6586, www.roswellag.org

## BAPTIST

**American, Free Will**, and **Southern Baptists** are all found throughout metro Atlanta. To find out more about Southern Baptists, visit www.sbc.net; for more on Free Will Baptists, go to www.nafwb.org; and for American Baptists, check out http://abc-usa.org. Some Baptist churches in the metro Atlanta area include:

- **Avondale Estates First Baptist Church**, 47 Covington Rd, Avondale Estates, 404-294-5284, http://afbc.com
- **Briarcliff Baptist Church**, 3039 Briarcliff Rd NE, Atlanta, 404-633-6103, www.briarcliffbaptist.org
- **Clairmont Hills Baptist Church**, 1995 Clairmont Rd, Decatur, 404-634-6231, http://clairmonthills.org
- **Druid Hills Baptist Church**, 1085 Ponce de Leon Ave NE, Atlanta, 404-874-5721, www.dhbc.org
- **Ebenezer Baptist Church**, 407 Auburn Ave NE, Atlanta, 404-688-7263, http://historicebenezer.org
- **First Baptist Church of Atlanta**, 4400 N Peachtree Rd, Atlanta, 770-234-8300, www.fba.org

- **Gwinnett Baptist Tabernacle**, 6690 Buford Hwy NE, Doraville, 770-448-2656,
- **Northside Drive Baptist Church**, 3100 Northside Dr NW, Atlanta, 404-237-8621, http://northsidedrive.org
- **Pleasant Hill Baptist Church**, 4278 Chamblee Tucker Rd, Atlanta, 770-939-1255, http://pleasanthillbc.org
- **Second-Ponce de Leon Baptist Church**, 2715 Peachtree Rd NE, Atlanta, 404-266-8111, wwwspdl.org
- **Wright Street Baptist Church**, 395 Wright St NE, Marietta, 770-422-5851, wrightstreetbaptistchurch.org

## CHRISTIAN SCIENCE

The Church of Christian Science was established by Mary Baker Eddy in 1879. Today the Mother Church is headquartered in Boston, with 2,000 branch churches in 80 countries around the world, including 8 in metro Atlanta. For more information on the Mother Church or Christian Science in general, visit www.christianscience.com. To learn more about Christian Science in Georgia, visit www.christiansciencega.com.

- **First Church of Christ Scientist Atlanta**, 150 Fifteenth St NE, Atlanta, 404-892-7838, http://christianscienceatlanta.com
- **First Church of Christ Scientist Decatur**, 446 Clairmont Ave, Decatur, 404-373-8383, http://decaturchurch.com
- **First Church of Christ Scientist Lilburn**, 1627 Hewatt Rd, Lilburn, 770-985-0562, http://christiansciencelilburnga.com
- **First Church of Christ Scientist Marietta**, 2641 Old Sewell Rd, Marietta, 770-565-7271

## CHURCH OF CHRIST

There are several Churches of Christ in metro Atlanta. To find one near you, check the Atlanta Yellow Pages, or consider the churches listed below. To find out more about the Church of Christ, visit http://church-of-christ.org, or the United Church of Christ website, www.ucc.org.

- **Atlanta Virginia Highland Church UCC**, 743 Virginia Ave NE, Atlanta, 404-873-1355, www.vhchurch.org
- **Hillcrest Church of Christ Decatur**, 1939 Snapfinger Rd, Decatur, 404-289-4573, www.hillcrestcoc.net
- **North Atlanta Church of Christ**, 5676 Roberts Dr, Dunwoody, 770-399-5222, www.nacofc.org

## CHURCH OF GOD

The **Worldwide Church of God** has about 42,000 members in 900 congregations around the world, including metro Atlanta. To find out more or to locate congregations in your area, visit them online at www.wcg.org. The **United Church of God** is also represented in metro Atlanta and around the world. For more information, visit www.ucg.org, or www.ucgatlanta.org. And, finally, information on **The Church of God** can be found at their homepage, www.thechurchofgod.org.

- **Mount Paran Church of God**, 2055 Mount Paran Rd NW, Atlanta, 404-923-8700, www.mountparan.com
- **Mt Paran Church of God North**, 1700 Allgood Rd, Marietta, 770-578-9081, www.mtparan.com,
- **Living Hope Christian Fellowship**, 5885 Mallory Park, College Park, http://atlanta.wcgweb.org
- **Pleasantdale Church of God**, 3434 Pleasantdale Rd, Doraville, 770-491-7071

## CHURCH OF GOD IN CHRIST

For more information about the Church of God in Christ, including churches throughout metro Atlanta, visit www.cogic.org. A few local Church of God in Christ congregations to consider are:

- **Greater Community Church of God in Christ**, 406 Roswell St, Marietta, 770-590-8510, www.greatercommunitycogic.com
- **Holy Fellowship Church of God in Christ**, 3691 Centerville Hwy, Snellville, 770-736-0207, www.holyfellowship.org

## CHURCH OF THE NAZARENE

For information about the Church of the Nazarene and a church locator service, try the main website for the Church of the Nazarene, www.nazarene.org. Area churches include:

- **First Church of the Nazarene**, 3861 Ernest W Barrett Pkwy, Marietta, 678-370-9292
- **Church of the Nazarene**, 170 Plaza Dr SE, Smyrna, 770-436-6784
- **East Point Church of the Nazarene**, 2736 Cheney St, East Point, 404-762-6417

## EVANGELICAL

A few of metro Atlanta's Evangelical churches are listed below. For a more complete listing, be sure to check the Atlanta Yellow Pages in print or online.

- **New Covenant Community Church**, 3147 Chamblee Tucker Rd, Atlanta, 770-451-2038, www.atlantanccc2.org
- **Christian Church of Atlanta Slavic Evangelic**, 3149 Old Atlanta Rd, Suwanee, 678-845-0420

## FRIENDS (QUAKERS)

Members of the **Society of Friends**, a.k.a. **Quakers**, can trace their church's roots back to some of the first European settlers. Persecuted in England for their beliefs, and then again in Massachusetts by their fellow Puritans, many Friends fled the Boston area to settle in other colonies along the eastern United States. Today Friends churches can be found throughout the world. To learn more about the Friends church, visit www.quaker.org. Local Friends meetinghouses include:

- **Atlanta Friends Meeting**, 701 W Howard Ave, Decatur, 404-377-2474, http://atlanta.quaker.org

## INDEPENDENT/INTERDENOMINATIONAL/NONDENOMINATIONAL

The following churches are just a few in metro Atlanta that identify themselves as independent, interdenominational, or nondenominational:

- **Buckhead Church**, 404-814-7000, 3336 Peachtree Road, Atlanta, http://buckheadchurch.org
- **Cumberland Community Church**, 3110 Sports Ave, Smyrna, 404-952-8834, www.cumberlandchurch.org
- **Free Gospel Interdenominational Church**, 957 Wylie St SE, Atlanta, 404-584-7874
- **Green Pastures Christian Ministries**, 5455 Flat Shoals Pkwy, Decatur, 770-987-8121, www.greenpastures.org
- **Gwinnett Church**, 678-812-4500, 1800 Satellite Blvd Duluth, www.gwinnettchurch.org
- **Martin Street Church of God**, 148 Glenwood Ave, Atlanta, 404-688-8545, www.mstcog.org
- **Midtown Church**, 3202 Paces Ferry Pl NW, Atlanta, 404-261-7100, www.midtownchurch.com
- **North Point Community Church**, 4350 North Point Pkwy, Alpharetta, 678-892-5000, www.northpoint.org
- **Smyrna Christian Church**, 910 Concord Rd SE, Smyrna, 770-435-1723, www.smyrnachristianchurch.org
- **Watermark Church**, 678-880-9092, 2126 Sixes Road, Canton, www.watermarkchurch.com

## JEHOVAH'S WITNESS

For information about Jehovah's Witness or to find a kingdom hall near you, visit www.watchtower.org or www.jw-media.org. A few include:

- **Chamblee, Dunwoody English and Korean Congregations**, 2300 Dunwoody Club Dr, Atlanta, 770-396-7171
- **College Park Congregation**, 4474 Scarborough Rd, Atlanta, 30349, 404-684-1492
- **Woodstock Congregation**, 2369 Cherokee Ln, Woodstock, 770-926-0639

## LATTER DAY SAINTS/MORMON

If you'd like to find out more about the Church of Jesus Christ of Latter-Day Saints, or search for a ward in your neighborhood, visit www.lds.org. A few metro Atlanta locations to consider are:

- **Atlanta Temple**, 6450 Barfield Rd, Sandy Springs, 770-393-3698, wwwldschurchtemples.com/atlanta
- **Church of Jesus Christ of Latter-Day Saints, Atlanta Stake**, 1947 Brockett Rd, Tucker, 770-934-4765
- **Church of Jesus Christ of Latter-Day Saints, Glenridge Ward**, 6449 Glenridge Dr NE, Atlanta, 404-256-2092

## LUTHERAN

Lutheranism came to the New World with the immigrants of the northern European countries, including Norway, Sweden, Denmark, Finland, and Germany. Today about two thirds of American Lutherans belong to the Evangelical Lutheran Church in America, www.elca.org, the largest conference of Lutherans in this country. Missouri Synod is the more conservative branch of the Lutheran church. Metro Atlanta Lutheran churches include:

- **All Saints Lutheran Church**, 722 Rockbridge Rd SW, Lilburn, 770-923-7283, www.aslc.org
- **Lord of Life Lutheran Church ELCA**, 5390 McGinnis Ferry Rd, Alpharetta, 770-740-1279, www.lordlife.org
- **Lutheran Church of the Messiah**, 465 Clairmont Ave, Decatur, 404-373-1682, www.lmessiah.org
- **Lutheran Church of the Redeemer**, 731 Peachtree St NE, Atlanta, 404-874-8664, www.redeemer.org
- **Rivercliff Lutheran Church**, 8750 Roswell Rd, Sandy Springs, 770-993-4316, www.rivercliflutheran.org/

## MENNONITE

Until the 19th century, most Mennonites were concentrated in rural farming communities, speaking German, and spurning much of the secular world. Since the 1800s, there have been divisions in the church, yielding the **Old Mennonite Church**, the **General Conference Mennonite Church**, the **Mennonite Brethren**, and the **Old Order Amish**. For more information about the Mennonite Church of the USA, visit www.mcusa.org, http://mennoniteusa.org. For more information about the Mennonite Church in metro Atlanta, contact the **Atlanta Mennonite Fellowship**, 404-627-5013, www.atlantamennonite.org.

## METHODIST (UNITED)

For more information on the United Methodist Church, visit their website, www.umc.org. If you'd like a complete listing of Methodist Churches in the metro Atlanta area, check the Atlanta Yellow Pages. A few local churches to consider are:

- **Atlanta First United Methodist Church**, 360 Peachtree St NE, 404-524-6614, www.atlantafumc.net
- **Brookhaven United Methodist Church**, 1336 N Druid Hills Rd NE, Atlanta, 404-237-7506, www.brookhavenumc.org
- **Druid Hills United Methodist Church**, 1200 Ponce de Leon Ave NE, Atlanta, 404-377-6481, www.druidhillsumc.org
- **North Springs United Methodist Church**, 7770 Roswell Rd NW, Atlanta, 770-396-0844, www.northspringsumc.org
- **Northside United Methodist Church**, 2799 Northside Dr NW, Atlanta, 404-355-6475, www.northsideumc.org
- **Sandy Springs United Methodist Church**, 86 Mount Vernon Hwy NE, Atlanta, 404-255-1181, www.ssumc.org

## ORTHODOX (COPTIC, EASTERN, GREEK, ALBANIAN, RUSSIAN)

For information on the **Orthodox Church in America**, visit www.oca.org, or try the **Greek Orthodox Archdiocese of America** at www.goarch.org/en/archdiocese. Two beautiful Orthodox churches in Atlanta are:

- **Greek Orthodox Cathedral of the Annunciation,** 2500 Clairmont Rd NE, Atlanta, 404-633-5870, www.atlgoc.org
- **St. Elias Antiochian Orthodox Church**, 2045 Ponce de Leon Ave NE, Atlanta, 404-378-8191, www.steliasofatlanta.org

## PENTECOSTAL/CHARISMATIC

If you'd like to learn more about the **Pentecostal/Charismatic Churches of North America**, or to find a local church, go to www.pccna.org. For more about the **International Communion of the Charismatic Episcopal Church**, check out www. iccec.org. Or try the **Pentecostal-Charismatic Theology Inquiry International** at www.pctii.org. A few Pentecostal churches in metro Atlanta to consider are:

- **Mableton Pentecostal Church**, 1000 Old Powder Springs Rd, Mableton, 770-941-6502
- **Rehoboth Community Church**, 1423 Akridge St NW, Atlanta, 404-758-2009
- **Seal of Life Ministry**, 6991 Peachtree Industrial Blvd, Norcross, 770-417-1928

## PRESBYTERIAN (USA)

A Protestant Church with its roots in 17th-century England, Presbyterianism was brought to the USA in the late 1600s by the Scottish and Irish. The largest US Presbyterian branch is the **Presbyterian Church (USA)**; find them online at www. pcusa.org. Area Presbyterian churches include:

- **Church of St. Andrew Presbyterian Church**, 5855 Riverside Dr, Atlanta, 404-252-5287, www.churchofstandrew.org
- **Druid Hills Presbyterian Church**, 1026 Ponce de Leon Ave NE, Atlanta, 404-875-7591, www.dhpc.org
- **Emory Presbyterian Church**, 1886 N Decatur Rd NE, Atlanta, 404-325-4551, www.emorypresbyterian.org
- **First Presbyterian Church of Marietta**, 189 Church St, Marietta, 770-427-0293, www.fpcmarietta.org
- **Korean Central Presbyterian Church**, 4011 Chamblee Dunwoody Rd, Chamblee, 770-458-1998
- **Mount Vernon Presbyterian Church**, 471 Mount Vernon Hwy NE, Atlanta, 404-255-2211, www.mvpchurch.org

## ROMAN CATHOLIC

In 2000, the Vatican reported that approximately 21% of the American population is Roman Catholic. That's about 60 million people in the USA. Here in Atlanta, there are over 100,000 Roman Catholic families, in over 100 parishes, in counties throughout the entire metro area. For more information about the Roman Catholic religion in Atlanta, or to search for local parishes, visit the Archdiocese of Atlanta online at www.archatl.com. For a complete listing of Catholic churches in your community, check the Atlanta Yellow Pages. A few to consider are:

- **Cathedral of Christ the King**, 2699 Peachtree Rd NE, Atlanta, 404-233-2145, www.cathedralofchristtheking.org
- **Immaculate Heart of Mary**, 2855 Briarcliff Rd NE, Atlanta, 404-636-1418, www.ihmatlanta.org
- **St. John Vianney Catholic Church**, 1920 Skyview Dr, Lithia Springs, 770-941-2807
- **St. Jude Catholic Church,** 7171 Glenridge Dr NE, Atlanta, 404-394-3896, www.stjudeatlanta.net
- **St. Paul of the Cross Roman Catholic Church**, 551 Harwell Rd NW, Atlanta, 404-699-1372 http://saintpaulofthecross.org
- **Shrine of Immaculate Conception**, 48 Martin Luther King Jr Dr, Atlanta, 404-521-1866, www.catholicshrineatlanta.org

## SEVENTH-DAY ADVENTIST

For information about the Seventh-Day Adventist church, check out www.adventist.org. For a comprehensive list of churches in metro Atlanta and around the world, visit Adventist Churches Online at www.adventist.org. A few local churches to consider are:

- **Alpharetta Seventh-Day Adventist Church**, 3315 Francis Rd, Alpharetta, www.alpharettasda.com
- **Cherokee Seventh-Day Adventist Church**, 101 Rope Mill Rd, Woodstock, 770-591-7304, www.tagnet.org/cherokee
- **Decatur Seventh-Day Adventist Church**, 2365 Candler Rd, Decatur, 404-284-6908, http://www.decatursdachurch.org
- **Marietta Adventist Church**, 1330 N Cobb Pkwy, Marietta, 770-427-7668, http://marietta.netadventist.org

## UNITY

For information about the Unity Church, or to find local congregations throughout metro Atlanta, visit the Association of Unity Churches' website, www.unity.org. You may also want to consider the following:

- **Atlanta Unity Church**, 3597 Parkway Ln, Norcross, 770-441-0585, www.atlantaunity.org
- **Unity North Atlanta Church**, 4255 Sandy Plains Rd, Marietta, 678-819-9101, www.unitynorth.org

## WESLEYAN

For more information about the Wesleyan Church, visit the Wesleyan Church online at www.wesleyan.org. A few local Wesleyan churches to consider are:

- **Decatur Wesleyan Church**, 3840 Kensington Rd, Decatur, 404-294-4402
- **Northside Wesleyan Church**, 2397 Beaver Ruin Rd, Norcross, 770-448-8861

## GAY AND LESBIAN FRIENDLY CONGREGATIONS

There are a number of gay-friendly churches and Synagogues in the metro Atlanta area. For full listings visit www.gaychurch.org, or Gays for God at www.godandgays.org.

- **Circle of Grace Community Church**, nondenominational Christian-feminist congregation; worships at various locations, including **Columbia Theological Seminary**; 1530 DeKalb Avenue, Ste A, Atlanta, 404-624-1140, www.circleof-graceatlanta.org
- **Congregation Bet Haverim (Jewish)**, 2676 Clairmont Rd NE, Atlanta, 770-642-3467, www.congregationbethaverim.org
- **Redefined Faith Worship Center**, African-American (black gospel) tradition, 743 Virginia Ave, Atlanta, 404-872-2133
- **Episcopal Church of the Epiphany**, 2089 Ponce de Leon Ave, Atlanta, 404-373-8338, www.epiphany.org
- **St. Mark United Methodist Church**, 781 Peachtree St, 404-873-2636, www.stmarkumc.org
- **Unity Fellowship Church of Atlanta**, 2001 Martin Luther King Dr, Atlanta, 404-752-5030, www.unityfellowshipchurchatl.org

## HINDU

Hinduism is as complex and multifaceted as the many gods it incorporates. Nearly 13% of the world's population is Hindu. Although most still live in India and other parts of Southeast Asia, there are now roughly one million Hindus in the United States, including a large population in metro Atlanta. To learn more, call the Atlanta Hindu Society, 770-248-9599, or contact the following Hindu temples:

- **BSS Hindu Temple**, 3518 Clarkston Industrial Blvd, Clarkston, 404-297-0501
- **Greater Atlanta Vedic Temple**, 770-381-3662, 492 Harmony Grove Rd SE, Lilburn, www.vedictemple.org
- **Hindu Temple of Atlanta**, 5851 Georgia Hwy 85, Riverdale, 770-907-7102, www.hindutempleofatlanta.org
- **Shiv Mandir of Atlanta**, Global Mall, 5675 Jimmy Carter Blvd, Ste 735, Norcross, 770-271-5398, www.shivmandiratlanta.org

# ISLAMIC

To learn more about the Islamic community in metro Atlanta, contact the Sahebozzaman Islamic Center of Atlanta at 770-642-9411, online at www.sicoa.org, or contact the Islamic centers and mosques below (for a complete listing, check the Atlanta Yellow Pages):

- **Al-Farooq Masjid of Atlanta**, 442 14th St NW, Atlanta, 404-874-7521, www.alfarooqmasjid.org
- **Atlanta Masjid of Al-Islam**, 560 Fayetteville Rd, Atlanta, 404-378-1600, www.atlantamasjid.com
- **Islamic Center of North Fulton**, 1255 Rucker Rd, Alpharetta, 678-297-0019
- **Masjid Omar bin Abdul Aziz**, 955 Harbins Rd NW, Norcross, 770-279-8606, www.masjidomar.org

# JEWISH

To learn more about the Jewish community in metro Atlanta, check out the **Atlanta Jewish Times**, 404-252-1600, http://atlantajewishtimes.com, a publication covering news and events for Atlanta's Jewish residents. Or visit the **Jewish Federation of Greater Atlanta** homepage, www.jewishatlanta.org. Below are a few local congregations to consider (for a complete listing of area Synagogues check the Atlanta Yellow Pages).

## CONSERVATIVE

- **Ahavath Achim Congregation**, 600 Peachtree Battle Ave NW, Atlanta, 404-355-5222, www.aasynagogue.org
- **Congregation Beth Shalom**, 5303 Winters Chapel Rd, Atlanta, 770-399-5300, www.bshalom.net
- **Congregation Etz Chaim**, 1190 Indian Hills Pkwy, Marietta, 770-973-0137, www.etzchaim.net

## ORTHODOX

- **Congregation Ariel**, 5237 Tilly Mill Rd, Atlanta, 770-390-9071, www.congariel.org
- **Congregation Beth Jacob**, 1855 LaVista Rd NE, Atlanta, 404-633-0551, www.bethjacobatlanta.org

## RECONSTRUCTIONIST

- **Congregation Bet Haverim**, 2676 Clairmont Rd, Atlanta, 404-315-6445, www. congregationbethaverim.org

## REFORM

- **Temple Beth David**, 1885 McGee Rd SW, Snellville, 770-978-3916, www.gwinnetttemple.com
- **Temple Beth Tikvah**, 9955 Coleman Rd, Roswell, 770-642-0434, www.bethtikva.com
- **Temple Kehillat Chaim**, 1145 Green St, Roswell, 770-641-8630, www.kehillatchaim.org
- **Temple Kol Emeth**, 1415 Old Canton Rd, Marietta, 770-973-3533, www.kolemeth.net
- **The Temple, Hebrew Benevolent Congregation**, 1589 Peachtree St NE, Atlanta, 404-873-1731, www.the-temple.org

## TRADITIONAL/CONSERVATIVE

- **Congregation B'nai Torah**, 700 Mt. Vernon Hwy, Atlanta, 404-257-0537, www. bnaitorah.org
- **Congregation Shaarei Shamayim**, 1810 Briarcliff Rd, Atlanta, 404-417-0472, www.shaareishamayim.com
- **Congregation Shearith Israel**, 1180 University Dr NE, Atlanta, 404-873-1743, www.shearithisrael.com

## NON–MOVEMENT AFFILIATED

- **Chabad Enrichment Center of Gwinnett**, 3855 Holcomb Bridge Rd, Norcross, 678-595-0196, www.chabadenrichment.org
- **Chabad of North Fulton**, 10180 Jones Bridge Rd, Alpharetta, 770-410-9000, www.chabadnf.org
- **Chabad of Cobb**, 4450 Lower Roswell Rd, Marietta, 770-565-4412, www. chabadofcobb.com

## NEW AGE/ALTERNATIVE SPIRITUALITY

Metro Atlanta is home to a variety of alternative religions and "new age" spirituality practices. Here you'll find everything from Wicca and Paganism to Kabbalah and meditation study. For more detailed listings of new age and spiritual happenings around town, be sure to check out the bulletin boards at local herb shops, health food stores, and metaphysical bookstores, or visit www.aquarius-atlanta.com.

## KABBALAH

If you're interested in finding out more about Kabbalah, be sure to visit www.kabbalah.com. For more information on Kabbalah study in Atlanta, contact the **Karin Kabalah Center of Atlanta**, 2531 Briarcliff Rd NE, Atlanta, 404-320-1038, www.karinkabalahcenter.com.

## MEDITATION CENTERS

The following meditation centers offer classes in meditation, guided meditation workshops, and more. In addition, the Siddha Yoga Meditation Center offers teachings in the lineage of their guru, Gurumayi Chidvilasananda, as well as weekly chanting and satsang. And Kashi Atlanta offers a weekly interfaith darshan (holy teaching) with Jaya Devi Bhagavati, chanting, and kirtan, and an annual weekend intensive with spiritual teacher and guru, Ma Jaya Sati Bhagavati.

- **Siddha Yoga Meditation Center of Atlanta**, 2531 Briarcliff Rd, Ste 100, Atlanta, www.symca.org
- **The InnerSpace–Atlantian Temple Meditation**, 6800 Roswell Rd Atlanta, 404-252-4540, www.theinnerspace.com
- **Kashi Atlanta Center for Yoga, Service and Community**, 1681 McLendon Ave, 404-687-3353, www.kashiatlanta.org
- **Shambhala Meditation Center of Atlanta**, 1447 Church St, Decatur, 404-370-9650, www.atlanta.shambhala.org

## PAGANISM/WICCA/WITCHCRAFT

If you'd like more information about Paganism, Wicca, or Witchcraft (and the various branches therein), go online to www.religioustolerance.org and www.beliefnet.com.

## SIKH

Founded just over 500 years ago, the Sikh faith now has a following of over 20 million people worldwide and is ranked as the world's fifth largest religion. Though only 220,000 Sikhs live in the United States, there is a large enough Sikh population here in metro Atlanta for three gurudwaras: **SEWA Gurudwara Sahib (Sikh Educational Welfare Association Inc.),** 10590 Woodstock Rd, Roswell, 678-819-2990, www.sewageorgia.org; **Gurudwara,** 1821 South Hairston Rd, Stone

Mountain, 404-808-6320; and the **Guru Nanak Mission Society of Atlanta Inc.**, 1158 Rockbridge Rd, Norcross, 770-931-3490. If you'd like to learn more about Sikhism, contact the gurudwaras directly, or visit www.sikhs.org.

## UNITARIAN UNIVERSALIST

The Unitarian Universalist Association (UUA) dates back to 1961, when the Universalism and Unitarianism movements officially merged. For more information about UUA, or to find a congregation near you, visit their website, www.uua.org. UUA churches in metro Atlanta include:

- **Emerson Unitarian Universalist Fellowship**, 2799 Holly Springs Rd, Marietta, 770-578-1533, www.emersonuu.org
- **First Existentialist Congregation of Atlanta**, 470 Candler Park Dr, Atlanta, 404-378-1327, www.firstexistentialist.org
- **Unitarian Universalist Congregation of Atlanta**, 1911 Cliff Valley Way NE, Atlanta, 404-634-5134, www.uuca.org
- **Unitarian Universalist Congregation of Gwinnett**, 12 Bethesda Church Rd, Lawrenceville, 770-717-7913, www.uucg.org
- **UU Metro Atlanta North Congregation**, 11420 Crabapple Rd, Roswell, 770-992-3949, www.uuman.org

LIKE MOST OF THE COUNTRY ATLANTA IS ON THE GREEN TRAIN, ADOPTING an increasing number of policies and ordinances that support sustainable living practices, while encouraging residents to make smarter decisions for the environment. More and more builders are building green residential and commercial developments because they say that's what the market expects. And the **Atlanta Regional Commission**, a non-profit group that acts as an advisor for much of metro Atlanta's growth, has added a Green Communities Certification program to offer communities the knowledge to improve their land use, recycling and waste reduction, green power, energy efficiency, water use, education, transportation, and air quality.

The moves are improving Atlanta's reputation nationwide. According to **SustainLane**'s 2008's ranking of 50 US cities, Atlanta came in 19th, leading the Southeast in the number of permits being sought for LEED-registered buildings. LEED, which stands for Leadership in Energy and Environmental Design, is a third-party certification program and benchmark for the design, construction, and operation of high-performance green buildings. In addition, in 2009 the federal government awarded Georgia $21 million to support green energy programs. The money is part of the US Department of Energy's Efficiency and Conservation Block Grant.

Atlanta protects its many trees with "no net loss" policy, and in 2013, the city was a finalist for a Green City Award from Waste & Recycling News. The award recognizes outstanding leadership and commitment to the introduction, education, and implementation of successful residential recycling programs.

Emory University has been recognized repeatedly for its environmentally related policies, practices, and academic offerings. For instance, the college made *Princeton Review*'s 2009 Green Rating Honor Roll.

One of Atlanta's biggest challenges is its vast urban sprawl. The city was rated one of the top five worst for land use by the Natural Resources Defense Council in 2011. Almost five hundred thousand Atlantans live in the city proper, while five million people are sprawled across the metro area. Most people commute, and single-passenger vehicles are the norm. To address the issue, city planners are working on numerous mass transportation initiatives, while educating, supporting and honoring developments that implement creative, progressive, mixed-use plans.

## GREENING YOUR HOME

The quickest and easiest way to have a green home is to buy one that is no bigger than you need—smaller homes consume fewer resources—and that is already well-insulated and energy-efficient, that incorporates nontoxic and sustainably produced materials, or that has features like solar-assisted hot water heating. There are numerous websites where you can search for green homes, plus most realtors these days and online search engines like Realtor.com offer a "green" category. Here are a few websites to check out:

- www.greenhomesforsale.com
- www.listedgreen.com
- www.livegreenproperties.com
- www.zillow.com
- www.trulia.com
- www.realtor.com
- www.frontdoor.com
- www.mls.com

### GREEN REMODELING

There are a number of contractors and businesses that offer green remodeling services in metro Atlanta. One place to start your hunt is the **Atlanta Regional Green Building Council** (www.usgbcga.org), an industry group that supports, advances, and promotes green building practices. Or for the do-it-yourself homeowner, there are a number of websites that offer tips, such as www.greenremodel.net, www.thisoldhouse.com, and www.hgtv.com.

In many cases, the greenest building materials are those that someone else has already used. Some businesses in Atlanta that sell recycled supplies are **Atlanta Salvage Outlet** (1034 Howell Mill Rd, 404-873-4416), **Home Resource Interchange** (750 Glenwood Ave, 404-624-4434), and **IMS Georgia Steel** (1635 Marietta Rd, 404-355-0486, www.imsgasteel.com/).

If it's new materials you require, **Bradco Supply** has two locations in Atlanta that carry a range of green building products (www.bradcosupply.com). And **American Building Surplus** (www.americanbuildingsurplus.com) lists regionally available green building products and services on its website. If you're doing structural work, consider using green-certified wood products, nontoxic or least-toxic glues and finishes, and low-VOC paint.

For more green building sources visit www.smithdalia.com, www.building-green.com, or www.greenhomebuilding.com.

## ENERGY EFFICIENCY

Reducing your home's energy consumption, particularly its consumption of energy produced by fossil fuels or other non-renewables, is probably the single most effective way to create a greener home. In most homes, furnaces and air conditioners, appliances, and lighting are the biggest energy hogs, and you'll get the most bang for your buck by weatherizing your home and making these systems work more efficiently. The following steps are typically recommended for boosting your home's energy efficiency:

- **Insulate and weatherize your home**. Poorly insulated walls, ceilings, and floors allow heated or cooled air to escape from your house, needlessly raising your energy use (and energy bill). Also, seal ductwork, insulate hot water pipes in non-conditioned spaces, and seal or caulk leaks around doors, windows, pipes, vents, attics, and crawlspaces. Replace or repair leaky old windows. These steps will also reduce drafts and increase comfort levels in your home.
- **Upgrade your heating and cooling systems**. Old furnaces and air conditioning units are usually much less efficient than new models. Once you've insulated and weatherized your home, consider replacing old units with new, efficient units, and make sure that they are properly sized for your home. A programmable thermostat can also help reduce energy consumption by adjusting the inside temperature automatically when you're at work or asleep.
- **Upgrade inefficient appliances**. Replacing old, inefficient washing machines, dishwashers, water heaters, and especially refrigerators with more efficient models can have a major effect on your energy consumption (and, in the case of washing machines and dishwashers, on your water consumption, too).
- **Install efficient lighting**. Compact fluorescent light bulbs use 75% less energy and last up to ten times longer than standard incandescent bulbs. They also generate less heat. For an assurance of quality, choose ENERGY STAR® bulbs.

Fortunately, you don't have to figure out how to accomplish all these things on your own. **The US Department of Energy** (http://apps1.eere.energy.gov/consumer/) has a website completely dedicated to helping citizens save on energy costs. They offer federal tax credits to help you pay for energy-saving improvements, and weatherization assistance for low income families. For a comprehensive whole-house energy assessment and energy recommendations, consider hiring a certified contractor to give your home an energy check-up. Georgia Power, Cobb

EMC, Southface Energy Institute, and Jackson EMC offer this service using nationally accepted ENERGY STAR analysis.

When you're ready to start investing in energy efficiency, low-cost loans and utility or manufacturer rebates are available for some projects. Also, both the state and federal government offer a number of tax credits and exemptions. For state credits, visit the Georgia Department of Revenue at www.etax.dor.ga.gov. For federal credits, visit **Energy Star's** website (www.energystar.gov) or talk to your accountant for details.

## RENEWABLE ENERGY

Consider buying green power from your local utility; look in the "Utilities" section of the **Getting Settled** chapter for details. If you are interested in going further in your support of renewables, not only can you make your home more energy-efficient, but you can make energy in your home. Atlanta gets plenty of sunny days year round, making **solar energy** a limitless resource. At **Atlanta Solar Technologies** (770-345-0638, www.atlantasolar.com)**,** you can buy everything from solar-powered radios and attic fans to complete power systems for your home or business. Also, check out **DirectSun Solar Energy and Technology** (770-864-0876, www.directsolarenergy.com). **Soenso Solar** (770-973-6298, www.soenso.com), provides a range of renewable energy sources including solar equipment and wind turbines. Significant federal and state tax credits and other incentives are available for those purchasing renewable energy systems; check **The Database of State Incentives for Renewable Energy** at www.dsireusa.org or the federal government's website, http://energy.gov/savings for specific information.

## WATER CONSERVATION

With Atlanta's current drought conditions, water conservation is not just a buzz word, it's a way of life. Experts have called the current drought "exceptional" and a 100-year drought that is directly affecting the state's drinking water supply. There are two lakes that supply drinking water to metro Atlanta—Lake Lanier and Lake Allatoona—and in recent years those lakes have dropped to record low levels. As a result, metro Atlanta has been under a year-round outdoor watering ban (although there are exceptions for certain businesses and homeowners watering by hand or watering produce).

Still, there are many ways you can conserve water indoors and outdoors. When using water indoors, try to wash only full loads of clothes or dishes, limit baths, and avoid leaving the water running. Also, consider updating your toilets if they are older than 1993. Older toilets use around 3.5 gallons per flush, while newer models use only 1.5 gallons. Some residents also keep a bucket in their shower to save the water they waste while the water is heating up. They can then use this to water new plants outside.

To conserve water outdoors, consider purchasing a rain barrel to gather rain water for your garden. Also, place plants only where they are best suited, and cover them with lots of mulch to preserve moisture. For more ideas on saving water, go to www.conservewatergeorgia.net.

## LANDSCAPING

When you are "greening" your home, don't forget to consider what you put on your yard.

Many pesticides and fertilizers can be harmful to pets and children, and should be avoided if possible. To avoid using these additives, try landscaping with native plants, which are adapted to the local climate and soils and practically take care of themselves. In addition, most native plants do not require constant watering and fertilization.

Also, consider starting a leaf compost in your back yard to make your own mulch. As mentioned previously, a top layer of mulch is like a warm blanket for your plants, allowing them to preserve moisture and survive drought.

To learn about Georgia's native plants, visit the **Georgia Native Plant Society** at www.gnps.org.

## ENVIRONMENTALLY FRIENDLY PRODUCTS AND SERVICES

Your pocketbook is one of your most powerful weapons in the environmental fight. Your decision to support environmentally friendly businesses not only helps those businesses but indirectly creates additional consumer demand for environmentally benign choices (a demand that could ultimately change the behavior of less environmentally focused businesses). Here are a few resources for finding green products and services.

- The Consumers Union guide to environmental labeling is online at **www.ecola-belindex.org**; the site includes a report card for various environmental claims and labels and assesses whether the claim is meaningful and/or verified.
- *Consumer Reports* maintains a website that assesses the environmental soundness of various products; visit **www.greenerchoices.org**.
- A few good directories of Atlanta's green businesses are **Green Atlanta**, www.atlantagreensource.com; **Living Green Pages,** www.livinggreenpages.com; and **The Green Chamber of the South**, www.greencs.org.

## FOOD

Most environmentally aware consumers know about the benefits of organic farming, but it is also important to buy locally produced food when possible.

Supporting local farmers keeps money circulating in the region and reduces the amount of greenhouse gases and other pollution associated with transporting the food from faraway fields. Most local co-ops and natural food stores, and some supermarkets, identify the geographic origin of their produce. Farmers' markets generally sell locally grown produce; check the **Shopping for the Home** chapter for more information. Or visit **www.pickyourown.org** to find a farmers' market in your area.

When buying food in the store, in addition to organic labels, look for certifications from **Salmon Safe** (www.salmonsafe.org), certifying that the source farm or vineyard uses watershed-friendly practices; the **Marine Stewardship Council** (www.msc.org), which certifies seafood as being from sustainable fisheries; and **Sustainable Farm Certification International** (www.sustainablefarmcert.com), which certifies farms and ranches for sustainable and humane practices. And to find an organic food store, visit **www.organicstorelocator.com**.

Finally, consider reducing the amount of meat in your diet. (Livestock production is an extremely resource-intensive activity.)

## GREEN MONEY

You can use environmental criteria to decide not only where to spend your money, but where to keep it. Some banks, including large national banks like Bank of America and Wells Fargo, are making efforts to become "greener" in their operations and lending practices. In 2012, Wells Fargo pledged $30 billion in new environmental investments, while Bank of America committed $50 billion to a ten-year plan to promote sustainability in all of its operations and lending practices. Examples of actions the banks plan to take are underwriting initial public offerings for "green" companies, making loans to consumers who buy hybrid vehicles, and helping developers to retrofit old factories and invest in renewable energy.

Green investing is also taking off, and many mutual funds now claim to invest only in environmentally and/or socially responsible companies. For more information about green investing, visit **Green Money Journal** (www.greenmoneyjournal.com) or **Green Investing** (www.sustainablebusiness.com).

## GREENER TRANSPORTATION

Probably the single best transportation choice you can make is choosing to live close to your place of work or in a place where you have a public transit option to get to work. The **Transportation** chapter lists alternatives to travel by automobile. However, when using a car is necessary or desirable, combine errands, carpool when possible, and ask your employer about telecommuting options. The **Drive Less/Save More** website (www.drivelesssavemore.com) offers more ideas for reducing the amount you drive, explains why driving less is good for your pocketbook, and offers a handy driving cost calculator to hammer the point home.

If you need or want to drive, consider driving a more fuel-efficient vehicle. You can even get (or convert to) a fully electric car, if you have the means. The most efficient mass production cars are gas-electric hybrids like the Toyota Prius or the Honda Civic hybrid. A hybrid car consumes less fuel, and you may be entitled to federal and state tax credits if you buy one. In Georgia, owners of hybrid or electric vehicles qualify for income tax exemptions and are allowed to use interstate HOV lanes when driving alone. Also, while there were few hybrid choices just ten years ago, there are multiple hybrid or electric vehicles on the market today.

Also, make sure that your car, whether hybrid or not, gets routine maintenance. A healthy engine will run more efficiently and emit less harmful fumes. And consider joining an auto club for roadside and travel assistance. **AAA Auto Club South,** www.aaasouth.com, is the largest in the Southeast.

## ALTERNATIVE FUELS

You can buy or modify cars to run on alternative fuels like pure ethanol or even natural gas, but by far the most popular alternative fuel is **biodiesel.** Biodiesel is essentially diesel fuel made from vegetable oil, and is usually sold blended with petroleum diesel fuel. The blend name designates the percentage of biodiesel: B100 is pure biodiesel, while B20 is 20% biodiesel and 80% petroleum diesel. To find current lists of stations that sell biodiesel or other alternative fuels in the metro Atlanta area, visit **www.biodiesel.org**. The **National Biodiesel Board** also has loads of information about biodiesel fuel on its website.

However, be aware that the use of biodiesel—particularly biodiesel blended with petro-diesel—is not without potential particulate pollution problems. If you already own a diesel-powered vehicle, biodiesel is a great choice that reduces dependence on oil. However, unless you plan to run your car on B100 exclusively, you might think twice about buying a car just so you can fuel it with biodiesel. (New passenger car models with cleaner-burning diesel engines may become available in the next few years, which could change the calculus.)

And although biodiesel is made from vegetable oil, it is *not* the same as straight vegetable oil (SVO) fuel (a.k.a. "French fry car fuel"); most diesel engines can run on pure biodiesel or biodiesel blends—at most, you'll have to replace a hose or two—but SVO fuel requires substantial modifications to your car (including, in most cases, a second fuel tank).

If your home has oil heat, note that B20 biodiesel also works in most oil-fired home furnaces.

## GREEN RESOURCES

The following are just a fraction of the resources on sustainability and environmental protection that are available in the region:

- **Beyond Pesticides,** www.beyondpesticides.org, works with allies to protect the public health and the environment from toxic pesticides. Provides useful information on alternative forms of pesticides in a quarterly news magazine, *Pesticides and You*, *Daily News* blog, and a bi-monthly bulletin, *School Pesticide Monitor.*
- **Clean Air Campaign,** 877-CLEAN-AIR, www.cleanaircampaign.org, a non-profit organization that works with local businesses and governments to improve air quality through smarter transportation plans. The group has partnered with more than 1,600 employers to design and implement commuter programs, protect public health through smog alerts, and offer incentives to commuters and employers, among other actions. Each day the campaign reduces traffic by more than 1.4 million vehicle miles, which keeps 700 tons of pollution out of the air.
- **Carbon Offsets,** almost everyone uses fossil fuels, whether indirectly or directly. Consider offsetting the resulting greenhouse gas emissions by purchasing or supporting **carbon offsets**. Carbon offsets fund projects that store carbon or reduce carbon emissions from other sources, such as tree planting projects, energy efficiency projects, and alternative energy investments. In theory, you can offset the carbon dioxide you generate by supporting these efforts. Offsets are available from sources like **Carbon Fund** at www.carbonfund.org, **Native Energy** at www.nativeenergy.com, and **Terra Pass** at www.Terrapass.com.
- **Earth Share of Georgia,** 404-873-3173, www.earthsharega.org, promotes environmental education, volunteerism, and charitable giving by partnering with businesses and communities across the state. The group supports 60 leading environmental groups in the state, as well as important activities like Earth Day.
- **Southface Energy Institute**, 404-872-3549, www.southface.org, is a non-profit corporation that provides environmental education and outreach programs to the community, including classes on residential energy codes, home energy rating systems, and EarthCraft House builder training.
- The US Department of Energy's **Energy Efficiency and Renewable Energy** website (www.eere.energy.gov) has some useful links and detailed (if not especially cutting-edge) information about renewable energy.

TODAY'S ATLANTA METROPOLITAN AREA ENCOMPASSES 28 COUNTIES and over 8,000 square miles, and even if you live right in the center of things, having access to a car will most likely be necessary at some point. In fact, travel to and from Atlanta's many outer suburbs requires a personal vehicle, as MARTA, the city's public transit system, covers only Fulton and DeKalb counties; public transportation options in the other counties are not comprehensive, if even available.

What follows are specifics about how to get around metro Atlanta by car and by public transportation, as well as tips for getting in and out of the city by Greyhound, Amtrak, and Southeast Stages, and contact information for Hartsfield-Jackson International Airport and the numerous airlines that fly in and out of there. Also covered here: what to expect from Atlanta traffic and tips for getting around on area roads and highways.

To get started, you may want to refer to the tips for finding your way around the city presented in this book's **Introduction.**

## GETTING AROUND BY CAR

Because metro Atlanta is so spread out, owning a car is pretty much a necessity. Depending on your point of view, or the day, cruising around the metro area can be an adventure or a headache. Unlike cities designed with easy-to-follow grid patterns, in Atlanta, streets that you believe to be parallel may eventually cross each other! Streets often change names with little or no warning; many roads that serve as major traffic routes are only two lanes wide; and, as you may have heard, there are over fifty streets with "Peachtree" somewhere in the name. Have patience. Major thoroughfares and highways serve as landmarks and can get you where you want to go. As in all major metropolitan areas, Atlanta drivers tend to be aggressive and may even be confrontational. Though road rage altercations are generally limited to horn honking and angry gestures, you should drive defensively and avoid drivers and situations that could be dangerous. Many savvy metro Atlanta drivers find elaborate short-cuts and use back roads to avoid dealing with boiling tempers on interstates and main thoroughfares. Use your map and experiment.

Here is an overview of some of the major highways and byways:

- **I-85** runs northeast through Gwinnett County toward Greenville, South Carolina, and southwest to the airport and Montgomery, Alabama. North of the downtown area it merges with I-75 to become the **Downtown Connector** (75-85). The Downtown Connector cuts directly through the downtown commercial sector, and I-75 and I-85 split again just south of the Lakewood Freeway.
- **I-75** extends north into Cobb and Cherokee Counties, heading toward Knoxville, Tennessee, and south to Henry County and eventually Florida.
- **I-20** runs east/west and joins Atlanta to Columbia, South Carolina and Birmingham, Alabama. It crosses the Downtown Connector just north of Turner Field. It is the road to take to both Zoo Atlanta and Six Flags Over Georgia.
- **I-285**, better known as "The Perimeter," circles around the city, crossing all the major highways at least once. The best known (and best avoided, if possible) interchange is "Spaghetti Junction," where I-285 crosses I-85 in a complex tangle of roadway.
- **Georgia 400** is an excellent commuter road that connects the Lenox Mall area and the financial district to the northern suburbs such as Roswell and Alpharetta. It meets I-85 near Lindbergh Drive and becomes a toll road just north of the Buckhead exit. If you travel GA 400 often, you may want to consider purchasing a GA 400 Cruise Card, which enables you to drive through the toll lanes without stopping. Contact the **State Road and Tollway Authority**, 404-365-7790, www.georgiatolls.com, for more information.
- **Peachtree Street** is the major thoroughfare cutting through Downtown, Midtown, and the heart of the Buckhead commercial district. It continues on to Lenox Mall and Phipps Plaza, eventually reaching I-285.
- **Piedmont Road** runs parallel to Peachtree between Downtown and Buckhead, although it crosses Peachtree in the northern section of Buckhead.
- **Ponce de Leon Avenue** travels east/west and links the downtown area to the city of Decatur and Stone Mountain.
- **Northside Drive** (which becomes **Cobb Parkway**) winds through Buckhead and Peachtree Battle, continuing on to Marietta.
- **Roswell Road** runs north and south from Buckhead through the cities of Sandy Springs and Roswell.

## TRAFFIC

At one time, Atlanta was called the "New York of the South," due, in part, to its bustling downtown and burgeoning arts scene. However, in the last two decades the city is more often compared to Los Angeles or Dallas for its urban sprawl, lack of comprehensive mass transportation, and horrendous traffic. Atlanta traffic problems are largely due to the incredible growth the city experienced since 2000. During this period, the metro area has added around 1 million new residents—up to 5.4 from 4.3 million. Those numbers are expected to continue to grow with 2020 estimates of 6.4 million, according to the Atlanta Regional Commission (ARC). Suburban sprawl has inched its way out to so many surrounding counties that metro Atlanta now encompasses more than 8,000 square miles of land. By some estimates, if growth continues at current rates, the North Georgia Mountains could actually become part of metro Atlanta in the next decade! This amazing growth in population, especially in suburban neighborhoods outside the I-285 perimeter, combined with the large number of corporations and offices located inside the perimeter, has made for the longest commute in the USA: an average of 36.5 miles roundtrip daily, according to the ARC. But even those who live and work intown are feeling the effects of commuting. With so many cars clogging the streets and interstates, commute time during peak hours now averages about an hour and half for a 30-mile drive, or 30 minutes for a mere 10-mile drive, even within the city limits!

In general, I-285 tends to be the most consistently congested during any given rush hour, with I-75 and I-85 southbound close behind. Georgia 400 is usually the least congested, except where it meets I-285 and I-85. None of this is set in stone though, since Atlanta's traffic problems are still evolving. Your best bet is to stay informed of the traffic situation whenever you plan to drive during heavy traffic times (generally 6 a.m. to 9 a.m. and 4 p.m. to 7 p.m., Monday–Friday). For up-to-the-minute traffic information to help you navigate metro Atlanta's streets and interstates, you may want to check out the websites offered by the **Georgia Department of Transportation**, www.511ga.com, **and WSB-TV's** *Triple Team Traffic* coverage at www.wsbtv.com/s/traffic. Also consider www.traffic.com/atlanta-traffic for real-time updates and road conditions, or search for phone apps that can alert you to traffic conditions. If you're not near a computer, you can call the Department of Transportation, 404-635-6800, for traffic information and road conditions. Radio stations **WSB-FM** (95.5FM) and **WYAY-FM** (106.7FM) offer traffic updates hourly and most of the other local radio stations offer traffic reports during morning and evening rush hours.

Commuting congestion leads to short tempers, high stress levels, and more aggressive driving tactics, and it's made Atlanta a much more dangerous place for pedestrians. According to the **Centers for Disease Control** (**CDC**) and the **Georgia Department of Human Resources**, over 50 pedestrians are killed here every year, making metro Atlanta the twelfth most dangerous city for pedestrians. One third of the fatalities typically occur on state or county roads that generally do not provide sidewalks for pedestrians. The other two thirds tend to occur intown, on some of Atlanta's busiest streets, including Buford Highway, Peachtree Street, Ponce de Leon Avenue, and Roswell Road. In almost all pedestrian fatality cases, the drivers are exceeding the posted speed limit. If you'd like more information on pedestrians in Atlanta, including helpful safety tips, or if you'd like to read the CDC's most current report, contact **Pedestrians Educating Drivers on Safety** (**PEDS**), 1447 Peachtree Street, Atlanta, 404-873-5667, www.peds.org.

## CARPOOLING

There are approximately 90 miles of High Occupancy Vehicle (HOV) lanes in the metro Atlanta area, running north and south along interstates 75 and 85, and east and west along I-20 from downtown to 285 east. All HOV lanes, which are available to vehicles carrying two or more occupants, and to all motorcycles and emergency vehicles, are strictly enforced. Single-passenger cars using the HOV lanes are ticketed. Many Atlantans take advantage of these lanes to decrease commute time to and from downtown by about 10 or 15 minutes, but finding someone to carpool with is not always easy. Your best bet is to check with co-workers to see if you can find anyone who lives close to you and would like to share a ride to work. If you don't have much luck there, you can contact the **Atlanta Regional Commission's Ride Find**, 1-877-433-3463, www.myridesmart.com. This organization may be able to put you in touch with others close to you who would like to share your commute. For more information on HOV lanes, including planned extensions, contact the **Department of Transportation**, 404-624-1300, www.dot.state.ga.us.

## EXPRESS LANES

In 2011, Atlanta added 16 miles of Express Lane along I-85. The lanes run north and south in Gwinnett from Old Peachtree Road to Chamblee Tucker Road. Commuters can pay to use the lanes, but they must have a Peach Pass Card and the cost to use the lane varies with traffic congestion. The maximum amount (charged at rush hours) is 90 cents a mile, so around $14 for a one-way 16-mile trip. Some vehicles can use the lane for free, such as those with three or more passengers, motorcyclists, transit vehicles, and emergency vehicles.

## CAR SHARING

Car sharing continues to draw interest in metro Atlanta. Car sharing companies provide cars in high-density urban areas across the country and charge their customers to use the cars by the hour or day. The concept works well with people who live in the city and find they only need or want a car, or second car, occasionally. In most cases, a customer must apply to be a member, and there are age and driver's history requirements. There is also a yearly membership fee—around $50.

Once drivers are set up, they can rent a car a day or month in advance, and choose from a range of vehicles based on their needs. They can also rent cars in other cities where the company operates.

Companies range from those that offer economy-style to high-end cars for customers looking more for a joyride than utility.

- **Zipcar**, 866-4-ZIPCAR, www.zipcar.com
- **Atlanta Driving Club**, 404-664-7125, www.atlantadrivingclub.com
- **Atlanta Joyrides,** 404-441-8669, www.atlantajoyrides.com

## CAR RENTAL

There are hundreds of car rental companies to choose from in metro Atlanta. For a complete listing, check the Atlanta Yellow Pages under "Automobile Renting." To help you get started, you may want to consider the following:

- **Alamo Rent-A-Car**, 800-462-5266, www.alamo.com
- **Avis Rent-A-Car**, 800-230-4898, www.avis.com
- **Budget Car and Truck Rental**, 800-527-0700, www.budget.com
- **Enterprise Rent-A-Car**, 800-261-7331, www.enterprise.com
- **Hertz Car Rental**, 800-654-3131, www.hertz.com
- **Thrifty Car Rental**, 800-847-4389, www.thrifty.com
- **Triangle Rent-A-Car**, 800-643-RENT, www.trianglerentacar.com

## TAXIS

While taxis are not as common in Atlanta as, say, New York, there are plenty to choose from. You can typically hail a cab in major parts of downtown and at the Atlanta Airport; for the rest of metro Atlanta you'll need to schedule a ride by phone or online.

There are a number of companies that serve the city—some consistent and clean, with amenities like handicap access—others dingy with less than stellar service. It's best to do your research online once you settle in. If you plan to use taxis regularly, familiarize yourself with what's available and check Yelp or Google for reviews. Also, to estimate your fare or learn about local taxis, visit www.taxifarefinder.com.

In the meantime, here are some of the largest and/or top rated taxi companies serving metro Atlanta:

- **Buckhead Safety Cab**, 404-875-3777, www.buckheadsafety.com; serving Buckhead, Lenox, and north Atlanta
- **Atlanta Checker Cab**, 404-351-1111, www.atlantacheckercab.com; serving metro Atlanta
- **Atlanta Royal Cabbies**, 404-584-6655, www.atlantaroyalcab.com; serving metro Atlanta

- **Norcross/Gwinnett Cab Company**, 770-458-1600; serving Norcross and other parts of Gwinnett County
- **Style Taxi**, 404-522-8294, www.styletaxi.com; serving north metro Atlanta

## BICYCLES

Despite increasing traffic (or perhaps because of it), many Atlantans make their commute via bicycle. Of course, this only works for those not traveling into the city from an outer suburb. Biking is becoming a popular alternative, although sometimes a dangerous one, for those who live and work in the same area. In Atlanta, bicycles are considered vehicles and, in the absence of a bicycle lane, must be ridden in traffic, often on busy, four-lane thoroughfares. The problem: most metro Atlanta roads do not offer bike lanes, and when bike lanes are added, they are generally on low-traffic streets like Fifth Street at West Peachtree, where many cyclists find they are not needed. However, there is a growing movement among bike enthusiasts and bike activists who are lobbying to make Atlanta streets safe for non-motorized vehicles. **Bicycle Georgia**, http://bicyclegeorgia. com, offers information on bicycle-related news stories, ride calendars, personals, discussion groups, bicycle advocacy organizations, and more. The **Atlanta Bicycle Campaign**, 404-881-1112, www.atlantabike.org, is an advocacy/social group committed to educating the public on bike safety. They even offer "Effective Cycling" classes to those who want to learn safe methods of riding in Atlanta traffic.

If you'd like to learn more about Georgia's bike laws, get the latest information on proposed bike lanes in Atlanta, or lodge a complaint with officials, contact the **Georgia Bicyclist and Pedestrian Coordinator**, 404-657-6692, www.dot. state.ga.us; the **Governor's Highway Safety Representative**, 404-656-6996, www.ghsa.org; or the **Atlanta Regional Commission**, 404-463-3100, www.atlantaregional.com.

Remember: even though metro Atlanta does not enforce a helmet law, it's always a good idea to protect yourself when you ride.

## PUBLIC TRANSPORTATION

### MARTA

The **Metropolitan Atlanta Rapid Transit Authority** (**MARTA**) is the public transportation system of Atlanta. It operates three train lines and the bus system. The MARTA north/south train line splits at the Lindbergh Center station to become the north/south and northeast/south lines. The north line continues to the Buckhead, Medical Center, and Dunwoody stations, the northeast line continues to the Lenox, Brookhaven, Chamblee, and Doraville stations. Regardless of where you choose to board the train, keep in mind the northeast/north/south rail line offers travelers a hassle-free ride to the airport.

For those who use MARTA regularly, it's a good idea to buy a Breeze card and forgo messing with tokens or cash fares. You can keep up to $300 on your Marta Breeze card, which can be purchased for $1 at any Marta RideStore. To learn more about Breeze cards, visit www.breezecard.com. MARTA operates five RideStores, which are located inside the Five Points, Sandy Springs, North Springs, and Airport stations, as well as its Lindbergh Headquarters building.

MARTA's rates have increased in the last decade, but it's still a much cheaper way to travel than driving a car. A one-way fare on the train and/or bus is $2.50, and seniors, disabled persons, or students pay half price. You can also purchase rides in bulk, 20 trips for $42.50, or by a pass, $23.75 for a week, $95 for a month.

MARTA offers a number of reduced fare programs. Seniors and the disabled can ride for half price, but they must use a Breeze card and purchase their card at a store in person. For a full list of special rates and offers from MARTA, such as student, group, or corporate discounts, visit www.itsmarta.com/fares-passes.aspx.

## TRAIN

MARTA's two train lines, the north/south (orange) line, which also contains the northeast/south line, and the east/west (blue) line, intersect at only one point: the Downtown Five Points station. For a single fare you can ride one line, transfer to the other line at Five Points, and transfer again to a bus for your final destination.

At the moment, the north/south line starts in North Springs, heads down to Buckhead, shoots through downtown, and ends up finally at the airport. The northeast/south line starts in Doraville, heads down to Brookhaven and Lenox Mall, and connects with the north/south line at Lindbergh, then travels the same route down to the airport. The east/west line extends from Hamilton E. Holmes (formerly Hightower) and proceeds through downtown and toward Decatur and beyond. A map of MARTA's train lines is available at www.itsmarta.com. Maps are clearly posted at all train stations and inside each train car.

Two stations serve residents living north of the perimeter: the Sandy Springs station and the North Springs station. The Sandy Springs station is located one mile northwest of the Dunwoody station at the intersection of Mt. Vernon Highway and Perimeter Center West. This station benefits residents of North Fulton County who wish to avoid a downtown (or Buckhead) commute. The North Springs station is located one mile north of Abernathy Road, east of Georgia 400, and west of Peachtree Dunwoody Road. This station, which serves people living along the northern Georgia 400 corridor, features a multi-level parking deck, and is accessible from both Georgia 400 and Peachtree Dunwoody Road.

Each MARTA rail station is 100% accessible to senior citizens and the disabled, with wide gates, escalators, and elevators. All of the trains offer special wheelchair spaces at the end of each rail car. MARTA also welcomes guide dogs on all of its trains and buses. No other pets are allowed.

Riding MARTA is a cheap and easy way to get around the city and is a great choice for downtown sporting events and trips to the airport. The rail system operates from 5 a.m. to 1 a.m., Monday–Friday, and from 6 a.m. to 12:20 a.m. on weekends and holidays. Trains are scheduled to run every 15 minutes on week-days, every 20 minutes on Saturdays, Sundays, and holidays.

## BUS

MARTA runs 91 bus routes throughout the city. Many bus routes connect the train stations to nearby neighborhoods or attractions. All buses accept cash, tokens, or Breeze cards. If you need a transfer card, ask the driver as you pay your fare. The driver can also assist riders who may have questions about identifying their stops.

Though some bus routes now offer 24-hour service, buses generally run from 5 a.m. to 1 a.m., Monday–Friday, and from 6 a.m. to 12:30 a.m. on weekends and holidays. To find out which routes run through your neighborhood, contact MAR-TA's Customer Information, 404-848-4711, or check www.itsmarta.com.

In a continuing effort to make mass transit accessible to everyone, MARTA now offers **ADA Complementary Paratransit Service**, buses equipped with wheelchair lifts. Residents can schedule a ride by calling 404-848-5000, and ser-vice runs through most of Fulton and DeKalb from 5 a.m. to 12:30 a.m., seven days a week and on holidays. However, they do not offer same-day service, so schedule your ride in advance. In addition, MARTA offers designated priority seating at the front of every regular bus for senior citizens and the disabled.

## EXPRESS SHUTTLES

During the summer, MARTA operates several express shuttles to help people reach local events and attractions without the hassle of traffic jams. These shuttles leave from designated stations and operate up to 90 minutes before the event. They will also bring passengers back to the station when the event ends. For instance, if you are heading out to a Braves game at **Turner Field**, you simply take a bus or drive to a convenient MARTA station, pay your fare, then take the train to the Five Points Station. Once you exit the train at Five Points, simply follow the signs leading to the shuttle, and there you are. There is no additional charge for the shuttle service as long as you are transferring from a MARTA bus or train. For those not using MARTA to get to the Five Points station, shuttle service is $2.50.

Besides the Braves shuttle, MARTA also operates a **Aaron's Amphitheatre Shuttle**, which departs from the Lakewood/Ft. McPherson station, and a **Six Flags Over Georgia Shuttle**, which departs from the Hamilton E. Holmes station.

For more information on MARTA's summer shuttle service, call 404-848-4711.

**MARTA PHONE NUMBERS AND WEBSITE**
- **Website**, www.itsmarta.com
- **Schedule Information**, 404-848-4711
- **General Information**, 404-848-5000
- **Customer Service**, 404-848-4800
- **Bus Services for Disabled**, 404-848-5389
- **TTY Service**, 404-848-5665

## XPRESS BUSES

Xpress, a public transportation service created by the state in 1999, is funded by the Georgia Regional Transportation Authority and 12 participating metro Atlanta counties. The service offers residents who live outside the perimeter (and largely outside of MARTA's reach) a straight shot into either Buckhead, Midtown, or downtown Atlanta. Since its first run, Xpress has been wildly popular with commuters, saving them both time sitting in their vehicles and money spent on gas or auto maintenance.

Xpress runs 33 routes in and out of Metro Atlanta Monday through Friday, from 5:30 a.m. to 8 p.m. Fares are $3 for one way, $5 for a round trip, or a 20-ride pass for $45, a 10-ride pass for $25, or a month's unlimited rides for $100. For more information on the Xpress commuter buses, call 404-463-4782 or go to www. xpressga.com.

## COBB COMMUNITY TRANSIT

Cobb County has its own bus system, which runs in and around Cobb County along 17 routes from 5 a.m. to midnight, Monday–Saturday (though not all buses run on Saturday). There is no bus service on Sunday. Fares are $2.50 for adults 18 and over, $1.50 for children under 18, free for children under 42 inches (with a paying adult), and $1 for senior citizens and the disabled. Along with its bus service throughout Cobb County, **Cobb Community Transit (CCT)** also offers limited express service to Atlanta, connecting with MARTA in Buckhead (Lenox Station), Midtown (Arts Center Station), and Downtown (Five Points Station), and with the state's Xpress bus service. Transfers to and from the trains and buses are free between the systems. For schedule information on either the CCT/MARTA connection or the Xpress connection, call 770-427-4444. Hearing-impaired customers can use the TDD line at 770-419-9183. Online, go to http://dot.cobbcountyga.gov/cct.

## GWINNETT COUNTY TRANSIT

Gwinnett County now has its own bus system, which runs local and express buses throughout Norcross and Lawrenceville, and to Gwinnett Place Mall and the Mall of Georgia, along 12 routes. Buses run from about 5 a.m. to midnight,

Monday–Saturday, except for express routes, which operate Monday–Friday. There is no bus service on Sunday. Fares are $2.50 for regular routes and $3.75 for express routes. Ten-ride ticket books can be purchased for $22.50 and $32.50. An express monthly pass costs $130. For complete schedule information and more, contact **Gwinnett County Transit** at 770-822-5010, or visit the county's website, www.gwinnettcounty.com.

## NATIONAL/REGIONAL TRAIN & BUS SERVICE

### AMTRAK

Atlanta's **Amtrak** passenger train station is located at 1688 Peachtree St NW. If you're looking to take a vacation, but prefer not to fly or drive, riding the rails may be for you. Amtrak offers competitive pricing and special saver fares for passengers throughout the year, traveling to many destinations in the USA. For the best rates, including internet-only discounts, check out www.amtrak.com. You can research Amtrak's train accommodations, plan your route, and even make your reservations online, sometimes at great savings. If you'd rather use the phone, you can get the same information (though not the same discounts) by calling 800-USA-RAIL (872-7245).

### GREYHOUND

You can find the **Greyhound Bus Terminal** in downtown Atlanta at 232 Forsyth Street SW. To make reservations or get schedule information, you have three choices: you can call the station directly at 404-584-1731, call Greyhound's National Reservation Line at 800-231-2222, or log onto Greyhound's website, www.greyhound.com.

### SOUTHEASTERN STAGES

**Southeastern Stages**, 260 University Avenue, SW, 404-591-2750, www.southeasternstages.com, offers nationwide connecting motorcoach service with daily schedules from Atlanta and Decatur to several cities throughout Georgia and the Southeast, including Athens, Augusta, Savannah, Charleston, and Columbia.

## AIR TRAVEL

### HARTSFIELD-JACKSON INTERNATIONAL AIRPORT

**Hartsfield-Jackson International Airport** is Atlanta's main airport. It also is the country's busiest airport, due largely to its housing of Delta Airlines, which is based in Atlanta. It was also ranked as one of the world's busiest airports in 2011. So, what do you need to know about Hartsfield? It's big—really big—and can be very confusing. And it's always under construction; and if you try to wait for someone in your car at the curb, you'll get a quick, no-nonsense warning, and maybe even a ticket, so it's better to circle the baggage claim exits over and over again. My best advice: know where you are going, but understand that you will be lost to some degree no matter what. Be patient and give yourself plenty of time to park and get to your terminal.

Hartsfield is located about ten miles south of the city, off of I-85, and unless it is rush hour, you shouldn't have much trouble with traffic. However, as smooth as the drive may be, parking can still be a hassle, especially during peak travel times (during the summer months and around holidays). If you're up to the challenge and choose to take a chance on finding a space, there are a few things to keep in mind. First, Hartsfield offers more than 30,000 public parking spaces, including approximately 14,500 deck spaces, 8,000 in Econo-lots, and 8,500 in Park & Ride lots, but all of these spaces can fill up fast. To stay on top of the parking situation at the airport, call the **Hartsfield-Jackson Parking InfoLine**, 404-530-6725. You'll hear a recorded message telling you which lots are full and which have spaces still available. This is a valuable service if you're on your way to the airport, but be sure to call as close to your departure time as possible, since the information changes throughout the day. You can also get updated parking information by tuning in to the airport's radio station, **WQO-AM 830**, or by going online to www.atlanta-airport.com.

Once you know that there are spaces available, you'll need to decide which lot you want to use. If you plan to park for just an hour or two, use the parking closest to the airport, where rates are $2 for 2 hours; $4 for 6 hours; $32 for 6 to 24 hours, or $36 for each additional day. For long-term parking, Hartsfield offers Econo-lots or covered parking decks on site. Or consider using one of the many Park & Ride lots located around the outer perimeter of the airport; the shuttles run on a tight schedule, so the wait is rarely long. In fact, it usually takes less time to use the shuttle at these lots than to drive in and out of parking decks looking for a closer space. Rates for Park & Ride lots start at $3 per hour, or a maximum $9 per day.

By far the easiest way to get to Hartsfield-Jackson is to use MARTA and avoid parking nightmares altogether. Most MARTA stations offer long-term parking for riders, and it only costs $2.50—the price of your fare. If this sounds like the choice for you, simply catch one of MARTA's southbound trains (on the north/south or northeast/south lines) and take it all the way to the end. MARTA will actually drop you off inside the airport. For more information on parking at the airport, including various rates and parking options, call the airport's customer service line at 877-ATL-PARK. For more information on taking MARTA to the airport, call 404-848-5000 or visit www.itsmarta.com.

Finally, if you just don't want to drive and you're carrying too many bags to take the train, you may want to consider taking an airport shuttle or hiring a car or limousine. The following services offer transportation to and from the airport (for a more complete listing, check www.atlanta-airport.com, under "Ground Transportation"):

- **AAA Airport Express**, 404-767-2000, www.aaaairportexpress.com
- **A & M Limo Corporation,** 770-955-4565, www.aandmlimo.com
- **Airport Metro**, 404-766-6666, http://airportmetro.com
- **Atlanta Starship Limousines**, 800-723-2145, www.atlantastarshiplimousines.com

Hartsfield-Jackson is home to both **Delta Airlines** and **AirTran**, is a focus center for Southeast Airlines, and houses almost every other major airline as well. Following is a list of airlines that fly into Hartsfield-Jackson. When making reservations or checking flight schedules, call the airlines or visit their website. For general airport information and flight delays, call Hartsfield-Jackson at 404-530-7300 or search online at www.atlanta-airport.com.

- **Aeromexico**, 800-237-6639, www.amconnect.com
- **Air Canada**, 888-247-2262, www.aircanada.ca
- **Air France**, 800-237-2747, www.airfrance.com
- **Air Jamaica**, 800-523-5585, www.airjamaica.com
- **AirTran Airways**, 800-247-8726, www.airtran.com
- **American Airlines**, 800-433-7300, www.aa.com
- **British Airways**, 800-247-9297, www.britishairways.com
- **Delta Air Lines**, 800-325-1999, www.delta.com
- **Frontier Airlines**, 800-432-1359, www.flyfrontier.com
- **Korean Air**, 800-438-5000, www.koreanair.com
- **Lufthansa**, 800-645-3880, www.lufthansa-usa.com
- **Southwest Airlines**, 800-I-FLY-SWA, www.southwest.com
- **Spirit Air**, 800-722-7117, www.spiritair.com
- **United Airlines**, 800-241-6522, www.ual.com
- **US Airways**, 800-428-4322, www.usairways.com

## DEKALB PEACHTREE AIRPORT

**DeKalb Peachtree Airport**, 2000 Airport Road, Chamblee, 770-936-5440, http://pdkairport.com, is the second busiest airport in Georgia (behind Hartsfield-Jackson) in the number of take-offs and landings each year: an average of approximately 202,000 per year over the last 30 years. What started as the site of Camp Gordon, a World War I Army training base, is now a 765-acre home to 447 aircraft (including 50 corporate jets), 4 runways, 25 large hangars, and 90 T-hangars. There is no regularly scheduled passenger or cargo service at DeKalb Peachtree; instead, the airport is used for corporate aircraft, charter service, pilot training, and recreational flights. Several large aviation service companies (**Epps**

**Air Service**, 770-458-9851, www.eppsaviation.com; **Mercury Air Group**, 770-454-5000, www.mercuryairgroup.com; and **Signature Flight Support**, 770-452-0010, www.signatureflight.com) operate out of DeKalb Peachtree, offering arrival/departure terminals, fuel sales, charter flights, hangar rentals, maintenance, and more. **Biplane Rides Over Atlanta**, 770-393-3937, http://biplaneridesoveratlanta.com, offers rides, sightseeing tours, and aerobatic flights. **American Air Flight Training**, 770-455-4203, www.fly-aaft.com; **Atlanta Aviation**, 678-904-1110, www.atlantaaviation.com; **Atlanta Flight School**, 770-457-1270, www.lanier-flightcenter.com; and **Quality Aviation**, 770-457-6215, www.qualityaviation.net, provide flight lessons by certified, experienced instructors, from the airport daily. DeKalb Peachtree Airport has also built a small picnic/visitor area complete with big wooden swings, picnic tables, and view stands for people who may not want to fly but want to watch people who do. It doesn't cost anything to sit and watch the planes take off, so if you like airplanes, it's a great place to spend an afternoon.

## FLIGHT DELAYS

Information about flight delays can be checked online on your airline's website, or at www.fly.faa.gov. Similarly, the site www.flightarrivals.com offers real-time arrival, departure, and delay details for commercial flights.

## CONSUMER COMPLAINTS—AIRLINES

To register a complaint against an airline, call or write the Department of Transportation: 202-366-2220, Aviation Consumer Protection Division, C-75 Room 4107, 400 7th Street SW, Washington, DC 20590.

I F YOU NEED TEMPORARY QUARTERS WHILE SEARCHING FOR YOUR HOUSE or apartment, metro Atlanta offers a variety of options, from inexpensive to those fit for royalty. There are even a growing number of special needs accommodations available at hotels throughout the city. In fact, all of the major hotels and motels listed below now offer rooms and services for the physically disabled, though services vary from location to location; if this is an issue, be very clear about specific needs when making a reservation. Whether a hotel, hostel, bed and breakfast, or short-term rental suits you, this section should give you a good start. Keep in mind that the prices listed below are per night and pre-tax. The current lodging tax in Atlanta is 13%, on top of a local sales tax of 4% to 7%, depending on the county.

## ROOM RESERVATION SERVICES

There are hundreds of hotels and motels throughout metro Atlanta, offering everything from the bare bones room-with-a-bed to opulent hotel suites with fresh-cut flowers, a separate bedroom suite, and thick, white robes. With so many options to choose from, it's often difficult to know where to start. Fortunately there are several reservation services and online travel agents that can help you find the hotel or motel that is right for you. Here are just a few to get you started:

- **Expedia**, 800-397-3342, www.expedia.com
- **Hotel Reservations Network**, 800-715-7666, www.hotel-discount.com
- **Hotels.com**, 800-246-8357, www.hotels.com
- **Orbitz**, 888-656-4546, www.orbitz.com
- **Priceline**, www.priceline.com
- **Quikbook**, 800-789-9887, www.quikbook.com

When making reservations through any discount site, it's important to ask about their cancellation policy and whether or not the rates they quote include hotel tax or any other charges. Most reservation services require a credit card for booking. A few may even require payment in full when making the reservation, though usually, payment for the room will be made directly to the hotel when you check out.

## INEXPENSIVE LODGINGS

If budget is more important than luxury, the following listings may be of interest. Most are chain hotels, with locations here and there throughout the city. All of them offer standard accommodations—bed, bath, towels, TV. Some may also offer additional amenities, so it might be a good idea to check around before making a decision on where to stay. Prices generally range between $100 and $150 per night, though you will want to confirm the rate with the hotel when making your reservation:

- **Best Western**, 800-780-7234, www.bestwestern.com; more than 40 locations in the metro Atlanta area
- **Cheshire Motor Inn**, 1865 Cheshire Bridge Rd, NE, 404-872-9628, http://cheshiremotorinn.scorpiohotels.com
- **Days Inn Hotels**, 800-329-7466, www.daysinn.com; more than 30 locations throughout metro Atlanta
- **The Highland Inn**, 644 N Highland Ave NE, Atlanta, 404-874-5756, www.the-highlandinn.com; located in the heart of Virginia Highland
- **Holiday Inn Hotels & Resorts**, 800-465-4329, www.ihg.com/holidayinn; more than 40 locations throughout metro Atlanta
- **Red Roof Inn**, 800-733-7663, www.redroof.com; locations throughout metro Atlanta
- **Sierra Suites**, 888-695-7608, http://hotelsierraalpharetta.com/alpharetta; a location in Alpharetta
- **Suburban Extended Stay Hotel**, 800-265-0363, www.suburbanhotels.com; several locations in metro Atlanta
- **Travelodge**, 800-578-7878, www.travelodge.com; locations throughout metro Atlanta
- **Wyndham Hotels and Resorts,** 800-999-3223, www.wyndham.com; several locations around metro Atlanta

## MEDIUM-PRICED LODGINGS

The following hotels range in price between $150 and $250 per night. Here you can expect rooms that are a little larger than what you'd find in the inexpensive hotels. You may also find additional amenities such as room service, internet access, and in-room mini-bars. Most are national chains, with several convenient locations throughout the metro Atlanta area:

- **Embassy Suites by Hilton**, 800-EMBASSY, http://embassysuites3.hilton.com/en/index.html; several locations in metro Atlanta
- **Homewood Suites by Hilton**, 800-445-8667, http://homewoodsuites3.hilton.com/en/index.html; 7 locations in metro Atlanta
- **The Omni Hotel at CNN Center**, 404-659-0000, 800-843-6664, www.omnihotels.com; located inside the CNN Center in downtown Atlanta
- **Radisson Hotels**, 800-333-3333, www.radisson.com; locations throughout metro Atlanta
- **W Hotels of Atlanta**, 770-396-6800, http://whotelsofatlanta.com; the W is a chic, modern hotel, and is actually on the cusp between mid-priced lodging and luxury. The W has three locations in Atlanta, in Downtown, Midtown, and Buckhead

## LUXURY LODGINGS

The following luxury hotels offer a wide variety of services and comforts for their guests. Rates begin at about $250 per night and go up from there, based on season and availability.

- **The Four Seasons Hotels and Resorts**, 75 14th St, Atlanta, 800-819-5053, www.fourseasons.com; first-class accommodations contained within a stunning neo-classical tower of rose and marble granite, overlooking both midtown and downtown Atlanta; the Four Seasons is arguably Atlanta's most upscale hotel.
- **Grand Hyatt Atlanta**, 3300 Peachtree Rd NE, Atlanta, 404-365-8100, 800-633-7313, www.grandatlanta.hyatt.com; first-class accommodations located in Buckhead, at the intersection of Peachtree Road and Piedmont Road, convenient to Lenox Mall and Phipps Plaza, as well as Buckhead's popular bar and nightclub scene.
- **InterContinental Buckhead**, 3315 Peachtree Rd, Atlanta, 404-946-9000, www.intercontinentalatlanta.com; a luxury hotel that combines international flair with southern elegance, the Intercontinental is located in the heart of Buckhead, and is home to chic restaurant Southern Art, and nightspot, the Bourbon Bar.
- **The Ritz Carlton Hotels of Atlanta**, 181 Peachtree St NE, Atlanta, 404-659-0400; 3434 Peachtree Rd, Buckhead, 404-237-2700; 800-241-3333, www.ritzcarlton.com; both the Downtown and Buckhead locations offer the first-class accommodations you'd expect from the Ritz.
- **Westin Hotels**, 7 Concourse Pkwy, 770-395-3900; 3391 Peachtree Rd NE, 404-365-0065; 210 Peachtree St NW, Atlanta, 404-659-1400; 4736 Best Rd, Atlanta, 404) 762-7676; 888-625-5144, www.starwoodhotels.com; offers first-class accommodations at four locations in metro Atlanta.

## BED & BREAKFASTS

To reserve a space in one of metro Atlanta's many bed and breakfast establishments, you may want to consider using a reservation service. Two to look into are **Bed and Breakfast Atlanta**, 404-875-0525, www.bedandbreakfastatlanta.com; and **Bed and Breakfast Inns Online,** www.bbonline.com. However, if you'd rather make your reservations directly with the bed and breakfast facility, you may want to try the following. Rates typically range between $100 and $300 per night:

- **King-Keith House Bed and Breakfast**, 889 Edgewood Ave, Atlanta, 404-688-7330, 800-728-3879, www.kingkeith.com; this 1890 Queen Anne–style home located in historic Inman Park boasts 12-foot ceilings and beautifully carved fireplaces.
- **Stonehurst Place**, 923 Piedmont Ave N, Atlanta, 404-881-0722, www.stonehurstplace.com; located in Midtown, a one-of-a-kind EarthCraft House, built in 1896 and on the National Register of Historic Places. Stonehurst was refurbished in 2008 with a strong focus on green living; it has two guest rooms and three suites, as well as lovely gardens and porches.
- **Sugar Magnolia Bed and Breakfast**, 804 Edgewood Ave NE, Atlanta, 404-222-0226; another charming 1892 Queen Anne Victorian home in historic Inman Park.
- **Virginia Highland Bed and Breakfast**, 630 Orme Cir NE, Atlanta, 404-892-2735, www.virginiahighlandbb.com; a friendly and comfortable bed and breakfast located within walking distance of Piedmont Park, the Atlanta Botanical Gardens, and countless restaurants and eclectic shops. Also, in 2006 the B&B's garden was designated an Audubon Wildlife Sanctuary, and its classic labyrinth was included in the World-Wide Labyrinth Project.
- **Whitlock Inn Bed and Breakfast,** 57 Whitlock Ave, SE, Marietta, 770-428-1495, www.whitlockinn.com; this Victorian bed and breakfast is in a national historic district. It's located one block from the Marietta Square and was called "the most beautiful bed and breakfast in Georgia," by *Country Inn Magazine*. Also hosts weddings and other events in a ballroom that seats 100 people.

## HOSTELS/YMCA

Atlanta's hostel market is pretty much non-existent. Below is one that is reputable and has been around for some time. For more options, check out www.hostelworld.com or www.hostelbookers.com for locations, pricing, and reviews. Also read the reviews to get a heads-up on hostels that overcharge or have other complaints. Rates range from $15 to $75 a night, based on location and accommodations.

- **Atlanta International Hostel**, 223 Ponce de Leon Ave, 404-875-9449, 800-473-9449, www.atlantahostel.com; prices start at $26.95 per night.

## SHORT-TERM LEASES

A short-term lease or corporate apartment may be a good bet if you plan on using temporary lodging for more than just a few weeks. Accommodations typically range from furnished studios to one- or two-bedroom apartments. And prices can range from $300 a week to $3,000 per month, depending on the establishment. A few to consider are:

- **Apartment Selector**, 770-552-9255, 866-494-3329, www.aptselector.com/atlanta; free service that can assist you in finding a corporate or short-term apartment that meets your needs.
- **Extended Stay America**, 800-804-3724, www.extendedstayamerica.com; locations throughout metro Atlanta, offering fully furnished studios with full kitchens, cable TV, and free voicemail service.
- **Post Corporate Apartments**, 770-434-6494, 800-643-POST, www.postproperties.com; tastefully furnished and fully equipped apartment homes include housewares, linens, washer and dryer, all utilities, and weekly housekeeping. Post has several locations throughout metro Atlanta, so call for more information.
- **Residence Inn by Marriott**, 800-331-3131, www.marriott.com/residenceinn; locations throughout metro Atlanta, offering suites that include a full-size kitchen, TV, linens, dishes and utensils, and daily maid service.
- **Studio Plus Deluxe Studios**, 800-804-3724, www.studioplus.com; 3 locations in metro Atlanta, offering deluxe studios that include a TV, kitchen, sofa sleeper, separate bedroom, fitness center, and weekly housekeeping.
- **Windsor Communities**, 800-888-RENT, www.windsorcommunities.com; 2 locations in metro Atlanta, offering tastefully furnished and fully equipped apartment homes ranging in size from studios to three-bedroom townhomes.

G EORGIA IS A BEAUTIFUL STATE THAT OFFERS RESIDENTS AND VISITORS a variety of landscapes. From the golden beaches of Georgia's coast to the beautiful mountains in the north, there are enough quick getaway destinations here to please any weekend wanderer.

Most of the following locales can be reached by car, though if you're planning to spend time on the islands dotting the coastline, you'll have about a six-hour drive and may have to ferry across once you reach the water. These island spots are generally not day trips from metro Atlanta, but are perfect for overnight, weekend, or even weeklong stays. Trips to the North Georgia Mountains can be done in a day, but with such magnificent views, many opt to stay longer.

## GEORGIA'S COAST

- **Cumberland Island**, off the coast of Georgia near St. Mary's, is 17 miles long and 1.5 to 3 miles wide. It is accessible by a ferry, which operates year-round from St. Mary's. There is a small ferry fee and reservations are required. Cumberland Island is a great place to visit if you are interested in walking tours and want to escape the typical tourist destinations. There are no restaurants or shops here, but you will find plenty of salt and freshwater marshes, white sand beaches, and live oak forests. Swimming and camping are available daily, though camp spaces must be reserved in advance. Most of the structures on the island date back to the pre–Civil War plantation era, though there are a few turn-of-the-20th-century buildings that were erected by the Thomas Carnegie family. For more information on visiting Cumberland Island or to make reservations, contact the **Superintendent** at P.O. Box 806, St. Mary's, GA 31558, 912-882-4335, 888-817-3421, www.cumberlandisland.com.
- **Jekyll Island**, off the coast of Georgia near Brunswick, is the smallest of Georgia's coastal islands, with 5,600 acres of highlands and 10,000 acres of

marshlands. In 1886, a group of wealthy businessmen bought the island and formed the Jekyll Island Club. Members of the club, including J.P. Morgan and William Rockefeller, vacationed here each winter in fabulous cottages, some of which are still standing. In 1947, the club was abandoned for economic reasons and the island was sold to the state. Today the Jekyll Island Authority maintains the island as a year-round resort, offering visitors a number of hotels, restaurants, and activities, including golf, water skiing, swimming, shopping, tennis, bicycling, and fishing. For more information on Jekyll Island, including lodging, dining, and entertainment options, contact the **Jekyll Island Convention & Visitors Bureau**, One Beachview Dr, Jekyll Island, GA 31527, 877-4-JEKYLL, www.jekyllisland.com.

- **St. Simons Island**, off the coast of Georgia near Brunswick, is another of Georgia's famous coastal islands. Originally home to several plantations in the pre–Civil War era, St. Simons flourished until Union troops, led by General Sherman, razed the estates, leaving only the slave quarters standing. Today, St. Simons Island is home to numerous museums, art galleries, family attractions, hotels, shops, and restaurants, as well as the fully inclusive **Sea Palms Golf and Tennis Resort**, 800-841-6268, www.seapalms.com. Besides golf and tennis, the resort offers three swimming pools, a private beach, a fitness center, a playground, outdoor buffets, and more. Rates vary depending on room size and the time of year. For more information on St. Simons Island, including a complete listing of hotels, restaurants, and entertainment options, contact the **St. Simons Visitors' Center**, 912-638-9014, 800-933-2627; or visit **St. Simons Online**, www.explorestsimonsisland.com.

- **Savannah**, located on the northern edge of Georgia's coast approximately 250 miles from Atlanta, has an abundance of history and architecture that few American cities can match. Having preserved its colonial grace and charm through the restoration of more than 1,400 historically significant buildings, Savannah has become one of the largest urban historic landmark districts in the USA, and also one of the state's most popular tourist destinations. In fact, an estimated 6.5 million visitors travel to this city each year. Savannah also hosts a number of parades year round, and the most popular is its St. Patrick's Day Parade. Each year an estimated 400,000 tourists descend on Savannah to attend the March 17th parade, which is the second largest of its kind in the country after Chicago. And as for dining and lodging, Savannah boasts numerous fine restaurants and cafés, and over 8,000 rooms in properties ranging from luxury hotels to small bed and breakfasts. Several airlines fly directly into Savannah International Airport, including AirTran, Comair, Continental Express, Delta Airlines, United, and US Airways. For more information on Savannah, contact the **Savannah Area Convention and Visitors' Bureau**, 101 East Bay St, Savannah, GA 31401, 877-SAVANNAH, http://savannah-visit.com.

- **Tybee Island**, located off the coast of Savannah, is one of the most popular of Georgia's coastal islands, due to its many beachside attractions, including a boardwalk, fishing pier, amusements, hotels, and vacation cottages. Tybee Island's beach runs the entire length of the island—with nearly four miles of Atlantic Ocean on one side and two miles of the Savannah River on the other. The northern tip of Tybee boasts the **Fort Pulaski National Monument**, 912-786-5787, www.nps.gov/fopu, and the **Tybee Museum and Lighthouse**, 912-786-5801, www.tybeeisland.com. The island can be reached by a causeway from Savannah and US 80. For more information, contact the **Savannah Area Convention and Visitors' Bureau**, 101 East Bay St, Savannah, GA 31401, www.savannah-visit.com.

## GEORGIA'S HEARTLAND

- **Athens**, approximately 65 miles northeast of Atlanta on the Atlanta Highway/GA-8, is home to the **University of Georgia**, 706-542-3000, www.uga.edu; the **Georgia Museum of Art**, 706-542-4662, www.uga.edu/gamuseum; and the **State Botanical Garden**, 706-542-1244, www.uga.edu/botgarden. Many Atlanta residents head over to Athens on weekends to see great college sports (UGA's football team, the Bulldogs, are a big draw) or to hear some of the up-and-coming local rock bands that frequent the clubs surrounding the university. Consider attending Athens' Ath Fest held every June for a taste of its local music and art scene, http://athfest.com. If you'd like more information on Athens, including where to stay or what to do while you're in town, contact the **Athens Convention and Visitors' Bureau**, 300 North Thomas St, Athens, GA 30601, 800-653-0603, www.visitathensga.com.
- **Macon**, about three hours south of Atlanta, is the largest city in Georgia's historic heartland. It is home to several popular tourist attractions including the **Ocmulgee National Monument**, 478-752-8257, www.nps.gov/ocmu, which traces the area's Native American heritage back 12,000 years, and the **Tubman African-American Museum**, 478-743-8544, www.tubmanmuseum.com, a showcase of African-American art, history, and culture. Macon also boasts the **Georgia Sports Hall of Fame**, 478-752-1585, www.gshf.org. For more information on Macon, including lodging, dining, and entertainment options, contact the **Macon Convention/Visitors' Bureau and Welcome Center**, P.O. Box 6354, Macon, GA 31208-6354, 478-743-3401, 800-768-3401, www.maconga.org.

## GEORGIA'S MOUNTAINS & STATE PARKS

- **Amicalola Falls**, located approximately 66 miles northwest of North Fulton County, offers visitors the chance to see the highest waterfalls (729 feet) in the state. Amicalola is also home to 17 tent and trailer sites, a 57-room lodge with restaurant, rental cottages, playgrounds, picnic shelters, and more set on 1,020 acres of lushly wooded land. Amicalola is a great place to visit if you want to

fish, camp, hike, or just relax. Call 706-265-4703, 800-864-7275 or visit www.
gastateparks.org/info/amicalola for additional information.

- **Black Rock Mountain State Park**, located astride the eastern Continental
  Divide in north Georgia, near the North Carolina border, is the highest state
  park in Georgia. Named for its sheer cliffs of dark-colored rock, Black Rock
  Mountain encompasses some of the most amazing scenery in all of Georgia's
  Blue Ridge Mountains—including a spectacular 80-mile view of the Southern
  Appalachians. The 1,502-acre park area is home to 52 tent and trailer sites, 10
  rental cottages, 11 walk-in campsites, 2 picnic shelters, a visitor's center, and a
  17-acre lake. Hiking, fishing, and primitive camping are available for visitors. For
  more information, call 706-746-2141, 800-864-7275, or visit www.gastateparks.
  org/info/blackrock.

- **Cloudland Canyon State Park**, located on the western edge of Lookout Mountain in northwest Georgia, near the Alabama border, attracts visitors with its
  3,485 acres of rugged geology and beautiful scenery. The park straddles a deep
  gorge cut into the mountain by Sitton Gulch Creek, and visitors are invited to
  hike its 4.5-mile waterfalls trail or 6.5-mile backcountry trail. If hiking isn't your
  thing, the park also offers 75 tent and trailer sites, a 40-bed group camp, rental
  cottages, picnic shelters, tennis courts, and swimming pools. Call 706-657-
  4050, 800-864-7275, or visit www.gastateparks.org/info/cloudland for more
  information.

- The **City of Dahlonega**, located approximately 63 miles northwest of Atlanta,
  was the site of the first major gold rush in the USA in 1828—20 years before gold
  fever hit California. Today Dahlonega offers ways to experience glimpses of the
  past with a visit to the **Gold Museum**, 706-864-2257, www.gastateparks.org/
  info/dahlonega, for gold panning and underground tours of the area's three
  major mines; many opt to visit during the annual Gold Rush Days celebration,
  the third weekend in October. Thousands of residents and visitors congregate
  on the town square to view over 300 arts and crafts exhibits, run a 5K race,
  listen to bluegrass music, and eat. A hog calling contest, king and queen cor-
  onation, and a number of children's activities add to the festivities. Dahlonega
  also plays host to several other non-gold-related festivals throughout the year,
  including the Bear on the Square Festival, held the third weekend in April,
  commemorating the bear that came to the square in the spring of 1996, www.
  bearonthesquare.com; the Fourth of July Family Day celebration, named one
  of the "Top Twenty Events in the Southeast" by the Southeast Tourism Society;
  and the Mountain Flower Festival of Arts, held the third weekend in May, showcasing the work of hundreds of local artists. For more information, contact the
  **Dahlonega-Lumpkin County Chamber of Commerce**, 706-864-3711, 800-
  231-5543, www.dahlonega.org.

- **Fort Mountain State Park**, located 8 miles east of Chatsworth, Georgia, along
  Highway 52, near the Tennessee border, derives its name from the 855-foot-
  long wall of rock that stands along the mountain's highest point. The theory is

that early Native Americans built the wall as protection against hostile invaders or for ancient ceremonies. Today the 3,428-acre park offers a variety of outdoor activities including 14 miles of hiking trails, a lake with a swimming beach, boat rentals and fishing, 74 tent and trailer sites, cottage rentals, and picnic sites. For more information, call 706-695-2621, 800-864-7275, or visit www.gastateparks.org/info/fortmt.

- **Hart State Park**, located in northeast Georgia at the South Carolina border, offers visitors several water-related outdoor activities, including boating, water skiing, bass fishing, and swimming on Lake Hartwell. Largemouth bass, black crappie, rainbow trout, and walleyed pike can be found in the park's 5,590-acre reservoir. Boat ramps and docks offer easy access, and a small man-made beach is designated for swimmers. There are also 76 tent and trailer sites, 2 rental cottages, 3 picnic shelters, and a 1.5-mile multi-use trail. For more information, call 706-376-8756, 800-864-7275, or visit www.gastateparks.org/info/hart.

- **Helen, Georgia**, approximately 80 miles north of Atlanta, is unlike any other community in Georgia. Originally a small, run-of-the-mill mountain town, Helen began a transformation process in 1968. Led by a group of area businessmen and local artist John Kollak, they turned the town into the Alpine Village replica that it is today. Kollak, inspired by the time he had spent in Bavaria, presented the Alpine Village idea, and Helen residents immediately began renovations. Today this quaint town offers over 150 import shops, 30 factory outlets, and a cobblestone alley of small boutiques and restaurants, with an array of old-world shopping, dining, and lodging opportunities. One of Helen's most popular annual events is the annual Oktoberfest celebration, which runs from mid-September through early November. German bands perform nightly, dancers in traditional Bavarian garb dance the polka and waltz, and visitors are invited to enjoy a selection of imported German wines and beers, warm pretzels, and specialty foods such as Bavarian wurst and sauerkraut. Contact the **Helen Welcome Center**, 706-878-1619, 800-858-8027, or the **Helen Convention and Visitors Bureau**, 706-878-2747, www.helenga.org, for more information.

- **Moccasin Creek State Park**, located approximately 20 miles north of Clarksville near the North Carolina border, is often referred to as the park "where spring spends the summer." Nestled in the Blue Ridge Mountains on the shores of Lake Burton, a Georgia Power Company reservoir, Moccasin Creek is a great starting point for high country exploration. Visitors are invited to tour the adjacent Lake Burton Fish Hatchery, operated by the Department of Natural Resources, which raises rainbow trout for lakes and streams across the Georgia Blue Ridge, or hike the 1-mile looping nature trail or the 1.5-mile trail up Moccasin Creek. Other activities include volleyball, basketball, horseshoes, camping, fishing, and boating. There are 54 tent and trailer sites with water and electrical hookups, wheelchair-accessible fishing piers, a public boat ramp, and boat rentals. If you'd like to find out more about Moccasin Creek State Park, including registering for a campsite, call 706-947-3194, 800-864-7275, or visit www.gastateparks.org/info/moccasin.

- **Sky Valley Resort & Country Club,** located about 120 miles northeast, or a two-hour drive, from busy Atlanta is a peaceful mountain city and resort. Atlantans have been coming to Sky Valley for decades to enjoy its mountain views and amenities. In fact, it was formerly Georgia's only ski resort, featuring three slopes maintained largely with man-made snow. However, Sky Valley has recently been revamped with a new clubhouse and updated 18-hole golf course. With gorgeous views due to its 4,100-feet elevation, a 12-acre lake, charming homes and accommodations, beautiful trails and waterfalls, it's a great all-around family resort. In addition, Sky Valley is only 30 minutes away from another popular mountain town, Highlands, NC, which houses numerous fine restaurants and shops, as well as its own theater, the Highlands Playhouse, and parades and events year round. For more information, call 706-746-5302 or go to www.skyvalleycountryclub.com or www.highlandsinfo.com.

- **Tallulah Gorge State Park**, located approximately 80 miles northeast of Atlanta, is Georgia's newest state park. One of the most spectacular gorges in the eastern USA, at 2 miles long and nearly 1,000 feet deep, this park is a favorite destination for Atlantans and North Georgians. The park was created through a partnership between the Georgia Department of Natural Resources and Georgia Power Company, and offers 50 tent and trailer sites, two lighted tennis courts, a picnic area, a 63-acre lake with beach, a visitors' center, and more than 20 miles of trails. For more information, call 706-754-7970, 800-864-7275, or visit www.gastateparks.org/info/tallulah. For reservations, call 706-754-7979.

- **Tugaloo State Park** is located on a rugged peninsula that juts into the Lake Hartwell reservoir in northeast Georgia, near the South Carolina border. Named by Indians for the river that once flowed near the park, Tugaloo offers year-round bass fishing, camping, volleyball, horseshoes, water skiing, swimming and hiking. There are 120 tent and trailer sites and 20 rental cottages on 393 acres of land. For more information, call 706-356-4362, 800-864-7275, or visit www.gastateparks.org/info/tugaloo.

- **Unicoi State Park and Lodge**, located just two miles from the Alpine village of Helen in northeast Georgia, is a popular and comfortable destination with its 100-room lodge and year-round schedule of activities. This 1,081-acre venue hosts over 80 tent and trailer sites, 30 rental cottages, lighted tennis courts, the lodge, a buffet-style restaurant, a craft shop, and a 53-acre lake. Visitors can enjoy a wide range of activities including hiking, camping, picnicking, swimming, boating, and an informative mountain culture and environmental program. Special Friday and Saturday night programs are scheduled throughout the year. For more information, call 706-878-2201, 800-864-7275, or visit www.gastate-parks.org/info/unicoi.

- **Vogel State Park**, about 11 miles south of Blairsville within the Chattahoochee National Forest, is one of Georgia's oldest and most popular state parks. Despite being one of the state's smallest parks, a mere 280 acres, it offers 110 tent and trailer sites, 36 rental cabins, 4 picnic shelters, and a 20-acre lake. Visitors are invited to enjoy the park's many family-oriented activities, including miniature golf, swimming, pioneer camping, pedal boats, and hiking along 17 miles of lush trails. For more information, call 706-745-2628, 800-864-7275, or visit http://gastateparks.org/info/vogel.

For those considering a visit to one of Georgia's State Parks, keep in mind that a Georgia Park Pass is required for all parked vehicles. Visitors may pay a daily parking fee of $5 or purchase an annual pass for $50, which is valid at all state parks. If you'd like to avoid the parking fee, try the state's Library Loan program. With your local library card, you can check out a Park Pass to use temporarily. For more information on parking passes, contact any of the state parks at the numbers listed above.

## NATIONAL PARKS

- **Chattahoochee River National Recreation Area**, located on Island Ford Parkway in Atlanta, consists of 16 land units along a 48-mile stretch of the Chattahoochee River. The park offers visitors a variety of recreational activities, including fishing, hiking, picnicking, and boating, as well as the chance to view a wide selection of natural flora and fauna, and Native American archeological sites. Restrooms, a bookstore, and wheelchair accessible trails are open to the public, and picnic tables are offered on a first-come basis. Camping is not allowed in the park. There are no entrance fees, though a daily parking fee of $3 for all park units has been instituted. For more information, call 678-538-1200, or visit www.nps.gov/chat.
- **Chickamauga and Chattanooga National Military Park**, located in north Georgia along the Tennessee border, was the first established National Military Park in the USA, back in 1890. The park honors the Civil War soldiers who fought at the Battle of Chickamauga in September 1863 and the Battle for Chattanooga in November 1863. Today the park, which consists of over 8,200 acres spread over Georgia and Tennessee, houses a Visitors' Center with exhibits on the battles, as well as a Civil War timeline. Several trails are available for walking or hiking, as well as audio tour tapes of the Chickamauga battlefield and seasonal tours of the Cravens House, which was a strategic location in the Battle of Lookout Mountain. For more information, call 706-866-9241, or visit www.nps.gov/chch.
- **Fort Frederica National Monument**, on St. Simons Island off the coast of Brunswick, was established in 1736 as the southernmost post of the British colonies in North America. The fort served as protection for Georgia and South Carolina from the Spanish, who had settled in Florida. Today the park is known for its exceptional beauty. Stately oak trees, well established and trailing grapevines, and Spanish moss give it an air of antiquity. Visitors are invited to view

exhibits on the history of Frederica, as well as the ruins of the fort's barracks. A number of special tours and activities are offered throughout the year for both adults and children, including the Fort Frederica Festival in March, the Fort Frederica 5K Easter Race, and the Holiday Open House in December. The park gift shop sells souvenirs, soft drinks, insect repellent (a must), and film. Lodging is not available in the park. For more information, call 912-638-3639 or visit www.nps.gov/fofr.

- **Fort Pulaski National Monument**, on Tybee Island, contains 5,365 acres of land, including some of the most pristine marshland on the Georgia coast. Named for Revolutionary War hero Count Casimir Pulaski, Fort Pulaski took 18 years to build and was the first military assignment for Robert E. Lee. Today this remarkably intact fort affords visitors the chance to tour the grounds and surrounding park and check out the fort's Civil War–era cannons, damaged walls, and parade grounds. There is also a quarter-mile trail for walking or hiking, a visitor center and museum, fishing and picnicking areas, and a boat-launching ramp that is open to the public. For more information, call 912-786-5787 or visit www.nps.gov/fopu.

- **Ocmulgee National Monument**, in Macon, is a memorial to the estimated 17,000 years of human habitation in this corner of North America. From Ice Age hunters, to Creek Indians, to the Mississippian culture that settled here from A.D. 900 to 1100, Ocmulgee preserves a continuous record of human life in the Southeast. Today the monument consists of two land units separated by three miles of wetlands along the Ocmulgee River. The park is open daily from 9 a.m. to 5 p.m., except for Christmas and New Year's Day. For more information call 912-752-8257, or visit www.nps.gov/ocmu.

For those considering a visit to a national park, either in Georgia or elsewhere in the USA, the **National Park Service** offers a camping and tour-reservation system. Check out www.nps.gov, or call 800-365-2267. A basic map and free brochures of national park locations can be obtained by calling 202-208-4747.

# NATIONAL FOREST SERVICE

If you're considering a camping trip, you may want to call the **National Forest Service's** toll-free reservation line, 877-444-6777, TDD 877-833-6777. There are nearly 40,000 nationwide campsites on national land, and you can make your reservations up to 240 days in advance. For more information, visit www.recreation.gov.

N UMEROUS ORGANIZATIONS IN ATLANTA AND IN THE SURROUNDING communities sponsor festivals, fairs, and feasts that draw crowds of enthusiastic participants every year. Because the area has such a mild climate, many of these events take place outdoors. *Creative Loafing* and the *Atlanta Journal-Constitution* often highlight annual celebrations, so keep your eyes peeled for information each month. For a complete list of annual events, contact the Georgia Department of Economic Development, 404-656-3590, www.georgia.org, or your county's visitors' bureau.

## JANUARY

- **ATC Resolution Run**—Start off the new year right with a run at Cobb Place in Kennesaw. One-mile at 12 noon, 5K/10K at 12:20 p.m. T-shirts go to the first 1,000 entrants. Race-day registration only. Call 404-231-9064 or go to www.atlantatrackclub.org
- **Dr. Martin Luther King Jr. Celebration**—Atlanta honors the birthday of the Civil Rights leader with three days of activities and events throughout the city. Call 404-526-8900 or visit www.thekingcenter.org
- **Chick-fil-A Bowl**—Annual college football post-season game (scheduled within a couple days before *or* after New Year's Day) that matches rivals from the Atlantic Coast Conference and the Southeastern Conference. Held at the Georgia Dome in downtown Atlanta. Call 404-223-4636, or visit www.chick-fil-abowl.com or www.gadome.com

## FEBRUARY

- **Black History Month Celebration**—Atlanta and surrounding communities play host to a wide variety of events celebrating African-American heritage and culture. For complete listings of scheduled activities, check the local newspapers during February, or contact your county's convention and visitors' bureau.

- **Groundhog Day**—Will he or won't he? Each year, Atlanta residents wait to find out whether General Beau Lee (Atlanta's favorite groundhog) will see his shadow. The event is held at Yellow River Game Ranch in Lilburn. Many visitors make a day of it, enjoying the ranch's picnic and play areas, and the 24-acre indigenous animal preserve. Call 770-972-6643, or visit www.yellowrivergameranch.com
- **Ringling Bros. Barnum & Bailey Circus**—Enjoy animals, clowns, trapeze artists, cotton candy … it's Ringling Bros. Barnum & Bailey Circus! Philips Arena, 404-249-6400, 404-878-3000, www.ringling.com
- **Southeastern Flower Show**—This 5-day festival of gardening inspiration, education, and fun for the entire family is one of the top three flower and gardening events in the USA. Highlights include guest speakers, a black-tie dinner, the annual Flower Power Party for young adults, and a silent auction. Local experts are on hand to demonstrate the latest in garden design and landscaping, the Daffodil Diner food court serves lunch and refreshments throughout the festival, and the Flower Show Marketplace sells garden supplies, as well as arts and crafts. Proceeds benefit the Atlanta Botanical Garden. www.sehort.org

## MARCH

- **Atlanta Film and Video Festival**—This 10-day festival showcases innovative animation, documentary, experimental, and student works by local, national, and international video and film makers. Highlights include screenings of work, educational seminars, guest speakers, and contests. Various locations throughout Atlanta, late March, www.atlantafilmfestival.com
- **Atlanta International Car Show**—Annual event that showcases over 500 new import and domestic vehicles being introduced to the public, with factory and dealer representatives on hand to answer questions. Highlights of the show include the concept car presentation, where the cars of tomorrow are unveiled today, and the Motor Sports Pavilion, featuring NASCAR cars and drivers up close and personal. Georgia World Congress Center, 770-916-1741, www.goautoshow.com
- **Atlanta St. Patrick's Day Parade**—A celebration of the popular Irish holiday, through the streets of Downtown and Buckhead. Many area bars offer green beer for the occasion. Downtown and Buckhead, www.stpatsparadeatlanta.com; most of Atlanta's surrounding cities have their own smaller parades and/or celebrations.
- **Conyers Cherry Blossom Festival**—Celebrate the arrival of spring and the flowering of the cherry blossoms with food, music, and activities for the entire family. This event is in the small town of Conyers, 30 minutes east of Atlanta. 770-602-2606, 800-CONYERS, www.conyerscherryblossom.com

- **Great Bunny Hop**—Families are invited to come visit the Easter Bunny, look for Easter eggs, and enjoy a wide array of fun activities at Zoo Atlanta. Zoo Atlanta, 404-624-5600, www.zooatlanta.org
- **WalkAmerica**—The March of Dimes' largest fundraising event and also one of the oldest fundraising walks in the USA. All proceeds from this 10K walk, held in Centennial Olympic Park, benefit the March of Dimes. Centennial Olympic Park, Atlanta, 404-350-9800, www.walkamerica.org, www.marchofdimes.com/georgia
- **Walking Tours of Historic Atlanta**—The Atlanta Preservation Center conducts a number of tours that showcase the rich historical tapestry of Atlanta, from the Civil War to the Civil Rights Movement. Available March through November. 404-688-3350, www.preserveatlanta.com

## APRIL

- **Atlanta Dogwood Festival**—Celebrate springtime in the South—highlighting Atlanta's history, culture, and beauty. Features include artists' booths, a children's area, canine Frisbee, live music, hot air balloons, and food. Piedmont Park, 404-329-0501, www.dogwood.org
- **Easter Sunrise Service**—Held at the top of the mountain, this nondenominational Easter service offers breathtaking views as the sun rises over the horizon. Stone Mountain Park, 770-498-5690, www.stonemountainpark.com
- **Georgia Renaissance Festival**—A great activity for the family, this festival offers visitors the chance to "journey back in time" to the Renaissance period, as they enter an elaborately detailed old-world village. Authentic food, detailed costumes, lively performers, and activities for all ages set the scene. Runs through June. Fairburn, 770-964-8575, www.garenfest.com
- **Inman Park Festival and Tour of Homes**—Offers residents and visitors the chance to get to know each other and tour some of the neighborhood's most interesting homes. Inman Park, 770-242-4895, http://inmanparkfestival.org
- **Jonquil City Jog 5K Run**—5K run through the city of Smyrna. Smyrna, 770-518-8002, www.symrnacity.com
- **Spring Jonquil Festival**—Residents of Smyrna celebrate spring and the blooming of their city flower, the jonquil, with music, food, activities, arts and crafts, and more. Village Green, Smyrna, 770-434-6600, www.smyrnacity.com
- **Taste of Marietta**—A sampling of the wide variety of foods found in Marietta, provided by area restaurants. Glover Park, Marietta, 770-429-1115, www.mariettasquare.com

## MAY

- **Atlanta Jazz Festival**—One of the country's largest free jazz festivals. Presented by the City of Atlanta Bureau of Cultural Affairs and running the entire month of May, the Atlanta Jazz Fest offers music lovers the chance to hear good, live jazz music at various venues throughout the city, with performers including local and national jazz musicians. Held at locations throughout Atlanta, 404-817-6815, www.atlantafestivals.com

- **Georgia Special Olympics Summer Games**—Emory University hosts this statewide Olympiad featuring intellectually disabled athletes, competing in a variety of events. Emory University, 404-521-6600, 866-946-7642, www.specialolympicsga.org
- **Kirkwood Festival and Tour of Homes**—A celebration of this historic Atlanta neighborhood, featuring live music, a children's area, food, history exhibits, and arts and crafts. The tour of homes features a variety of architectural styles, with homes ranging from elaborate restorations to works-in-progress. Bessie Branham Park, 404-377-4253, www.historic-kirkwood.com
- **Lasershow**—An amazing outdoor light show, set to music ranging from classical to southern rock. Runs through October. Stone Mountain Park, 770-498-5690, www.stonemountainpark.com
- **Sweet Auburn SpringFest**—Celebrates the rich history of Atlanta's Auburn Avenue, former home of Martin Luther King, Jr., with food, music, and entertainment along the avenue. Auburn Avenue, Atlanta, 404-886-4469, www.sweetauburn.com
- **Taste of Alpharetta**—Sample a wide variety of foods found in Alpharetta, provided by area restaurants. Alpharetta, 800-294-0923, www.alpharetta.ga.us

## JUNE

- **AtlantaFest Christian Music Festival**—Features the best in traditional and contemporary Christian music, as well as food, activities and fellowship. Stone Mountain Park, 770-498-5690, www.atlantafest.com, www.stonemountainpark.com
- **Atlanta Symphony Orchestra Summer Concert Series**—The ASO performs under the stars at Atlanta's Chastain Park. For more information, including the concert schedule and play list, contact the ASO directly. Alpharetta Verizon Wireless Amphitheater at Encore Park, 404-733-5010, www.vzwamp.com
- **Shakespeare's Birthday Party**—A free family-friendly event put on by the Georgia Shakespeare Company at Oglethorpe University. The event features arts, crafts, performances, music, and more; 404-264-0020, www.gashakespeare.org
- **Virginia Highland SummerFest**—Offers residents and visitors the chance to discover the neighborhood, sample food from local restaurants, visit the numerous galleries and boutiques that line Highland Avenue, meet new people, and listen to great local music. Virginia Highland, 404-222-8244, www.vahi.org/summerfest.html

# JULY

- **ATC Decatur-DeKalb YMCA 4 Mile**—The Atlanta Track Club, in conjunction with the local YMCA, sponsors this four-mile run through the City of Decatur. Decatur-DeKalb YMCA, 404-231-9064, www.atlantatrackclub.org
- **Coca-Cola Summer Film Festival**—Each summer the Fox Theatre hosts a series of films, which may include recently released movies, family-oriented movies, and classic films. The schedule changes annually, so be sure to contact the theater for more information. Fox Theatre, Atlanta, 404-881-2100, www.foxtheatre.org
- **Fantastic Fourth Celebration**—Fireworks, food, music, and games are offered throughout Stone Mountain Park in honor of Independence Day. Stone Mountain Park, 770-498-5690, www.stonemountainpark.com
- **Fourth in the Park**—Marietta's Independence Day celebration features food, music, activities, and fireworks. Marietta Square, 770-794-5601, www.mariettasquare.org
- **July 4th Celebration**—Lake Lanier Islands' Independence Day celebration features food, music, activities, and fireworks, as well as the opportunity to watch the sun set over the water. Lake Lanier Islands, 770-932-7200, www.lakelanierislands.com
- **Peachtree Road Race**—The famous 10K race attracts runners and spectators from around the world. The race begins at Lenox Mall and winds down Peachtree to Piedmont Park. Spectators fill the outdoor patios of all of the Buckhead restaurants along Peachtree, and line the sidewalks as well. Runners who participate get a Peachtree Road Race T-shirt and the satisfaction of competing in the largest 10K road race in the world. Lenox Square Mall to Piedmont Park, 404-231-9064, www.atlantatrackclub.org
- **Pied Piper Parade, Concert, and Fireworks**—Fourth of July festival on the square in Decatur, featuring a parade, live music, and spectacular fireworks. Downtown Decatur, 404-687-2576, www.dcvb.org
- **Star Spangled Celebration**—This concert and massive fireworks display over Lenox Square in Buckhead is well attended, to say the least. In recent years, crowds as large as 200,000 have descended on the mall parking lot to watch the show. Those not wanting to fight the crowds for this Independence Day celebration may opt to stay home and watch the party on TV. Lenox Square Mall, Atlanta, 404-233-6767, www.simon.com

# AUGUST

- **Decatur BBQ, Blues & Bluegrass Festival**—Annual BBQ, bluegrass and blues festival held on the Decatur Square. Downtown Decatur, 404-687-2576, www.decaturbbqfestival.com
- **Smyrna's Birthday Celebration**—Annual festival celebrating the history of Smyrna. Village Green, Smyrna, 770-434-6600, www.cobbcvb.com

# SEPTEMBER

- **Annual Marietta Streetfest**—This annual street festival features live entertainment, dining, and a classic car show. Marietta Square, 770-794-5710, www.marietta.com/marietta-streetfest
- **Art in the Park**—Enjoy local arts and crafts on the historic Marietta Square. Marietta Square, 404-966-8497, www.artparkmarietta.com
- **Arts Festival of Atlanta**—This week-long arts festival celebrates the work of local artists, jewelers, dancers, and musicians. Bring your checkbook. Locations around Atlanta, 770-941-9660, http://atlantaartsfestival.com
- **Atlanta Cup Soccer Tournament**—One of the premier soccer tournaments in the USA. Offers competitive play for boys' and girls' teams, ages 10 through 19. Matches are held over Labor Day weekend, and all proceeds benefit the Georgia Soccer Foundation. Locations throughout Atlanta, www.atlantacup.com
- **ATC Singleton 5 Mile & 10 Mile Race**—The Atlanta Track Club sponsors this annual five- and ten-mile race through Stone Mountain Park. Stone Mountain Park, 404-231-9064, www.atlantatrackclub.org
- **DragonCon**—The largest sci-fi, fantasy, and comic book convention in the USA, it features presentations, gaming tournaments, contests, auctions, performances, and exhibits. Many popular artists, actors, and authors of the sci-fi/fantasy/comic book genres attend to answer questions and sign autographs. Various locations throughout Atlanta, 404-669-0773, www.dragoncon.org
- **Grant Park Tour of Homes**—Discover the unique beauty of Grant Park and tour some of the neighborhood's most interesting homes, including recently renovated bungalows and restored Victorians. Grant Park, 404-903-5526, www.grantparktour.org/tour
- **Gwinnett County Fair**—Boasts traditional carnival rides, games of luck and skill, and good old-fashioned fair food. County Fairgrounds, Lawrenceville, 770-963-6522, www.gwinnettcountyfair.com
- **JapanFest**—Celebrates Japanese culture by featuring street performers, authentic Japanese cuisine, traditional dance, martial arts and bonsai demonstrations, a tea ceremony, and Japanese folk music. Gwinnett Conference Center, 404-842-0736, www.japanfest.org
- **North Georgia State Fair**—This state fair attracts visitors from across metro Atlanta and north Georgia. Traditional carnival rides, games, live entertainment, and food are the big attractions. Jim Miller Park, Marietta, 770-528-8989, http://northgeorgiastatefair.com
- **Roswell Arts Festival**—Enjoy local food and entertainment on Roswell's historic square. Proceeds go to support Roswell's Parks and Recreation Department. Roswell, 770-641-3705, www.roswellartsfestival.com
- **Sandy Springs Festival**—Festival includes food, music, arts and crafts, a 10K road race, and family-oriented activities. Sandy Springs, 404-851-1328, www.sandyspringsfestival.com

- **Yellow Daisy Festival**—Celebrates the blooming of the rare confederate yellow daisy, which can only be found within a 50-mile radius of Stone Mountain Park, by showcasing the work of over 400 local artists and crafters. Live entertainment, a children's corner, music, and food are also featured. Stone Mountain Park, 770-498-5690, www.stonemountainpark.com

# OCTOBER

- **AIDS Walk**—Annual walk through Midtown raises awareness and money for AIDS research. Midtown, 404-876-9255, www.aidswalkatlanta.com
- **Atlanta Marathon**—The Atlanta Track Club sponsors this annual event, which follows a course that takes participants on a tour through Atlanta. Atlantic Station, Midtown, 404-231-9064, www.atlantatrackclub.org
- **Atlanta Pride Festival**—A celebration of Atlanta's lesbian and gay community, featuring activities, games, music, food, and more. This festival is open to anyone who wants to show support for the gay and lesbian communities, regardless of sexual orientation. Check website for dates and locations, 404-929-0071, www.atlantapride.org
- **Atlanta Greek Festival**—Greek history and culture are honored at the Atlanta Greek Festival. Authentic food, performances, and more are highlights of this popular annual event. Greek Orthodox Cathedral of the Annunciation, 404.633.5870, www.atlantagreekfestival.org
- **Candler Park Fall Fest**—Weekend-long festival held in Candler Park, features live music, arts and crafts from neighborhood artists, food, and games. Candler Park, http://fallfest.candlerpark.org
- **Cobb County Classic Rodeo**—Annual, classic rodeo at Miller Park, begins at 8 p.m. and runs until 10:30 p.m. Jim Miller Park, Marietta, 770-528-8875, http://cobbcountyrodeo.com
- **Cagle's Fall Hayrides**—The dairy offers daily tours of the farm, hayrides, and a cornfield maze to walk through. Cagle's Dairy, Canton, 770-345-5591, http://caglesfamilyfarm.com
- **Boo at the Zoo**—Zoo Atlanta offers a fun alternative to door-to-door trick-or-treating, with Halloween games, treats, and more. Children (and adults) are invited to attend this Halloween event in costume. Zoo Atlanta, 404-624-5600, www.zooatlanta.org
- **Goblins in the Garden**—It's the Atlanta Botanical Garden's take on Halloween, where little ones are invited to join in a parade and receive treats while touring the garden. Atlanta Botanical Garden, www.atlantabotanicalgarden.org
- **Halloween in Roswell**—The city of Roswell offers a number of spooky events to get kids and adults in the Halloween mood. Try one of Roswell's ghost tours, visit the Manor Haunted House, or hear eerie folk tales in the gardens outside Bar-

rington Hall. Hours vary and admission prices are very reasonable, with children often admitted free. Roswell Square, 770-640-3253, www.visitroswellga.com

- **Stone Mountain Highland Games**—Annual festival featuring traditional Scottish games (both spectator and participatory), Scottish food, and music. Stone Mountain Park, 770-521-0228, www.smhg.org
- **Taste of Atlanta**—Come for a sampling of the wide variety of foods found throughout Atlanta, provided by local restaurants at Atlanta's newest intown destination mall, Atlantic Station. Atlantic Station, 404-875-4434, www.tasteofatlanta.net
- **Tour of Southern Ghosts**—Annual storytelling festival, featuring professional storytellers dressed in antebellum costume, is open to the public from mid-October to Halloween night. Guests are led through Stone Mountain Park's Antebellum Plantation by candlelight to hear six different southeastern-based ghost stories. Stone Mountain Park, 770-498-5690, www.stonemountainpark.com

## NOVEMBER

- **ATC Run Around the Rock 5 M/10M/15M**—Hosted by the Atlanta Track Club, multiple races around Stone Mountain, including a one-mile race for children. Stone Mountain Park, 404-231-9064, www.atlantatrackclub.org
- **Atlanta Half Marathon and Thanksgiving Day 5K**—The Atlanta Track Club sponsors this annual event, run along the 1996 Olympic marathon course. Outside Turner Field, Downtown, 404-231-9064, www.atlantatrackclub.org
- **Holiday Celebration**—A celebration of the holiday season, featuring music, food, activities, and gifts market. Stone Mountain Park, 770-498-5690, www.stonemountainpark.com
- **Lighting of the Tree**—The annual lighting of the Gwinnett Historic Courthouse, complete with carolers, Christmas tree, and holiday decorations, helps set the mood for the upcoming holiday season. Historic Courthouse, Lawrenceville, 770-882-5450, www.gwinnettcounty.com
- **Lighting of Macy's Great Tree**—The annual lighting of this enormous Christmas tree traditionally draws a large crowd, and many Atlanta residents view this Thanksgiving night activity as the official start of the holiday season. Lenox Square Mall, Atlanta, 404-233-6767, www.simon.com
- **Veterans Day Parade**—This parade begins on West Peachtree Street and makes its way to Centennial Olympic Park. The parade pays tribute to the veterans of the armed forces who have served in uniform and risked their lives to keep our country safe. Downtown, 404-521-6600, http://gavetsdayparade.org

# DECEMBER

- **Atlanta Symphony Orchestra Holiday Concerts**—Feature season-appropriate compositions performed by the Orchestra, the ASO Chorus, and the ASO Opera. Symphony Hall, 404-733-4900, www.atlantasymphony.org
- **Christmas at Bulloch Hall**—Christmas decorations, music, and more highlight this annual holiday event at Roswell's historic Bulloch Hall. Roswell, 770-640-3253, www.visitroswellga.com
- **Christmas at Callanwolde**—Christmas decorations, musical performances, and art are part of this annual holiday event. Callanwolde Fine Arts Center, Atlanta, 404-872-5338, www.christmasatcallanwolde.org
- **Christmas at the Wren's Nest**—This annual celebration of Christmas, at the historical Wren's Nest, features food, music, and holiday decorations. Home of author Joel Chandler Harris, 404-753-7735, www.wrensnestonline.com
- **Peach Drop**, Atlanta's answer to New York's ball drop on Times Square; revelers at this New Year's Eve celebration count down the minutes to the New Year in anticipation of the dropping of the great peach. Family events held all day on New Year's Eve. Underground Atlanta, 404-523-2311, www.peachdrop.com
- **The Marietta Pilgrimage, Christmas Home Tour**—A tour of six private, historic Marietta homes, lovingly restored and decorated for the holidays. Historic District, Marietta, 770-429-1115, www.mariettapilgrimage.com
- **An Old Fashioned Marietta Christmas**—An old-time Christmas celebration, featuring music, food, fun, and games for the entire family. Marietta, 770-429-1115, www.mariettasquare.com
- **The Nutcracker**—The annual Atlanta Ballet production of this beloved Christmas classic is a favorite among local residents. Fox Theatre, 404-881-2100, www.foxtheatre.org, 404-873-5811, www.atlantaballet.com
- **Chick-fil-A Bowl Parade**—This parade heralds the upcoming Chick-fil-A Bowl (which falls within a couple of days before or after New Year's Day), with both of the participating college football teams, their school bands, and their fans partying through Downtown. Downtown, 404-586-8537, www.peachbowl.com
- **Santa on the Square**—Children (and adults) can visit Santa and view his Marietta workshop on weekends throughout December. Santa's Workshop, Glover Park, Marietta, 770-429-1115, http://santaonthesquare.com.

THOSE INTERESTED IN LEARNING MORE ABOUT THE HISTORY OF ATLANTA, or just getting a feel for the city, may want to consider the following list of books.

## CHILDREN/YOUNG ADULTS

- *The Atlanta Braves Baseball Team* by Thomas S. Owens and Tom Owens (Enslow Publishers). A comprehensive history of the Atlanta Braves' Organization, from their early days to their championship runs of the 1990s. (ages 9–12)
- *The Atlanta Braves* by John F. Grabowski (Lucent Books) (ages 9–12)
- *Competitive Edge (Hardy Boys Casefile #111)* by Franklin W. Dixon (Simon Pulse). The Hardy Boys must discover who's out to sabotage the 1996 Olympic Games—before it's too late. (young adult)
- *Happy Birthday Martin Luther King* by Jean Marzollo and J. Brian Pinkney (Scholastic). A brief biography (with pictures) for young children. The authors are especially sensitive when it comes to King's death. (ages 4–8)
- *Leaving Atlanta* by Tayari Jones (Warner Books). A novel set in 1979 Atlanta during the infamous Atlanta child murders. The story centers on the relationships of three fifth graders as they struggle with family issues, and the string of murders that has left the city terrified. (young adult)
- *On the Mound With ... Greg Maddux* by Matt Christopher (Little Brown). A biography of Atlanta Braves' pitcher Greg Maddux, considered by many to be one of the best pitchers in Major League Baseball. (ages 9–12)

## NONFICTION

### ART/ARCHITECTURE

- *AIA Guide to the Architecture of Atlanta* by Isabelle Gournay (University of Georgia Press). Profiles the various architectural styles of the city.

- *American Paintings at the High Museum of Art* by Judy L. Larson, Donelson Hoopes, and Phyllis Peet (Hudson Hills Press). Covers the three centuries of American art on permanent display at the High Museum of Art.
- *Atlanta Architecture—Art Deco to Modern Classic, 1929–1959* by Robert M. Craig and Richard Guy Wilson (Pelican Publishing Co.). A scholarly review of the art deco and modern classic architectural styles in Atlanta.

## BIOGRAPHIES

- *The Autobiography of Martin Luther King Jr.* by Martin Luther King Jr. and Clayborne Carson (Warner Books). This autobiography, written by Carson, is based on thousands of King's essays, notes, letters, speeches, and sermons, and offers a glimpse of King's life.
- *Born to Rebel: An Autobiography* by Benjamin E. Mays (University of Georgia Press). Starting life humbly as the son of a sharecropper, he went on to become the President of Morehouse College for almost three decades and the first black president of the Atlanta School Board.
- *Ted Turner: It Ain't As Easy As It Looks: A Biography* by Porter Bibb (Johnson Books). An in-depth portrait of the often outspoken, larger-than-life media mogul.

## FOOD

- *Atlanta at the Table* by Frances Schultz and Dot Griffith (Wyrick & Co.). A look at how Atlanta entertains—from fancy balls to down-home Sunday dinners. Each chapter includes photos and recipes.
- *Cooking Atlanta Style: Delicious Recipes from Atlanta's Best Restaurants, Hotels and Caterers* (Longstreet Press); and *More Cooking Atlanta Style* (St. Simons Press, Inc.), by Margaret E. Norman. A compilation of interesting recipes from some of the best chefs in Atlanta.

## GUIDES

- *147 Fun Things to do in Atlanta* by Karen Foulk (Into Fun Company Publications)
- *Around Atlanta with Children: A Guide for Family Activities* by Denise Black (Peachtree Publishers). A look at places to visit and things to do with children in Atlanta.
- *The Atlanta Dog Lover's Companion* by Marilyn Windle and Phil Frank (Avalon Travel Publishers). Highlights places to go and things to do with dogs in Atlanta
- *Atlanta Walks: A Comprehensive Guide to Walking, Running, and Bicycling Around the Area's Scenic and Historic Locales* by Ren and Helen Davis (Peachtree Publishers).

- *Gardening Around Atlanta* by Avis Aronovitz (Eldorado Press). Atlanta as seen through its lush and diverse gardens.
- *Ponce de Leon: An Intimate Portrait of Atlanta's Most Famous Avenue* by George Mitchell (Argonne Books). A glimpse of Ponce de Leon Avenue some twenty years ago.
- *Sideways Atlanta: A Field Guide to Offbeat Attractions in the "City Too Busy to Hate"* by Suzanne Winterberger and Bill Tomey (Creative Intelligence Agency). A look at some of Atlanta's little known, yet memorable, events and places.

## HISTORY

- *Archival Atlanta: Electric Street Dummies, the Great Stonehenge Explosion, Nerve Tonics, and Bovine Laws: Forgotten Facts and Well-Kept Secrets From Our City's Past* by Perry Buffington and Kim Underwood (Peachtree Publishers). An offbeat look at Atlanta's history.
- *Atlanta: An Illustrated History* by John Lewis (Hill Street Press).
- *Atlanta and Environs, A Chronicle of Its People and Events* (Volumes I, II, and III) by Franklin M. Garrett (University of Georgia Press). Chronicles the people and events shaping Atlanta from 1820 to 1976, by one of Atlanta's most respected historians.
- *Atlanta and the War* by Webb Garrison (Rutledge Hill Press). A look at the city before, during, and after the Civil War.
- *Atlanta on My Mind* by Stanley Skoryna (Home Museum Press). A 335-page compilation of facts and details about the city.
- *Atlanta Rising: The Invention of an International City, 1946-1996* by Frederick Allen (Longstreet Press). Chronicles 50 years of Atlanta history, concluding with the 1996 Olympic Games.
- *Atlanta Then and Now* by Michael Rose (Thunder Bay Press). Chronicle of Atlanta's growth and change over the last century.
- *Atlanta—Voices of the Civil War* by the editors of Time Life Books (Time Life Books). An audio presentation through letters, diaries, and personal recollections of the events surrounding the Atlanta campaign.
- *Black Atlanta in the Roaring Twenties* by Herman Skip Mason, Jr. (Arcadia Publishing). A compelling look, through pictures and stories, at Atlanta's black culture during the jazz age.
- *Emblems of Conduct* by Donald Windham (University of Georgia Press). A memoir of the author's Depression-era Atlanta youth.
- *The Legacy of Atlanta: A Short History* by Webb B. Garrison (Peachtree Publishers). An abbreviated paperback history of Atlanta, highlighting important people and events.
- *Pickin' on Peachtree: A History of Country Music in Atlanta* by Wayne W. Daniel (University of Illinois Press). Traces the roots and growth of country music, from county fairs to Atlanta radio, to national recording deals.

- **The Temple Bombing** by Melissa Faye Greene (Ballantine Books). An exploration of the events surrounding the racially motivated bombing of Atlanta's oldest synagogue in 1958.
- **To 'Joy My Freedom: Southern Black Women's Lives and Labors After the Civil War** by Tera W. Hunter (Harvard University Press). Chronicles African-American working women from slavery to their struggles as free domestic laborers, using Atlanta as a backdrop.
- **Where Peachtree Meets Sweet Auburn** by Gary Pomerantz (Penguin Books). Atlanta history as seen through the lives of two families and two mayors, one black and one white.

## SPORTS

- **The History of the Atlanta Falcons** by Michael E. Goodman (Creative Education). A look at Atlanta's professional football team.
- **None But the Braves: A Pitcher, A Team, A Champion** by Tom Glavine, Nick Cafardo (with an introduction by Greg Maddux) (HarperCollins Publishers). World Series MVP and Braves' pitcher Tom Glavine tells the inspiring story of how the Braves went from "worst to first."

## FICTION

- **The Answer Man** by Roy Johansen (Bantam). Ken Parker, owner of an Atlanta-based polygraph service, soon finds himself caught up in two high-profile murder cases, and he's the prime suspect. (Mystery)
- **Atlanta** by Sara Orwig (Onyx Books). The final book in Orwig's southern Civil War trilogy (which also includes New Orleans and Memphis) begins as Sherman makes his way through Atlanta, and tells the story of Yankee Colonel Fortune O'Brien and southern beauty Claire Dryden. (Romance)
- **Atlanta Graves** by Ruth Birmingham (Berkley Publishing Group). Debut novel featuring Sunny Childs, an Atlanta private investigator, as she tries to solve an art theft and catch a killer before her company defaults on its bank loan. (Mystery)
- **Atlanta Heat** by Robert Coram (Signet Book). A rookie detective tries to solve a double homicide with help from one of Atlanta's most famous crime reporters. (Mystery)
- **The Blue Place** by Nicola Griffith (Perennial). Former cop Aud Torvingen finds herself becoming personally involved, as she investigates a puzzling art theft and murder. (Mystery)
- **The Dog Star** by Donald Windham (Hill Street Press). Chronicles the life of 15-year-old Blackie Pride as he roams the streets of post-Depression Atlanta. (General Fiction)

- **Down On Ponce** by Fred Willard (Longstreet Press). Debut novel by Atlanta resident Fred Willard offers a sometimes humorous yet noir-esque look at a handful of interesting characters from one of the seediest parts of town. (Mystery/Suspense)
- **Downtown** by Anne Rivers Siddons (Harper Torch). *Downtown* tells the story of a plucky young Irishwoman, Smoky O'Donnell, who arrives in Atlanta in 1966 to find herself working at *Downtown*, a small, hip magazine. (General Fiction) Other books by local author Anne Rivers Siddons include *Off Season, Outer Banks, Hill Towns, Homeplace, Fox's Earth, Heartbreak Hotel, Low Country, King's Oak*, and *Peachtree Road*.
- **Driving Miss Daisy** by Alfred Uhry (Theatre Communications Group). The play, which was adapted into the 1989 Academy Award–winning film of the same name. (Fiction/Play)
- **Gone With the Wind** by Margaret Mitchell (Warner Books). The consummate saga of love and struggle during the Civil War. (General Fiction/Literature)
- **The Kidnapping of Aaron Greene** by Terry Kay (William Morrow & Co.). Average "Joe" Aaron Greene is kidnapped on his way to work and held for $10 million. The catch is that the kidnappers want a powerful Atlanta bank to pay the ransom, not Aaron's parents. When the bank refuses, a storm of controversy erupts. Where is Aaron? And why would anyone want to kidnap him? (Mystery) Other books by local author Terry Kaye include *The Runaway, Shadow Song, The Book of Marie, The Valley of Light*, and *To Dance with the White Dog*.
- **The Last Night of Ballyhoo** by Alfred Uhry (Theatre Communications Group). A play depicting life in Atlanta's Jewish community of the late 1930s. (Fiction/Play)
- **Looking for Atlanta** by Marilyn Dorn Staats (University of Georgia Press). Margaret Hunter Bridges, an aging Atlanta debutante, tries to find herself and make sense of her life amidst the pain of a messy divorce and the accidental death of her daughter. (General Fiction)
- **A Man in Full** by Tom Wolfe (Bantam). Set in Atlanta, this 700+ page novel explores (and satirizes) the lives of several interesting southern characters. (General Fiction)
- **Irish Eyes** by Kathy Hogan Trocheck (Avon). One of several Callahan Garrity mysteries set in Atlanta. (Mystery)
- **A Plague of Kinfolks** by Celestine Sibley (HarperTorch). Atlanta political journalist turned columnist and mystery writer Sibley tells another Kate Mulcay story set in Atlanta and woven around eccentric characters and humorous, down-home situations. (General Fiction)

## AMBULANCE

For emergency ambulance service in the greater Atlanta area dial 911. If you are calling DeKalb County from another county in the metropolitan area, dial 404-294-2493.

## ALCOHOL & DRUG DEPENDENCY

- **Alcoholics Anonymous**, metro Atlanta Central Office, 404-525-3178, http:// atlantaaa.org
- **Atlanta Recovery Center**, 877-413-3073, http://atlantarecoverycenter.com
- **Georgia Alliance,** 877-315-6907, www.georgiaalliance.org
- **Georgia Alliance for Children**, 404-588-0708, www.gac.org
- **Living Recovery,** 888-507-LIFE, www.livingrecovery.com
- **Narcotics Anonymous**, 800-711-6375, www.grscna.com
- **National Substance Abuse HelpLine**, 800-378-4435
- **Northside Hospital Recovery Center**, Alcohol & Drug Services, 404-851-8961, www.northside.com

## ANIMALS

- **Animal Bites**, 911
- **Animal Control, Cherokee County**, 770-345-7270, www.cherokeega.com
- **Animal Control, Cobb County**, 770-499-4136, http:// cobbcountyga.gov
- **Animal Control, DeKalb County**, 404-294-2996, www.dekalbcountyanimals-ervices.com
- **Animal Control, Fulton County**, 404-794-0358, www.fultoncountyga.gov
- **Animal Control, Gwinnett County**, 770-339-3200, www.gwinnettcounty.com

- **Atlanta Dead Animal Removal**, 404-330-6333, www.atlantaga.gov/government/publicworks.aspx
- **Atlanta Humane Society**, 404-875-5331, www.atlantahumane.org
- **Cherokee County Humane Society**, 770-928-5115, www.cchumanesociety.org
- **Cobb County Humane Society**, 770-428-5678, www.humanecobb.org
- **Gwinnett County Humane Society**, 770-798-7711, www.gwinnetthumane.com
- **Metro Atlanta Animal Emergency Centers**, 770-455-7077, www.atlantaanimalalliance.com/emergency.htm
- **PAWS Atlanta (the DeKalb County Humane Society)**, 770-593-1155, www.pawsatlanta.org

## AUTOMOBILES

- **Abandoned Vehicle Removal**, 404-658-6666, www.atlantapd.org
- **American Automobile Association (AAA)**, 800-AAA-HELP, www.aaa.com
- **Atlanta Police Property** (number to call for impounded cars), 404-853-4330, www.atlantapd.org
- **State Department of Drivers Services**, 404-362-6500, www.dds.ga.gov

## PARKING VIOLATIONS

- **Parking Collections**, 404-658-6886, www.atlantaga.gov
- **Parking Violations**, 404-658-6935, www.atlantaga.gov
- **Traffic Court—General Ticket Information**, 404-658-6940, www.atlantaga.gov

## BIRTH & DEATH RECORDS

- **State of Georgia, Department of Vital Records**, 404-679-4702, http://health.state.ga.us

## CONSUMER COMPLAINTS AND SERVICES

- **Atlanta Bar Association**, 404-521-0781, www.atlantabar.org
- **Atlanta Chamber of Commerce**, 404-880-9000, www.metroatlantachamber.com
- **Better Business Bureau of Metropolitan Atlanta**, 404-766-0875, www.atlanta.bbb.org
- **Consumer Product Safety Commission**, 404-730-2870, 800-638-2772, www.cpsc.gov
- **Federal Trade Commission**, 404-656-1390, 877-382-4357, www.ftc.gov
- **State Attorney General Consumer Affairs Division**, 404-656-3300, www.law.state.ga.us
- **State Insurance Commissioner**, 404-656-2070, 800-656-2298, www.inscomm.state.ga.us

- **State Consumer Affairs Office**, 404-651-8600, 800-869-1123, www.consumer.ga.gov
- **US Attorney General, Northern District of Georgia**, 404-581-6000, www.justice.gov/usao/gan
- **US Public Interest Research Group (USPIRG)**, 404-892-3403, http://uspirg.org, www.pirg.org

## CRISIS

### CHILD ABUSE AND NEGLECT

- **Cherokee County Child Protective Services**, 770-720-3610, www.cherokeega.com
- **Cobb County Child Protective Services**, Region 17, 770-528-5015, www.cobbcountyga.gov
- **DeKalb County Child Protective Services**, Region 14, 404-370-5066, www.co.dekalb.ga.us/dfcs
- **Fulton County Child Protective Services**, Region 13, 404-699-4399, http://dfcs.dhr.georgia.gov
- **Gwinnett County Child Protective Services**, Region 15, 770-995-2122, www.gwinnettcounty.com
- **State of Georgia Division of Family and Children Services**, 404-463-7291, http://dfcs.dhr.georgia.gov

### CRIME

- **Crime in Progress**, 911
- **Atlanta Police Department**, (404) 546-7290, www.atlantapd.org, www.atlantapd.org/phonedirectory.aspx
- **Cherokee County Sheriff's Office**, 678-493-4200, www.cherokeega-sheriff.org
- **Cobb County Sheriff's Office**, (770)499-4600, www.cobbsheriff.org
- **Cobb County PD Crime Prevention Unit**, 770-499-3909, http://police.cobbcountyga.gov
- **DeKalb County Police Department**, 678.937.2852, http://web.co.dekalb.ga.us/dk_police
- **DeKalb County PD Crime Prevention Unit**, 678.937.2852, http://web.co.dekalb.ga.us/dk_police
- **Fulton County Police Department**, 770-495-8738, www.fultonpolice.org
- **Gwinnett County Police Department**, 770-513-5000, www.gwinnettcounty.com
- **Gwinnett County PD Crime Prevention Unit**, 770-623-2610, www.gwinnettcountysheriff.com
- **State Patrol Office**, 404-624-7000, http://dps.georgia.gov
- **Victim-Witness Assistance Program**, 404-865-8127, www.atlantava.org

## RAPE AND SEXUAL ASSAULT SERVICES
- **Cherokee/Cobb Rape Crisis Center**, Crisis Line, 770-427-3390
- **DeKalb Rape Crisis Center**, Crisis Line, 404-377-1428, http://dekalbrapecrisi-center.org
- **Georgia Network to End Sexual Assault**, 678-701-2700, www.gnesa.org
- **Grady Hospital Rape Crisis Center**, Crisis Line, 404-616-4861
- **Gwinnett Sexual Assault Center**, Crisis Line, 770-476-7407

## DISCRIMINATION

- **Cobb and Douglas County Community Services Board**, 770-429-5000, www.cobbcsb.com
- **DeKalb County Community Relations Commission**, 404-371-2393, www.co.dekalb.ga.us
- **Fulton County Human Services Department**, (404) 613-7944, www.fultonhumanservices.org
- **Georgia Commission on Equal Opportunity (Employment)**, 404-656-1736, http://gceo.state.ga.us
- **Georgia Commission on Equal Opportunity (Housing)**, 404-656-7708, http://gceo.state.ga.us/housing.htm
- **Gwinnett County Community Services Department**, 770-822-8880, www.gwinnettcounty.com
- **State Department of Community Affairs**, 404-679-4840, www.dca.state.ga.us
- **US Government Employment Discrimination Department**, 800-669-4000, www.eeoc.gov
- **US Government Health & Human Services, Office for Civil Rights**, 800-368-1019, www.hhs.gov/ocr
- **US Government Housing Discrimination Department**, 800-669-9777, www.fairhousinglaw.org

## ELECTED OFFICIALS AND GOVERNMENT

### BOARD OF ELECTIONS
- **Board of Elections (Cherokee County)**, 770-479-0595, www.cherokeega.com
- **Board of Elections (Cobb County)**, 770-528-2300, www.cobbelections.org
- **Board of Elections (DeKalb County)**, 404-298-4020, www.co.dekalb.ga.us
- **Board of Elections (Fulton County)**, 404-730-7072, www.fultoncountyga.gov
- **Board of Elections (Gwinnett County)**, 770-822-8787, www.gwinnettcounty.com
- **Secretary of State, Elections Division**, 404-656-2871, www.sos.georgia.gov

### CITY OF ATLANTA
- **Atlanta City Council**, 404-330-6030, www.atlantaga.gov

- **Atlanta Mayor's Office**, 404-330-6100, www.atlantaga.gov/mayor

## COUNTY OFFICIALS
- **Cherokee County Government**, 678-493-6000, www.cherokeega.com
- **Cobb County Government**, 770-528-1000, http://cobbcountyga.gov
- **DeKalb County Government**, 404-371-2000, www.dekalbcountyga.gov
- **Fulton County Government**, 404-730-4000, www.fultoncountyga.gov
- **Gwinnett County Government**, 770-822-8000, www.gwinnettcounty.com

## STATE GOVERNMENT
- **Georgia State Government Official Website**, www.georgia.gov
- **Georgia Secretary of State**, 404-656-2881, www.sos.georgia.gov
- **Georgia Governor's Office**, 404-656-1776, http://gov.georgia.gov

## EMERGENCY

For fire, police, or medical emergencies in the greater Atlanta area dial 911. If you are calling DeKalb County from another county in the metropolitan area, dial 404-294-2493.

## ENTERTAINMENT

### FINE ARTS
- **Alliance Theatre**, 404-733-5000, www.alliancetheatre.org
- **Arts at Emory**, 404-727-5050, http://arts.emory.edu
- **Atlanta Ballet**, 404-892-3303, www.atlantaballet.com
- **Atlanta Coalition of Performing Arts**, 404-894-3481, www.atlantaperforms.com
- **Atlanta Entertainment Online**, http://atlantaentertainment.com
- **Atlanta Symphony Orchestra**, 404-733-4949, www.atlantasymphony.org
- **Ballethnic Dance Company**, 404-762-1416, www.ballethnic.org
- **City of Atlanta Office of Cultural Affairs**, 404-817-6815, http://ocaatlanta.com
- *Creative Loafing* **Online Happenings Calendar**, www.creativeloafing.com
- **Fulton County Arts Council**, 404-730-5780, http://fultonarts.org
- **TicketMaster**, 800-745-3000, www.ticketmaster.com

### VENUES
- **Atlanta Civic Center**, 404-523-6275, www.atlantaciviccenter.com
- **Center Stage Atlanta**, 404-885-1365, www.centerstage-atlanta.com/
- **Chastain Park Amphitheater**, 404-233-2227, www.classicchastain.com
- **The Fox Theatre**, 404-881-2100, www.foxtheatre.org

- **The Georgia Dome**, 404-223-9200, www.gadome.com
- **The Gwinnett Civic Center Arena**, 770-813-7500, www.gwinnettciviccenter.com
- **Aaron's Amphitheater**, 404-443-5090, www.livenation.com
- **Rialto Center for the Arts**, 404-651-1234, www.rialtocenter.org
- **Philips Arena**, 404-878-3000, www.philipsarena.com
- **Variety Playhouse**, 404-524-7354, www.variety-playhouse.com
- **Woodruff Arts Center**, 404-733-5000, www.woodruffcenter.org

## HEALTH AND MEDICAL CARE

- **AIDS Hotline—CDC National**, 800-342-AIDS
- **Alzheimer's Association, Georgia Chapter**, 404-728-1181, http://alz.org/georgia/
- **American Cancer Society**, 800-ACS-2345, www.cancer.org
- **American Lung Association of Georgia**, 770-434-5864, www.lung.org
- **North Georgia Health District/Cherokee County Health Department**, 770-345-7371, www.nghd.org/CherokeeHealth/
- **Board of Health (Cobb County)**, 770-514-2300, www.cobbanddouglaspublichealth.org
- **Board of Health (DeKalb County)**, 404-294-3700, www.dekalbhealth.net
- **Board of Health (Fulton County)**, 404-765-4146, www.fultoncountyga.org
- **Board of Health (Gwinnett County)**, 770-963-5142, www.gwinnettcounty.com
- **Diabetes Association of Atlanta**, 404-527-7150, www.diabetesatlanta.org
- **Epilepsy Foundation—Georgia Chapter**, 678-306-1210, www.epilepsyga.org
- **Families First**, 404-853-2800, www.familiesfirst.org
- **Georgia Poison Control Center**, 800-222-1222, www.georgiapoisoncenter.org

### PHYSICIAN REFERRAL SERVICES

- **Atlanta Medical Center Physician Referral**, 404-265-3627, www.atlantamedcenter.com
- **Children's Healthcare of Atlanta**, 404-250-KIDS, www.choa.org
- **DeKalb Medical Center Physician Referral**, 404-501-9355, www.dekalbmedicalcenter.com
- **Emory Health Connection**, 404-778-7777, www.emoryhealthcare.org
- **Georgia Academy of Family Physicians**, 800-392-3841, www.gafp.org
- **Atlanta Millennium Healthcare**, 770-390-0012, www.millennium-healthcare.com
- **Southern Regional Medical Center (Riverdale)**, 770-991-8000, www.southernregional.org

## HOUSING

- **Atlanta Housing Authority**, 404-892-4700, www.atlantahousing.org

- **Atlanta Neighborhood Development Partnership**, 404-522-2637, www. andpi.org
- **City of Atlanta Housing Code Enforcement**, 404-330-6190, www.atlantaga. gov/government/planning.aspx
- **US Department of Housing and Urban Development, Georgia**, 404-331- 5136, www.hud.gov/local/index.cfm?state=ga

## IMMIGRATION

- **Department of Homeland Security**, www.dhs.gov, www.whitehouse.gov/ deptofhomeland
- **General Government Questions**, 800-688-9889, www.usa.gov
- **Social Security Administration**, 800-772-1213, www.ssa.gov
- **US Bureau of Consular Affairs**, www.travel.state.gov
- **US Bureau of Citizenship and Immigration Services (USCIS)**, 800-375-5283, www.uscis.gov
- **US Customs and Border Protection**, www.cbp.gov
- **US Department of State, Visa Services**, http://travel.state.gov
- **US Immigration Online—Green Cards, Visas, Government Forms**, www. immigrationdirect.com

## LEGAL REFERRAL

- **AAA Attorney Referral Service of Georgia**, 404-252-8808, http://aaaattorney-referralservice.com
- **Atlanta Bar Association**, 404-521-0781, www.atlantabar.org
- **Atlanta Legal Aid Society**, 404-524-5811, www.atlantalegalaid.org
- **Atlanta Volunteer Lawyers Foundation**, 404-521-0790, www.avlf.org
- **Legal Aid Georgia**, www.georgialegalaid.org

## LIBRARIES

See also **Libraries** in **Cultural Life** and end-listings in the **Neighborhood Profiles**.

- **Cherokee County Central Library**, 770-345-7565, www.sequoyahregionalli-brary.org
- **Cobb County Central Library**, 770-528-2320, www.cobbcat.org
- **DeKalb County Central Library**, 404-370-3070, www.dekalblibrary.org
- **Fulton County Central Library**, 404-730-1700, http://afpls.org
- **Gwinnett County Central Library**, 770-822-4522, www.gwinnettpl.org
- **Smyrna Public Library**, 770-431-2860, http://smyrnalibrary.org

## MARRIAGE LICENSES

- **Cherokee County Probate Court**, 678-493-6160, www.cherokeega.com
- **Cobb County Probate Court**, 770-528-1900, http://cobbcountyga.gov
- **DeKalb County Probate Court**, 404-371-2601, http://web.co.dekalb.ga.us/probate_court
- **Fulton County Probate Court**, 404-730-4692, www.fultoncountyga.gov/probate-court
- **Gwinnett County Probate Court**, 770-822-8250, www.gwinnettcourts.com

## MUNICIPALITIES

### CITY OF ATLANTA

- **Atlanta City Council**, 404-330-6030, www.atlantaga.gov
- **Atlanta City Hall**, 55 Trinity Ave, Atlanta, 404-330-6000, www.atlantaga.gov
- **Atlanta Mayor's Office**, 404-330-6100, www.atlantaga.gov/mayor

### METRO ATLANTA

- **City of Alpharetta**, 678-297-6000, www.alpharetta.ga.us
- **City of Austell**, 770-944-4300, www.austellga.gov
- **City of Avondale Estates**, 404-294-5400, www.avondaleestates.org
- **City of Canton**, 770-704-1500, http://canton-georgia.com
- **City of Chamblee**, 770-986-5010, www.chambleega.com
- **City of Decatur**, 404-370-4100, www.decaturga.com
- **City of Lawrenceville**, 770-963-2414, www.lawrencevillega.org
- **City of Lithonia**, 770-482-8136
- **City of Marietta**, 770-794-5501, www.mariettaga.gov
- **City of Norcross**, 770-448-2122, www.norcrossga.net
- **City of Roswell**, 770-641-3727, www.roswellgov.com
- **City of Smyrna**, 770-434-6600, www.symrnacity.com
- **City of Stone Mountain**, 770-498-8984, www.stonemountaincity.org
- **City of Woodstock**, 770-592-6007, www.woodstockga.gov

## PARKS AND RECREATION DEPARTMENTS

### COUNTY DEPARTMENTS

- **Cherokee County Parks and Recreation Department**, 770-924-7768, www.crpa.net
- **Cobb County Parks and Recreation Department**, 770-528-8800, http://prca.cobbcountyga.gov
- **DeKalb County Parks and Recreation Department**, 404-371-2631, www.co.dekalb.ga.us/parks

- **Fulton County Parks and Recreation Department**, 404-730-6200, www.fultoncountyga.gov/fcprd
- **Gwinnett County Parks and Recreation Department**, 770-822-8875, www.gwinnettcounty.com

## CITY DEPARTMENTS

- **Alpharetta Parks and Recreation Department**, 678-297-6100, http://alpharetta.ga.us
- **Atlanta City Parks and Recreation Bureau**, 404-817-6788, www.atlantaga.gov
- **Chamblee Parks and Recreation Department**, 770-986-5016, www.chambleega.com
- **City of Decatur Parks and Recreation Department**, 404-377-0494, www.decatur-ga.com
- **Marietta Parks and Recreation Department**, 770-794-5601, www.mariettaga.gov
- **Roswell Parks and Recreation Department**, 770-641-3760, www.roswellgov.com

## POLICE

- **Atlanta,** emergency, 911; non-emergency, 404-853-3434, www.atlantapd.org
- **Cherokee County,** emergency, 911; non-emergency, 678-493-4200, www.cherokeega-sheriff.org
- **Cobb County**, emergency, 911; non-emergency, 770-499-3900, http://cobbcountyga.gov
- **DeKalb County**, emergency within DeKalb County, 911; emergency outside DeKalb County, 404-294-2493; non-emergency, 404-294-2519, http://web.co.dekalb.ga.us/dk_police
- **Fulton County**, emergency, 911; non-emergency, 404-730-5700, www.fultonpolice.org
- **Gwinnett County**, emergency, 911; non-emergency, 770-513-5000, www.gwinnettcounty.com
- **Georgia State Patrol**, 404-624-7000, http://dps.georgia.gov
- **US Marshal's Service, Northern District of Georgia,** 404-331-6833, www.justice.gov/marshals

## POST OFFICE

For a list of post offices with extended hours, see **Mail Delivery** in the **Helpful Services** chapter. For addresses of neighborhood post offices, check the end-listings in the **Neighborhood Profiles**.

- **US Postal Service**, 800-275-8777, www.usps.com

## ROADS

### STREET MAINTENANCE

- **Atlanta**, www.atlantaga.gov/government/publicworks.aspx: days, 404-330-6654; nights, weekends, and holidays, 404-65-WORKS
- **Cherokee County**, 770-345-5842, www.cherokeega.com/ccweb/departments/public_works
- **Cobb County**, http://gps.cobbcountyga.gov: days, 770-528-3666; nights, weekends, and holidays, 770-419-6201
- **DeKalb County**, www.co.dekalb.ga.us/publicwrks/index.htm: days, 404-297-3840; nights, weekends, and holidays, 404-294-2523
- **Fulton County**, 404-612-7400, www.fultoncountyga.gov/publicworks-home
- **Gwinnett County**, 770-822-7474, www.gwinnettcounty.com

### ROAD CONDITION/TRAFFIC INFORMATION

- **Atlanta Traffic Report**, www.traffic.com/Atlanta-traffic-reports
- **Georgia 511**, www.511ga.org
- **Georgia DOT Traffic Information**, 404-624-1300, ext. 1000, www.georgia-navigator.com
- **Triple Team Traffic**, www.wsbtv.com/s/traffic

## SANITATION AND GARBAGE

- **Atlanta Public Works Department,** 404-659-6757, www.atlantaga.gov
- **City of Austell Sanitation Department**, 770-944-4300, www.austellga.gov
- **City of Decatur Sanitation Department**, 404-377-5571, www.decaturga.com
- **City of Marietta Sanitation Department**, 770-794-5581, www.mariettaga.gov
- **City of Smyrna Sanitation Department**, 770-319-5338, www.smyrnacity.com
- **Cobb County Garbage Pick Up**, 770-528-2500, www.cobbcountyga.gov
- **DeKalb County Sanitation Department**, 404-294-2900, www.co.dekalb.ga.us
- **Fulton County Garbage Pick Up**, 404-730-7400, www.fultoncountyga.gov
- **Gwinnett County Garbage Pick Up**, 770-822-5187, www.gwinnettcounty.com

### RECYCLING

- **City of Atlanta Recycling Hotline**, 404-792-1212, www.atlantaga.gov
- **Cobb County Recycling Information**, 770-528-1135, www.cobbcounty.org
- **DeKalb County Recycling Information**, 404-294-2900, www.co.dekalb.ga.us
- **Fulton County Recycling Information**, 404-730-8097, www.fultoncountyga.gov
- **Gwinnett County Recycling Information**, 770-822-5187, www.gwinnettcounty.com

## SCHOOLS

- **Georgia Department of Education**, 404-656-2800, www.doe.k12.ga.us
- **Atlanta City Schools**, 404-827-8599, www.atlanta.k12.ga.us
- **Cherokee County Schools**, 770-479-1871, www.cherokee.k12.ga.us
- **Cobb County Schools**, 770-426-3300, www.cobb.k12.ga.us
- **DeKalb County Schools**, 678-676-1200, www.dekalb.k12.ga.us
- **Fulton County Schools**, 404-768-3600, www.fulton.k12.ga.us
- **Gwinnett County Schools**, 770-963-8651, www.gwinnett.k12.ga.us

## SENIORS

- **American Association of Retired Persons (AARP)**, Georgia Office, 404-881-0292, www.aarp.org/ga
- **The Center for Positive Aging**, 404-872-9191, www.centerforpositiveaging.org
- **Cobb Senior Services**, 770-528-5364, http://cobbcountyga.gov
- **Fulton County Office of Aging**, 404-730-6000, www.fultoncountyga.gov
- **Georgia Association of Homes & Services for the Aging**, 404-872-9191, www.gahsa.org
- **Georgia Council on Aging**, 404-657-5343, www.gcoa.org
- **Georgia Health Care Association**, 678-289-6555, www.gnha.org
- **Gwinnett Coalition for Health and Human Services**, 770-995-3339, www.gwinnettcoalition.org
- **Medicare Fraud & Abuse Hotline**, 800-447-8477, www.medicare.gov
- **National Caucus & Center on Black Aged**, Atlanta Office, 404-892-6222, www.ncba-aged.org
- **Retired Senior Volunteer Program (RSVP) of Metro Atlanta**, 404-206-5005, www.seniorcorps.org
- **Social Security Administration**, 800-772-1213, www.ssa.gov

## SHIPPING SERVICES

- **DHL**, 800-225-5345, www.dhl.com
- **FedEx**, 800-463-3339, www.fedex.com
- **LTL Freight**, 800-610-6500, www.yrc.com
- **UPS**, 800-742-5877, www.ups.com
- **US Postal Service Express Mail**, 800-222-1811, www.usps.com

## SPORTS

- **Atlanta Braves**, 404-522-7630, http://atlanta.braves.mlb.com
- **Atlanta Falcons**, 404-223-8000, www.atlantafalcons.com/

- **Atlanta Hawks**, 404-827-3865, www.nba.com/hawks
- **The Masters Tournament**, 706-667-6000, www.masters.com
- **Clark Atlanta University Athletic Department**, 404-880-8126, www.cau.edu
- **Emory University Athletic Department**, 404-727-6547, www.emoryathletics.com
- **Georgia State University Athletic Department**, 404-651-3166, www.georgiastatesports.com
- **Georgia Tech Athletic Department**, 404-894-5447, www.ramblinwreck.com
- **Morehouse College Athletic Department**, 404-215-2669, http://athletics.morehouse.edu
- **Morris Brown College Athletic Department**, 404-220-0270, www.morrisbrown.edu
- **Oglethorpe University Athletic Department**, 404-364-8422, www.oglethorpe.com
- **University of Georgia Athletic Department**, 706-542-1231, www.georgiadogs.com

## TAXES

### FEDERAL, WWW.IRS.GOV
- **Forms**, 800-829-3676
- **Income**, 800-829-1040

### STATE, WWW.DOR.GA.GOV
- **Forms**, 404-417-6011
- **Income**, 404-417-3210
- **Refunds**, 404-656-6286
- **Taxpayers Assistance**, 404-417-2300

### CHEROKEE COUNTY, WWW.CHEROKEEGA.COM
- **Property Tax**, 770-479-0439
- **Tax Assessor**, 770-479-0433

### COBB COUNTY, HTTP://COBBCOUNTYGA.GOV/TAX
- **Property Tax**, 770-528-8600
- **Tax Assessor**, 770-528-3100

### DEKALB COUNTY, WWW.CO.DEKALB.GA.US
- **Property Tax**, 404-298-4000
- **Tax Assessor**, 404-371-2471

## FULTON COUNTY, WWW.FULTONCOUNTYGA.GOV

- **Property Tax**, 404-730-6100
- **Tax Assessor**, 404-730-6400

## GWINNETT COUNTY, WWW.GWINNETTCOUNTY.COM

- **Property Tax**, 770-822-8800
- **Tax Assessor**, 770-822-7200

## TAXI SERVICE

- **Buckhead Safety Cab**, 404-875-3777, www.buckheadsafety.com
- **Atlanta Checker Cab Company**, 404-351-1111, www.atlantacheckercab.com
- **Norcross/Gwinnett Cab Company**, 404) 477-4988, http://norcrosstaxi.com
- **Style Taxi**, 404-522-8294, www.styletaxi.com

## TELEPHONE

- **AT&T**, 800-222-0300, www.att.com
- **Alltel**, 800-501-1754, www.alltelwireless.com
- **MCI**, 800-444-3333, www.mci.com
- **Sprint**, 800-877-4646, www.sprint.com
- **Verizon**, 800-343-2092, www22.verizon.com

## TOURISM AND TRAVEL

- **Atlanta Convention & Visitor's Bureau**, 404-521-6600, www.atlanta.net
- **Georgia Department of Economic Development**, 800-VISIT GA, www.georgia.org
- **Georgia State Parks and Historic Sites**, 404-656-2770, 800-864-7275, www.gastateparks.org
- **National Park Service**, 800-365-2267, www.nps.gov
- **National Forest Service Reservation Line**, 877-444-6777, www.reserveusa.com

## TRANSPORTATION

- **Amtrak**, 800-872-7245, www.amtrak.com
- **Atlanta Regional Commission's Ride Find**, 1-87-RIDEFIND, www.myridesmart.com
- **Cobb Community Transit**, 770-427-4444, www.360cobb.com/Transportation/CobbCommunityTransit.html
- **DeKalb Peachtree Airport**, 770-936-5440, www.pdkairport.com
- **Greyhound Bus**, 800-231-2222, www.greyhound.com
- **Gwinnett County Transit**, 770-822-5010, www.gwinnettcounty.com

- **Hartsfield-Jackson International Airport**, 404-530-7300, www.atlanta-airport.com
- **MARTA**, 404-848-4711, www.itsmarta.com

## UTILITY EMERGENCIES

### ELECTRICITY
- **City of Acworth**, 770-917-1234
- **City of Buford**, 770-945-6761
- **City of Lawrenceville**, 770-963-2414
- **City of Norcross**, 770-448-2112
- **Cobb EMC**, 770-429-2100, 770-429-2110
- **Georgia Power Company**, 811, 888-891-0938
- **Jackson EMC**, 770-963-6166, 800-325-8597
- **Sawnee EMC**, 770-887-2363, 800-635-9131
- **Snapping Shoals EMC**, 770-786-3484
- **Walton EMC**, 770-267-2505, 800-342-6582

### GAS
- **Atlanta Gas Light 24-Hour Line**, 770-994-1946

### LOCAL PHONE
- **AT&T,** 800-CALL-ATT, www.att.com
- **Comcast**, 800-COMCAST, www.comcast.com
- **Vonage,** 800-705-7092, www.vonage.com

### WATER
- **City of Atlanta Water Emergency**, 404-658-7220
- **City of Austell Water Emergency**, 770-944-4321
- **City of Marietta Water & Sewer Emergency**, 770-794-5230
- **City of Roswell Water Emergency**, 770-640-4100
- **Cobb County Water Emergency**, 770-419-6201
- **DeKalb County Water Emergency**, 770-270-6243
- **Fulton County Water Emergency**, 770-640-3040
- **Gwinnett County Water Emergency**, 678-376-7000

## VOTING

For a list of voting stations, refer to **Voting** in the **Getting Settled** chapter. For Board of Elections officers, see above under **Elected Officials and Government**.

- **Cherokee County**, www.cherokeega.com
- **Cobb County**, www.cobbelections.org
- **DeKalb County**, https://dklbweb.dekalbga.org/voter
- **Fulton County**, www.fultoncountyga.gov
- **Georgia Secretary of State**, **Elections Division**, 404-656-2871, www.sos.state. ga.us/elections
- **Gwinnett County**, 770-822-8787, www.gwinnettcounty.com

## WEATHER INFORMATION

- 770-603-3333, www.weather.com, www.nws.noaa.gov, www.accuweather.com

## ZIP CODE INFORMATION

- 800-275-8777, www.usps.com

# INDEX

S ARAH SPEARS STEWART IS A FREELANCE WRITER/EDITOR/PHOTOGRA-pher who has lived and worked in Atlanta all her life. She's written for the *Rockdale Citizen* and the *Atlanta Business Chronicle*, and worked as a communications specialist for the state of Georgia. Currently she's the public relations and marketing specialist for Chart Your Course International, an employee management and leadership development business located outside Atlanta. Stewart lives in Marietta with her husband and two sons. To connect with Stewart, search for her on LinkedIn.com or visit www.sarahspearsstewart.com.

# READER RESPONSE

We would appreciate your comments regarding this sixth edition of the *Newcomer's Handbook® for Moving to and Living in Chicago.* If you've found any mistakes or omissions or if you would just like to express your opinion about the guide, please let us know. We will consider any suggestions for possible inclusion in our next edition, and if we use your comments, we'll send you a free copy of our next edition. Please e-mail us at readerresponse@firstbooks.com, or mail or fax this response form to:

**Reader Response Department**
**First Books**
**6750 SW Franklin, Suite A**
**Portland, OR 97223-2542**
**Fax: 503.968.6779**

Comments: _____

_____

_____

_____

_____

_____

_____

_____

_____

Name: _____

Address: _____

_____

_____

Telephone: ( ____ ) _____

Email: _____

**6750 SW Franklin, Suite A**
**Portland, OR 97223-2542**
**USA**
**P: 503.968.6777**
**www.firstbooks.com**

# RELOCATION RESOURCES

Utilizing an innovative grid and "static" reusable adhesive sticker format, **Furniture Placement and Room Planning Guide...Moving Made Easy** provides a functional and practical solution to all your space planning and furniture placement needs.

### MOVING WITH KIDS?

Look into *The Moving Book: A Kids' Survival Guide*.

Divided into three sections (before, during, and after the move), it's a handbook, a journal, and a scrapbook all in one. Includes address book, colorful change-of-address cards, and a useful section for parents.

Children's Book of the Month Club "Featured Selection"; American Bookseller's "Pick of the List"; Winner of the Family Channel's "Seal of Quality" Award

And for your younger children, ease their transition with our brand-new title just for them, *Max's Moving Adventure: A Coloring Book for Kids on the Move.* A complete story book featuring activities as well as pictures that children can color; designed to help children cope with the stresses of small or large moves.

### NEWCOMERSWEB.COM

Based on the award-winning *Newcomer's Handbooks,* **NewcomersWeb.com** offers the highest quality neighborhood and community information in a one-of-a-kind searchable online database. The following areas are covered: Atlanta, Austin, Boston, Chicago, Dallas–Fort Worth, Houston, Los Angeles, Minneapolis–St. Paul, New York City, Portland (Oregon), San Francisco, Seattle, Washington DC, and the USA.

## NEWCOMER'S HANDBOOKS®

Regularly revised and updated, these popular guides are now available for Atlanta, Boston, Chicago, China, Dallas–Ft. Worth, Houston, London, Los Angeles, Minneapolis–St. Paul, New York City, Portland, San Francisco Bay Area, Seattle, and Washington DC.

"Invaluable ...highly recommended" – Library Journal

If you're coming from another country, don't miss the **Newcomer's Handbook® for Moving to and Living in the USA** by Mike Livingston, termed "a fascinating book for newcomers and residents alike" by the *Chicago Tribune.*

**FIRST BOOKS**

**6750 SW Franklin Street**
**Portland, Oregon 97223-2542**
**Phone 503.968.6777 · Fax 503.968.6779**
**www.firstbooks.com**